Understanding International Law through Moot Courts

Understanding International Law through Moot Courts

Genocide, Torture, Habeas Corpus, Chemical Weapons, and the Responsibility to Protect

Henry F. Carey and Stacey M. Mitchell

LEXINGTON BOOKS
Lanham • Boulder • New York • Toronto • Plymouth, UK

Published by Lexington Books
A wholly owned subsidiary of Rowman & Littlefield
4501 Forbes Boulevard, Suite 200, Lanham, Maryland 20706
www.rowman.com

10 Thornbury Road, Plymouth PL6 7PP, United Kingdom

British Library Cataloguing in Publication Information Available

Library of Congress Cataloging-in-Publication Data

Understanding international law through moot courts : genocide, torture, habeas corpus, chemical weapons, and the responsibility to protect / Henry F. Carey and Stacey M. Mitchell.
pages cm
Includes bibliographical references and index.
ISBN 978-0-7391-7065-6 (cloth : alk. paper) — ISBN 978-0-7391-7066-3 (electronic)
1. International criminal law--Study and teaching. 2. Moot courts. I. Carey, Henry F., 1953- editor of compilation. II. Mitchell, Stacey M., editor of compilation.
KZ1237.U53 2014
341—dc23
2013047494

™ The paper used in this publication meets the minimum requirements of American National Standard for Information Sciences—Permanence of Paper for Printed Library Materials, ANSI/NISO Z39.48-1992.

To Michael and Christopher Mitchell, the loves of my life

and

For Faye, John-Henry and Miho Carey, the loves of mine

Contents

Chapter 1

Crucial Topics for International Law Analysis, Debate, and Moot Courts

In a rapidly globalizing world debates persist about the appropriateness of prosecutions of violators of international criminal law in international venues, whether these are *ad hoc* or permanent. This of course is closely linked to, and in fact stems from, the centuries-old debate about the seeming inviolability of the principles of state sovereignty and non-intervention.[1]

Efforts to hold heads of state, political elites, and members of society responsible for war crimes, crimes against humanity, and genocide through conventional trials (international, domestic) and/or truth and reconciliation commissions frequently run up against sovereignty as one of a number of defenses utilized by the accused. Moreover, because these crimes are "extraordinary" offenses, due partially to their "organic and group component," the apportionment of individual responsibility becomes an especially tricky matter.[2] How responsible are political elites for the trespasses committed by those farther down the chain-of-command? How should blame be apportioned if perpetrators (the state, soldiers) sincerely believe they were merely targeting "enemies"? Where is the permissible boundary between national security concerns and the protection of civil liberties? These and other questions are worth exploring, particularly in a post-9/11 world.

The Focus on Moot Courts

It has been said that "[t]he international law course provides a legal lens through which students may view the world and its many opportunities and challenges."[3] *Understanding International Law through Moot Courts* exemplifies a growing commitment of scholars and educators to the importance of providing undergraduate and graduate international affairs/political science students with an education not only in the principles of international law, but also the fundamentals of legal analysis and writing. As Dana Zartner suggests:

> the application of the pedagogical tools of law school to political science classes . . . would improve students' research, writing, and speaking skills. These tangible benefits weigh evermore important as a check to the increasing number of students coming into college with minimal experience writing comprehensive research papers. Concepts such as identifying an issue, creating a thesis, developing hypotheses, gathering evidence, and clearly presenting an argument are as crucial for the field of political science as they are for law.[4]

The use of these educational tools in political science courses is therefore beneficial to students interested in pursuing a career in many fields including, but by no means limited to, the legal profession.[5]

Although these teaching techniques are certainly familiar to law school professors, their use in the political science classroom is a fairly recent development. As Carey and Beck discuss, for much of the twentieth century, the subject of international law was either completely marginalized in international relations courses or taught by political scientists from a purely descriptive perspective. Over the past few decades an increasingly inter-dependent international environment, the growing visibility of international legal institutions, and greater efforts by countries to prosecute political leaders for violations of international criminal law are just some of the many factors that have made international law increasingly relevant for international affairs courses.[6]

Yet many political science professors have *limited* their efforts to explaining the relationship between international law and the interests and behavior of states.[7] As Welling Hall discusses, much of this is demonstrated in international relations textbooks which still tend to *downplay* the significance and effectiveness of international law. In her survey of textbooks used in international relations courses she found that international law is most often presented as being of secondary importance to state interests. It appears to exist in a vacuum, devoid of any larger connection to regime formation, dispute resolution, and so forth. International law is most often reduced to a type of ideology or worldview; worse still a "myth." Because these textbooks are often the first experience undergraduate students have with international law they frequently come away with serious misconceptions and biases.[8]

This book attempts to be both a work of scholarship and teaching within the fields of law and politics. By using the medium of hypothetical litigations, inspired by real world situations but using fictitious names to avoid any necessary misrepresentation of anyone living or dead, the book aspires to raise all the important legal, as well as political problems and challenges associated with international litigation. All five cases are set in either the International Criminal Court (ICC) or the International Court of Justice (ICJ). Each includes legal briefs for both sides (prosecutor or plaintiffs/appellants or defendants/respondents). The legal briefs are admittedly not as comprehensive as would be provided by actual litigation, which would number in pages far exceeding this entire book for each brief. However, scholars, teachers, and students will benefit from the issues raised in these briefs by debating their merits. Readers can respond by arguing that we got the presentation right or wrong, with other arguments, interpretations, and justifications. We aim to provoke in a scholarly way our readers and our moot court participants, whether in an armchair, classroom, or auditorium. There is certainly no reason why professors might not want to revisit these cases, among their students or colleagues, using the same or different facts, from those presented.

On a more general note, increased discussions about international law pedagogy have created a greater awareness of the types of tools—such as this textbook—that professors can utilize in the classroom to promote greater student comprehension of international law, including its sources and its application to real-world events. Some of these discussions have taken place in forums including International Studies Association conferences.[9] Moreover, there are now entire journals devoted exclusively to simulations and other innovative pedagogical techniques; a good example being *Simulation and Games.*[10] Added to this are the efforts by organizations including the American Society of International Law (ASIL) to promote greater public awareness of the importance international law has in our everyday lives; information which ASIL presents to students, professionals, and the public at large in an easily accessible and comprehensible form.[11]

Despite certain obstacles, enthusiasm for the use of these inventive techniques has not withered.[12] Several scholars advocate the use of an interdisciplinary approach (holistic approach) that incorporates a variety of techniques ranging from the analysis of different approaches to the study of international law—feminism, legal realism, identity politics—to the legal analysis of cases (the Issue, Rule, Analysis, Conclusion or "IRAC" approach),[13] to student debates, to hybrid methods involving the use of information-based technology;[14] all of these referred to more broadly as "active learning techniques."

Shaw defines active learning techniques as those "that ask students to participate in constructing their own knowledge."[15] As aptly stated by Carter, active learning techniques (the use of case studies specifically) are useful in that they permit "Students . . . [to] see learning less as a passive activity than as a shared responsibility between themselves and their instructors . . . [they] become 'stakeholders' in their own education, and more learning ensues."[16] Active learning techniques emphasize cooperative learning wherein students work together to find answers to various problems or puzzles posed by their professor;

this quite different from the "zero-sum" competitive environment traditionally encountered at universities.[17] For international affairs courses cooperative learning is quite beneficial:

> The study of international relations is defined by problems and challenges that are interdisciplinary . . . students need to be prepared for research and problem-solving in a variety of issue areas. Cooperative learning techniques that provide for the sharing of expertise and research findings with peers provide students with skills that are critical for success in the world today.[18]

The benefits scholars associate with active learning (or cooperative learning) techniques, including "problem-based learning" (PBL) techniques such as moot courts, are many. They are credited with improving student participation, cognitive and affective learning, interest in particular subject area(s), long-term retention of course material, self-esteem, and better relations with instructors.[19] As Cox discusses, active learning techniques are a fundamental part of experiential learning. Grounded in the educational philosophies of Dewey, Piaget, and Kolb among others, experiential learning emphasizes the link between human knowledge and human experience and inquiry.[20] Experiential learning of course has direct implications for the teaching of international law in that its use permits international law to move beyond a set of abstract concepts to something that more directly impacts our daily lives.[21]

A conclusion reached by many of these studies is that not every active learning technique is suitable for every classroom.[22] In any event for students studying international law or international affairs, PBL techniques can be especially useful. As Ambrosio contends, "the central assumption of PBL is that students learn more and acquire skills more effectively if they are tasked to solve problems."[23] PBL techniques engage students more fully in the learning process and encourage them to think critically in a collaborative setting; "to apply, integrate and retain information."[24] The process of PBL involves what Burch refers to as the "learning cycle" which includes the presentation of a problem/issue to students, followed by initial analysis of the problem, research, and an end stage at which time students report the results of their research to the instructor.[25]

Of course one of the more useful problem-based pedagogical techniques is the simulation exercise, which includes the use of mock trials and moot courts.[26] Ringel describes moot courts as "academic simulations of appellate advocacy that educate students about the law and the judicial process. Students, acting as lawyers or judges, 'try' a case before an appellate court."[27] Moot courts are considered to have a number of benefits for students; chief among these, the fact that they allow students the hands-on experience of preparing substantive legal arguments (both written and oral).[28] They also provide students with a degree of familiarity with the legal procedures of international courts, as well as leadership skills, a collaborative work ethic, and greater self-esteem. As Ringel, Zartner, and others suggest moot courts are useful not merely for political science courses, but for a wider range of disciplines (e.g., history, sociology) because of their inherent value as a means of imparting analytical, writing, and speaking skills to students.[29]

Towards this end, *Understanding International Law through Moot Courts: Genocide, Torture, Habeas Corpus, Chemical Weapons, and the Responsibility to Protect,* is an especially useful supplement to international law curricula for undergraduate and graduate students alike. *Understanding International Law through Moot Courts* approaches the topic of international prosecutions for violations of human rights and international criminal law from a different angle compared to other texts utilized in classrooms.[30] It moves beyond description of existing cases and/or the assessment of the historical and current factors that continue to help or more accurately impede international prosecutions, to the actual points of law argued by prosecutors and defendants alike in hypothetical cases involving violations of international criminal law. More specifically the text examines the legal implications that surround the foreign policy decisions made by political actors in response to real-world scenarios.

Moreover, *Understanding International Law through Moot Courts* fills a gap in the existing moot court literature much of which is largely limited to articles and conference papers, or specifically targets law students.[31] This text is concerned primarily with demonstrating the application of international law to specific—though hypothetical—cases heard before the ICJ and the ICC. These moot court briefs and case judgments help students formulate legal arguments that will be applicable to other similar cases; they provide students with excellent sources of international law, as well as a greater comprehension of topics ranging from jurisdictional disputes to matters of evidence. They are therefore useful for formulating the arguments necessary for writing a superior moot court brief.

Constructing a Moot Court

The Layout of the Text

Each moot court brief included in this text addresses contemporary controversies in international affairs; issues ranging from the application of the newly emerging Responsibility to Protect (R2P) doctrine, to the torture of detainees, to the derogation from international due process protections. These briefs are based on five actual moot courts organized by co-author Henry F. Carey at International Studies Association Conferences held between 2008 and 2010 and used in some of his classes since, including International Law, Human Rights, and International Criminal Law (both undergraduate and graduate levels). The cases could also be used in any senior capstone course, as well as in any law school. The contents of this book benefited from legal briefs written for the five ISA panels between 2008, 2009 and 2010 and are authored by Henry F. Carey and Stacey Mitchell. In addition, George Andreopoulos wrote chapter 2, which discusses the interrelationship between human rights and international criminal law, and which has become increasingly important to the development of case decisions of international courts. Dave Benjamin and Stephanie Wolf authored the legal briefs of the Chemical Weapons/Necessity defense case. Aaron Fichtelberg and Robert J. Beck wrote the defense brief for the Torture case; Robert Weiner the defense brief for both respondents in the genocide case. In addition, Stephanie Bromfield wrote the Genocide judgment, Becky Sims, the R2P judgment, and Rick Crawford the judgment for the Chemical Weapons/Necessity Defense Case. All the remaining materials were prepared by co-authors Carey and Mitchell. Some of their materials were initially presented at the moot courts organized by Carey at the International Studies Association meetings of 2008, 2009, and 2010, but have been substantially revised. Judicial opinions were not included in the ISA moot courts and were added here. All of the original presenters at those five moot courts held were then notified and consented to the use of their initial drafts or chose to become authors of sections in this book, as indicated above. We want to express our profound gratitude to all those who participated in these five moot courts at the ISA conferences and who stimulated our thinking at these initial moot courts, which also constituted the first wave of ISA "innovative panels" commissioned by its leadership. Due to space limitations in an already lengthy book, we have omitted an extensive bibliography that the authors had prepared for each of the five moot court chapters. They contain court case and scholarship on all the legal issues presented in each case, as well as historical materials that inspired each of the five moot courts in the book. The authors would be happy to provide any of these five bibliographies to interested teachers and scholars.

The first case in this book concerns application of the United Nations Convention on the Punishment and Prevention of Genocide (UNGC). The issue of contention in case two concerns the failure of a president to adhere to the R2P doctrine; specifically his decision to deliberately withhold necessary aid to his population in the wake of a natural disaster and his refusal to grant foreign aid workers access to the effected groups. Case three involves the legality of the use of chemical weapons by a head of state against an invading army. Case four addresses issues of liability associated with the use of torture by state actors. In the final case the parties are contesting the legality of a government's derogation from providing *habeas corpus* protections for suspected terrorists detained by that government. Although all of these cases are "hypothetical," most bear a striking resemblance to criminal events that have recently taken place (or are still taking place in some cases).

After each set of briefs and legal judgments is an appendix which includes an example moot court. Each case also includes an introduction that lays out the facts of the case in question, discusses (where applicable) issues associated with the material and contextual elements of the crimes(s) in question, provides additional topics for classroom discussion, and also places the issues of contention between the parties within the broader context of foreign affairs and international relations. With respect to the latter, providing students with a sufficient background will enable them to better understand the legal issues involved in each of the hypothetical cases. This of course will aid them in constructing better arguments. Students will likely have additional questions about the examples used, and instructors should feel free to supplement this text with relevant articles and materials addressing, for example, the factual and legal circumstances surrounding the use of torture by the Bush Administration, as well as controversies surrounding the current ICC indictment of President Omar Hassan al-Bashir of the Sudan. Lastly, each introduction defines and explains the various legal terms and concepts utilized by the parties in their briefs and includes helpful hints about preparing a successful moot court.

Designing a Moot Court

Although the moot courts used by instructors are informal, taking place in a classroom as opposed to a competitive forum like the Jessup International Moot Court Competition, it is still important that instructors provide students with the "rules of the road." In other words, they should clearly state at the outset the purpose of the moot court(s), the roles student will have in the exercise (as judges, legal counsel etc.), the parties they will be representing, the time allotted for student preparation, and the necessary deadlines for briefs and other related assignments. Shaw in particular emphasizes the importance of clarifying the objectives of simulations like moot courts; letting students know that they are not merely "playing a game."[32]

In terms of primary assignments, student attorneys are required to write legal briefs, based on either the facts presented in these chapters or new facts that they develop as modifications or entirely new, but analogous situations, as we describe later in this chapter. It is important for lawyers to start with the relevant treaty law, then proceed to any clear principles of customary international law, as stated by the International Committee of the Red Cross (ICRC) or human rights treaty bodies. Students then need to utilize case law from actual trials, which though not technically binding, consists of the most authoritative interpretations of both statutes and customs. They will certainly need case law on acts of omission that lead to destruction, and case law more clearly defining intent. In genocidal cases, there are often crimes against humanity committed by both sides. In this situation evidence of intent from the facts is also quite relevant.

Students will make oral arguments based on their legal research on new soft law developments in court cases, case law, and general comments by treaty bodies, in order to make more specific arguments about the implications of treaty texts. Students will learn some fairly complex arguments from the start, such as the difference between treaty and customary international law. They will find that some states contend that they are bound by no treaty that they have not ratified, and then, only to those provisions of ratified treaties for which they have not posited reservations at the time of ratification. However, others can try to hold that country to rules of customary international law. A counter-argument would hold that certain provisions are either not part of such customary law, or that the state in question has been a persistent objector to the treaty or customary law provisions at hand. Here, one can turn to persuasive soft law, treaty body case law or general comments for human rights and the analyses of the ICRC on customary international laws of war and the various provisions of the Geneva Conventions, including sections from the two 1977 Protocols which, though not universally ratified, are possibly binding under customary international law.

Additionally, students will need to understand *how* to apply human rights law, not only to civil, but also to criminal cases, as orthodox legal interpretations (to which the United States does not adhere!) hold that human rights law applies always, including in armed conflict, where international criminal law has been more thoroughly established. These criminal laws in treaties, however, do not displace human rights laws, even if every human rights violation does not automatically result in a crime being committed. An additional legal issue is the applicability of Common Article three of the four 1949 Geneva Conventions. It lists the minimum standards accepted as binding under customary international law—though technically, they only apply to non-international armed conflict. This provided a large loophole for the Bush administration to argue that Common Article three did not apply to its counter-terrorism policies, until the Supreme Court held in the 2006 *Hamdan* decision that it did apply, upholding the long-held view of the ICRC. If the prohibitions and protections do apply, then torture is absolutely banned, *habeas corpus* must be protected, as well as other rights protected by civilized nations.

The briefs included in this text are intended to be a source from which student lawyers can model their legal briefs and court judgments. Other assignments—weekly reports, outlines for briefs—are at the discretion of the instructor. Before beginning the written brief, students need to familiarize themselves with the facts of their particular case (stipulated and/or disputed), as well as the lower court's ruling. As stated previously, it will also be helpful for moot court participants to do some extra research into the actual case or event on which their moot court case is based. If the facts are not the same as those in the textbook, then the students need to establish which facts are not in dispute with a consensus document reached before the trial. The set of facts can be based on a real situation or an imaginary one. Even with an imaginary situation, the date selected is crucial because it would imply what laws and legal institutions existed at that moment, including newly developed case law relative to the case date. Also, in the interest of avoiding any legal liability, all names of persons in this book are fictitious, though actual events and legal statutes, cases and documents are used. We leave it to professors and students to decide whether or not to use real historical figures and names.

We also emphasize that teachers probably should alter the facts so that the briefs and judgments written by students will address different legal and factual interpretations. By choosing and developing their own sets of facts, students will create their own legal arguments, legal briefs, and judgments. Professors will need to review the student selection of facts for each case to make sure there is ample room for legal arguments on both sides of an issue. Generally, the list of facts should be kept to a minimum so that everyone involved can focus only on legal arguments. If a case lacks witnesses, then the proceedings will resemble an appellate trial, which only concern legal arguments. Each case up to the five in this book should have a tentative list of facts submitted two weeks prior to oral argument, with the list finalized in consultation with the professor within a week of the trial.

Given the lack of familiarity most undergraduate and graduate students will have with international law, legal research, and legal writing, instructors need to be prepared for the various questions which will no doubt arise as students begin work on their briefs. Instructors should encourage students to ask for this assistance, as well as to look for guidance from other professors and fellow members of their moot court group. There are also a number of excellent resources about legal writing and research that students can consult including *Legal Writing*, 2d ed. by Richard J. Neumann and Sheila J. Simon (2011), *Just Writing: Grammar, Punctuation, and Style for the Legal Writer*, 3d ed. by Anne Enquist and Laurel Currie Oates (2009), and *The Legal Writing Handbook: Analysis, Research, and Writing*, 5th ed. by Laurel Currie Oates and Annie Enquist (2010) just to name a few.

Students should become familiar with both international legal sources, as well as legal databases for major legal systems, especially the United States and the United Kingdom. Databases such as Lexus/Nexus and Heinonline.org are available in most universities and many colleges. Appointments with or presentations by research librarians in law and social science libraries would help as well, especially if professors are unfamiliar with these sources. Research on soft law, which is not binding but is persuasive, can be easily located on the home page of the UN High Commissioner on Human Rights. Human rights case law, also non-binding, can be derived from all of the UN human rights treaty bodies, as well as the Inter-American and European Courts of Human Rights and, since the 2009 Lisbon Treaty, the Court of Justice of the European Union. Finally, the most important case law will come from the ICJ; for criminal trials from the two *ad hoc* International Criminal Tribunals for Yugoslavia and Rwanda, the Special Court for Sierra Leone, and the ICC.

More generally for those students responsible for writing a legal brief it is advisable for them to anticipate what the opposing side will argue. On this point Kee states:

> Why do we do this? Some advocates argue that the way to build the strongest case for your client is to first build the case for the other side. In so doing you effectively identify the weaknesses in your own case and the challenges you will need to meet. Being aware of all the weak points in your case allows you to build stronger arguments.[33]

This of course is advice that is equally applicable to writing position or research papers.

As for the actual format for the briefs, besides the examples in this book, students can also look to examples of moot court briefs found on the Philip C. Jessup International Law Moot Court Competition page of the International Law Students Association website at http://www.ilsa.org/jessuphome, as well as the Telders International Law Moot Court Competition whose web address is found at www.grotiuscentre.org/TeldersMootCourt.aspx. Of course students can also look to the actual briefs filed by parties in cases before the ICC or ICJ which are available on their respective websites for guidance.

Reference citations for each brief included in this book are in endnote format. This is purely a matter of style and students should feel free to cite their sources in the body of the brief, or in footnote format unless otherwise instructed by their professor. It may be advisable for student lawyers to include a table of contents or an outline for their legal briefs and judgments. This is beneficial for those reading the brief including, but not limited to, student judges. Once legal briefs for each side are completed, they must be circulated and/or posted so that members of the opposing side, as well as the judge(s) can prepare for the actual moot court and the written judgment that the latter should write.

For the oral argument stage of any international moot court, the outline of each case depends on the time available. For all moot courts the judge(s) begin the proceedings by announcing the established facts of the case, which are not to be contested in oral arguments, and the indictments of a criminal case, based on alleged violations of specific statutes, such as at the ICC, or pleadings in a civil trial, such as before the ICJ, the European or Inter-American Courts of Human Rights, or the Court of Justice of the European Union. Each attorney or set of attorneys presents their opening statements, followed by their arguments, after which judges are permitted to ask questions of each side. Student lawyers must be prepared to answer these questions; referencing relevant points of law in their answers. After each side presents its closing arguments, the judge(s) will then issue their ruling, with the written version to follow after the case ends. Final versions of student legal briefs can also be evaluated after a post-trial submission. Students find more clarity from the actual trial, particularly on how to organize legal arguments, based on the three main sources of international law: treaties and statutes, customary international law, and principles from domestic legal systems. Instructors will need to clearly establish beforehand the time allotted for opening statements, arguments, and so forth.

Throughout the process it is helpful for instructors to emphasize the value and importance of group cooperation. As Lamy suggests cooperation enables students to "support their peers with critical and constructive feedback."[34] Cooperation *between* teams is also crucial. The primary disagreements between both sides in a moot court exercise are not over the facts of the case per se, but rather the legal interpretation of these facts. As stated above, it is therefore necessary for both sides to come to an agreement beforehand regarding which facts are to be stipulated. Students should feel free to make modifications as they see fit, keeping in mind of course that both sides *must* agree to whatever changes are made. This also applies to the crimes charged.

In terms of the actual design of the moot court, the shape it acquires is a function of a number of factors: class size, the number of separate cases the instructor wishes to address in his/her course, and the number of different actors the instructor wishes to include in the moot court among others. Assuming only one moot court will take place a large class permits the utilization of multiple attorneys, as well as expert witnesses for each side. This is similar in some respects to the design utilized by Ambrosio in his mock trial of Saddam Hussein in which he divided students into three groups: the prosecution, defense, and judges. To better distribute the workload he further divided prosecution and defense groups by issue area; with each sub-group assigned to research and write about their one particular issue area (violation of humanitarian law against the Kurds, the 1980 invasion of Iran, the 1990 invasion of Kuwait, and the use of chemical weapons). Student-attorneys for both sides were responsible for writing briefs, presenting their oral arguments at trial, and responding to questions raised by the judges (who were then responsible for writing a report about their final decision).[35]

Professors have the option of using class time on one specific case or any number and combinations of the five in this book, Students are permitted to select a case of interest to them; to pick which side he/she wishes to argue; choose to stand as an expert witness (and for which side), or as a judge. When multiple lawyers are used for each side, each attorney usually argues the charges associated with one of the sets of crimes. For example, in a recent moot court, one student lawyer for the prosecution made the argument for charges associated with crimes against humanity; the other for war crimes. Similar to Ambrosio's moot court, student attorneys are assigned briefs and judges are required to submit final reports. For larger classes with student roles needed, students will role-play as expert witness and be expected to write a witness affidavit. Again class size matters. For smaller classes, or larger classes using all five moot courts in the same semester, the use of expert witnesses is unnecessary. Professors can also consider whether or not to designate the type of "team leaders" used by Ambrosio.[36] In any event and regardless of class size, the fact that each student is made responsible for a particular part of the moot court process prevents the possibility of "free riding" which often occurs in group projects.[37]

As indicated above and below, instructors will find it necessary to begin the course semester with both basic instruction about international civil and criminal law. In addition to case law etc., instructors should make every effort to ensure that students become familiar with the general principles of law, such as *nullum crimen sine lege*,[38] their application, and the sources of law that apply to each crime. Students will also need to become knowledgeable about the different modes of liability available under international law. An excellent, initial source for civil cases is the Statute of the International Court of Justice, and for criminal cases the Rome Statute of the ICC.[39]

As a general rule, the moot courts in this book are designed to have situations which are not clear cut in the law. Judges are to interpret the law. Professors will also have to guide and mentor each group of lawyers, judges, and where applicable, witnesses, on the legal arguments of each case, as well as specific roles. This is especially true for undergraduates with limited legal backgrounds. Difficult concepts like criminal disobedience as self-defense, necessity defenses for alleged crimes like torture, as well as denial of fundamental due process rights to individuals will require extensive explanation. Students need to learn the difference between criminal and illegal behaviour (most illegal acts are not crimes, such as breaching a contract or being an illegal immigrant). However, many legal issues are involved in arguing and deciding criminal cases. Students need to learn how to identify legal issues and how to make legal arguments. Judges and lawyers also need to decide what laws are relevant, from the facts given for each case, or the facts that teachers and students decide to alter to create similar but distinct cases to those in this book. Judges start with the prosecution or plaintiffs' arguments. If these arguments fail, then judges do not have to consider the defendants' arguments. That said, judges can rule to partly convict or find liability.

Judges are aided by both sides' legal briefs and oral arguments. Judges have to decide what are the best arguments, as well as conduct independent legal research to verify what has been submitted and to identify additional legal issues. While judges are free and encouraged to decide these cases according to their understanding of legal and moral mandates, these are hypothetical international courts. They exist to combat impunity—so long as legal due process and criteria are rigorously applied and provided. The fact that most domestic courts defer to existing power structures is the *raison d'etre* for an international court to assert its jurisdiction.

It is important to state that professors must not do the work for their students, lest they simply repeat what they are told. At the same time, before they attempt to read relevant cases, students need to be guided in identifying the legal issues in dispute, especially if they are not political science or criminal justice majors. Seven years of classroom experience in using these cases shows that any determined student can rise to the occasion with a little help. Reviewing the case materials in this book is a great first step, from which students can come up to date with more recent cases and specialized law journal articles on the substantive issues of law raised in each case. Particular attention should be made in all cases on the mental ("intent and knowledge") and material (particular acts identified in the law) elements. Instructors may recommend that students consult relevant portions of international law textbooks, such as by Alina Kaczorowka, William Slomanson, Malcolm Shaw, or Malcolm Evans, or international criminal law textbooks, such as by the late Antonio Cassese or the forthcoming, third edition from Gerhard Werle and his colleagues.

Instructors will also find it helpful to review particular case-law where either subjective or objective tests of the mental element were used. For the cases at the ICJ and the ICC, an additional source of international law is the principles of the major legal systems. An international court, with less than two decades of case decisions, does not yet have a standard and will look to domestic legal systems for an answer as to what standards to apply, such as for the mental element. Similarly, intention may also raise issues of what constitutes "intent" (*mens rea* and "knowledge"; the latter based on either an objective, reasonable person test, or a subjective test). Furthermore, legal standards might also find negligence and recklessness as potential, lower standards of the mental element. Criminal cases will also raise a civil law concept—the contextual element—which will not be familiar to most American or British students. The example of torture will be especially instructive, since as a war crime, it requires armed conflict as context, but as a crime against humanity, under current law construed narrowly, requires a "widespread or systematic attack" as context. Instructors will also find it useful to read portions of cases, such as from the International Criminal Tribunal for the Former Yugoslavia (ICTY) and the Special Court for Sierra Leone, where the courts have a broader interpretation of this contextual element.

Regarding sources of law, these will differ somewhat between the ICC and ICJ to the extent that the former utilizes as its primary source the Rome Statue. Instructors should ensure that students become familiar with the various sources of international law: international treaty, customary law, and case law (as a secondary source).[40] With respect to customary international law it is derived from state practice that is "based on sense of legal obligation."[41] As Werle discusses, customary law "can be determined by the totality of states' behavior" which in turn is measured by the nature of the practice in question (its length, uniformity etc.), applicable treaty practice, state legislation and court decisions, and indirectly by the "decisions of international courts and the practices of international organizations."[42] Customary international law will become an *important* independent source of law students can consult in constructing their legal briefs. In addition to the Rome Statute, students will find it extremely useful to familiarize themselves with other treaties such as those described above. This of course is just a starting point. An excellent source for these and other applicable treaties is the website of the International Committee for the Red Cross (ICRC) at www.icrc.org/ihl. Another excellent source is the United Nations Treaty Collection at http://treaties.un.org.

Student lawyers should also be made cognizant of the variety of defenses available to the accused.[43] The introductory chapter for each case will discuss in greater detail procedural and substantive defenses raised by the accused. One possible defense is sovereign immunity.[44] Of the two categories of sovereign immunity (functional or *ratione materiae*, and personal or *ratione personae*), an exception is made for functional immunity when it comes to *jus cogens* violations. In other words, in cases in which the crimes are those to which universal jurisdiction applies, they were committed as official acts (agent was acting on behalf of the state), and regardless of whether or not the agent of such acts is in office, sovereign immunity *does not* apply.[45] Students should be aware of the conditions under which both types of immunity apply and whether (if ever) personal immunity applies to international crimes.

The first step is to establish facts from which both sides can argue their case. This should take about 25 percent of prep-trial preparation. Another 25 percent of pre-trial teaching will be learning the basics and nuances off the three elements of crime for criminal cases and the sources of law for both criminal and civil cases. Aside from research on the material elements of any criminal case, most students will have the most difficult time learning two other key elements, legal research on objective and subjective tests of the mental element and standards of intent and knowledge, as well as possible lower standards of intent for two other terms of art: negligence and recklessness.

More generally for other defenses—necessity, duress—there are two tests to determine the mental state of the defendant: an objective and a subjective test. With respect to the defense of necessity, for example, an objective test would ask: were the actions of the defendant *reasonable*; those which a reasonable person would have chosen in a similar set of circumstances?[46] By contrast, the subjective test pertains to what the defendant perceived at the time. For duress, for instance, the mental state is one of fear of imminent harm. Student attorneys for both sides should be prepared to address both tests in their arguments.

For moot court cases before the ICC, student attorneys must be able to address the mental, material, and contextual elements of the crimes being charged in their legal briefs and oral arguments. The mental element is laid out in Article 30 of the Rome Treaty.[47] Consistent with the civil law tradition of strict legality, the elements required for each crime under the court's jurisdiction are now clearly spelled out in an addendum to the Rome Treaty and are available on the ICC's website.[48] Students are strongly advised to become familiar with this addendum.

It is advisable for instructors to make students aware of the fact that much of the interpretation of international criminal law boils down to semantics. In moot courts student lawyers will be required to debate the definitions associated with the elements of the various international crimes. For instance: what does "attack" mean when it comes to crimes against humanity? What is "widespread" or for that matter "systematic"? What is meant by "persecution"?

Contextually, students and scholars should be aware that the reputation of international prosecution is very much in flux. Impunity is certainly being reduced to some extent. On the other hand, there are many new dilemmas and disadvantages perceived. To cite just one example: A new, influential precedent has been the wholesale reversal of Kenyan public opinion regarding the ICC's trial of the sitting president and vice president of Kenya, both indicted for various crimes against humanity. Five years later, they ran as a team and won their offices without violence. Instead of favoring ICC prosecution based on the desire to prevent and punish these crimes, the Kenyan public now opposes prosecution, presumably because 1) a way to ethnic peace through collaboration was found, 2) the perception of Western bias and/or 3) demands that complimentary jurisdiction be respected due to the fact that a credible domestic investigation into the atrocities was conducted. The authors of this book recently published a book addressing such themes, which we would like to recommend to interested readers, *Trials and Tribulations of International Prosecution*, published by Lexington Books in 2013.

Lastly it is important to once again return to the topic of the role of instructors in moot court exercises. As a type of PBL it is important that students are responsible for constructing their moot court arguments and/or fulfilling other criteria relevant to their particular role in the moot court process. It is often recommended that instructors occupy a neutral position; as facilitators of the process; to answer questions students have about where to obtain information useful to their arguments; about various interpretations of the law; and about their expected role in the moot court. In this regard the role of instructors is especially critical in the period leading up to the actual moot court.

As Shaw states more generally with regard to simulations, they "involve giving up some control of the classroom to students, so instructors should be flexible. By their very nature, simulations are frequently unpredictable. This is a virtue. Unexpected events often hold a great deal of educational potential."[49] In some circumstances, however, instructors in classes in which moot courts are held should be prepared to step in if students appear to be having difficulty making their arguments and/or responding to the questions posed by student judges.[50] Moreover, in some instances, instructors may need to assist the judge in formulating his/her questions to both attorneys in an effort to ensure that judges and attorneys address all relevant issues. At the same time instructors "must resist the temptation to take over the class."[51]

One final note: for a successful moot court, participants need to stay focused and on point. This of course is a quality that comes with practice and will likely prove difficult for those students who lack experience with public speaking. At the same time, students should refrain from simply "reading lines" from a pre-prepared statements. Successful arguments are simply a matter of adequate preparation.

Notes

1. For an excellent discussion about the importance of the principles of sovereignty and non-intervention see Jack Donnelly, *Universal Human Rights: Theory and Practice,* 2d ed. (Cornell University Press, 2003). Fichtelberg reminds us that the supposedly negative impact international courts have on these core principles is a criticism frequently voiced by realist scholars. Aaron Fichtelberg, "Criminal Tribunals," in *The International Studies Encyclopedia,* ed. Robert A. Denemark, (Blackwell Publishing; Blackwell Reference Online, 2010), http://www.isacompendium.com/subscriber/tocnode (accessed November 14, 2010).

2. For further information about the "extraordinary" nature of these crimes see Mark Drumbl, *Atrocity, Punishment and International Law* (Cambridge: Cambridge University Press, 2007), 24.

3. Henry F. Carey and Robert J. Beck, "Teaching International Law," in *The International Studies Encyclopedia,* ed. Robert A. Denemark (Blackwell Publishing;

Blackwell Reference Online, 2010), available at: www.isacompendium.com (accessed April 2, 2011). Hardbound edition: (Oxford: Blackwell, 2010), 6801-6819.

4. Dana Zartner, "An Interdisciplinary Approach to Teaching International Law: Using the Tools of the Law School Classroom in Political Science," *PS: Political Science & Politics* 42 (January 2009): 189.

5. Zartner, "An Interdisciplinary Approach."

6. Carey and Beck, "Teaching."

7. Carey and Beck, "Teaching."

8. B. Welling Hall, "The Standing of International Law in Undergraduate IR Texts," *International Studies Perspectives* 4 (2003): 145-147.

9. At the 49th annual conference in San Francisco, California in 2008, for example, scholars and educators addressed topics ranging from the appropriate texts for use in undergraduate international law courses to the utilization of information technology as a pedagogical aid. See for example C.J. Joyner, "Choosing an Appropriate Basic Text and Developing Course Materials" (roundtable presentation at the annual International Studies Association conference, San Francisco, CA, March 28, 2008); also John Gamble, "Developing a Website Devoted to International Law Teaching," (roundtable presentation at the annual International Studies Association conference, San Francisco, CA, March 28, 2008).

10. Active learning techniques are also addressed in *International Studies Association Compendium, International Studies Perspectives, Human Rights Quarterly, PS: Political Science and Politics,* and *Journal of Political Science Education.* There is also a host of online resources that will prove useful for instructors including the Active Learning in International Affairs Section of ISA at http://sitemaker.umich.edu/alias.isa/home and the APSA Teaching and Learning Conference, www.apsanet.org/conferencepapers.

11. A good example of ASIL's efforts include publications such as *International Law: 100 Ways it Shapes our Lives,* at www.asil.org (accessed April 2, 2011). For further comments about ASIL educational efforts see John Gamble, "Teaching or Getting off the Lectern: Impediments to Improving International Law Teaching," 13 *ILSA Journal of International and Comparative Law* 379 (2007).

12. These obstacles, according to Gamble, include a greater emphasis placed on research rather than teaching in universities, and a lack of enthusiasm for teaching indicated by the actions (or lack thereof) on the part of international professional organizations. Gamble, "Teaching or Getting off the Lectern," 383-385.

13. See Zartner, "An Interdisciplinary Approach," 190.

14. On this latter technique see Robert J. Beck, "Teaching International Law as a Partially Online Course: The Hybrid/Blended Approach to Pedagogy," *International Studies Perspectives* 11, no. 3 (August 2010): 273-290.

15. Caroline M. Shaw, "Designing and Using Simulations and Role-Play Exercises," in *The International Studies Encyclopedia,* ed. Robert A. Denemark (Blackwell Publishing), www.isacompendium.com/public/book?id=g9781444336597_9781444336597 (accessed June 9, 2011). Shaw provides an excellent overview of the literature about the effectiveness of simulations and role-playing in classrooms more generally, as well as their actual design and use (best practices).

16. Ralph G. Carter, "Teaching with Case Studies," in *The International Studies Encyclopedia,* ed. Robert A. Denemark (Blackwell Publishing), www.isacompendium.com (accessed June 9, 2011).

17. Steven L. Lamy, "Cooperative Learning in International Relations," in *The International Studies Encyclopedia,* ed. Robert A. Denemark (Blackwell Publishing, 2010),

www.isacompendium.com/public/book?id=g9781444336597_9781444336597 (accessed June 9, 2011).

18. Steven L. Lamy, "Cooperative Learning."

19. Shaw, "Designing." It must be noted that Shaw does not refer to simulations as a type of PBL. This connection is made by other authors (see above; for those who make a *distinction* between simulations and PBL techniques, see Lamy, "Cooperative Learning"). There is nevertheless a great deal of overlap between these techniques. The benefits of active learning techniques to which Shaw refers are those outlined by Greenblat. See C. S. Greenblat, "Teaching with Simulation Games: A Review of Claims and Evidence," *Teaching Sociology* 1, no. 1 (1973): 62-83; they are also similar to those described by Lamy in "Cooperative Learning."

20. Eric Cox, "Experiential Learning and Learning Styles," in *The International Studies Encyclopedia,* ed. Robert A. Denemark (Blackwell Publishing, 2010), www.isacompendium.com/public/book?id=g9781444336597_9781444336597 (accessed June 9, 2011). In his article Cox relies heavily on Kolb's theory of experiential learning. For further information regarding the central premises of Kolb's argument, see A.Y. Kolb and D.A. Kolb, "Learning Styles and Learning Spaces: A Review of the Multidisciplinary Application of Experiential Learning Theory in Higher Education," in *Learning Styles and Learning: A Key to Meeting the Accountability Demands in Education*, ed. R.R. Sims and S.J. Sims (New York: Nova Science, 2006), 45-91.

21. Moreover, as Cox and others argue, experiential learning has value for *all* types of learning styles (and variations thereof). The styles to which Cox refers in his piece include Kolb's four styles of learning (diverging, assimilating, converging, and accommodating), as well as the seven distinct intelligences proposed by Gardner ("linguistic, logical-mathematical, musical, bodily-kinesthetic, spatial, interpersonal, and intrapersonal," quoted in Cox, "Experiential"). For a further information see D.A. Kolb, *Experiential Learning: Experience as the Source of Learning and Development* (Englewood Cliffs, NJ: Prentice Hall, 1984) and H. Gardner, *Intelligence Reframed: Multiple Intelligences for the 21st Century* (New York: Basic Books, 1999); for more information about the literature addressing the effectiveness of the Kolb and Gardner models more generally, see Cox, "Experiential."

22. In fact a multitude of different techniques, in addition to traditional lectures, may be appropriate in order to address various learning styles exhibited by students in international affairs courses. As Cox reminds us in "Experiential Learning," "students may learn differently from different learning techniques, active learning components of courses should not be seen as discrete units in a class replacing traditional teaching, but rather as integrated parts of the classroom that combines traditional teaching methods with alternative teaching approaches." On a separate note, Cox's article is an especially useful source for other techniques available to political science instructors—including internships and service-learning—and the literature associated with same. For Carter's discussion about learning styles and case-based studies see "Teaching."

23. Thomas Ambrosio, "Trying Saddam Hussein: Teaching International Law through an Undergraduate Mock Trial," *International Studies Perspectives*, 7 (2006): 159.

24. Kurt Burch, "A Primer on Problem-Based Learning for International Relations Courses," *International Studies Perspectives,* 1 (2000): 31. On the value and application of PBL, see also Lamy, "Cooperative Learning."

25. Burch, "A Primer," 34-36 and of course Kolb, *Experiential Learning.*

26. Shaw distinguishes simulations from role-playing and games; the latter two geared towards an individual's response to a particular set of circumstances given the

parameters of his/her "character," and "competitive play with clear rules about how players 'win' the exercise," respectively. By contrast, in simulations participants are placed in real-world scenarios that involve more "complex interactions," and are given greater freedom with respect to achieving relevant goals or outcomes. Shaw, "Designing," 2.

27. Lewis S. Ringel, "Designing a Moot Court: What to Do, What not to Do, and Suggestions for How to Do it," *PS: Political Science and Politics*, 37, no. 3 (2004): 460; also "Writing Successful Moot Court Cases for In-Class Simulations," *Law and Courts* (Winter 2004): 9-17.

28. Zartner's discussion about how to conduct moot courts is especially instructive (Zartner, "An Interdisciplinary Approach"). Also helpful is Ringel, "Designing a Moot Court," and Charles R. Kerr "Costs and Benefits of Undergraduate Moot Court: A Literature Review" (paper presented at the annual meeting of the Northeastern Political Science Association, Providence, RI, 2002).

29. Ringel, "Designing a Moot Court," 459.

30. See for example Malcolm N. Shaw, *International Law*, 6th edition (Cambridge, UK: Cambridge University Press, 2008); and William Schabas and Nadia Bernaz, *Routledge Handbook of International Criminal Law* (New York: Routledge, 2010).

31. See, for example, Christopher Kee, *The Art of Argument: A Guide to Mooting* (New York; Cambridge: Cambridge Univ. Press, 2006).

32. Shaw, "Designing," 11.

33. Kee, *The Art*, 21.

34. Lamy is referencing the suggestions Johnstone et al. make with respect to cooperative learning more generally. See Lamy "Cooperative Learning." 4; also D.W. Johnson, R.T Johnson, and K.A. Smith, "The State of Cooperative Learning in Postsecondary and Professional Setting," *Educational Psychology Review* 19 (2007): 15-29.

35. Although as he states the drawback to this approach was the fact that "it limited a student's research, writing, and debate to only one issue area," at the same time this approach "helped structure the exercise." Ambrosio, "Trying," 164.

36. Team leaders are responsible for keeping their group on task, reporting to the instructor on the progress of their group and giving opening and closing arguments during the actual moot court. Ambrosio, "Trying," 164-165.

37. Although Carter addresses free riding in association with classroom discussions of case studies it is certainly also applicable to moot courts. Carter, "Teaching," 5.

38. *Nullum crimen sine lege* is the principle that forbids retroactive application of the law to a crime. As this concerns international crimes, at the time a crime is committed "a written or unwritten norm must have existed upon which to base the criminality under international law." Gerhard Werle, *Principles of International Criminal Law*, 2d edition (The Hague: T-M-C-Asser Press, 2009), 37. This principle is spelled out in Article 22 of the Rome Statute. However, there is an exception. Although "courts may not create a new criminal offense" as Cassese discusses, the *ad hoc* tribunals and other courts can "only *adapt* [emphasis in original] provisions envisaging criminal offenses to changing social conditions—as long as that adjustment . . . is consonant with, or even required by, *general principles* [emphasis in original]." Antonio Cassese, *International Criminal Law*, 2d edition (Oxford: Oxford University Press, 2008), 46. This principle is exemplified by the expansion of the definitions of armed conflict and genocide adopted by the Courts in the *Tadić* (IT-94-1-A) and *Rutaganda* (ICTR-96-1-T) cases before the International Criminal Tribunal for the Former Yugoslavia and the International Criminal Tribunal for Rwanda, respectively. For further discussion on expansive applications of this principle see also Werle, *Principles*, 38. For other general principles of international criminal law, see Cassese, *International Criminal Law*, 32-52.

39. ICJ statute available at: http://www.icj-cij.org/documents/?p1=4&p2=2&p3=0. ICC Statute available at: http://untreaty.un.org/cod/icc/statute/romefra.htm. Per the ICC Statute, individual criminal responsibility includes: direct liability (individually and jointly), aiding and abetting, incitement, attempt to commit, and so forth. See Rome Statute, Art. 25(3).

40. When it comes to international courts case law is an influential source of law. Yet precedent generated by other international courts is *not* legally binding on the ICC. In other words rulings by the Appellate Chamber of International Criminal Tribunal for Rwanda (ICTR) will be binding on the Trial Chambers (lower courts) within the ICTR, but not on the ICC. Likewise decisions reached by other international courts are not binding on the ICTR. Interestingly while the ICTR and the International Criminal Tribunal for the Former Yugoslavia (ICTY) are bound by their own judicial precedent (at least the Trials Chambers are) the ICC is not even bound by its own judicial precedent. Werle, *Principles*, 57; 61-62; see also Rome Statute, Art. 21. As discussed in the introduction to case one the fact that the ICC bases its decisions first and foremost on the Rome Statute demonstrates the Court's strong foundation in civil law traditions.

41. Werle, *Principles*, 51.

42. Werle, *Principles*, 51. For his full discussion on other sources of international criminal law, see Principles, 49-59.

43. Under the ICC Statute jurisdictional and inadmissibility issues are covered by Articles 17-19; due process guarantees Articles 55 (investigatory stage) and 67 (trial stage). For further discussion about due process rights afforded the accused and challenges associated with same, see William A. Schabas, *An Introduction to the International Criminal Court*, 3d edition (Cambridge, UK: New York: Cambridge University Press, 2007), 205-210

44. The concept of sovereign immunity derives from the principle of sovereign equality between states (basis for functional immunity) and the belief that government officials should be able to conduct their legitimate affairs in other countries without fear of prosecution (the basis of personal immunity, see above). The latter notion is based on the premise that criminal prosecution infringes on international relations. Werle, *Principles*, 235. This is paraphrased from a quote Werle uses from Cassese, *International Criminal Law*, 303.

45. This notion is grounded in customary international law derived in large part from the work of the Nuremberg and Tokyo Tribunals and has now become a general principle of international law, enshrined in, among other treaties, the Rome Statue of the ICC. See Rome Statute, Art. 27. The bar is raised much higher for personal immunity. As Cassese states: "even accused of international crimes, the state agent entitled to personal immunities is inviolable and immune from prosecution on the strength of the international rules on such . . . immunities." Cassese, *International Criminal Law*, 320. Of course this immunity lasts only as long as the official's tenure in office and depends on whether the prohibited conduct is included in a treaty that implicitly or explicitly excludes personal immunity as a procedural defense. For example, personal immunity for those in office is prohibited by Article 27(2) of the ICC Statute. As Werle and Cassese both indicate this prohibition is also grounded in customary international law (at least for international courts). For a fuller discussion about the distinctions between personal and functional immunity see Cassese, *International Criminal Law*, 302-314; see also Werle, *Principles*, 234-241.

46. The reasonableness test is spelled out in Article 31(1)(c) of the Rome Statute.

47. Intent is not the same thing as motive. Whereas the former concerns the aim of the act, the latter represents the reason for the act. For an excellent discussion regarding

the distinctions between intent and motive, see Larry May, *Genocide: A Normative Account* (New York: Cambridge University Press, 2010), 138-143.

48. International Criminal Court, Elements of the Crimes, UN. Doc. PCNICC/2000/1/Add.2 (2000), http://www.icc-cpi.int/NR/rdonlyres/336923D8-A6AD-40EC-AD7B-45BF9DE73D56/0/ElementsOfCrimesEng.pdf.

49. Shaw, "Designing," 11.

50. For more on this point see Ambrosio, "Trying," 166.

51. Carter, "Teaching," 7. For further discussion regarding the role of instructors as facilitators in cooperative learning exercises see Lamy, "Cooperative Learning," 3.

Chapter 2

The "Turn to Protection": International Human Rights Law/ International Humanitarian Law and the Implications of their Convergence

By George Andreopoulos

When students look at the treaties and statutes directly relevant to the cases in this book, many gaps appear. Certainly, criminal statutes, primarily drawn from international humanitarian law (IHL), are narrower, as well as require higher standards of proof, than do the human rights treaties. The latter are drawn upon in litigation before human rights courts, where the respondents are states, not individuals, and there the standard of proof is the preponderance of evidence, not proof beyond a reasonable doubt. In a criminal case, the statute, read narrowly, is expected to guide us in identifying the contextual, mental, and material elements of a prohibited act. International human rights law (IHRL), on the other hand, requires the respondent state to, among other things, investigate, punish, prevent, and pay reparations for acts of commission, as well as for acts of omission. This chapter is designed to introduce students to the important task of deciding how to apply both bodies of law to a set of critical cases. Additionally, the chapter will also point to broader issues, beyond the five cases in this book, which illustrate how the convergence between IHRL and IHL has affected the application of these laws in armed conflict situations and in other human rights disputes.

In the last twenty years, accountability for gross and systematic violations of IHRL and IHL has become a major world order issue. Within the span of a decade, the international community has established, through United Nations Security Council (UNSC) Resolutions, and a series of agreements, two *ad hoc* international tribunals, the International Criminal Tribunal for the Former Yugoslavia (ICTY) and Rwanda (ICTR); a series of hybrid courts, including the Special Court for Sierra Leone (SCSL), the Serious Crimes Panel for East Timor (SCPET) and the Extraordinary Chambers in the Courts of Cambodia (ECCC); and last, but not least, the International Criminal Court (ICC). To these developments one should add domestic courts operating on the basis of the principle of universal jurisdiction,[1] the European and American Human Rights regional courts through their impact on domestic law systems,[2] and the proliferation of non-judicial mechanisms, primarily in the form of truth and reconciliation commissions (TRCs).[3] Some analysts have argued that we are witnessing a trend towards the globalization of accountability, manifested through the dynamic interplay of international and domestic justice options.[4] To be sure, the extent to which the institutionalization of accountability options constitutes part of a varied mosaic, or of a truly universal and irreversible trend, is a matter of dispute.[5] However, even some realist and neorealist critics are far from dismissive as to its potential implications.[6]

This focus on accountability, and, in particular, on the proliferation of judicial mechanisms, has been accompanied by a host of arguments seeking to justify it. Some of the most commonly cited arguments include establishing the truth;[7] preventing vigilantism;[8] rehabilitating renegade states by promoting a culture of accountability;[9] marginalizing extremist leaders, thus facilitating the process of national reconciliation;[10] and individualizing guilt as opposed to assigning collective guilt to particular national or ethnic groups.[11] In addition, strong claims have been made as to the tribunals' contribution to general, as well as to specific deterrence. In particular, the United Nations Secretary-General has repeatedly raised the stakes by attributing general deterrence effects to these mechanisms, thus identifying them as contributing factors to the maintenance of international peace and security. Due to the (largely untested) proposition that judicial mechanisms deter violations during ongoing conflicts and also prevent the recurrence of conflict, the international community has sought to ensure that they are included in all recent ceasefire agreements and constitute integral components of any attempt to promote the rule of law and, by extension, democracy in post-conflict societies.

These mechanisms have dealt with the most serious international crimes: genocide, war crimes, and crimes against humanity. Given their subject matter jurisdiction, they have drawn upon IHRL and IHL and, in the process, have contributed to the growing convergence of these two bodies of law, as well as to the development of international criminal law (ICL); the latter is a relatively new and hybrid branch of law which "derives its origin from and . . . draws upon"

IHRL and national criminal law.[12] This chapter will focus on IHRL and IHL, the more established bodies of international law dealing with atrocity crimes,[13] and explore their growing convergence in the context of international litigation, as well as on the political consequences of such convergence. In addressing these issues, the chapter will examine the main features of these two bodies of law, as well as their key differences, and critically discuss the advantages derived from and the problems posed by the intersection between these two bodies of law. This chapter suggests that the convergence has led to mixed results: on the legal front, it has contributed to the further clarification and specificity of the general (chapeau) elements, as well as of the underlying offences that constitute these international crimes, and, in the process, has addressed some of the gaps in the ongoing quest for accountability; on the political front however, it has contributed to the erosion of the transformative potential of the human rights discourse. As a result of the latter, this development should give more comfort to policy-makers and less comfort to human rights advocates.

Conceptual and Legal Framework

International tribunals constitute a subset of institutions of international justice. As such, their establishment, functions, and effects constitute an integral part of disciplinary debates about the role of law and legal institutions in international relations. Within the realm of realism, realist and neorealist scholars consider law and legal institutions as primarily a reflection of state calculations of self-interest based on the distribution of power in the international system. They attribute their existence to the performance of valuable functions for states. In a nutshell, politics structure rules.[14]

Within the realm of liberal IR theories, institutionalist scholars recognize that, although states are self-interested actors, rules can have an impact on state behavior primarily because they alter incentives so that states are rendered *more* rather than *less* cooperative.[15] In this context, legal institutions are an expression of states' ability to develop common approaches to world order issues based on mutual policy adjustments. Within the same realm, other scholars have used as their starting point the disaggregated model of the state which presupposes that states should not be conceived as units, and that their constituent parts, like various groups of government officials, courts, and legislatures, can define state preferences and act purposively in world politics.[16]

Going a step further, critical scholars, and in particular those associated with the constructivist school have argued that law and legal institutions can have an independent effect on state conduct by reshaping values held by and identities of national governments and in the process have an independent impact on outcomes in international politics. Some scholars in this tradition have been studying, either independently or in collaboration with international lawyers, the phenomenon of "legalization" which has been defined as "a form of institutionalization characterized by three components: obligation, precision, and delegation."[17] In this context, the causal arrow between politics and rules has been reversed and the fundamental premise is that rules can, and under certain circumstances, do structure politics; the critical question is to identify the relevant causal pathways and the circumstances under which this structuration can materialize.

Any approach that seeks to attribute a role to these legal processes and mechanisms that is more than epiphenomenal, will have to draw from the institutionalist framework broadly defined, namely a framework that encompasses liberal and critical theory perspectives.

Moving to the applicable legal framework, the rules relevant for our subject matter are primarily drawn, as mentioned earlier, from two bodies of law: IHRL and IHL. These two bodies share a fundamental commitment to human dignity irrespective of the status of the law's beneficiaries (civilians, combatants, detainees), as well as of the situational context (peace, public emergency, international/non-international conflict). This was best encapsulated in the Martens Clause, which first appeared in the preamble to the 1899 Hague Convention II,[18] and has been reaffirmed in the 1949 Geneva Conventions and the 1977 Additional Protocols.[19] In addition, both bodies of law have traditionally been state-centered, although they have exhibited different forms of state-centrism. IHRL has been premised on an antagonistic relationship between the individual and the state. The state is perceived as the primary source of abusive conduct and a right "provides . . . the rational basis for a justified demand . . . that the actual enjoyment" of the substance of the right in question be . . . socially guaranteed against standard threats."[20] While this emphasis is shifting and the abusive conduct of non-state entities (families, communities, armed groups, multinational corporations) is coming under increasing scrutiny, it would be fair to say that, in IHRL, the state remains the main source of "standard threats." IHL, on the other hand, has been shaped by expectations of reciprocity in interstate conduct.[21] Traditionally the emphasis in IHL has been placed on state interests both during and after war, as opposed to the protection of individuals and groups; this manifested in the importance attached to, among other things, the collective sanctions of classical international law, namely reprisals during conflict and reparations after conflict.[22]

The differences between IHRL and IHL have been more pronounced than their similarities. To begin with, the human rights discourse places emphasis, as the term indicates, on rights; the humanitarian discourse, on the other hand, places emphasis on needs.[23] This differentiation is also reflected in their respective legal frameworks. The emphasis on rights provides IHRL with less flexibility, since the rights discourse, being more absolute, leaves little room for negotiation or compromise (at least in theory). Humanitarianism's emphasis on needs indicates that IHL must privilege access to those in need; to ensure access to those in need, humanitarians must have a more flexible approach to their legal framework, since access has to be negotiated with those entities (state authorities, armed groups) that can affect it.

Another key difference relates to their main area of concern. Despite their shared commitment to human dignity, traditionally IHRL has focused on the relations between states and their own nationals in peacetime, or in situations of public emergency, while IHL has been concerned with the treatment of combatants and non-combatants by their opponents in conflict situations, as well as with the means and methods of warfare.[24] Having said that, as we shall see below, the changing nature of conflict situations and the concomitant impact on our understanding of the concept of *protected persons,* have been contributing factors to the growing convergence of these two bodies of law.

Last, but not least, a key difference between IHRL and IHL lies in their approach to the loss of human life.[25] IHRL has much stricter rules for the loss of human life, while IHL, being applicable in conflict situations, operates within a context in which the loss of (combatant) life is taken for granted, and allowance is also made for "collateral damage"; a controversial and rather ill-defined concept that encompasses the incidental loss of civilian life in the context of lawful military operations. More specifically, and leaving aside the issue of the death penalty,[26] under IHRL, killing is lawful if it is required to protect life (proportionate) and there are no other means, such as capture or non-lethal incapacitation, that would prevent the threat to life. Thus, under IHRL an intentional, premeditated, and deliberate killing cannot be legal because such killing can never constitute the sole objective of an operation. In this context, a "shoot to kill" policy would clearly be in violation of IHRL.[27] Under IHL, on the other hand, killing is lawful when the target is a combatant, or in case of a civilian only for such time as the person "directly participates in hostilities."[28]

Before we proceed with the advantages, as well as the challenges posed by the intersection of these two bodies of law, a brief examination of the concepts of crimes against humanity, genocide and war crimes, as well as of the contribution of the evolving jurisprudence of the two *ad hoc* tribunals is in order.

Crimes against Humanity

Crimes against humanity refer to acts that violate fundamental tenets of human dignity (murder, extermination, enslavement, deportation, among others); are committed as part of a widespread or systematic attack against (primarily, but not exclusively) any civilian population, which is instigated, condoned or tolerated by a state or non-state authority; and can be committed during war or peace.[29] Crimes against humanity are usually divided into two categories: "murder type" offenses that can be perpetrated against any civilian population, and more targeted "persecution type" offenses which can be perpetrated against any collectivity on "political, racial, national, ethnic, cultural, religious, gender . . . or other grounds that are universally recognized as impermissible under international law" as stipulated in the Statute of the ICC. The crime of genocide is an offspring of the "persecution type" offenses.

Since its appearance in the Charter of the Nuremberg Tribunal, the concept has undergone a considerable evolution. In the Charter, the concept was anchored to the other two crimes in the indictment, namely crimes against the peace and war crimes. This meant that only those crimes against humanity that resulted from inter-state aggression would be punishable, what came to be known as the "war nexus requirement."[30] Genocide, as is noted below, was the first crime against humanity to be de-linked from the war nexus requirement. Recent jurisprudential developments indicate that such de-linking now applies to all crimes against humanity. As the ICTY Appeals Chamber noted in the *Tadić* case, "It is by now a settled rule of customary international law that crimes against humanity do not require a connection to international armed conflict . . . customary international law may not require a connection between crimes against humanity and any conflict at all."[31] Moreover, the term "any" in reference to civilian population indicates that crimes against humanity could be committed against any civilians irrespective of their defining characteristics. As the ICTY Trial Chamber noted in the *Vasiljević* and *Kunarac* cases, a crime against humanity could "in principle be committed against a state's own population if that state participates in the attack."[32] Last, but not least, in discussing the policy element in the commission of crimes against humanity, the ICTY ruled, in the *Tadić* case, that state policy does not constitute anymore a requirement for their commission: "In this regard the law in relation to crimes against humanity has developed to take into account forces which, although not those of the legitimate government, have de facto control over, or are able to move freely within, defined territory."[33] Thus, crimes against humanity could be committed by non-state entities.

Genocide

Genocide is the most serious crime against humanity. According to the 1948 Convention on the Prevention and Punishment of the Crime of Genocide, genocide refers to

> any of the following acts committed with intent to destroy, in whole or in part, a national, ethnical, racial or religious group, as such: (a) Killing members of the group; (b) Causing serious bodily or mental harm to members of the group; (c) Deliberately inflicting on the group conditions of life calculated to bring about its physical destruction in whole or in part; (d) Imposing measures intended to prevent births within the group; (e) Forcibly transferring children of the group to another group.

In addition to the commission of genocide, the convention also made conspiracy, incitement, attempt, and complicity in genocide punishable under international law.

What primarily distinguishes genocide from other crimes against humanity is its intentionality.[34] Intentionality indicates, in addition to the criminal intent that accompanies the underlying offence (e.g., killing), the existence of an aggravated criminal intention (*dolus specialis*) to commit this offence in order to destroy the targeted group as such.[35] The Statute of the ICC contains the same definition of genocide as the one found in the 1948 Convention.

The Genocide Convention has certain noticeable strengths and weaknesses. Among its strengths are: first, the delinking of this crime against humanity from the war nexus requirement. In its very first article, the Convention characterizes genocide as a crime under international law, "whether committed in time of peace or in time of war;" second, the provision for the international criminal responsibility of all individuals for the commission of this crime, irrespective of their status (i.e., whether rulers, public officials, or private individuals); and, third, the prospect for the use of force under international auspices for the prevention and suppression of acts of genocide. Concerning the last issue, it is worth noting that, with Article VIII of the Convention, member states "may call upon the competent organs of the United Nations to take such action under the Charter . . . as they consider appropriate" to deal with situations involving genocide. Since one of these "competent organs" is the Security Council, the international community had at its disposal, ever since the entering into force of the Convention, the option of authorizing coercive measures, including, if necessary, the use of force, for humanitarian purposes (prevention and suppression of genocide).[36]

The Convention's weaknesses include: (1) the exclusion of certain groups from the list of those groups whose persecution would constitute the crime of genocide (in particular, social and political groups); and (2) its enforcement provisions. Concerning the latter, according to Article VI of the Convention, those responsible for the commission of genocide "shall be tried by a competent tribunal of the State in the territory of which the act was committed," or by an international penal tribunal. This meant that, for a long period of time, there was no credible forum for judicial enforcement. Until the establishment of the ICC,[37] the only possible legal venue would have been the courts of the country in which the crime was committed. Thus, unless a regime responsible for the commission of genocide were to be overthrown and the successor regime were to embark on legal proceedings against the perpetrators of the predecessor regime, a remote possibility indeed, nothing could be done to punish those responsible for the commission of such acts.

The Genocide Convention was first used in international proceedings in 1993, when the then Republic of Bosnia and Herzegovina (RBiH) instituted proceedings against the then Federal Republic of Yugoslavia (FRY) before the International Court of Justice (ICJ). The Republic of Bosnia and Herzegovina argued that former members of the Yugoslav Peoples' Army, together with Serb military and paramilitary forces, had engaged, with the assistance of FRY, in acts that amounted to breaches of the Genocide Convention. This petition was followed by RBiH requests for provisional measures that would enable RBiH to exercise its inherent right of individual or collective self-defense. After almost fourteen years of proceedings, the ICJ eventually rendered its Judgment in February 2007.[38] In a decision that generated great controversy, the Court found that Serbia had not committed genocide, had not conspired to commit genocide and had not been complicit in genocide, in violation of its obligations under the Convention. However, it also ruled that Serbia had violated the obligation to prevent genocide in respect of the genocide that had occurred in Srebrenica, and had violated its obligations under the Convention by having failed to fully cooperate with the ICTY.[39]

With the establishment of the ICTY and ICTR the Genocide Convention was finally invoked before international criminal proceedings. The evolving jurisprudence of these two tribunals has been instrumental in the clarification of key elements of the crime of genocide. Concerning "the intent to destroy,"[40] for example, the ICTY ruled in the *Krstić* case that the targeting of Bosnian men of military age in Srebrenica constituted such intent, since "this selective destruction of the group would have a lasting impact upon the entire group."[41] Moreover, the issue of "direct and public incitement to commit genocide," which constitutes one of the forms of criminal participation, has received considerable attention in both tribunals due to the role of the media.[42] The media were instrumental in creating and perpetuating a criminal mindset that legitimized the carrying out of mass killings.[43] In particular, the ICTR Trial Chamber in the *Nahimana* case noted the power of the media to both create and destroy important human values; this power, the Court stated "comes with great responsibility. Those who control such media are accountable for its consequences.[44] Last, but not least, concerning the act of "complicity in genocide," another form of criminal participation, both Courts have ruled that an accomplice, to be considered as such, must provide the type of support which has a "substantial effect on the perpetration of the crime."[45]

War Crimes

War crimes are serious violations of treaty and customary rules applicable in armed conflict situations, whether these are international or non-international. The body of rules and customs that cover armed conflict situations is known as the laws of war, or international humanitarian law. IHL is traditionally divided into the "Hague law" and the "Geneva law." Although there is a clear overlap, the former refers to the set of rules found in the Hague Conventions that provide for the various categories of lawful combatants, and cover issues relating to the means and methods of warfare, as well as to the treatment of those who do not take part in hostilities (civilians), or no longer take part in them (wounded and sick, prisoners of war). The latter refers to the set of rules found in the 1949 Geneva Conventions and the 1977 Additional Protocols, and cover issues relating to the treatment of those who do not, or no longer take part, in hostilities.[46] Having said that, this traditional distinction is undoubtedly less relevant today. Even Additional Protocol I, which is usually characterized as "Geneva" law, contains many "Hague" law provisions that are provisions relating to the means and methods of warfare.[47]

In a similar vein, the international tribunals have been instrumental in clarifying and refining key elements of war crimes. For example, one of the key elements of the grave breaches subcategory of war crimes concerns the status of protected persons. The jurisprudence of the ICTY on this issue has demonstrated the ability of international courts to maintain conceptual relevance in light of the changing context of warfare. In particular, in the *Čelebići Camp* case, the Appeals Chamber of the ICTY relied on a broad and purposive interpretation of the Geneva Conventions to rule that, given the nature of the conflict, nationality should not be the defining criterion for the protected status of persons; instead, the ICTY ruled that ethnicity trumped nationality in the determination of such status. Thus Bosnian Serbs, detained in the camp by Bosnian Muslims, should be regarded as "having been in the hands of a party to the conflict . . . of which they were not nationals," and, therefore, as protected persons.[48] Likewise, in examining the commission of "outrages upon personal dignity," the ICTY ruled in the *Kunarac* case that, in order to incur criminal liability, the accused must have had the intention to commit such act or omission, as well as knowledge of the possible, not actual, consequences of such act/omission.[49]

The Growing Convergence between IHRL and IHL: Issues and Challenges

The emerging jurisprudence of international tribunals has clearly impacted the development of both bodies of law. Before, however, we can examine this issue, it is important to situate it within the broader context of the evolving dynamics of the post-cold war environment.

The end of the cold war marked a shift in the discussion of security and of the nature of the threats that seek to undermine it. From an exclusive preoccupation with state security issues and an emphasis on inter-state aggression, the discussion shifted towards non-military challenges and their impact on human security with a concomitant emphasis on the welfare of individuals and collectivities. An early indication of this shift was reflected in the United Nations Secretary-General's report *An Agenda for Peace* in which a key task for the international community would be "to address the deepest causes of conflict: economic despair, social injustice and political oppression."

This concern with human security issues was also reflected in a series of UNSC resolutions adopted during the same period, beginning with resolution 688 on the aftermath of Iraq's eviction from Kuwait and aimed at the protection of the Iraqi civilian population. It was followed by resolutions 794 on Somalia, 941 on Bosnia-Herzegovina, 955 on Rwanda, and 1203 on Kosovo, Federal Republic of Yugoslavia, among others.[50] The high or low point (depending on one's view about all this) came on the eve of the opening of the 1999 United Nations General Assembly session with Kofi Annan's call, as a last resort, to humanitarian arms "in the face of massive and ongoing abuses"; a call that came in the midst of an ongoing debate about the legality and legitimacy of the use of force in defense of the Kosovar Albanians, an operation sharply counterposed to the international community's perceived lack of response (more accurately abandonment) in the case of Rwanda.

Thus, on the immediate aftermath of the cold war, human protection emerged as a key world order issue. The enabling factors clearly included a shift to non-military challenges to human welfare, and the proliferation of intra-state conflicts, in which the deliberate targeting of civilians, as opposed to combatants, often constituted the main aim of the parties to the conflict. These factors combined to highlight the need for a protective framework that could transcend traditional, and no longer sustainable on normative grounds, dichotomies, such as the ones between war and peace and between types of conflict (international vs. non-international armed conflicts).

In addition to the transcendence of established dichotomies, the exigencies of protection necessitated a reconsideration of sovereignty, a foundational metanorm of international society. Certainly, as several studies have demonstrated, sovereignty was never absolute; key principles of sovereignty, such as the autonomy of domestic structures, have been routinely compromised through a variety of coercive interventionary activities undertaken by more powerful states and/or international institutions.[51] What the exigencies of protection added to these conditionalities was the expectation that domestic authorities would adhere to a certain degree of responsible conduct towards the people under their jurisdiction; conduct that would be consistent with international human rights and humanitarian norms and standards. Moreover, these expectations were to be explicitly premised on the idea that sovereignty entails such conduct, and that any protective activities should be framed not in the intrusive language of *coercive interference against the sovereign prerogatives of domestic authority structures,* but as *legitimate action in the realization of the duty to protect the people from abusive authorities.* Hence this duty was designated by its proponents as the responsibility to protect (R2P).[52]

Yet, this was not a new concern, as some critics argued, pointing to the long-standing debate on the legality and legitimacy of humanitarian intervention. These critics were skeptical of the transition from a discourse of intervention to one of protection.[53] According to them, there was more continuity than change in that transition; a continuity that deepened the grounding of humanitarianism in human rights and in the process reinforced the transformation of human rights from a discourse of resistance to that of an "apology for state violence."[54]

Addressing the different aspects of this ongoing debate is beyond the scope of this chapter. One aspect of this discussion though is directly relevant to our concerns, since it involved the interplay between human rights and humanitarianism. More specifically, it raised critical questions on the meaning of the "turn to protection" and its implications for the growing convergence between the international human rights and international humanitarian legal regimes.

What did the emphasis on protection entail for the relevant legal regimes? To begin with, this emphasis provided space for the further expansion of both bodies of law. As indicated above, the work of the courts has been instrumental in providing greater specificity and in refining key elements of these international crimes. For example, in the case of crimes against humanity, the jurisprudence of the tribunals has contributed to the clarification and precise determination of the general requirements (chapeau elements) that a criminal act must meet before it can qualify as a crime against humanity, as well as of the underlying offenses which would form the basis of the charges against the perpetrators of such acts.[55]

Moreover, and related to the previous point, the *ad hoc* tribunals have been instrumental in the clarification of elements that are common to these international crimes. A good example here is the notion of "attack" which is relevant both in the context of IHL and war crimes, as well as of crimes against humanity.[56] According to the 1977 Geneva Protocol I, "'attacks' means acts of violence against the adversary, whether in offence or in defence."[57] According to IHL, "attack" can only be envisaged in the context of a situation of armed conflict (whether international or non-international). This is not the case though for the notion of "attack" in the context of crimes against humanity. As the ICTY Appeals Court noted in the *Kunarac* case, "attack" in the context of crimes against humanity is broader since "it encompasses any mistreatment of the civilian population;" however, it is not confined to the use of armed force.[58] Therefore, prosecutors would argue that, in the context of crimes against humanity, "attack" is not in itself a crime, but the vehicle for the commission of such crimes, as opposed to its status in IHL where it constitutes an independent violation.[59]

However, the turn to protection can have spillover effects beyond the advances in the area involving the criminalization of human rights and humanitarian law violations. Any discussion about the normative status of R2P will have to take into consideration the evolving jurisprudence on protection.[60] This jurisprudence not only clarifies and refines key concepts and elements, but builds precedents which can be subsequently used in support of protection-related initiatives before other fora. For example, this jurisprudence can support proceedings before the ICJ instituted by one country against another for the respondent's failure to exercise its protection obligations, as well as a request by an organ or a specialized agency of the United Nations for an advisory opinion from the ICJ on the status of R2P in international law. Last, but not least, these developments will also inform deliberations before the political organs of the United Nations system (in particular the Security Council) concerning whether a particular country's situation calls for an R2P-related response.

Five Examples of the Application of IHL and IHRL

A few examples would illustrate the importance of the above mentioned developments, and, in particular, the impact of the turn to protection. Examples would be drawn from genocide, R2P, torture, arbitrary detention, and the state of necessity defense. These examples would include a discussion of both the aforementioned convergence between IHRL and IHL, as well as of any potential tensions between them; tensions where the judge will have to choose the most appropriate legal framework. Such situations would include disputes relating to arguments raised by persistent objectors to customary international law or treaty interpretations.[61] Needless to say, given the space constraints involved, this discussion cannot be exhaustive.

In a case involving individuals charged with the commission of genocidal acts before the ICC, the evolving jurisprudence of the *ad hoc* tribunals would be an important source in the clarification and applicability of the general elements of the crime of genocide, as well as in the determination of its underlying offenses. Concerning the general elements, in addition to the earlier remarks on the "intent to destroy," a reference should be made to the notion of the protected group: a national, ethnic, racial, or religious group. A critical question here is the basis for the designation of the protected group as such: is such designation to be based on some objective feature of the society under examination, or on subjective grounds? In the *Kayishemu and Ruzindana* case, the ICTR noted that such designation can originate from several sources that include self-identification (that is when the group distinguishes itself from other groups), as well as identification by others; in the latter case, the "others" would, of course, include the perpetrators of genocidal acts.[62] One of the key reasons for emphasizing the subjective perspective in the classification of a group as such relates to the need to establish the requisite genocidal intent of the perpetrator; to do so, what matters is whether the targeted individual(s) was/were perceived by the perpetrator as being member(s) of the group in question, irrespective of the objective characteristics of the said group. The ICTY Trial Chamber reached the same conclusion in the *Jelisić* case when it noted that "it is more appropriate to evaluate the status of a national, ethnical or racial group from the point of view of those persons who wish to single that group out from the rest of the community."[63]

Concerning the underlying offenses, a good example would be the notion of the deliberate infliction on a group of conditions of life calculated to bring about, in whole or in part, its destruction. What are some of these conditions that, while they do not have the immediate impact of killing, can bring about the destruction of a group? In the *Kayishema* and *Ruzindana* case, the ICTR Trial Chamber noted that such actions would include "rape, the starving of a group of people, reducing required medical services below a minimum, and withholding sufficient living accommodation for a reasonable period, provided the above would lead to the destruction of the group in whole or in part."[64]

A second example involving protection issues comes from the debate surrounding the applicability of R2P. Let us assume that a major natural disaster occurs in a country ruled by an authoritarian regime.[65] Not only is the ruling government's response inadequate, but the government places strict controls on the amount of aid and its distribution. Could such acts constitute crimes against humanity that would incur criminal liability and trigger recourse to R2P? This question was raised in connection with the Burmese government's response to Cyclone Nargis. In such a case indictments could be issued for crimes against humanity. Following our earlier discussion of the notion of attack, which, in the context of crimes against humanity "encompasses any mistreatment of the civilian population" such acts could constitute "extermination," or "other inhumane acts." In this context, the prosecution could argue that since the government refuses, limits, or directs aid in a way that results in the commission of the underlying offenses (e.g., extermination), those responsible should be held criminally liable for acts of commission, as well as omission, that constitute crimes against humanity.[66] However, defense lawyers would argue that, absent a widespread or systematic attack on a civilian population, read narrowly, there is no criminal liability for crimes against humanity.

What would be the factual basis for a charge of, for example, murder in this context,? If people who had survived the initial storm ended up losing their lives because of the fact that aid, though available, was not received promptly by the intended recipients, then this act/omission could plausibly constitute the basis for a charge of murder. However, before one can proceed with such a charge, the element of criminal intent has to be addressed. For murder as a crime against humanity, the required intent (mental element) encompasses both direct and indirect intent.[67] Unless there is evidence directly linking officials to policies whose deliberate purpose was the elimination of the victims (direct intent), the most likely basis for the charge of murder would be an awareness on the part of the said officials that death was a probable consequence of such acts/omissions (indirect intent).[68]

In addition to the issue of criminal liability, such behavior on the part of the ruling regime could result in the adoption of a UNSC resolution, which, in invoking R2P, would authorize the delivery of humanitarian assistance against the wishes of the said regime.[69] A UNSC resolution adopted along these lines would have to refer to the protection clause of the 2005 World Outcome Document.[70] This would involve the application of soft law, a non-binding resolution about R2P. While R2P has been, since 2005, reaffirmed in several resolutions adopted by the UNSC[71] this development would not render, according to the defense, those violating its provisions criminally liable. The prosecution, on the other hand, would argue that public officials have an obligation to ensure that their country adheres to its obligations under the UN Charter, including the agreement to "accept and carry out the decisions of the Security Council." Moreover, if the situation in question were to occur in an African Country, the resolution would have to include a reference to Article 4(h) of the African Union's Constitutive Act.[72] Last, but not least, such a case would offer a good opportunity to a humanitarian agency of the UN system (like UNHCR) to seek, with the support of the UN General Assembly, an advisory opinion from the ICJ as to the legal status and content of R2P.

Another example involves the use of torture, an issue area which has received extensive attention in recent years.[73] Under international human rights law, a key requirement for the commission of torture is the "public official" requirement, which is contained in Article 1 of the Convention against Torture.[74] In its earlier decisions in *the Čelebići Camp* and *Furundzija* cases, the ICTY noted that the definition of torture in said Convention, including the public requirement, was part of customary international law.[75] Subsequently, however, in the *Kunarac* case, the ICTY drew a distinction between international human rights law and international humanitarian law as far as the elements in the definition of the offense, in particular with regard to said requirement.[76] The Appeals Chamber noted that "The Torture Convention was addressed to States and sought to regulate their conduct, and it is only for that purpose and to that extent that the Torture Convention deals with the acts of individuals acting in an official capacity."[77] It then went on to state that the definition of torture as provided for in the Convention "reflects customary law as far as the obligation of States is concerned"; this, however, "must be distinguished from an assertion that this definition wholly reflects customary international law . . . generally."[78] Thus, the Appeals Chamber concurred with the Trial Chamber "that the public official requirement is not a requirement under customary international law in relation to the criminal responsibility of an individual for torture outside of the framework of the Torture Convention."[79] Thus, by confining the public official requirement to the framework of the Torture Convention, the ICTY reaffirmed that, individuals, who engage in torture practices while in the service of non-state entities, can be held criminally liable at the international level; such entities would include non-state armed groups, and private military and security companies (PMSCs) in the service of state, as well as of non-state entities (like multinational corporations-MNCs).[80] While the Torture Convention is not a criminal statute, torture constitutes a criminal offense under the Statutes of the ICTY, the ICTR, and the ICC and can be prosecuted as such. Moreover, in countries which have incorporated the Torture Convention, as well as the Geneva Conventions, into domestic law the perpetrators of torture practices can be prosecuted before domestic courts.

Another controversy surrounding torture, relates to the use of "enhanced interrogation techniques" in the "war on terror." During the Bush administration, the United States advanced a highly restrictive understanding of torture and sought to draw a distinction between it and other forms of cruel, inhuman, or degrading treatment. This effort reached its apogee with the controversial memorandum prepared by then Assistant Attorney-General and currently federal judge Jay S. Bybee.[81] In that memorandum, Bybee suggested that the definition of the term "severe pain," as used in Section 2340A of the U.S. Code which defines torture, must rise to the level "that would ordinarily be associated with a sufficiently serious physical condition or injury such as death, organ failure, or serious impairment of body functions-in order to constitute torture."[82] Bybee reached that conclusion simply on the basis of the U.S. position during the drafting of Article 1 of the UN Convention Against Torture and other Cruel, Inhuman or Degrading Treatment or Punishment; not only was such a position not reflective of the consensus reached by the states participating in the said convention, but as the UN's then Special Rapporteur on Torture noted, this memo "did not address the practices and case law of the Committee in the state reporting, inquiry, and complaints procedures."[83] It is important to note here that the work of the treaty-based monitoring organs, such as the Committee against Torture, constitutes an important source in the determination and clarification of the nature of member states' obligations under the said treaties. The Bybee memorandum constituted, until it was superseded by a follow-up memorandum at the end of 2004, the legal basis for the interrogation techniques applied to detainees in Guantanamo and other detention facilities.

The arbitrary deprivation of liberty is another issue area which has generated considerable controversy during the "war on terror," is. Both bodies of law expressly prohibit it. In IHRL, Article 9 of the Universal Declaration of Human Rights (UDHR) and Article 9 of the International Covenant on Civil and Political Rights (ICCPR) protect individuals from arbitrary arrest and detention. Although the prohibition of arbitrary arrest or detention is not considered as a non-derogable right under the ICCPR, human rights case law, as well as the work of the Human Rights Committee (ICCPR's monitoring organ), have consistently reaffirmed its importance.

More specifically, the HRC, in General Comment 29, noted the following in its discussion of the role of procedural guarantees in securing non-derogable rights:

> It is inherent in the protection of rights explicitly recognized as non-derogable in Article 4, paragraph 2, that they must be secured by procedural guarantees, including, often, judicial guarantees. The provisions of the Covenant relating to procedural safeguards may never be made subject to measures that would circumvent the protection of non-derogable rights . . . In order to protect non-derogable rights, the right to take proceedings before a court to enable the court to decide without delay on the lawfulness of detention, must not be diminished by a State party's decision to derogate from the Covenant.[84]

In a similar vein, the Inter-American Court of Human Rights (IACtHR), in its advisory opinion in the *Habeas Corpus Case*, ruled that "writs of habeas corpus and of *amparo* are among those judicial remedies that are essential for the protection of various rights whose derogation is prohibited by Article 27(2) and that serve, moreover, to preserve legality in a democratic society." The IACtHR went on to conclude that the writ of *habeas corpus* is among those judicial guarantees which are "essential" for the protection of non-derogable rights.[85] Thus, in a *habeas corpus* trial, where criminal liability is not at issue, the main arguments would focus on the legal weight that should be attributed to the interpretive work of treaty bodies. Plaintiffs would naturally argue in favour of the more expansive, soft-law definitions, while the defendants would argue that states are only bound by treaty text ("black letter law"), as modified by any reservations or understandings registered at the time of ratification.

In IHL, the arbitrary deprivation of liberty is prohibited under Article 3 common to the Geneva Conventions. Common Article 3 provides for the humane treatment of all "persons taking no active part in the hostilities." As the International Committee of the Red Cross (ICRC) study on Customary IHL noted, the arbitrary deprivation of liberty is not compatible with such a treatment.[86] Moreover, all four Geneva Conventions have very specific rules on the reasons for which individuals may be detained. For example, Article 42 of the Fourth Geneva Convention (on the protection of civilian persons) provides for the internment of protected persons "only if the security of the Detaining Power makes it absolutely necessary."[87] According to Article 43, any person so detained "shall be entitled to have such action reconsidered as soon as possible by an appropriate court or administrative board . . . if the internment is maintained, the court or administrative board shall periodically, and at least twice yearly, give consideration to his or her case, with a view to the favourable amendment of the initial decision, if circumstances permit."[88]

The conditions of internment/detention were addressed by the ICTY in the *Čelebići Camp* case. Echoing the *travaux preparatoires* of the Geneva Conventions, the Trial Chamber noted that the drafters "only permitted internment . . . as a last resort" and made it subject to strict rules.[89] More specifically, such a measure would be justified if the individuals concerned were engaged in "activities prejudicial or hostile to the security of the State." While the Court acknowledged the difficulty in arriving at a precise definition of this concept, and that the detaining authorities had wide discretion as regards the concept's content and the choice of means, such discretion was not unlimited. The Court stipulated that acts prejudicial to security would include "espionage, sabotage and intelligence activities . . . The clause cannot simply refer to an individual's political attitude towards the state."[90]

In addressing the choice of means, the Trial Chamber emphasized that the adopted measures of constraint "should not affect the fundamental right of the persons concerned to be treated with humanity";[91] this was clearly consistent with basic precepts of IHRL. Equally important was the Court's reaffirmation of the fundamental nature of the procedural safeguards entrenched in Article 43 of the Fourth Geneva Convention: "An initially lawful internment clearly becomes unlawful if the detaining party does not respect the basic procedural rights of the detained persons and does not establish an appropriate court or administrative board as prescribed in Article 43 of Geneva Convention IV."[92]

The Bush administration steadfastly resisted the application of the Geneva Conventions to "war on terror" detainees, including the provisions concerning the procedure for determining the lawfulness of such detentions. The main argument has been that the Geneva Conventions were not applicable to Al-Qaeda detainees, because the organization is not a party to them; concerning the Taliban, the Bush administration, while acknowledging that Afghanistan is a party to these Conventions, concluded that Taliban detainees were not entitled to POW status.

The Obama administration, in an effort to address these issues announced the establishment of a review process to determine long-term detention and specifying that such detention will continue "only when lawful and necessary to protect against a significant threat to the security of the United States."[93] In addition, in an effort to demonstrate its support for a strong international legal framework, the administration indicated its acceptance of Article 75 of Additional Protocol I and of Additional Protocol II.[94] It is worth noting here that Article 75 has been clearly influenced by Article 14 of the International Covenant on Civil and Political Rights.

While this is an important step forward, since Article 75 specifies the minimum protections for detainees, its legal implications are unclear. On the one hand, this confirms earlier statements as to the acceptance of these minimum requirements by the United States. Article 75 was never cited as a reason for the U.S. reluctance to ratify Additional Protocol I,[95] so any argument about persistent objection by the defense in relation to this article, would presumably not apply. On the other hand, in terms of treaty law, Article 75 applies in situations of international armed conflicts, but not in situations of non-international armed conflicts. According to the U.S. Supreme Court in the *Hamdan* case[96] the conflict with Al-Qaeda is at least governed by common Article 3 of the Geneva Conventions, therefore it is, by implication, a non-international one. Does this mean that Article 75 does not apply to Al-Qaeda detainees? Not according to the ICRC whose study on Customary International Humanitarian Law concluded that all the rules on fundamental guarantees are applicable in both international and non-international conflicts.[97] This argument would be reinforced by the special status that the Geneva Conventions confer upon the ICRC. However, the defendants could argue that the interpretive work of the ICRC in relation to the Geneva Conventions carries no more legal weight than the corresponding work (general comments) of the monitoring organs (treaty bodies) of the main human rights treaties.

Nothing captures better the momentum generated by the convergence of these two bodies of law than the renewed emphasis on procedural safeguards for detainees in situations which privilege, par excellence, the securitization of responsive action. As noted earlier, Article 75 of Additional Protocol I reflects the influence of IHRL on IHL (in particular, Article 14 of the ICCPR). Moreover, as the ICTY indicated in the *Čelebići Camp* case, failure to adhere to these safeguards would unquestionably transform the legal status of adopted security measures.

Last, but not least, a few remarks on the state of necessity defense are in order. In the International Law Commission's (ILC) Draft Articles on State Responsibility, necessity/state of necessity "denotes those exceptional cases where the only way a State can safeguard an essential interest threatened by a grave and imminent peril is, for the time being, not to perform some other international obligation of lesser weight or urgency."[98] According to the ILC, necessity constitutes one of the defenses precluding the wrongfulness of an act of the state invoking it. States have invoked this defense on several occasions before international tribunals with varying degrees of success.[99] The ICC statute also provides such defense for individuals, as do both civil and common law systems, though they are more rare in the latter.

An occasion in which such an issue might surface would involve a state faced with an imminent/actual threat, resulting from an unlawful act, which would place its very survival at stake. If the state in question possesses weapons of mass destruction, then the question would arise as to whether the state could resort, in invoking necessity, to the use of such weapons in response to the said threat emanating from an unlawful act. From a human rights/humanitarian perspective, two key characteristics of weapons of mass destruction are: the indiscriminate nature of their effects and the superfluous injury or unnecessary suffering caused by their use.[100] In any interpretive endeavour, IHL would take, as the *lex specialis*, precedence over IHRL.[101] What guidance would IHL provide in this context? The ICRC study on customary rules of IHL has identified the prohibition of the use of weapons, which are by nature indiscriminate and are of a nature to cause superfluous injury or unnecessary suffering, as customary rules in both international and non-international conflicts.[102] However, while these rules are not contested, there is contestation when it comes to specific weapons. Some countries have argued that it is the rule itself that renders such weapons illegal, while others have argued that it depends on the weapon under consideration; namely, if there is no treaty or specific customary rule prohibiting the use of the weapon under consideration, then the existence of the general rule itself is not enough to declare the use of the said weapon illegal.

If one adopts the former argument, then the use of chemical, biological, and nuclear weapons would be considered illegal, irrespective of the existence of specific treaties prohibiting these weapons. If one adopts the latter argument, then there would be a differentiation between say nuclear weapons, for which there is no treaty prohibiting their use, and chemical weapons, for which such a treaty exists.[103] In the *Nuclear Weapons Case*, the most well-known case relating to the effects of such weapons, both Russia and France argued, in their submissions to the ICJ, in favour of the latter; however, most other states assessed their legality on the basis of the general rule itself.[104]

The ICJ's advisory opinion, upon its examination of both treaty and customary international law, added another layer of uncertainty to the whole debate. It ruled on the one hand that "the threat or use of nuclear weapons would generally be contrary to the rules of international law applicable in armed conflict, and in particular the principles and rules of humanitarian law," while it qualified, on the other hand, this decision by its inability to conclude definitely, "in view of the current state of international law, and of the elements of fact at its disposal," "whether the threat or use of nuclear weapons would be lawful or unlawful in an extreme circumstance of self-defence, in which the very survival of a State would be at stake."[105]

What are the implications of the above discussion for the necessity defense argument in support of the use of such weapons in response to an extreme threat? To a great extent the validity of such argument would be determined by the existence of a specific customary or treaty rule prohibiting the use of the weapon or weapons under consideration.

There is another side to this turn on protection though. The expansion of the relevant legal space has reinforced the convergence of particular dimensions of protection in human rights and humanitarianism. Within human rights, the international criminalization of a growing number of human rights violations has reinforced the emphasis towards the enforcement/reactive dimension of protection at the expense of the preventive one. Within humanitarianism, the international criminalization of atrocities committed in non-international conflicts has deepened its traditional emphasis on *jus in bello*, as opposed to *jus ad bellum* issues. *Where these two developments intersect is on a violations-centered* approach which privileges consequences over causes.

To be more precise, this expansion has reinforced the dominance of the legal discourse over the political discourse within the human rights universe. It has contributed to the ongoing displacement of questions of power and interests which are viewed as contentious, "value-laden" and obstacles to progress.[106] The growth of the legal discourse, which is reflective of the transformation of complex political issues "into legal questions, and then into questions of legal 'rights,'"[107] has privileged particular aspects of protection that are easily amenable to adjudication. There is no doubt that there is something very positive about this development since it signals the widespread acceptance of human rights within the international community, as the product of a legal consensus rather than as the imposition of a particular political agenda.[108] However, the advances in legalization have a dark side: not only have they marginalized issues pertaining to the distribution of power and wealth that are the causes of endemic violations, but, in the process, have made, as one analyst aptly noted, "other forms of collective emancipatory politics less available."[109]

The transition has been easier within the humanitarian universe, since humanitarianism has historically emphasized an impartial and neutral approach to protection issues. Notwithstanding the ongoing debates about the relevance and resilience of the traditional/emergency model in the delivery of humanitarian assistance, there is no doubt that IHL has been more immune to discussions about causes (*jus ad bellum*) than its human rights counterpart.[110] A key factor in this, although by no means the only one, has been the unique status of the ICRC (the primary exponent of the traditional model) within IHL; there is no human rights organization with comparable status within IHRL. While IHL has progressively incorporated more human rights principles and norms in its provisions, a trend that began in earnest with the adoption of the 1949 Geneva Conventions, this "humanization" did not seriously challenge IHL's perennial emphasis on the consequences of the uses of armed force as opposed to its causes.[111] If anything, this humanization, with the concomitant emphasis on alleviating suffering and ensuring protection has reinforced the legalization of human rights advocacy.

Concluding Remarks

The last twenty years have witnessed a turn to protection manifested primarily through the proliferation of justice options for victims of human rights and humanitarian law violations. In the process, the relevant bodies of law, IHRL and IHL, have been strengthened as a result of the work of key mechanisms of accountability, in particular (but not exclusively) of the two *ad hoc* tribunals, the ICTY and ICTR. Their evolving jurisprudence has contributed to the clarification and greater specificity of key concepts and elements of these two bodies of law and has reinforced their growing convergence. Such convergence and its contribution to human protection can fill an important gap in the continuing quest for accountability, and reinforce the centrality of human rights and humanitarian norms and standards in the development of the rule of law. However, these developments have also raised some serious concerns because they have, in the process, reinforced a focus on human rights issues amenable to adjudication. The ongoing privileging of the consequences over the causes of human rights violations is a challenge that this turn to protection has yet to address.

Notes

1. Stephen Macedo, ed., *Universal Jurisdiction: National Courts and the Prosecution of Serious Crimes under International Law* (Philadelphia: University of Pennsylvania Press, 2003).

2. Theodora Christou and Juan Pablo Raymond, *European Court of Human Rights: Remedies and Execution of Judgments* (London: British Institute of International and Comparative Law, 2005); and Jo M. Pasqualucci, *The Practice and Procedure of the Inter-American Court of Human Rights* (New York: Cambridge University Press, 2003).

3. Priscilla B. Hayner, "Fifteen Truth Commissions—1974 to 1994: A Comparative Study," *Human Rights Quarterly* 16, no. 4 (1994): 597-655; Priscilla B. Hayner, *Unspeakable Truths: Confronting State Terror and Atrocity* (New York: Routledge, 2001); and Audrey R. Chapman and Patrick Ball, "The Truth of Truth Commissions: Comparative Lessons from Haiti, South Africa, and Guatemala," *Human Rights Quarterly* 23, no.1 (2001): 1–43.

4. Richard A. Falk, "Assessing the Pinochet Litigation: Whither Universal Jurisdiction?" in *Universal Jurisdiction*, ed. Macedo, 97-120.

5. See, among others, Geoffrey Robertson, *Crimes Against Humanity: The Struggle for Global Justice* (New York: New Press, 2000); David Wippman, "Atrocities, Deterrence, and the Elements of International Justice," 23 *Fordham Int'l L. J.* 473 (1999); Bruce Broomhall, *International Criminal Justice and the International Criminal Court: Between Sovereignty and the Rule of Law* (Oxford, UK: Oxford University Press, 2003);

and William Schabas, *An Introduction to the International Criminal Court* (New York: Cambridge University Press, 2001).

6. Henry A. Kissinger, *Does America Need a Foreign Policy?* (New York: Simon and Schuster, 2001); and Jack Snyder and Leslie Vinjamuri, "Trials and Errors; Principle and Pragmatism in Strategies of International Justice," *International Security* 28, no. 3 (Winter 2003/04): 5-44.

7. Richard J. Goldstone, *For Humanity: Reflections of a War Crimes Investigator*, Castle Lectures Series (New Haven, CT: Yale University Press, 2000).

8. Istvan Deak, "Resistance, Collaboration and Retribution during World War II and Its Aftermath," *The Hungarian Quarterly* (Summer 1994): 62-74.

9. Gary J. Bass, *Stay the Hand of Vengeance: The Politics of War Crimes Tribunals* (Princeton, NJ: Princeton University Press, 2000).

10. Payam Akhavan, "Beyond Impunity: Can International Criminal Justice Prevent Future Atrocities?" 95 *Am. L. Int'l L.* 7 (January 2001).

11. Gerard Prunier, *The Rwanda Crisis: History of a Genocide* (New York: Columbia University Press, 1999).

12. Antonio Cassese, *International Criminal Law* (New York: Oxford University Press, 2003).

13. For a discussion of the term atrocity crimes, see David Scheffer, *All the Missing Souls: A Personal History of the War Crimes Tribunals* (Princeton, NJ: Princeton University Press, 2012), 428-430.

14. Edward Hallett Carr, *The Twenty Years Crisis, 1919-1939: An Introduction to the Study of International Relations* (London: Macmillan, 1939); Kenneth N. Waltz, *Theory of International Politics* (Reading, MA: Addison-Wesley, 1979); John J. Mearsheimer, "The False Promise of International Institutions," *International Security* 19, no. 3 (Winter 1994/1995): 5-49.

15. Robert O. Keohane and Helen V. Milner, ed., *Internationalization and Domestic Politics*, Cambridge Studies in Comparative Politics (New York: Cambridge University Press, 1996).

16. Andrew Moravcsik, "Taking Preferences Seriously: A Liberal Theory of International Politics," *International Organization* 51, no. 4 (1997): 513–53 and Anne-Marie Slaughter, *A New World Order* (Princeton, NJ: Princeton University Press, 2004).

17. Kenneth W. Abbott, Robert O. Keohane, Andrew Moravcsik, Anne-Marie Slaughter, and Duncan Snidal, "The Concept of Legalization," *International Organization* 54, no. 3 (Summer 2000): 17-35.

18. The text of the Martens Clause in the 1899 Hague Convention II is as follows: "Until a more complete code of the laws of war has been issued, the high contracting Parties deem it expedient to declare that, in cases not included in the Regulations adopted by them, the inhabitants and the belligerents remain under the protection and the rule of the principles of the law of nations, as they result from the usages established among civilized peoples, from the laws of humanity, and the dictates of the public conscience"; Adam Roberts and Richard Guelff, ed., *Documents on the Laws of War*, 3d ed. (New York: Oxford University Press, 2000), 70.

19. See J.B. Scott, ed., *The Hague Conventions and Declarations of 1899 and 190*, 3d ed. (New York: Oxford University Press, 1918), 101-102 and George Andreopoulos, "The International Legal Framework and Armed Groups," *Human Rights Review* 11(2) (June 2010): 228.

20. Henry Shue, *Basic Rights: Subsistence, Affluence, and U.S. Foreign Policy* (Princeton, N.J.: Princeton University Press, 1980), 13. Having said that, it is important to note that the relation between human rights and the state is more complex, since rights

also need institutional arrangements to guarantee them; arrangements for which the state is responsible. Therefore, rights seek both to enable and constrain the state. For a very good discussion of the institutionally referential role of rights, see Christian Reus-Smit, "On Rights and Institutions," in *Global Basic Rights,* ed. Charles R. Beitz and Robert E. Goodin (New York: Oxford University Press, 2009), 29-37.

21. Theodor Meron, "The Humanization of Humanitarian Law," 94 *Am. J. Int'l L.* 239 (2000).

22. Meron, "The Humanization of Humanitarian Law," 243.

23. Michael Barnett, *The Empire of Humanity. A History of Humanitarianism* (Ithaca, NY: Cornell University Press, 2011), 16.

24. It is important to stress that IHRL has a greater reach than IHL, since the former is also applicable during conflict situations, as confirmed by the International Court of Justice in its Advisory Opinion on the *Legality of the Threat or Use of Nuclear Weapons* (1996). However, in the determination of the applicable rules in conflict situations, IHL, being the *lex specialis,* will take precedence over IHRL.

25. Needless to say, the list is by no means exhaustive. Our brief treatment addresses some, not all, of the key similarities and differences.

26. While allowance is made for the death penalty in the International Covenant on Civil and Political Rights (ICCPR), subsequent international, as well as regional legal instruments prohibit it and there is a growing consensus in the international human rights community on the need to work towards its eventual abolition.

27. UNGA, Human Rights Council, Report of the Special Rapporteur on Extrajudicial, Summary or Arbitrary Executions, *Study on Targeted Killings* (May 28, 2010) www.ohchr.org/english/bodies/hrcouncil/docs/14session/A.HRC.14.24.Add6.pdf.

28. For a treatment of this concept, see Nils Melzer, *Interpretive Guidance on the Notion of Direct Participation in Hostilities Under International Humanitarian Law* (ICRC, 2009) http://www.icrc.org/eng/assets/files/other/icrc-002-0990.pdf.

29. Cassese, *International Criminal Law,* 73.

30. Beth Van Schaack, "The Definition of Crimes Against Humanity: Resolving the Incoherence," 37 *Colum. J. Transnat'l. L.* 787 (1999).

31. International Criminal Tribunal for the Former Yugoslavia, *Prosecutor v. Dusko Tadić,* Decision on the Defense Motion for Interlocutory Appeal on Jurisdiction, para. 141 at http://www.icty.org/x/cases/tadic/acdec/en/51002.htm.

32. Guenael Mettraux, *International Crimes and the Ad Hoc Tribunals* (New York: Oxford University Press, 2006), 165.

33. ICTY, *Prosecutor v. Tadić,* Case No: IT-94-1, Opinion and Judgment, para. 654 (May 7, 1997) at http://www.icty.org/x/cases/tadic/tjug/en/tad-tsj70507JT2-e.pdf.

34. For more on this, see George Andreopoulos, ed., *Genocide. Conceptual and Historical Dimensions* (Philadelphia, PA: University of Pennsylvania Press, 1994).

35. Cassese, *International Criminal Law,* 103-105; Schabas, *An Introduction to the International Criminal Court,* 36-41.

36. George Andreopoulos, "On the Prevention of Genocide. Humanitarian Intervention and the Role of the United Nations," in *Concepts and Strategies in International Human Rights,* ed. George Andreopoulos (New York: Peter Lang, 2002).

37. The Rome Statute, the treaty establishing the ICC, entered into force on July 1, 2002.

38. International Court of Justice, *Case Concerning Application of the Convention on the Prevention and Punishment of the Crime of Genocide, Bosnia and Herzegovina v. Serbia and Montenegro,* Judgment of February 26, 2007, available at the following website: www.icj-cij.org/docket/files/91/13685.pdf.

39. ICJ, *Bosnia*, Judgment.

40. This is a general (chapeau) element of the crime of genocide. See below for a discussion of general elements and underlying offenses of the crimes under consideration.

41. ICTY, *Prosecutor v. Radislav Krstić*, Case No: IT-98-33-T, Judgment, para. 595 (August 2, 2001).

42. The others are: genocide, conspiracy to commit genocide, attempt to commit genocide, and complicity in genocide.

43. Mettraux, *International Crimes and the Ad Hoc Tribunals*, 255.

44. Mettraux, *International Crimes and the Ad Hoc Tribunals*, 255.

45. Mettraux, *International Crimes and the Ad Hoc Tribunals*, 258.

46. Cassese, *International Criminal Law*, 47-48.

47. Examples of "Hague" law provisions in Additional Protocol I are Articles 37 and 38 which refer, respectively, to the prohibition of perfidy and to the use of recognized emblems. Roberts and Guelff, *Documents on the Laws of War*, 442-443.

48. ICTY, *Prosecutor v. Zejnil Delalić, Zdravko Mucić, Hazim Delić and Esad Landžo (Čelebići Camp case)*, Case No: IT-96-21-A, Appeals Chamber Judgment, para. 106 (February 20, 2001) at http://www.icty.org/x/cases/mucic/acjug/en/cel-aj010220.pdf.

49. Mettraux, *International Crimes and the Ad Hoc Tribunals*, 102.

50. UNSC, Security Council Resolution 688, S/RES/688 (1991) (April 5, 1991); Security Council Resolution 794, S/RES/794 (1992) (December 3, 1992); Security Council Resolution 941, S/RES/941 (1994) (September 23, 1994); Security Council Resolution 955, S/RES/955 (1994) (November 8, 1994); and Security Council Resolution 1203, S/RES/1203 (1998) (October 24, 1998).

51. For an analysis of the conditionality of sovereignty, in particular in its Westphalian and international legal variants, see Stephen D. Krasner, *Sovereignty. Organized Hypocrisy* (Princeton, NJ: Princeton University Press, 1999).

52. See on this, International Commission on Intervention and State Sovereignty, *The Responsibility to Protect*, http://responsibilitytoprotect.org/ICISS%20Report.pdf; and Gareth Evans and Mohamed Sahnoun, "The Responsibility to Protect," *Foreign Affairs* 81(6) (2002): 99-110.

53. See, for example, David Rieff, "Humanitarianism in Crisis," *Foreign Affairs* 81(6) (2002): 111-121 and Fabrice Weissman, "'Not In Our Name:' Why Medecins Sans Frontieres Does Not Support the 'Responsibility to Protect,'" *Criminal Justice Ethics* 29(2) (2010): 194-207.

54. Anne Orford, *Reading Humanitarian Intervention. Human Rights and the Use of Force in International Law* (Cambridge, UK: Cambridge University Press, 2003), 187.

55. Examples of chapeau elements of crimes against humanity include the concepts of "attack," "any civilian population," and "widespread or systematic"; examples of underlying offenses include "murder," "extermination," "deportation," and "enslavement"; for a good discussion, see Cassese, *International Criminal Law*, 64-95, and Mettraux, *International Crimes and the Ad Hoc Tribunals*, 155-190.

56. In the ICC statute, the contextual element for crimes against humanity is a "widespread or systematic attack directed against any civilian population." For the alleged offences to constitute war crimes, they must have been committed in the context of and associated with an armed conflict.

57. Roberts and Guelff, *Documents on the Laws of War*, 447.

58. ICTY, *Prosecutor v. Dragoljub Kunarac, Radomir Kovač and Zoran Vukovič*, Case No: IT-96-23 & IT-96-23/1-A, Judgment, para. 86 (June 12, 2002); see Mettraux, *International Crimes and the Ad Hoc Tribunals*, 157.

59. Mettraux, *International Crimes and the Ad Hoc Tribunals*, 157.

60. There is an ongoing debate in the scholarly literature as to the precise designation of R2P (concept, principle or norm?). It is beyond the scope of this chapter to address this debate. For a brief overview, see Alex J. Bellamy, *Responsibility to Protect: The Global Effort to End Mass Atrocities* (Cambridge, UK: Polity Press, 2009), 4-7.

61. The issue of persistent objector is raised in the context of the development of rules of customary international law. The designation refers to a state (or states) which initially and continuously object(s) to a particular rule; such a state is not bound by the rule in question in situations where that rule has become customary international law.

62. International Criminal Tribunal for Rwanda, *Prosecutor versus Clément Kayishema and Obed Ruzindana,* Case No:ICTR-95-1-T, Judgment, para 98 (May 21, 1999); see also Mettraux, *International Crimes and the Ad Hoc Tribunals,* 224.

63. Quoted in Mettraux, *International Crimes and the Ad Hoc Tribunals*, 224.

64. ICTR, *Kayishema and Ruzindana*, Judgment, para 116.

65. Characterizing a disaster as natural carries strong political connotations. Many so-called natural disasters (e.g., floods, hurricanes, earthquakes) have led to loss of life and property that were clearly disproportionate to the scale of the event. The extent of the resulting devastation has often been the result of human (criminal) negligence and lack of appropriate responsive action. This is why many analysts have argued that designating a disaster as simply natural silences the human element and offers comfort to negligent or outright criminal regimes. The discussion of this issue is beyond the scope of this chapter.

66. For a similar argument, see Stuart Ford, "Is the Failure to Respond Appropriately to a Natural Disaster A Crime Against Humanity? The Responsibility to Protect and Individual Criminal Responsibility in the Aftermath of Cyclone Nargis," 38 *Denver J. Int'l L. & Pol'y* 227 (2010).

67. Ford, "Is the Failure to Respond Appropriately," 245.

68. Ford, "Is the Failure to Respond Appropriately," 245.

69. Gareth Evans, "Facing Up to Our Responsibilities," *Guardian* (May 12, 2008), http://www.guardian.co.uk/commentisfree/2008/may/12/facinguptoourresponsbilities. It is interesting to note though that there was no consensus among proponents of R2P as to the applicability of the concept in the context of Cyclone Nargis. Asia-Pacific Centre for the Responsibility to Protect, *Cyclone Nargis and the Responsibility to Protect,* Myanmar Briefing, No. 3 (May 16, 2008), www.r2pasiapacific.org/documents/Burma_Brief2.pdf.

70. UN General Assembly, *2005 World Summit Outcome,* (September 20, 2005), para 139, www.ilo.org.

71. United Nations Security Council Resolutions 1674 (2006), 1755 (2007) and 1769 (2007) are examples of such resolutions.

72. *Constitutive Act of the African Union* which is, available at the following website: www.au.int/en/sites/default/files/ConstitutiveAct_EN.pdf. Article 4(h) provides for "the right of the Union to intervene in a Member State pursuant to a decision of the Assembly in respect of grave circumstances, namely: war crimes, genocide and crimes against humanity." Although the Act does not refer to R2P (in fact, it antedates the ICISS Report on R2P), and frames the action in terms of the Union's right to intervene, as opposed to the targeted government's obligation to protect, it is clear from the deliberations surrounding the adoption of this provision that such action would be undertaken in circumstances in which the government of the country concerned is unable or unwilling to meet its protection obligations. For more on Article 4(h) of the Constitutive Act, see Ben Kioko, "The right of intervention under the African Union's Constitutive Act: From Non-interference to Non-intervention," *International Review of the Red Cross* 85, no. 852 (December 2003): 807-825; and Dan Kuwali, "Art. 4(h) + R2P: Towards a Doctrine of

Persuasive Prevention to End Mass Atrocity Crimes," 3 *Interdisc. J. Hum. Rts. L.* 55 (2008-2009).

73. The best scholarly treatment is by Darius Rejali, *Torture and Democracy* (Princeton, NJ: Princeton University Press, 2007).

74. Convention against Torture and Other Cruel, Inhuman or Degrading Treatment or Punishment (1984), www.ohchr.org/english/law/cat.htm.

75. ICTY, *Čelebići*, Trial Judgment, para. 442 (November 16, 1998) and *Prosecutor v. Anto Furundžija*, Case No: IT-95-17/1-T, Judgment, paras. 159-160 (December 10, 1998).

76. ICTY, *Kunarać et. al.* Appeals Judgment (June 12, 2002).

77. ICTY, *Kunarać et. al.* Appeals Judgment, para 146.

78. ICTY, *Kunarać et. al.* Appeals Judgment, para 147.

79. ICTY, *Kunarać et. al.* Appeals Judgment, para 148.

80. Examples of the latter would include the private contractors working for Titan and CACI in Iraq who were involved in the Abu-Ghraib prisoner abuse case and for whom the United States Army was ostensibly responsible, and the personnel of private international, as well as domestic, security firms working for the oil companies in the Niger Delta, who have been involved in numerous incidents of abusive conduct against the local population; see P.W. Singer, "Outsourcing War," *Foreign Affairs* 84(2) (2005): 119-132 and Rita Abrahamsen and Michael C. Williams, *The Globalization of Private Security, Country Report: Nigeria* (January 2005) available at the following website: http://users.aber.ac.uk/rbh/privatesecurity/country%20report-nigeria.pdf.

81. U.S. Department of Justice, Office of Legal Counsel. Memorandum for Alberto R. Gonzales, Counsel to the President, *Re Standards of Conduct for Interrogation under 18 U.S.C. §§2340-2340A*.

82. U.S. Department of Justice, *Re Standards of Conduct for Interrogation*, 6.

83. Manfred Nowak, "What Practices Constitute Torture?: US and UN Standards," *Human Rights Quarterly* (2006): 813. The Committee that Nowak refers to is the Committee against Torture, the monitoring organ of the Convention against Torture.

84. United Nations, *International Covenant on Civil and Political Rights, General Comment no. 29: States of Emergency (Article 4)*, CCPR/C/21/Rev.1/Add.11 (August 31, 2001), paras 15 and 16.

85. *Habeas Corpus in Emergency Situations (Arts. 27[2] and 7[6] of the American Convention on Human Rights)*, Advisory Opinion OC-8/87 (January 30, 1987), Inter-Am. Ct. H.R. (Ser. A) No. 8 (1987)

86. Jean-Marie Henckaerts and Louise Doswald-Beck, *Customary International Humanitarian Law. Volume I: Rules* (Cambridge, UK: Cambridge University Press, 2005), 344. The ICRC study characterizes such prohibition as a customary rule of IHL.

87. Roberts and Guelff, *Documents on the Laws of War*, 315.

88. Roberts and Guelff, *Documents on the Laws of War*, 315.

89. ICTY, *Čelebići*, Trial Judgment, para 572.

90. ICTY, *Čelebići*, Trial Judgment, para 567.

91. ICTY, *Čelebići*, Trial Judgment, para 570.

92. ICTY, *Čelebići*, Trial Judgment, para 583.

93. The White House. Office of the Press Secretary, *Fact Sheet: New Actions on Guantanamo and Detainee Policy* (March 7, 2011) at http://www.lawfareblog.com/wp-content/uploads/2011/03/Fact_Sheet_-_Guantanamo_and_Detainee_Policy.pdf.

94. White House. Office of the Press Secretary, *Fact Sheet: New Actions on Guantanamo*. It is important to note here that the United States has not ratified either Protocol.

95. Abraham Sofaer, "The Position of the United States on Current Law of War Agreements," 2 *Am. U. J. Int'l L. & Pol'y* 460 (1987).

96. See *Hamdan v. Rumsfeld*, 548 U.S. 557 (2006).

97. Henckaerts and Doswald-Beck, *Customary International Humanitarian Law*, 299-383.

98. UN International Law Commission, *Draft Articles on Responsibility of States for Internationally Wrongful Acts, with Commentaries.*

99. For a discussion of some of these cases, see the ILC commentary.

100. There is no standard definition of weapons of mass destruction. For a recent study that surveys different definitions, see W. Seth Carus, *Defining "Weapons of Mass Destruction,"* Revised and Updated, Center for the Study of Weapons of Mass Destruction, Occasional Paper, No. 8 (National Defense University Press, Washington, D.C., January 2012), www.ndu.edu. Nuclear, biological, and chemical weapons would be included in all definitions; see the appendices in Carus' study.

101. IHRL has dealt much less with the issue of weapons and their appropriate use than IHL. IHRL is primarily relevant in the context of riots and other types of public disturbances that fall below the level of intensity that would characterize non-international armed conflict situations, and addresses the types of weapons that law enforcement authorities can legitimately use in their efforts to restore order.

102. Henckaerts and Doswald-Beck, *Customary International Humanitarian Law*, 237-250.

103. Convention on the Prohibition of the Development, Production, Stockpiling and Use of Chemical Weapons and on their Destruction at http://www.opcw.org.

104. Examples would include Mexico, Netherlands, Sweden, the United Kingdom, and the United States; see Hanckaerts and Doswald-Beck, *Customary International Humanitarian Law*, 243.

105. International Court of Justice, *Legality of the Threat or Use of Nuclear Weapons.* Advisory Opinion of 8 July 1996.

106. See Tony Evans, "International Human Rights Law as Power/Knowledge," *Human Rights Quarterly* 27 (2005): 1052.

107. David Kennedy, *The Dark Sides of Virtue. Reassessing International Humanitarianism* (Princeton, NJ: Princeton University Press, 2004), 33.

108. For a discussion of the pitfalls of legalism, see Bronwyn Leebaw, "The Politics of Impartial Activism: Humanitarianism and Human Rights," *Perspectives on Politics* 5(2) (2007): 226-227.

109. Kennedy, *The Dark Sides of Virtue*, 33.

110. For a recent discussion of the different approaches to humanitarian action, see Michael Barnett, *Empire of Humanity: A History of Humanitarianism* (Ithaca, NY: Cornell University Press, 2011), 32-46.

111. On the influence of human rights on IHL, see Meron, "The Humanization of Humanitarian Law." This does not mean that the humanization of IHL has not raised other questions among its proponents. One of the key concerns is that the influence of human rights law may adversely affect IHL's relevance in the battlefield. On this issue, see the Geoffrey Best, *War and Law Since 1945* (New York: Oxford University Press, 1994), especially pages 370-401.

Chapter 3

Alleged Genocide and Failure to Prevent and Punish Genocide: Nolandia versus Notoria and Idealia

With Robert Weiner and Brittany Bromfield

The first moot court raises two main legal questions emerging from the Convention on the Prevention and Punishment of the Crime of Genocide (hereafter, Genocide Convention): a) Did a genocide occur? and b) When must a third party country "prevent and punish" such a genocide? The first issue debates the implications and applications of the definition of genocide and applies them to a set of facts. The second asks whether there are defenses to an obligation to prevent genocide, such as requiring UN Security Council (UNSC) sanction of any armed intervention, and if not, then does that responsibility for genocide prevention by a state party extend only inside that same state party's own territory or beyond into one or more third state party's territory where genocide prevention is required? This case involves a similar scenario to that addressed in the *Bosnia v. Serbia* case before the International Court of Justice (ICJ), but with facts drawn from the situation in Darfur, Sudan. The difference in this moot court from the actual *Bosnia v. Serbia* case is that there are two different defendants; one a perpetrator state (Notoria) being sued by another state (Nolandia) which is linked to the persecuted minority in Nolandia. The second defendant (Idealia) is a third party state, geographically removed from Notoria but with a worldwide military presence and superpower interests, who is being sued by the same plaintiff for its failure to take action to prevent the genocide.

This case, held at the ICJ under Article 9 of the Genocide Convention (which grants the ICJ authority to resolve disputes arising under that treaty's authority), is distinguished from International Criminal Court cases, which target individuals, such as that currently pending against representatives of the Government of Sudan.[1] The case against members of the Sudanese government was initiated at the behest of the UNSC. However, the facts of the case in this chapter are similar to the alleged genocide in the Darfur region of Sudan. In the Sudan, the government in 2003 sent in an Arab militia—the *Janjaweed* ("devils on horseback")—to address the "problem" of a counter-insurgency. Goldsmith writes: "the retaliation . . . went beyond simple counterinsurgency, with entire villages being attacked. Sudanese planes bombed villages and then government troops and . . . *Janjaweed* entered the targeted villages, raping the women, killing people that were left, and polluting the water supply before burning the villages to the ground."[2] The President of Sudan, Omar Hassan Ahmed al-Bashir, and two other alleged agents of the government, including Ali Muhammad Ali Abu-Al-Rahman, head of the *Janjaweed*) were subsequently indicted by the ICC for crimes against humanity and war crimes.[3] In 2010 al-Bashir was indicted for genocide for his use of the *Janjaweed*, the Sudanese Armed forces, and other security and intelligence forces to selectively target certain civilian populations (the Fur, Masalit, and Zaghawa) in the Darfur region.[4] The indictments against al-Bashir and his accomplices are intended by the ICC and international community to deter individuals from invoking reasons of state for individual crimes and to combat impunity.[5] In *Notoria*, however, individual criminal responsibility is not at issue.[6] This moot court illustrates that jurisdiction over cases of genocide is one which the ICJ shares with the ICC and which is sometimes described as a "dual regime of responsibility for genocide."[7]

Notoria is a civil suit. As with civil suits more generally, the burden of proof is lower than in a criminal lawsuit. All that is required is a "preponderance of evidence." Cases of genocide can go before the ICJ though clearly it is difficult to punish a state with imprisonment. It is not exactly clear, therefore, whether the standard of guilt or liability at the ICJ is probability or proof of guilt beyond a reasonable doubt, or somewhere in between. In any event the larger problem in this case is how to apply a legal standard—intent to destroy a racial, religious, ethnic, or national group—to concrete situations. Generally, genocides are thought to be situations of mass murder of minority civilians, not merely incidents of attacks that destroy villages of distinct type, where counter-insurgency or counter-terrorism strategies are seemingly impelled by the need to find the enemy embedded in civilian living situations. The United States never recognized the situation in Bosnia, though some, such as the Minister Counselor of the U.S. Mission to the United Nations, deemed the situation in Bosnia to meet the legal criteria of the Genocide Convention. Of course, the United States considered Bosnia from the viewpoint of politics, not just law, but that situation also divided academic opinion; this similar to the current situation in Syria which has created division over whether or not the targeting of Sunni civilians by a Alawite, quasi Shia regime is just a civil war or also genocide.

Situations resembling the alleged genocides in Bosnia and Syria are much harder to prove than the systematic and clearly attempted extermination in Rwanda. There, most of the executions were of civilians who were already detained and/or were clearly non-combatants. In the former situations, those who were subjectively viewed as enemy combatants were thus killed, supposedly because they were militarily dangerous, not because the killers wanted to eliminate part of those groups "as such"—certainly not to a level of proof beyond a reasonable doubt. In their defense Croat and Serb defendants accused of genocide at the International Criminal Tribunal for Yugoslavia (ICTY) often pointed to the fact that women and children were usually spared. On the other hand, in the case of Srebrenica especially, detained males from the enemy ethnic group were systematically executed in cold blood; this clear evidence of genocide. However, a few notorious incidents do not mean an entire war was genocidal. As discussed in greater detail below, Bosnia failed as the plaintiff to prove that Serbia committed genocide in its case before the ICJ, even though the Court did indicate that genocide had occurred in Bosnia. Those legal arguments and evidence adduced are available online at the ICJ website.

According to the Genocide Convention, genocide is an intent crime; killings and other facts connoted by genocide are only evidence of the intent to destroy in part an ethnical, religious, national, or racial group. Technically, one does not actually have to kill anyone, as long as there is a plan or other manifested intent to destroy part of one or more of the groups in question. However, in practice, there has never been a declared genocide without actual mass murder. Killing a legally protected person, usually a non-combatant civilian or a soldier who has surrendered, is clearly evidence of a war crime and possibly a crime against humanity. The act does not rise to the level of genocide *unless* the murder was part of a plan to destroy part of one of these four types of groups (and not cultural or political groups, which negotiations between the Soviet Union and the United States, among other UN member states, excluded in order to reach an agreement). If one destroys a racial group, but that was not the intent, then one is not guilty of genocide. One may be guilty of something else, but not of genocide. If one intended and failed, then that person would still be guilty of genocide.

The real issue is not the target, but the mental element, especially whether or not the Genocide Convention contemplates an objective or subjective test. The latter is a strong defense, but it is critical to underscore that intent is not judged, even in a subjective test, by what the defendant *said* was intent, but what was the actual intent of the defendant.

In the second half of this case, the question becomes: what are the obligations of state parties to prevent genocide? Often politically, the issue is divisive because states seek to legalize humanitarian intervention without UNSC sanction, thus violating the UN Charter's Article 2(4) prohibition against armed attacks against sovereign states' political independence or territorial integrity. The

Genocide Convention turns that issue on its head, by asserting that states have not merely a possible option to intervene, but an obligation to do so, though the form of intervention may not constitute an armed attack. The Convention's requirement to "prevent and punish genocide" is undefined, other than to offer an option where states "may" ask UN bodies to take action to prevent and punish genocide. Obtaining UNSC approval to sanction intervention is neither mandatory nor an exclusive prerogative.

Humanitarian interventions, unlike those sanctioned by the UNSC under the doctrine of R2P, are at best putatively "illegal, but legitimate." NATO's intervention to prevent genocide in Bosnia in 1995 and Kosovo in 1999, the former under UNSC sanction and the latter not, both resulted not primarily from the influence of international norms against genocide, as is commonly believed, but from domestic factors such as the mass media, public opinion polls, and election cycles. That Bosnia had suffered a genocide was quite incidental to the U.S. decision to intervene, in no small part because the Clinton administration decided to avoid the "g" word, much as it did in its decision not to intervene contemporaneously in the Rwandan genocide, to circumvent the legal obligations of the Genocide Convention to prevent and punish genocide.

As part of the trial of *Bosnia v. Serbia* at the ICJ, two "provisional protective measures" were issued in April and September 1993. The then Federal Republic of Yugoslavia (FRY, later renamed Serbia and Montenegro) was ordered explicitly "*to do everything in its power to prevent the crimes of genocide and to make sure that such crimes are not committed by military or paramilitary formations operating under its control or with its support.*" At that trial's conclusion, Serbia was absolved of genocide, but it was found guilty of not preventing the genocide. In this particular case, the ICJ suggested that military officers and civilian leaders were guilty; only missing was the requisite level of proof, much of which was denied to the ICJ because the crucial evidence (the Supreme Defense Council records) had been granted to the ICTY on the condition that they not be revealed to anyone else.

Another category where soldiers might not be convicted of genocide would include situations where the particular atrocities occurred in combat and not in detention where the "acts may speak for themselves" as genocide. In combat, the motive of soldiers might be that the enemies were killed because they were the enemy. Some ostensibly non-combatant civilians might number among the victims as collateral damage, but because of the context, there might not be independent witnesses and other evidence from which "guilt beyond a reasonable doubt" could be established. In *Bosnia v. Serbia*, the ICJ accepted that acts of genocide certainly were perpetrated by Bosnian Serb forces, but could not find conclusive evidence of the specific Serb intent to destroy the ethnic Bosniaks as a group in whole or in part. What made the Serbian government less likely to be held liable for genocide is that the test of the mental element of the crime of genocide is subjective, as determined by the Genocide Convention. Instead of the presumptive objective test for the *mens rea* (guilty mind), based on what the reasonable person would have thought, this statute asserts that what matters is the subjective mind of any defendant. Thus, it would not matter that a reasonable person would have or should have known about the protective status of noncombatant civilians. So long as the defendant state thought that they were enemy combatants and not intended civilian targets from a racial, ethnic, religious, or national group to be destroyed in whole or in part, their acts would not be genocide, though they might constitute other crimes.

In the European Court of Human Rights case, *Jorgić v. Germany* on July 12, 2007, the Court held that rendering an area "ethnically homogeneous," is not genocide unless the ethnic cleansing meets the Conventions' requirement of "deliberately inflicting on the group conditions of life calculated to bring about its physical destruction in whole or in part," and the mental element is also present. Similarly, the ICTY held that while "there are obvious similarities between a genocidal policy and the policy commonly known as 'ethnic cleansing,' a clear distinction must be drawn between physical destruction and mere dissolution of a group."[8] The expulsion of a group or part of a group does not in itself suffice for genocide.

The ICJ's holding in *Bosnia* effectively concluded that Serbia was legally complicit in genocide by not preventing it, while having both the duty and the power to do so. Rulings in the ICJ can be contrasted with the ICTR. In the ICTR most of the convictions for genocide concerned paramilitary and military officials who were far easier to convict because they killed civilians in such a way that clearly demonstrated intent (in detention without due process). In the ICJ to hold a country responsible for genocide or failing to prevent genocide, its leaders must knowingly attack or fail to attack those who could attack a part of one of the four protected civilian groups set for destruction. A civilian leader would have to be linked to a plan, based on eye witness testimony or written documentation that indicated what may be clear, but hard to prove beyond a reasonable doubt, that the civilian leader intended to eliminate a part of a group. For countries to be liable, it may be harder to hold them responsible for genocides perpetrated by military officers acting in rogue fashion, as opposed to the civilian leaders who ordinarily are head of government and head of state. Only when military officers are heads of government and/or state would their actions be more likely to make the country liable for perpetrating or failing to prevent genocide.

Facts of the Case

The Republic of Notoria is the largest country in Africa, measuring over nine hundred thousand square miles. Since 2003 the country has been involved in an on-again, off-again conflict with three main rebels from the region of Killalli. Killalli is thousands of miles from the capital of Notoria, which is located in the eastern portion of the country. The people of Killalli and the inhabitants of the North (including those who make up the *Satanakunda*) are members of different ethnic groups. The Killanian victims are African Muslims, who in turn live in both Killalli and the capital.

The alleged violence which took place in Killalli consisted of the destruction of villages and the displacement and/or killing of large numbers of civilian inhabitants, primarily ethnic African Muslims living in villages, who are largely non-combatant civilians of the same ethnicity as some of the rebel groups fighting for secession of Killalli from Notoria. The group that is largely responsible for these actions is the ethnic Arab Muslim, *Satanakunda*, a paramilitary group associated with the Government of Notoria. A UN Commission of Inquiry sent to the region concluded in 2004 that the violence that was being perpetrated against the inhabitants of Killalli was *not* genocide. However, most NGOs and governments allege that it was genocide. The basis for this conclusion was the Commission's perception that the attacks were primarily aimed at rebels and/or otherwise intended to prevent rebel activity. In any event a hybrid African Union-UN peacekeeping force was dispatched to the region in 2007 to address the humanitarian disaster and to attempt to implement force separation among those rebel groups that had agreed to a cease-fire with the government. The mission was authorized by the UN Security Council under Chapter VI, as a voluntary mission without authority to use force except in its own self-defense. The UNSC was veto-deadlocked over the attempt to authorize a Chapter VII mission that would authorize "all means necessary" to establish peaceful conditions. The United States of Idealia is a permanent member of the UNSC, but did not attempt to propose a public initiative for a Chapter VII peace enforcement mission because it was clear from private discussions that other permanent UNSC members would veto such a resolution. The hybrid peacekeeping force has been subjected to attacks from the rebel groups in Killalli, as well as against humanitarian aid workers. The peacekeeping mission has been unwilling, unable, or is not authorized to protect either the humanitarian relief workers or the villagers who have been murdered in paramilitary attacks by the *Satanakunda*.

Notoria has also been engaged in a decades-long civil war with rebels in the south of the country since the late 1950s. Most recently the South declared its independence, following a plebiscite that indicated overwhelming support in the South for a separate state. Notoria, surprisingly, accepted the secession in the South, but not in Killalli. Although Notoria has launched its own investigations into the genocide, the President of Notoria was nevertheless indicted by the International Criminal Court in 2010 for genocide, crimes against humanity, and war crimes. Nolandia sued the Government of Notoria in the ICJ for violation of the United Nations Convention on the Prevention and Punishment of the Crime of Genocide and sued the United States of Idealia for its failure to prevent the genocide in Killalli. The Republic of Notoria and the United States of Idealia have both ratified the Genocide Convention.

Similar to the Republic of Notoria, Idealia is also being held responsible for its failure to prevent genocide in the Killalli region. The United States of Idealia is a developed Western country and sometimes claims to be the "leader of the free world." News polls and other surveys taken in 2004-2005 demonstrate that a majority of the citizens of Idealia believed Notoria had perpetrated genocide in Killalli. The Foreign Minister of Idealia expressed the view in 2005 that genocide was occurring to the people of the Killallian region of Notoria, though no additional action was undertaken by the United States of Idealia. It was not clear whether the Foreign Minister was speaking for himself or his government.

Idealia has abundant resources, including a large military that it occasionally uses unilaterally to respond to humanitarian, natural and man-made disasters, as well as to security threats throughout the world. Idealia sometimes engages in unilateral attacks on sovereign states without the approval of the UN Security Council, on which it holds a permanent seat.

All three countries have standing before the International Court of Justice, Notoria and Nolandia on an obligatory basis and Idealia on an optional basis, which it has exercised in order to peacefully resolve its legal obligations in this case.

Legal Matters and Other Issues for Discussion

Genocide, unlike most crimes against humanity and war crimes, is a violation of peremptory, non-derogable, *jus cogens* norms. This means genocide and similar *jus cogens* norms such as the prohibitions on torture, rape, and murder, cannot be contradicted by any other legal claim, such as might be made from interpreting treaties or customary international law. *Jus cogens* norms are always valid. The relatively uncontroversial concept of *jus cogens* does not mean that compliance *de facto* is high or that defining the crime or its remedies is simple, only that *de jure* interpretations are unequivocal. Rooted in natural law genocide's status is derived not only from the strongest ethical and moral claims, but also from the treaty banning the crime. By comparison positive law derives principles of law from reason and the laws of the state.[9] Positive law—the dominant paradigm today—is based on consent, often though not always manifested in treaties. Certain behaviors are therefore prohibited by positive law, not social norms based on claims of natural law or even *jus cogens*.

With regard to the crime of genocide more specifically, unlike the Statute of ICC, genocide is not included in the Statute of the ICJ. This marks yet another important distinction between the two courts and is a good starting point for a classroom discussion about sources of law utilized by international courts and, by extension, the differences between civil law and common law systems. Under civil law systems, the main sources of law are codes, based on strict legality. The alleged offender "may only be held criminally liable and punished if at the moment when he performed a certain act the act was regarded as a criminal offence by the relevant legal order."[10] The ICC is partly a system more grounded in civil law traditions. Its chief source of law is the 1998 Rome Statute, which also specifies that the traditional sources of international law also apply. Under the Statute's Article 21, judges may also take into consideration existing treaties, "the principles and rules of international law," the laws of states, and its own precedents).[11] Moreover, the legal precedents established by the *ad hoc* tribunals—the ICTY, the ICTR—and other international courts are also influential though not technically binding on the ICC unless the jurisprudence comes to be considered by the judges as binding under customary international law, presumably because most states have shown a sense of legal obligation and have obeyed these rules.

Of course, in practice, customary international law can be argued in the eye of the beholder. As with common law, judges can "discover" and clarify binding, customary law under the fiction that they themselves are not creating new law—which, of course, they are. Given the paucity of genocide cases, even after nearly two decades of the *ad hoc* tribunals, the role of judges in attempting to define and apply genocide to specific facts is particularly acute for legal, practical, and political reasons. There is still no consensus among states and scholars of what genocide really means, when real world cases are considered.

Compared to civil law systems, "judge-made law" is much more influential in common law systems.[12] Common law systems are therefore more flexible with regard to the applicable sources of law available to prosecutors and defendants alike. Though technically not bound by precedents, the ICJ utilizes the flexibility of common law jurisprudence through Article 38 of the ICJ Statute. The latter specifies international conventions, international customary law, and generally accepted principles as its sources of international law, with relevant jurisprudence/case law and scholarly opinion offering evidence of these three legal sources of international law.[13]

On a separate note, students will benefit from an examination of the ICJ's rules of procedure, which outlines rules regarding written pleadings, oral arguments, witness testimony and the like. Students should make note of the fact that the questions included in the appendix to this chapter could be used in their moot courts. Per Article 62 of the Rules of the Court, questions can also be asked of witnesses and experts, if the teacher and students choose to introduce different or more facts in this case, or if contested facts are to be introduced through the use of witnesses and cross-examination to accommodate more student participants.

According to Article 9 of the Genocide Convention, the ICJ is permitted to hear disputes between States Parties to the Convention regarding "the interpretation, application or fulfillment of the present Convention, including those relating to the responsibility of a State for genocide or for any of the other acts enumerated in Article III."[14] Based on its interests in the ethnic minority that also lives in Nolandia that is being destroyed in the Killallian region of Notoria, Nolandia alleges that Notoria is liable for the commission of genocide and complicity to commit genocide[15] largely through its conspiracy to murder and its support to an ethnic Arab militia, the *Satanakunda*. It also alleges that the government of Notoria knowingly permitted the *Satanakunda* to commit genocide, along with other violent human rights violations against the ethnic African Muslim, Killallian group and for failing to prevent this genocide in violation of Articles 1, 8 and 9 of the Genocide Convention.[16]

Nolandia and even an otherwise uninvolved superpower, Idealia, are both accused of violating the Convention for failure to prevent and punish genocide which are acts of *omission*. Unlike crimes of commission "properly defined," crimes of omission (sometimes called "crimes of commission by omission") are those in which the accused has a specified duty to act—sometimes for third parties even "extraneous to criminal law"—as well as the capacity to act.[17] Minus this capacity, the actor is not liable for the offense. Superior responsibility is one such example which will also be discussed in upcoming chapters. Crimes of omission rest on the assumption that, had the accused adhered to his/her duty, the crime in question would *not* have taken place.[18] Notoria might be sanctioned for its *failure* to act to prevent harm to the civilian group in question; to effectively control the actions of its military and militia.

Duttwiler argues, the crime of omission—aside from superior responsibility—is grounded less in treaty and/or customary law than it is in general principles of law.[19] He concludes that "there is in international law a general principle of law which states that for the purposes of criminal law, omission is normatively equivalent to action, if there was a special legal duty to act and prevent the harm in question."[20] The ICC Statute specifically mentions crimes of omission such as the failure to prevent and punish genocide; so there is clearly no ambiguity in the existence of an obligation other than what that obligation requires. The jurisprudence (statutes and case law) of the ICTR and the ICTY has also referred to crimes of omission,[21] though few persons have actually been convicted of such.

In three of the cases—*Mucić et. al., Krnojelac, Aleksovski*[22]—culpable omission was associated with willful mistreatment (e.g., deprivation of materials necessary for survival) of detainees. In the *Prosecutor v. Blaškić*, the ICTY Appeals Chamber held that the defendant's use of civilians (Bosniak Muslims) as human shields was a culpable omission per Article 7(1) of the Court's Statute which (paraphrasing) forbids the planning, instigation, ordering, committing or aiding and abetting of "grave breaches" of the Geneva Conventions, war crimes, genocide. and/or crimes against humanity.[23] Lastly, as Rana discusses, an ICTR case, the *Mpambara* case,[24] in which the Trial Chamber held that culpable omission—as a failure to prevent and punish—must be determined by three factors: the accused must be bound by a specific duty; he/she must be aware of and have willfully refused to discharge his/her duty; and the crime actually took place.[25] Interestingly, although the defendant was acquitted and his acquittal upheld on appeal, in another ICTR case, the defendant was convicted for culpable omission; the Court in this latter instance looking to the Rwandan Penal Code for guidance.[26]

The respondent's legal brief challenges the definitions of state and individual responsibility for genocide under international law. Notoria contends that neither it nor Idealia are liable for failure to prevent genocide under the terms of the Genocide Convention. In their review of both sets of legal briefs students will note the fact that both sides frequently refer to *Bosnia v. Serbia*.[27] This case was the first of its kind.[28] As indicated above Serbia was sued by Bosnia for its violation of the Genocide Convention, including the act of genocide in Srebrenica,[29] as well as a failure to prevent and punish the crime of genocide. Serbia was found liable by the ICJ for its act of omission),[30] but *not* liable for perpetration of the crime of genocide in Srebrenica due to the Serbian government's lack of effective control over the Bosnian-Serb army.[31] Instead, the Bosnian-Serb army perpetrated the genocidal murders of detainees in Srebrenica after receiving orders from the Bosnian-Serb government, not necessarily from identifiable actors who could be accountable from the government of the neighboring country of Serbia.[32]

In the present case, with respect to commission, Respondent Notoria's defense hinges on the argument that Notoria lacked the *dolus specialis* necessary for genocide. Unlike many other crimes under international law, conviction for the commission of the crime of genocide requires the demonstration of a *dolus specialis* on the part of the accused. As the ICTR Trial Chamber stated in the first genocide conviction in history in the August 1998 decision, *Akayesu:* "Special intent of a crime is the specific intention, required as a constitutive element of the crime, which demands that the perpetrator clearly seeks to produce the act charged."[33]

As Schabas writes this special intent is made up of three components; specifically the "offender must intend to destroy the *group* [emphasis added], the offender must intend that the group be destroyed in whole or in part, and the offender must intend to destroy a group that is defined by nationality, race, ethnicity or religion."[34] This special intent "describes a particular, additional mental element that goes beyond simply reflecting the material elements of the crime"[35] and as a consequence can be even more difficult to demonstrate, compared to direct intent (*dolus directus*) and certainly recklessness (*dolus evantualis*).[36] A higher standard of proof is required. As Cassese makes clear, more often than not—given a lack of direct evidence (e.g., a paper trail of the sort left behind by the Nazis)—courts must infer genocidal intent from the facts of the case.[37] This of course can be problematic in absence of evidence of a pre-existing genocidal plan (a sufficient, though not necessary component of genocide).[38]

Despite nearly two decades of genocide litigation, great uncertainty remains over the definition and application of this legal term. Part of the problem might be political or cultural, not legal. Much of the contemporary popular understanding is informed by the Holocaust, where the destruction of the Jewish and Roma people occurred during detention, as occurred at Srebrenica. However, in most genocides, civilians have been killed deliberately or recklessly in combat or recklessly and intentionally during marches and/or as a consequence of deprivation. Thus, there is a high degree of interpretation of motives, with recklessness and negligence falling outside the intent required by the text of the Genocide Convention for the crime of genocide.

Another issue of contention is the definition of a group or a part of a group, as well as what destroying a part of a group involves. The first task is to determine whether one of the four groups named, racial, ethnical, religious, or national, applies to a set of facts.[39] The absence of a working definition of "group" raises issues of both objective (what reasonable people regard as membership criteria as well as certain statistical criteria), *and* subjective aspects of group membership, what the individuals in a supposed group feel about their membership. As the author of the defense briefs in this chapter has written elsewhere, Robert Weiner argues that genocide scholars have long criticized the exclusion of political, social, and economic groups from the Genocide Convention.[40] May proposes changing the legal definition of genocide in the Convention to protect groups whose identity is publicly recognized (having "*both* stable in-group perception *and* out-group perception of the members as all forming a coherent group") and significant to group members themselves. This would reduce the ambiguity in membership criteria, while also expanding them to include political and cultural groups that were excluded during treaty negotiations in 1948.[41]

In recent years international jurisprudence has expanded the definition of "group" to include subjective and objective qualities of group membership.[42] In *Rutaganda*, the ICTR held that "for the purposes of applying the Genocide Convention, membership of a group is, in essence, a subjective rather than an objective concept. The victim is perceived by the perpetrator of genocide as belonging to a group slated for destruction. In some instances, the victim may perceive himself/herself as belonging to the said group."[43] Despite the subjective expansion of the definition of "group," international courts have as of yet to include any of the aforementioned excluded groups (e.g., political, economic) under the protective rubric of the Genocide Convention.

Idealia is being sued because of its alleged failure to prevent genocide under Articles 1, 8, and 9 of the Genocide Convention.[44] Its inclusion reflects the commonly expressed exasperation at the failure of the international community, both the UN Security Council and major world powers to protect the victims of genocide in cases where decisive action would have prevented the genocides in Rwanda, Srebrenica, if not all of Bosnia, Aceh, Indonesia, Cambodia, (the list goes on), and perhaps for not trying in more intractable, arguable genocides in Sri Lanka, Syria, Chechnya, Ivory Coast, and Kenya.[45] Applicant/Plaintiff Nolandia contends that Idealia held an *erga omnes* obligation to respond to the genocidal crisis, where advocates of R2P legal doctrine argue triggers, at least the option of intervening to stop a genocide, and perhaps mandates some response, however limited the options, even if only to call a genocide as such, as well as to impose economic sanctions, blockades and coercive diplomacy to induce peace talks and a cease-fire, as well as arresting or sanctioning indicted genocidal leaders—among the remedies that might satisfy the Convention's requirement of state parties to prevent and punish genocide. *Erga omnes* obligations are "obligations towards all other member states of the international community, . . . [which] at the same time confer on any state the right to require that [in this case] acts of genocide be discontinued."[46] The ICJ in *Bosnia* affirmed that the duty to prevent and punish the crime of genocide was an *erga omnes* obligation not subject to territorial limitations. However, this legal conclusion does not appear to have much political effect, since neither the UN Security Council nor the United States, among other countries, ever formally recognized either Bosnia or Rwanda as genocides, even though action was belatedly undertaken in the former and effectively withdrawn in the latter. In Sudan, the U.S. accusation of genocide was ephemeral, the statement of Secretary of State Colin Powell, whose authority to speak for the country was strong, but did not result in an explicit position of that country. Whether or not this consistent political reluctance of states to deem genocides in real cases has affected the possible reluctance of courts to find genocides in general and has resulted in the new legal concept of "acts of genócide" is worthy of study. It could be argued that customary international law has been emerging where state action and sense of legal obligation is modifying the perceived meaning of the Genocide Convention. Additionally, the frequent veto-deadlocks at the UN Security Council, which reflects political and security considerations, arguably may not constitute *legal* criteria for determining the meaning of the Genocide Convention's legal terms.

Erga omnes obligations are closely associated with a newly emerging international doctrine referred to as the R2P. Discussed in greater detail in the next case section, R2P requires states such as Idealia and also Notoria "to protect . . . populations from genocide, war crimes, ethnic cleansing and crimes against humanity [including their own populations],"[47] even if no threat to the peace, as required by Article 39 in Chapter VII of the UN Charter, is present.

Idealia's argument in defense of its actions is instructive because it explains in detail its legal rationale for inaction. The UNSC's invocation of Article 39 authority in Libya in 2011[48] established an important political, if not also a legal precedent, even if the implementation by NATO resulted in an unauthorized regime change and not so much protection over the longer term. On other occasions, such as at the time of writing, the possible genocide in Syria, the veto-deadlock in the Security Council has led to inaction. Former U.S. Ambassador to the UN, John Bolton, opposed any mandatory responsibility to protect or intervene per Chapter VII of the UN Charter. As Glanville writes:

> It would seem that it was primarily the intervention of . . . Bolton that prevented a firmer declaration . . . In 2005 Bolton acted on behalf of the United States to ensure that this freedom [to interpret international obligations as states see fit] would be preserved. The United States was reluctant to bind itself to respond to particular cases in particular ways. Consequently, it sought to reject any suggestion that it might be obliged to act when states fail to protect their populations.[49]

At most, Bolton suggested that states had a moral responsibility to act and that the response to humanitarian crises should be determined on a case-by-case basis within the purview of the UN Security Council.[50]

The issues associated with third-party intervention are an excellent topic for classroom discussion and debate. Is UNSC approval necessary for military intervention or can states act on their own to stop mass atrocities? Frequent UN member state condemnations of the unilateral interventions to stop the atrocities and arguable genocides of Vietnam in Cambodia; India in Bangladesh/East Pakistan and Tanzania in Uganda suggest that if the R2P justifies intervention, it would only be when the UNSC authorizes an intervention. These actions were widely condemned. In these particular instances military intervention to stop an egregious international crime as it is taking place runs afoul of the UN Charter (the highest source of international law); specifically Article 2(4) which states: "All Members shall refrain . . . from the threat or use of force against the territorial integrity or political independence of any State, or in any other manner inconsistent with the Purposes of the United Nations." Advocates of unilateral humanitarian intervention without UNSC authorization argue that Article 2(4) provides a legal opening, when an intervention truly does support one of the main Purposes of the UN: protection of human rights. Under these conditions, what else could Idealia or any other concerned country have done to meet their obligation as state parties to the Genocide Convention to prevent and punish genocide? Are there other Articles within the UN Charter that would give support to the notion of unilateral intervention?

Moreover, does simple acknowledgment of a crime as genocide lead to a military response? As indicated above members of the Government of the United States of Idealia have officially referred to the violence in Notoria as "genocide." Again this is a similar situation to the U.S. response to the genocide in Darfur. It is obvious from that particular set of facts that mere acknowledgment of genocide does not necessary provoke a forceful response. Should it though? This is part and parcel of Nolandia's argument.

MEMORIAL OF THE KINGDOM OF NOLANDIA

COMES NOW the Kingdom of Nolandia and for their Memorial to the Court, asks the following:

QUESTIONS PRESENTED

Does the violence in Killalli constitute genocide under international law? How can the intent of the Government of the Republic Notoria be measured absent evidence of a direct order or other "smoking gun"?

For purposes of application of the United Nations Convention on the Punishment and Prevention of Genocide (Genocide Convention), what are the criteria that distinguish an ethnic or racial group under international law?

Can the actions of an irregular militia—the *Satanakunda*—be attributed to the Government of Notoria if these acts were not the result of a direct order from the government and took place outside the purview of government officials?

If it is found that the Government of Notoria did not commit genocide, did it then fail to *prevent* genocide and if so how can this failure be determined? What are the legal foundations of a state's obligation to prevent genocide?

Did the United States of Idealia violate its duty to prevent genocide? What is the scope of this duty under international treaty and customary law?

STATEMENT OF LAW

The crime of genocide is an extraordinary offense that violates *jus cogens* norms and which "shocks the conscience of mankind." It is rooted in natural law that supersedes all treaty law.

The Republic of Notoria and the United States of Idealia are signatories to the Genocide Convention and are therefore obligated by its terms.[51]

The black Muslim population of Notoria is a group protected by the Genocide Convention.

The attacks perpetrated against black Muslims in Notoria by the *Satanakunda* militia meet the criteria of acts prohibited under the Genocide Convention.

Notoria is directly responsible for the genocide based on its support of the *Satanakunda* and its own participation in the killings. Notoria has violated Articles 1, 2, and 3 of the Genocide Convention.

Notoria is also in violation of Articles 1, 8, and 9 of the Genocide Convention for failing to prevent and punish the genocide from occurring within its territory. Notoria acted contrary to its obligations to protect its population which is a responsibility that is deeply rooted in international customary law. Therefore, even if the Court finds that Notoria was not actively involved in the commission of genocide, Notoria must be held responsible for failing to prevent it.

The United States of Idealia is in violation of Articles 1, 8, and 9 of the Genocide Convention for its failure to prevent genocide in Notoria; a crime which it publicly recognized and condemned. Idealia failed to adhere to its obligations to prevent such atrocities under customary international law.

STATEMENT OF JURISDICTION

The Court has the jurisdiction to hear this case under Article 9 of the Genocide Convention which grants this Court to hear disputes "between the Contracting Parties relating to the interpretation, application or fulfillment of the present Convention, including those relating to the responsibility of a State for genocide or for any of the other acts enumerated in Article III."[52]

SUMMARY OF ARGUMENTS

The violence in Killalli meets the definitional requirements for the crime of genocide outlined in Article 2 of the Genocide Convention. The civilian population in Killalli was targeted by the Government of Notoria on the basis of their group identity. The Government of Notoria directly, and through its provision of assistance to the extremist militia the *Satanakunda,* is responsible for the commission of genocide in violation of Articles 1, 2, and 3 of the Convention. Moreover, Notoria is liable for its failure to prevent and punish genocide as per Articles 1, 8, and 9 of the Convention, pursuant to past decisions of this Court, and the newly emerging R2P norm.

The Government of Idealia, through its failure to come to the aid of the people of Killalli, acted in contravention of its obligations pursuant to Articles 1, 8, and 9 of the Genocide Convention, past decisions of this very Court, and evolving customary international law, not to mention an *erga omnes* obligation as genocide violates a peremptory norm of international law.

ARGUMENTS

I. Respondent Notoria is in Violation of International Law by Failing to Fulfill its Duties Under the Genocide Convention to Prevent and Punish Genocide Occurring within its Territory

A. THE SITUATION OCCURRING IN NOTORIA CONSTITUTES GENOCIDE

Article 2 of the Genocide Convention defines genocide as:

> [A]cts committed with the intent to destroy, in whole or in part, a national, ethnic, racial, or religious group and includes any of the following:
> (a) Killing members of the group;
> (b) Causing serious bodily harm to members of the group;
> (c) Deliberately inflicting on the group conditions of life calculated to bring about its physical destruction in whole or in part;
> (d) Imposing measures intended to prevent births within the group;
> (e) Forcibly transferring children of the group to another group.[53]

This definition is wide-ranging and includes a number of crimes intended to destroy a group based solely on a particular characteristic. This definition covers acts committed in the state of Notoria. The Notorian government and its sponsored militia group, the *Satanakunda*, are responsible for the murders of tens of thousands of black Muslim Notorians residing in the Killalli region of the country. These killings have been carried out systematically, and are aimed at destroying the black Notorian population in the Killalli region of Nortoria. These acts have been carried out in a manner which fulfills Articles 2(a), 2(b), and 2(c) of the Convention.

The Respondents claim that this is *not* genocide because there is not a group being singled out on the basis of nationality, ethnicity, race, or religion. We argue that, contrary to Respondents' position, at least one of these classifications is met in this case. We have a clash between Muslim-Arabs and Muslim-blacks who may have lived together and even intermarried over the past two decades yet still primarily identify themselves—and more importantly each other—by their racial groupings. The specific targeting of the black Muslim population indicates an intent to destroy a group based simply on differing racial characteristics.

International jurisprudence is now clear on the fact that group identity comprises subjective *and* objective components. In terms of group identity, the International Criminal Tribunal for Rwanda (ICTR) dealt with a similar issue with respect to the identities "Tutsi" and "Hutu." Both groups were members of the same religion and of similar racial/ethnic makeup due to years of intermarriage. As Cassese states:

> for the TC [Trial Chamber] in *Akayesu* the question of whether or not a multitude of personas made up a group protected by the rules against genocide was primarily a question of fact: the court had to establish whether (i) those persons were *in fact treated* as belonging to one of those protected groups; and in addition (ii) they *considered themselves* as belong to one of such groups.[54]

What matters especially is the manner in which the target population is *perceived* by the attacking group. The Trial Chamber of the International Criminal Tribunal of the Former Yugoslavia (ICTY) in *Jelisić* ruled that:

> to attempt to define a national, ethnical, or racial group today using objective and scientifically irreproachable criteria would be a perilous exercise whose result would not necessarily correspond to the perception of the persons concerned by such categorisation. Therefore it is more appropriate to evaluate the status of a national, ethnical, or racial group from the point of view of those persons who wish to single that group out from the rest of the community. The Trial Chamber consequently elects to evaluate membership . . . using a subjective criterion.[55]

Moreover, it is worth noting that the UN Commission of Inquiry sent to Killalli to assess the abuses perpetrated by the *Satanakunda* concluded in its 2004 report that group identity in Killalli is largely a matter of individual perception. Therefore whether or not members of the target group in Killalli were in fact black or more likely of "mixed" racial origins is *less* of an issue than the fact that they were perceived as such by the Government of Notoria.

Additionally, evidence of the fact that the situation in Notoria is genocide is further substantiated by the international discourse which has emerged. It is not insignificant in that the legislature of the United States of Idealia passed a resolution declaring and condemning the situation in Killalli as genocide. This classification was affirmed by Idealia's Foreign Minister for Human Rights a short time thereafter.

B. NOTORIA BREACHED ITS DUTY UNDER THE GENOCIDE CONVENTION BY ENGAGING IN THE COMMISSION OF GENOCIDE

Article 1 of the Genocide Convention states that: "The Contracting Parties confirm that genocide, whether committed in time of peace or in time of war, is a crime under international law which they undertake to prevent and punish."[56] As a party to the Genocide Convention Respondent Notoria is legally prohibited from *committing* genocide. Moreover, Article 4 states that: "Persons committing genocide or any of the other acts enumerated in article III shall be punished, whether they are constitutionally responsible rulers, public officials or private individuals."

Article 3 of the Genocide Convention states that the following acts shall be punishable: "(a) Genocide; (b) Conspiracy to commit genocide; (c) Direct and public incitement to commit genocide; (d) Attempt to commit genocide; (e) Complicity in genocide."[57]

Notoria is responsible for the massacres which occurred in Killalli. Evidence collected by internationally respected human rights organizations demonstrates that the Notorian military has been directly involved in the attacks against the black Notoria population in Killalli. The Government of Notoria has also provided weapons, funding, and other "encouragement" to the *Satanakunda* militia group. These acts are in violation of Articles 3(a) and (e) of the Genocide Convention, respectively.

The crime of genocide is one in which the *actus reus* and *mens rea* must align. Genocide requires a special intent or *dolus specialis* on the part of the perpetrator to destroy a group protected by the Genocide Convention in whole or in part.[58] The ICTY Trial Chamber in *Stakić* stated that all crimes outlined in Article 3 of the Genocide Convention require demonstration of this special intent.[59]

According to case law of the *ad hoc* Tribunals this special intent may be inferred from context among other things. The ICTY Appeals Chamber stated in *Jelisić* for example:

> As to proof of specific intent, it may, in the absence of direct explicit evidence, be inferred from a number of facts and circumstances, such as the general context, the perpetration of other culpable acts systematically directed against the same group, the scale of atrocities committed, the systematic targeting of victims on account of their membership of [sic] a particular group, or the repetition of destructive and discriminatory acts.[60]

Respondent Notoria will claim that the military may have been engaged in crimes against humanity, at the very least war crimes, through its reckless conduct which resulted in the deaths of thousands of civilians. However, as indicated above, the special intent for genocide can be derived from the actual behavior of its perpetrators.[61] It is true that the military forces of Respondent Notoria were fighting a civil war against rebel forces within the region of Killalli. However, it is also true that their violent behavior "deliberately and systematically" murdered eleven targeted members of the black Muslim population of Killalli on the basis of that group's perceived racial-ethnical identity. Based on the evidence, a reasonable person could certainly be expected to conclude from the factual record that genocide indeed had and is still occurring.

Moreover, the Government of Notoria did in fact render substantial material, logistical, and other support to the *Satankunda* militia; a group who by their very actions demonstrate the intent to destroy the black Muslim population of Killalli. Therefore through the actions of its military, and by way of its support for the *Satankunda* militia, the Respondent Government of Notoria has demonstrated the special intent required for complicity and commission of the crime of genocide. Notoria has violated international criminal law and must be held responsible for its actions.

C. NOTORIA BREACHED ITS DUTY UNDER THE GENOCIDE CONVENTION BY FAILING TO PREVENT GENOCIDE WITHIN ITS TERRITORY

Respondent Notoria is also in violation of international law for its *failure* to prevent and punish the genocide occurring within its territory. Therefore, even if the Court finds that Respondent Notoria was not actively involved in the commission of the crime of genocide, Notoria must be held responsible for failing to prevent the crime of genocide pursuant to Articles 1, 8, and 9 of the Convention. This obligation occurs when a state learns, or should normally have learned, of the existence of a serious risk that genocide will be committed.

a. Notoria has Violated its Obligations under the Genocide Convention

Article 9 of the Genocide Convention imposes extensive obligations on states to prevent or be held accountable for genocide. Article 8 calls upon member states to "call upon the competent organs of the UN" in the event genocide is occurring. Nortoria failed to do this. Even if the Court should find that there is not enough evidence to conclusively prove that the Government of Notoria directly participated in the genocide of black Muslim Notorians in the Killalli province, Respondent may still be held liable for its complicity in the genocide arising from its failure to prevent the massacres conducted by the *Satanakunda*; a crime of culpable *omission*.

In this case Respondent Government of Notoria is legally responsible for the violence in Killalli because it knowingly failed to protect its citizenry from the violence unleashed by the *Satanakunda*. The facts of this case demonstrate that the Government clearly possessed knowledge of the violence occurring in Killalli and as a sovereign state the means with which to stop it.

b. Notoria has Violated its Obligations under the Principle of State Responsibility

In addition to being in breach of its obligations under the Genocide Convention, Notoria is in violation of the International Law Commission's (ILC) Draft Articles on State Responsibility, which have risen to the level of customary international law.[62] An "internationally wrongful act" is considered by the ILC to be an act or omission that: "(a) Is attributable to the State under international law; and (b) constitutes a breach of an international obligation of the State."[63] Such actions or omissions are those which violate preemptory norms of international criminal law. A breach of an international obligation is defined by Article 12 of the ILC Draft Articles as "an act of that State that is not in conformity with what is required of it by that obligation, regardless of its origin or character."[64]

Notoria is responsible for making sure that those individuals within its control do not commit violations of international law. Even if this Court concludes that Respondent Notoria was not a direct participant in the genocide either by way of the actions of its military or more specifically the *Satanakunda* acting as a "direct organ" of Notoria, as a sovereign state the Government of Notoria clearly failed to control its military, as well as the *Satanakunda* militia group within its borders, thereby allowing the genocide to continue in contravention of international law.[65] The actions of its military and the *Satanakunda* are therefore attributable to Respondent under customary international law. With respect to the military, Article 7 of the Draft Articles holds that states are nevertheless liable for the actions of their entities even when these actions "[exceed their] authority or [contravene] instructions."[66]

Similar to Respondent Idealia, Respondent Notoria has an obligation, spelled out in the ILC Draft Articles, as well as the 2005 World Summit Resolution, to protect members of its own population from crimes against humanity, ethnic cleansing, war crimes, and genocide.[67] The failure of Respondent Notoria to protect its population is a violation of its obligations pursuant to customary international law and the Genocide Convention.

c. Notoria has Violated its Obligations Pursuant to the Decisions of the International Court of Justice

Furthermore, a finding that Respondent Notoria is criminally responsible for its failure to act would be wholly consistent with this Court's jurisprudence. Notoria is liable under international law for failing to prevent genocide pursuant to the 2007 holding of the International Court of Justice in *Application of the Convention on the Prevention and Punishment of the Crime of Genocide (Bosnia and Herzegovina v. Serbia and Montenegro).*[68]

As this Court stated in *Bosnia*: "it is self-evident . . . that if a State is not responsible for any of the acts referred to in Article III, paragraphs (a) to (e) of the Convention, this does not mean its responsibility cannot be sought for a violation of the obligation to prevent genocide and the other acts referred to in Article III."[69] This Court held that the obligation to prevent genocide is "both normative and compelling";[70] a State must "take all measures to prevent genocide which

[are] within its power, and which might . . . [contribute] to preventing the genocide."[71] In other words, the state has an obligation to exercise *due diligence* which in turn is a function of its capacity (physical, legal) to act.[72] Moreover, the state's obligation to act to prevent genocide arises "at the instance the State learns of, or should normally have learned of, the existence of a serious risk that genocide will be committed."[73]

In *Bosnia v. Serbia*, this Court ruled that the leadership of Serbia, including President Slobodan Milošević, was fully aware there was a serious possibility of genocide occurring in Srebrenica and was therefore responsible for the violations of international criminal law that ensued.[74] As this applies to the present case, Respondent did indeed have the capacity to act to prevent the genocide from occurring. Moreover, being aware of the possibility of genocide or more accurately the actual *perpetration* of genocide clearly obligated Notoria and all of its agents to take preventative action to avoid further harm to the black population of Killalli.

Unlike this Court's ruling in *Bosnia*, Applicant also contends that Respondent Notoria did in fact exercise *effective* control over the chief perpetrators of the offenses addressed in this case In *Bosnia*, this Court held that:

> the conduct of an organ or person furnishing aid or assistance to a perpetrator of the crime of genocide cannot be treated as complicity in genocide unless at least the organ or person acted knowingly . . . in particular, was aware of the specific intent (*dolus specialis*) of the principal perpetrator. If that condition is not fulfilled, that is sufficient to exclude categorization as complicity.[75]

As stated above, the facts of the case demonstrate that Notoria did in fact knowingly provide aid and assistance to the *Satanakunda*; aid which helped facilitate the genocide. Moreover, leaders of the Respondent Government of Notoria certainly had control over the military. As such the government is therefore absolutely liable for their actions. The Respondent's actions demonstrate the *dolus specialis* required for complicity in the crime of genocide pursuant to Article 3(e) of the Genocide Convention.

II. Respondent Idealia has Violated International Law by Failing to Fulfill its Duties Under the Genocide Convention by not Taking Action to Prevent the Genocide Occurring within Notoria

A. THE GENOCIDE CONVENTION ESTABLISHES A CLEAR DUTY TO TAKE ACTION TO PREVENT GENOCIDE

The obligation to prevent genocide imposes a duty on States Parties to the Genocide Convention to intervene to stop killings under the terms of the treaty, the full title of which underscores its object and purpose which is both preventative *and* punitive. Operative Article 1 of the Genocide Convention establishes a clear duty to (i) prevent *and* to (ii) punish genocide. These two distinct duties are not qualified or limited and the breach of one or both incurs state responsibility. Thus, the ICJ ruled in *Bosnia (Provisional Measures)* that Yugoslavia was required under the Genocide Convention to "take all measures within its power to prevent the commission of the crime of genocide."[76]

Moreover, this Court in its February 2007 Judgment in *Bosnia* held that a state can be held responsible for breaching the obligation to prevent genocide provided that genocide was actually committed, which it was in this case, and provided it had the means to do so. The duty to prevent genocide is further supported by Articles 8 and 9 of the Genocide Convention which reference, respectively, (i) the option for States Parties to call upon the UN to take action under the Charter in fulfilling its obligations of prevention or suppression (which would not be referenced absent a clear duty); and (ii) the recognition that state responsibility attaches to the failure to prevent or punish genocide.

Preambular language in the Genocide Convention further supports the view that the duty to prevent is part and parcel of the purpose of the UN and a duty of its Member states insofar as they are obliged to take action to maintain international peace and security. The failure to take action to prevent genocide constitutes a threat to that purpose: "[A]cts of genocide identified by the present Convention are crimes against the Law of Nations, and that the fundamental exigencies of the civilization, international order and peace require their prevention and punishment."[77] This view is buttressed by the *Advisory Opinion on Reservations to the Genocide Convention* in which it was held that the crime of genocide "shocks the conscience of mankind, results in great losses to humanity, and which is contrary to moral law and to the spirit and aims of the United Nations."[78] Security Council practice further supports the proposition that states have a duty to act to prevent genocide.

In addition, a number of high level panels support the existence of a duty to prevent. The UN Secretary-General's establishment in 2004 of a High Level Panel on Threats, Challenges, and Change affirms a responsibility to protect as referenced in its report,[79] and as affirmed by the General Assembly's adoption in September 2005 by 191 states the 2005 World Summit Outcome which recognizes that atrocity crimes are a matter of universal concern.[80] A panel of eminent international law experts has opined in a recent report that "in the context of atrocity crimes, the focus is no longer on States' sovereign rights, but also on their responsibilities," and that "States have responsibilities not only with regard to other States but also towards populations, including the civilian populations of other States."[81]

B. IDEALIA HAS FALLEN SHORT OF MEETING ITS DUTY TO PREVENT INSOFAR AS ITS ACTIONS TO DATE FAIL TO MEET THE THRESHOLD FOR PREVENTIVE ACTION TO STOP GENOCIDE

The Genocide Convention is silent as to the precise scope of the duty to prevent genocide. Nonetheless, state practice and the progressive development of international human rights law and its system of human rights protection provide guidance as to the range of measures which fall within the scope of the duty to prevent. A state Party may choose among a range of measures to undertake to prevent or punish genocide. Prevention may entail support for democratic institutions, rule of law, development assistance, the promotion of arms control and disarmament, and the like. In the instant case, the Respondent has fallen well short of its duty to prevent under the Genocide Convention given the substantial range of methods and means at its disposal. What actions Idealia has taken do not at all rise to the threshold required to satisfy its duty to prevent genocide. Whereas the national legislature of the United States of Idealia adopted a resolution declaring the attacks being carried out in Killalli to be genocide, a characterization endorsed by the Foreign Minister for Human Rights of Idealia in 2005, these measures do not constitute preventive measures and were, in any case, pronouncements of a purely domestic political nature. Neither does the sponsorship of Idealia of Security Council Resolution 1665 constitute the duty to prevent.

C. EVEN ASSUMING THAT THE GENOCIDE CONVENTION DOES NOT ESTABLISH A CLEAR DUTY FOR STATES TO PREVENT GENOCIDE, THE DUTY TO PREVENT ATTACHES BY VIRTUE OF THE FACT THAT GENOCIDE IS INDISPUTABLY A PEREMPTORY NORM OF INTERNATIONAL LAW AND, MOREOVER, AN OBLIGATION ERGA OMNES

The prohibition of genocide qualifies as a rule of customary international law[82] and as a *jus cogens* norm per Judge Elihu Lauterpacht in the September 1993 *Provisional Measures* ruling in *Bosnia*: "the prohibition of genocide . . . has generally been accepted as having the status not of an ordinary rule of international law but of jus cogens. Indeed, the prohibition of genocide has long been regarded as one of the few undoubted examples of jus cogens."[83]

The duty to prevent genocide, as a *jus cogens* norm, trumps any incompatible obligation, even one dictated by the UN Charter. In its *Advisory Opinion in the Reservations to the Genocide Convention* the ICJ held: "the principles underlying the Convention are principles which are recognized by civilized nations as binding on States, even without any conventional obligation."[84] This view is supported by pronouncements of the United Nations Security Council on the subject of states' duty to prevent genocide, urging, in an operative paragraph in the context of the Rwandan genocide, "all States and relevant organization to cooperate in countering radio broadcasts that incite acts of genocide, hatred and violence."[85] Acts of genocide have become internationalized under the UN Charter and developments in human rights law and are thus no longer a matter within the exclusive domestic jurisdiction of states.

Genocide further constitutes an obligation *erga omnes*, norms in respect of which all states have a legitimate interest in enforcing. The prohibition of genocide has been identified as an *erga omnes* norm by the ICJ in *Barcelona Traction case* (*Belgium v. Spain*),[86] and thereby confers on any state to proceed against another state for failure to prevent and/or punish the crime of genocide. In the *Barcelona* case, all states were held to have an interest in the protection of *erga omnes* obligations. Professor Toope has argued persuasively that the

Court's ruling clearly vests a right to expect the performance of an *erga omnes* obligation insofar as it recognized a class of obligations owed by a state "towards the international community as a whole" and according to which all states had a legitimate "interest in their protection."[87] He reasons that individual states may thus be burdened with a duty under customary international law to enforce the obligation to prevent genocide.[88] In the instant case, Nolandia is asserting its legitimate right pursuant to the international law concept of *erga omnes* and attaching to the crime of genocide to take action in respect of Idealia's failure to take preventive action.

III. Respondent Idealia, Which has the Military Means to Prevent the Commission by Respondent Notoria of Ongoing Genocide Consisting of Killing, Raping, and Burning by the Satanakunda in Killalli, is Obligated under International Law to take Such Action in the Absence of Action by the UN Security Council

A. ALL STATES PLEDGE UNDER UN SECURITY COUNCIL TO TAKE JOINT AND SEPARATE ACTION TO PROTECT HUMAN RIGHTS

By classifying genocide as an "international crime," Article 1 of the Genocide Convention is indicating intent for all states to recognize, prevent, and punish such a crime. While Respondent's argument concerning the primary responsibility of the UN to maintain international peace and security is generally without dispute, the UN Charter is not absolute in its requirements that all actions go through the Security Council.

The United Nations Security Council is obviously the preferred forum for instigating an action such as military intervention to prevent genocide like that in Notoria. If the Security Council, however, is unable or unwilling to act, then responsibility moves to individual member states. Each member of the UN, on becoming party to the treaty, pledges to uphold all components of that treaty, including the protections of human rights. Article 55 requires states to promote "universal respect for, and observance of, human rights and fundamental freedoms for all without distinction as to race, sex, language, or religion,"[89] and Article 56 requires states to take "joint and separate action"[90] to achieve these goals. Moreover, as the prohibition on genocide has reached the status of a *jus cogens* norm, all states have a responsibility to prevent genocide from occurring. This universal nature of the crime entitles all states, whether or not they have a direct interest in the situation, to take action to prevent the occurrence of genocide, even in the absence of United Nations Security Council action.

B. RISING RECOGNITION OF THE LIMITED NATURE OF SOVEREIGNTY AND THE RESPONSIBILITY OF STATES TO PROTECT PERSONS IN OTHER COUNTRIES REQUIRED IDEALIA TO ACT

The R2P is an emerging norm of customary international law, one which adheres to a more limited notion of state sovereignty and allows for the breach of sovereignty when a state is grossly in violation of international human rights law. Created through a Canadian-led commission charged by former UN Secretary-General Kofi Annan to develop this concept, the resulting report entitled *The Responsibility to Protect* was released in December 2001. Since that time, R2P as a norm of international law has been endorsed by two UN Secretary-General reports, as well as by the US Institute for Peace.[91] This concept has also been recognized in the judicial decisions of the International Court of Justice. For example, in the *Bosnian Genocide* case, the ruling of the ICJ finding Serbia in violation of its international legal obligations for failing to prevent the massacre at Srebrenica, provides strong persuasive authority concerning the affirmative responsibility of states to prevent genocide through humanitarian intervention.[92]

The Court stated in its *Bosnia* decision that State Parties to the Genocide Convention must use all means at their disposal to prevent any person, group of persons, or state entity from committing an act of genocide or any other act prohibited by the treaty. The Court also held that a state may be held responsible for failure to uphold the provisions of the Genocide Convention for failing to prevent genocide if it had the means to do so, but simply refrained from acting.[93]

This international legal principle of R2P is largely based on restricted notions of sovereignty, which recognize that sovereignty not only implies the duty to respect the sovereign integrity of other states, but also "summons the concomitant duty of the government to respect the fundamental rights of all peoples within the state and take action to protect them."[94] Given this emerging norm, there must come a point at which states have an obligation to intervene in the affairs of another state to protect the greater good. As stated by former UN Secretary-General Kofi Annan in his address before the 2000 Millennium Summit, "[I]f humanitarian intervention is, indeed, an unacceptable assault on sovereignty, how should we respond to a Rwanda, to a Srebrenica—to gross and systematic violations of human rights that offend every precept of our common humanity?"[95] This is where R2P comes in, the motivating factor of which is the drive to stop or prevent human suffering. The report does recognize that this is not an action to be taken lightly, as sovereignty is a foundational core of the international system. Therefore, the report has developed what is called the "threshold of last resort," which means before using force to protect, governments are legally bound to pursue all reasonable peaceful means available to them to resolve the situation, including an appeal to the UN Security Council. The timetable for this pursuit, however, must be contingent on the situation at hand: "If human rights conditions worsen, or the threats to the security of persons in that state escalate, the lawful justification—and need—for military intervention will rise correspondingly."[96]

If the UN Security Council is unable or unwilling to act, there must be resort to an alternative method of preventing the human rights abuses. This is what we saw in the case of NATO intervention in Kosovo, as characterized by the Independent International Commission on Kosovo (2000), chaired by Richard Goldstone and Carl Tham. The report deemed the NATO intervention unavoidable because, "diplomatic options had been exhausted, and two sides were bent on a conflict which threatened to wreak humanitarian catastrophe."[97] The Commission held that NATO intervention was legitimate. The situation in Notoria is arguably worse than that in Kosovo. The massacres in Killalli have been widespread and have been categorized as genocide. The United States of Idealia, a state party to the Genocide Convention, as well as a member of the United Nations, has the obligation (and the means) to intervene to protect the black Muslim population in Killalli, Notoria. Under international law, Idealia is obliged to do so.

IV. Respondent Idealia, by Classifying the Situation in Killalli as Genocide, is Obligated by International Law to Act

A. IDEALIA HAS CLASSIFIED THE SITUATION AS GENOCIDE AND IN SO DOING TRIGGERS ITS RESPONSIBILITY TO ACT

a. There is a Clear Finding of Genocide in the Instant Case, Affirmed by the Pronouncements of Idealia [as Referenced in Part (a) relating to Applicant's Arguments in Support of its Application re: Respondent Notoria]

Idealia's contention that the situation in Notoria does not constitute genocide is belied by the facts of the case as argued above and, moreover, Idealia is estopped from claiming that the situation is not genocide in light of its own characterization of the situation as genocide, in particular the pronouncement of its Foreign Minister. A state can be held responsible for breaching the obligation to prevent genocide, provided that genocide was actually committed. As argued above, genocide was committed in this case, thereby triggering responsibility on the part of Idealia to take action to prevent genocide.

b. The Genocide Convention Imposes Individual State Responsibility under International Law on the Part of States for the Failure to Prevent Genocide Wherever it Occurs

Article 9 of the Genocide Convention expresses the principle of state responsibility for genocide, an obligation which extends to the duty to prevent genocide. Article 1, which articulates the clear duty to prevent—as well as punish—genocide, together with Article 9, places upon states the dual duties to prevent and to punish genocide among states inter-se, in addition to establishing responsibility to punish individuals for committing the crime of genocide. This view is supported by the observation of Judge Lauterpacht in *Application of the Genocide Case (Bosnia Herzegovina v. Yugoslavia) (Provisional Measures).* Under Article I of the Genocide Convention, Idealia has the obligation to prevent and punish genocide. This obligation occurs when a state learns, or should normally have learned, of the existence of a serious risk that genocide will be committed. A finding of genocide imposes an obligation to act to prevent the crime. This view is supported by state practice showing that states understand

and act in accordance with the belief that a declaration of genocide carries with it legal responsibility to act. Examples include the pronouncement by the United States during the Rwanda crisis that that United States was not prepared to declare that genocide was taking place in Rwanda because "there are obligations which arise in connection with the use of the term," a view also supported by Secretary General Boutros Boutros Ghali.[98]

c. Idealia's Duty to Act to Prevent the Crime of Genocide does not Infringe Upon the Principle of State Sovereignty, as Notoria's Conduct has Internationalized the Situation in its Territory

Contrary to the Respondent's claim, participation as a States Party to the Genocide Convention by definition internationalizes the matter of genocide and renders a claim of noninterference in the domestic affairs of a state null and void. In addition, (and as argued above) the UN Charter and subsequent accretions of the UN human rights system combine to transform the international understanding of the principle of territorial integrity and non-interference in the domestic affairs of states.[99] Indeed there is near universal agreement that mistreatment of citizens is a matter in which states and international organizations may take interest and in which UN Member States and, in the case of genocide, all states, have a legitimate interest.[100] States that have ratified the Charter cannot assert that genocide, one of the most egregious violations of human rights law, is a matter of the exclusive domestic jurisdiction of any one state.[101] Insofar as the crime of genocide is concerned—massive violations of the most fundamental of all rights, the right to life—it represents a high level threat to the maintenance of international peace and security which is a matter of international, and not purely a domestic, concern. The renewed attention given in recent years to R2P against atrocities further supports this proposition.[102] This is further bolstered by the fact that the crime of genocide is both an obligation *erga omnes* and *jus cogens*. As such, there can be no question as to the application of the principle of state sovereignty and/or interference in domestic affairs in a case of genocide.

SUMMARY AND PRAYER FOR RELIEF

Both Respondents in this case, the Republic of Notoria and the United States of Idealia, are signatories of the Genocide Convention and therefore both are obligated by its terms. Respondent Notoria is liable for commission of the crime of genocide, as well as failure to prevent the crime of genocide, a crime of culpable omission. Agents of the Government of Notoria directly participated in the campaign of violence launched against the black Muslim population of Killalli and Respondent Notoria also rendered support to the *Satanakunda* in this campaign. Notoria is also responsible for its failure to stop the *Satanakunda's* actions once these actions became known to Respondent. Consequently Respondent is liable for complicity in the crime of genocide. Respondent Idealia is liable for its failure to come to the aid of the black Muslim population of Killalli in contravention of its obligations under the Genocide Convention. Idealia had knowledge of the crimes occurring in Killalli and failed to put a stop to these crimes. Wherefore, Applicant prays that this Court find that both Respondents have failed to meet their legal obligations to stop the genocide in Killalli.

RESPONDENTS' COUNTER-MEMORIAL

COMES NOW the Republic of Notoria and the United States of Idealia and for their Counter-Memorial to the Court, asks the following:

QUESTIONS PRESENTED

Can states be held liable under the terms of the United Nations Convention on the Prevention and Punishment of the Crime of Genocide (Genocide Convention)?

Can a state be held liable for genocide when its actions and the conditions present within its borders do not demonstrate the special intent required for the crime of genocide under international law, and if the groups involved fail to meet the criteria for protected groups set forth under Article 2 of the Genocide Convention?

Can the Government of the Republic of Notoria be held legally responsible for the actions of an entity—an irregular militia, the *Satanakunda*—that took place thousands of miles from the capital of Notoria and which were *not* the result of a direct order from the officials of the Government of Notoria?

Can the military of the Republic of Notoria be held responsible for the crime of genocide if its actions constituted reckless behavior and not the actions demonstrating the *dolus specialis* required for the crime of genocide under international law?

Is the Government of Notoria liable for a failure to prevent the crime of genocide given that a). the government has no direct control over the chief perpetrators responsible for the violence in Killalli and that b). the actions of the irregular militia in question were conducted beyond the purview of government officials?

Is the United States of Idealia in violation of the Genocide Convention for failing to prevent or punish genocide in Notoria, where Idealia has no troops on the ground and where a peacekeeping mission already exists and where the UNSC could sanction that peacekeeping mission under UN Charter, Chapter VII to "take all means necessary to prevent and punish genocide."

Is unilateral intervention to stop genocide warranted under the terms of the Genocide Convention? Or in the alternative is the appropriate response of States

Parties to the Genocide Convention to be taken through the UN Security Council?

STATEMENT OF LAW

Respondents Government of the Republic of Notoria and United States of Idealia are signatories to the Genocide Convention,[103] and are therefore obligated by its terms.

Respondents Government of Notoria and the United States of Idealia cannot be held liable under the Genocide Convention as Article 4 of the Convention holds *individuals* criminally liable for genocide, not States.

Respondents contend that the violence that has been occurring in Killalli is the result of fighting between rebel groups and the *Satanakunda* militia group. The numbers of deaths that have resulted are also a consequence of starvation and disease. These conditions do not constitute genocide pursuant to the terms of Article 2 of the Genocide Convention.

Much of the violence in the Killalli region has been caused by rebel groups within that region. Respondent Notoria concedes that while the *Satanakunda* militia group and the military of Notoria may be responsible for some of the violence in the Killalli region, this violence was conducted outside of the knowledge of the Government of Notoria. With regard to the military, Respondent conceded that the military may have acted in a reckless manner in its campaign against the rebels in Killalli. However, at the most these troops are responsible for crimes against humanity and at the very least war crimes. Neither of these crimes necessarily imply anything about genocide. Both fall outside Applicant's claim, as well as the jurisdiction of this Court.

With respect to the *Satanakunda* Respondent Notoria has no relationship with the militia group. The *Satanakunda* are a separate entity from the Government of Nortoria, the government therefore has no control over their actions. Respondent Government of Notoria contends that it also lacks effective control over the actions of tprehe *Satanakunda* militia group because of the geographical distance separating the region of Killalli from the capital of Notoria. Notoria had no knowledge of the violence or risk of violence perpetrated against the civilian population of Killalli by the *Satanakunda*. Had Notoria possessed such knowledge it would have acted to stop or prevent the violence from occurring. Therefore Notoria cannot be held liable for failure to prevent pursuant to Articles 1, 8, and 9 of the Genocide Convention.

Moreover, Respondents contend that the population of the Killalli region of the Republic of Notoria is similar in ethnic, religious and racial makeup to the population of the northern regions of Notoria due to years of inter-marriage and co-habitation. Therefore the population of Killalli cannot be categorized as a separate national, ethnical, racial or religious group and consequently is not protected by terms of the Genocide Convention.

Additionally, Respondent Notoria contends that it does not have and has never demonstrated the *dolus specialis* required for the crime of genocide under international criminal law. As genocide is the only crime with which this case is concerned, absent a demonstration of the *dolus specialis* there can be no finding of genocide.

The particular identity of the population of Killalli, Respondent Notoria's lack of genocidal intent, and its absence of effective control over the *Satanakunda* militia group means that genocide has *not* been proven to take place beyond a reasonable doubt. Consequently there is no responsibility to prevent genocide. Respondent Notoria therefore has not violated Articles 1, 2, 3, 8, and 9 of the Genocide Convention.

If this Court should find that genocide did occur in Killalli, Respondent United States of Idealia is not liable for a failure to prevent the crime of genocide in this case pursuant to Articles 1, 8, and 9 of the Genocide Convention. Respondent Idealia contends that to unilaterally intervene in the internal affairs of a sovereign state such as Notoria would be a violation of Article 2 of the Charter of the United Nations.[104] Moreover, Article 8 of the Genocide Convention requires that action to prevent the crime of genocide be taken through the Security Council of the United Nations; a position confirmed in paragraph 139 of the 2005 World Summit Outcome Resolution.[105] Idealia is currently taking the appropriate steps to deal with the crisis in Killalli pursuant to international law.

SUMMARY OF ARGUMENTS

Notoria is not in violation of its duties under the Genocide Convention. First, the Genocide Convention is inapplicable to the situation in question as the Convention establishes an obligation on the part of states not citizens and secondly, the civilians of Killalli do not constitute a protected group under Article 2 of the Convention. Moreover, Notoria did not have the resources to either commit or prevent genocide in this case given the geographical distance and the absence of any direct connection or control over the *Satanakunda*. Regardless, the events occurring in Killalli do not amount to genocide, but are the unfortunate consequence of civil war. Thus Notoria's failure to respond applies only to the prevention of war crimes at the least, crimes against humanity at the most.

Idealia's response to the violence in Killalli is fully consistent with its obligations under international law. Idealia has, through the UN Security Council, taken the appropriate measures to prevent the violence through its support of a UN hybrid peacekeeping mission. These actions reflect an adherence to Article 2 of the UN Charter.

ARGUMENTS

I. Respondent Notoria is not in Violation of International Law by Failing to Fulfill its Duties under the Genocide Convention because the Situation in Killalli is not Genocide

II. Respondent Idealia is not in Violation of International Law by Failing to Fulfill its Duties under the Genocide Convention because the Situation in Killalli is not Genocide

A. THERE IS NO CLEAR STATE RESPONSIBILITY OF NOTORIA AND IDEALIA FOR THE SITUATION OF GENOCIDE IN KILLALLI

To begin with, Notoria is not responsible for the commission of genocide in Killalli, since the intent of the drafters of the Genocide Convention was not to hold *states* responsible for genocide. The Genocide Convention does not establish state responsibility for the commission of acts of genocide, but rather focuses on the responsibility of individuals who should be punished for this heinous crime. Article 4 of the Genocide Convention reads: "Persons committing genocide or any of the other acts enumerated in article 3 shall be punished, whether they are constitutionally empowered rulers, public officials or private individuals."[106]

Furthermore, as Judge Owada pointed out in his separate opinion on the February 26 2007 judgment of the International Court of Justice (ICJ) in *Application of the Convention on the Prevention and Punishment of the Crime of Genocide (Bosnia and Herzegovina v. Serbia and Montenegro)* that States cannot "*accept direct international responsibility for . . . [genocide] and be held to account under the Convention* [italics in original]."[107]

The text of the Genocide Convention clearly focuses on individual responsibility and one should not read into the text of the Convention or imply more than what was meant according to a strict interpretation of the language. A perusal of the *Travaux Préparatoires* for the Genocide Convention clearly shows that there was no intention to establish state responsibility for genocide.[108]

According to the *Joint Declaration* by Judges Shi and Koroma in the *Bosnia* case: "'interpretation must be based above all on the text of the treaty.'"[109] For example, the above-mentioned judges observed that, according to the canons of interpretation reflected in Article 31 of the Vienna Convention on the Law of Treaties, "A Treaty shall be observed in good faith in accordance with the ordinary meaning to be given to the terms of the treaty in their context and in the light of its object and purpose."[110]

Furthermore, according to Judge Owada, in his separate opinion, as the Nuremberg Tribunal famously stated, "crimes against international law are committed by men, not by abstract entities."[111] Moreover, Judges Shi and Koroma go on to say in their Joint Declaration in *Bosnia*: "As an international criminal instrument, the Convention envisages the trial and punishment of individuals for the crime of genocide. It does not impose criminal responsibilities on the State as a State."[112] And, according to the eminent jurist Hersh Lauterpacht, "'*The Convention thus subjected individuals to the direct obligation and sanction of international law.*'"[113]

B. GENOCIDE IS NOT OCCURRING IN KILLALLI, THEREFORE NOTORIA AND IDEALIA HAVE NOT FAILED TO FULFILL THEIR DUTIES UNDER THE GENOCIDE CONVENTION TO PREVENT GENOCIDE

Next it is important to stress that what has been occurring in Killalli since 2003 is not genocide. Therefore Respondents Notoria and Idealia have not failed to fulfill their duties under the Genocide Convention. What has been occurring in Killalli since 2003 has been a rebellion and civil war. A finding of genocide cannot be made in connection with the effects of the conflict on the population, such as the burning of villages, the killing of civilians, and the displacement of large numbers of people. These are all the unfortunate results of a civil war. The Government of Notoria is trying to deal with a violent revolution perpetrated by rebel groups in Killalli.

Moreover, the statistics gathered as evidence about the scale of the casualties and deaths of the civilian population may not be accurate either due to the fact that many civilians have perished as a result of starvation and disease. If genocide has *not* been proven to take place beyond a reasonable doubt, then there is no responsibility to prevent it. As the ICJ ruled in *Bosnia* "A state can be held responsible for breaching the obligation to prevent genocide only if genocide was actually committed."[114]

Therefore, as the ICJ has noted in *Bosnia*, "however, if neither genocide nor any of the other acts listed in Article III of the Convention are ultimately carried out, then a state that omitted to act when it could have done so cannot be held responsible *a posteriori,* since the event did not happen which, under the rule set out above, must occur for there to be a violation of the obligation to prevent."[115] The acts referred to in Article 3 of the Genocide Convention are:

> (a) Genocide;
> (b) Conspiracy to commit genocide;
> (c) Direct and public incitement to commit genocide;
> (d) Attempt to commit genocide;
> (e) Complicity in genocide.[116]

Furthermore, the obligation of a state to prevent genocide, depends on the capacity of a state to do so.[117] For example, this capacity could depend on the "geographic distance of the State concerned from the scene of events, and the strength of the political links, as well as links of all kinds, between the authorities of the State and the main actors in the events."[118] Obviously the geographical distances in Notoria are too vast for the central Government of Notoria to prevent genocide, as well as to assume that the President of Notoria has any knowledge of atrocities which are committed. After all, Notoria is the largest country in Africa, measuring some 967,500 square miles.

Additionally, the "links" between the Government of Notoria and paramilitary formations wreaking havoc in the civil conflict in Killalli are neither clear nor firm. Consequently Respondent Government of Notoria does not exercise complete effective control over paramilitary formations such as the *Satanakunda*.

The President of Notoria as Head of State and Commander-in-Chief of the armed forces of Notoria may not have any knowledge of the atrocities that have been committed in the civil conflict that has been taking place since 2003, and in any event, may not have direct control over his commanders. Therefore he cannot be held responsible for the actions of his lesser commanders in the field. What is occurring in Notoria is *not* genocide, but a civil war which began in 2003 when three main groups rebelled against the central government.

Notoria has suffered from civil conflict ever since it gained its independence in 1956. The civil war in Killalli has been characterized as a chaotic scene where fragmented rebel organizations have been attacking international peacekeepers and humanitarian aid workers, and elements of the *Satanakunda* militia have been attacking each other. Moreover, efforts to resolve the war in Killalli have now been complicated by the outbreak of conflict between the Northern part of Notoria and the newly independent Republic of Southern Notoria which emerged in July 2011.

The democratic government of the United States of Idealia prefers to deal with these two problems simultaneously through multilateral diplomatic efforts rather than through the application of unilateral military force which, in any event, has been made moot with the dispatch of a hybrid international peacekeeping force by the UN Security Council to Killalli in 2007.

C. SPECIAL INTENT TO COMMIT GENOCIDE AGAINST A PROTECTED GROUP IN NOTORIA HAS NOT BEEN PROVEN

Under international criminal law the crime of genocide is based on a deliberate plan that has been drawn up by governments, and or individuals to kill a group of people based on their nationality, ethnicity, race or religion—whether in whole or in part. As the ICJ ruled in *Bosnia*, "the intent must be to destroy at least a substantial part" of the targeted group.[119] Proving intent is critical and central to proving that genocide has taken place in Killalli. The burden of proof is on the prosecution to prove that a special intent (*dolus specialis*) was involved in the killing of a group and or its members. Admittedly, this is a narrow legal definition, but as Allan A. Ryan has written, "As difficult as genocides may be to prevent or prosecute, they are fiendishly difficult to define and the process of definition can be highly politicized, subjective, and emotional, as we try to make the definition fit the events we want to call genocide."[120]

Intent may not only refer to the physical extermination of a group, but it can also refer to the state of mind (*mens rea*), that is, the state of mind of perpetrators of the genocide must be demonstrated very clearly as apart from the motivation to commit genocide. But where is the documentation that proves beyond a reasonable doubt that the responsible government officials of Respondent Notoria, especially the President of Notoria, are guilty of having the *mens rea,* and demonstrating an explicit, as well as implicit, special intent to commit genocide? It is critical that special intent be proven in the case of alleged *genocidaires.* Moreover, as the ICJ stated in its judgment in *Bosnia*: "The specific intent is also to be distinguished from other reasons or motives the perpetrator may have" and "great care must be taken in finding in the facts a sufficiently clear manifestation of that intent"[121] and of course the intent must be related to the group as such. No such genocidal plan beyond a reasonable doubt has been proven to exist in the case of the leadership of Notoria.

For example, in 2009, the Pre-Trial chamber of the International Criminal Court (ICC) ruled that the President of Notoria could *not* be charged with genocide, as the Prosecutor-General had failed to provide sufficient evidence which would establish beyond a reasonable doubt that the facts showed that acts of genocide had been committed in Killalli.

In February 2010 the original finding of the Pre-Trial chamber was reversed by the Appeals Court of the ICC. Consequently the Pre-Trial chamber issued a new finding which led to charging of the President of Notoria with three counts of genocide. However, the reversal of the Pre-Trial chamber's original decision was arrived at on the basis of questionable grounds, making the revised arrest warrant for the President of Notoria on the grounds of genocide easier to achieve. For example, the new decision of the Pre-Trial chamber was based on far less stringent grounds than their original decision. It called for evidence of the commission of acts of genocide to be based only on "reasonable grounds" as opposed to evidence of genocide "beyond a reasonable doubt." Nor can the President of Notoria be accused of failing to prevent genocide in Killalli, if one tries to use *Bosnia* as a precedent, since the ICJ found that genocide had *not* been committed in Bosnia-Herzegovina, with the exception of Srebrenica. What occurred in Bosnia-Herzegovina was not genocide, but ethnic cleansing. Consequently, this Court did not award compensation to Bosnia-Herzegovina.

The tragic killings which have occurred in Notoria have taken place within the context of a civil war and are an unfortunate by-product of the fighting. They are not the result of any attempt to systematically exterminate a group of people, "in whole" or even "in part."

Moreover, one needs to prove in the case of Notoria that a "protected group" is being subjected to genocide. The Genocide Convention itself does not even provide a clear definition of what is meant by a "group," but rather creates a set of categories of groups. The Convention does not afford any guidance as to what constitutes the clearly defined boundaries of a protected group. Four categories of groups are identified by the Genocide Convention as protected groups: national groups, ethnical groups, racial groups, and religious groups. In the case of Killalli, in terms of objective criteria, it is hard to clearly distinguish between the two opposing sides in the civil conflict due to such factors as the history of coexistence and intermarriage of these different groups. If the opposing groups are intermingled, how then can genocide be committed against a non-existent protected group? The question that has been raised in connection with proving the commission of genocide in Killalli is whether or not the tribes that have been specifically targeted—"black Muslims"—fit into the category of a protected group from an objective point of view.

But the case for genocide in this instance rests more on subjective than objective criteria. This point in turn raises a discussion about the notion of the "imagined community,"[122] whereby group identity is a matter of perception. In this instance groups that are supposedly being attacked and their attackers perceive themselves as constituting separate distinct groups. The attackers in this case, popularly referred to as *Satanakunda* ("devils on horseback" or "camels"), are said to refer to their victims in a derogatory fashion. But this hardly meets the evidentiary standards as to what constitutes a "protected group" from an objective point of view.

Furthermore, this differentiation is all highly subjective in a civil conflict, where the "fog of war" is a prevalent factor that further confounds the issue of group identity. In the case of Killalli a UN Commission of Inquiry concluded in 2004 that it found *no* evidence of genocide. The Commission did not find genocidal intent, despite "the systematic killing of civilians belonging to particular tribes, of large scale causing of serious bodily or mental harm to members of the population belonging to certain tribes, and of massive and deliberate infliction on those tribes of conditions of life bringing about their physical destruction in whole or in part"[123] But as a result the Commission concluded that, despite the high death toll and the sheer scale of criminal activity, the intention of the militia and government forces "was to murder all those men they considered as rebels, as well as forcibly expel the whole population so as to vacate the villages and prevent rebels from hiding among, or getting support from the local population."[124]

The UN Commission of Inquiry found that it was hard to distinguish between the two groups identified as "Africans" and "Arabs," in terms of objective factors, because of the history of coexistence and intermarriage of the two groups. As the Commission of Inquiry on Killalli pointed out, the subjective identification of what constitutes a "protected group" raises the notion of an "imagined community," whereby the groups that are being attacked as well as the attackers perceive themselves as comprising separate groups, as there is a process of self-identification at work. In terms of perception, this draws a distinction between groups that could be identified as "Arab" and those as "African." In some cases the two groups could only be distinguished from each other only in terms of the language that they spoke. Finally, Notoria is working through its own judicial process to investigate claims of Genocide.

III. Respondent Idealia is not Obligated to Unilaterally take Action Against Notoria Because to do so Would Violate Notoria's Sovereignty in Contravention to International Law

Even if this Court should find that genocide did occur in Killalli, Idealia is not obligated to act unilaterally against Notoria, because this would violate Notoria's sovereignty. State sovereignty is a principle which has provided the foundation of world order for over 360 years, ever since the appearance of the Treaty of Westphalia in 1648. The central element of international order is the principle of state sovereignty. The sovereignty of the state should be considered inviolable and sacrosanct. It is necessary to protect state sovereignty against unilateral military intervention by a state so as to preserve world order.

State sovereignty is enshrined as a basic principle of the UN Charter, especially in Article 2. For example, Article 2 of the UN Charter recognizes the sovereign equality of all state members. Furthermore the inviolability of state sovereignty has also been recognized in section 7 of Article 2 of the Charter, in which the United Nations is prohibited from intervening in matters which fall essentially within the domestic jurisdiction of a state, except in connection with an enforcement action undertaken by the Security Council of the United Nations.[125] In the final analysis, it is the position of Idealia that it is the responsibility of the entire international community, acting through the Security Council of the United Nations, to intervene in Notoria, if necessary with a Chapter VII type of peacekeeping force, to prevent and punish genocide.

IV. Respondent Idealia is not Obligated under International Law to Act Unilaterally in Absence of Action by the United Nations Security Council

Idealia recognizes that it has an *erga omnes* obligation to respond to cases of genocide. However, Idealia would be acting illegally if it engaged in unilateral military intervention in Killalli, since according to Article 2(4) of the UN Charter, a state may not use force or threaten to use force against another state in their relations with each other.[126] For example, the military intervention by NATO in Kosovo in 1999 was also deemed to be illegal, since it took place without the authorization of the Security Council. Unilateral military action by Idealia, under the guise of exercising state responsibility to prevent genocide according to Article 1 of the Genocide Convention, could mask neocolonial efforts at intervening in a matter which falls within the domestic jurisdiction of Notoria.

Additionally, per section 139 of the 2005 World Summit Resolution, the only type of action that is recommended to take place under the newly emergent "Responsibility to Protect" norm is "collective action, in a timely and decisive manner, through the UNSC, in accordance with the Charter, including Chapter VII, on a case-by-case basis."[127]

Idealia is exercising its state responsibilities by supporting the decision of the UN Security Council to deploy a peacekeeping force in Killalli in 2007, with the approval of the Government of Notoria. This hybrid peacekeeping force—an amalgamation of UN peacekeepers with a previously deployed African peacekeeping force—has been operating in Notoria since 2007, with Idealia supporting the periodic renewals of its mandate. Therefore the question of unilateral military action is moot. The current democratic administration of Idealia, rather than opting for unilateral military action in Killalli, prefers to use a multilateral diplomatic approach in dealing with situation in Killalli. Respondent Idealia has fully supported the efforts of the ICC to arrest the President of Notoria who is charged with three counts of genocide, has provided logistical aid for the international peacekeeping force in Killalli, and has furnished a significant amount of humanitarian aid for the internally displaced persons in Killalli.

SUMMARY AND CONCLUSIONS

Both Respondents in this case readily admit that they are signatories of the United Nations Convention on the Prevention and Punishment of the Crime of Genocide and are obligated by its terms. However, in this case the perpetration of the crime of genocide in the Killalli region of the Republic of Notoria has not been proven beyond a reasonable doubt. What has been occurring in the country since 2003 is a civil war between rebel groups in Killalli and various militia groups including the *Satanakunda*. Respondent Notoria had no knowledge of any campaign of violence launched by the *Satanakunda* and, in any event, lacked effective control over the militia due to the militia's lack of official status as well as simple geography. Moreover, the groups "targeted" by the *Satanakunda* do not meet the criteria of protected groups under the Genocide Convention and there has been no demonstration of the dolus specialis required for the commission of genocide; a fact buttressed by the 2004 report by the UN Commission of Inquiry. Respondent United States of Idealia is not obligated to prevent the crime of genocide through unilateral intervention. To do so would be in contravention of existing international treaty and customary law; specifically the Genocide Convention and the UN Charter, as well as the 2005 World Summit Outcome Resolution, respectively. Respondent Idealia is taking the appropriate steps to deal with crisis in Killalli commensurate with its responsibilities under international law. For the foregoing reasons, Respondents respectfully request that this Court enter an Order dismissing the Application.

JUDGMENT

PART ONE: Nolandia versus the Republic of Notoria

Basis for the Court's Jurisdiction

The International Court of Justice has jurisdiction to resolve, in accordance with international law, legal disputes submitted to it by states (jurisdiction in contentious cases).[128] This Court has jurisdiction for the both parts of this trial because both parties are states parties to the UN Genocide Convention, which in turn requires them to prevent and punish genocide and which grants the ICJ jurisdiction on matters, under Article 9:

> Disputes between the Contracting Parties relating to the interpretation, application or fulfillment of the present Convention, including those relating to the responsibility of a State for genocide or any of the other acts enumerated in Article 3, shall be submitted to the International Court of Justice at the request of any of the parties to the dispute.

The first part of this case has been initiated by the plaintiff Nolandia, who alleges that the defendant, Republic of Notoria, committed and failed to prevent genocide in its region of Killalli. Having ratified of the Genocide Convention and having previous submitted to binding ICJ jurisdiction, Nolandia and Nortoria have standing to resolve this dispute, which the Genocide Convention has given to the ICJ as a locus of jurisdiction. Because the facts of the case and the basis of jurisdiction have been established, the Court now proceeds in the following section to judge this case.

Judgment

This Court finds respondent Notoria liable for genocide and for failing to prevent and punish this genocide that has occurred in its own country. This section is dedicated to analyzing legal questions in order to determine that genocide occurred and what the judge will consider prior to making the judgment.

The Republic of Notoria has denied that (1) genocide has occurred and that if any type of violence did occur, that it was (2) unknowledgeable and incapable of preventing, controlling, and punishing the violence, and therefore (3) not liable for the criminal charges. Notoria argues that violence in Notoria is a civil war, not genocide, and has occurred in response to rebellion against the central government. The violence cannot be racially based since, it claims, that the two groups have had similar intermarriage. Notoria claims that is had no knowledge of genocide, nor was there any formal relationship with the paramilitary *Satanakunda*.

Legal Question A—Was there an Intent to Destroy?

Punishable acts of genocide include (a) Genocide, (b) Conspiracy to commit genocide, (c) Direct and public incitement to commit genocide, (d) Attempt to commit genocide, and (e) Complicity in genocide. Notoria and its associated paramilitary, the *Satankunda*, an ethnic Arab, Islamic militia, have sought to repress a rebellion by ethnic African Muslim by attacking defenseless ethnic African civilians in Killalli. Conspiracy to commit Genocide means that one group "aims at exterminating the whole or a substantial part of the group."[129] To prove intent, international case law states evidence of genocidal intent can be the existence of a plan, a large number of victims destroyed from a racial, religious, ethnic or racial group. Destruction of cultural institutions, monuments, etc. can also act as proof of genocide.[130] For example, the Bosnian Serb President ordered the Bosnian Serb forces to destroy and remove the Muslim population in Srebrenica by planning to "create an unbearable situation of total insecurity with no hope of further survival or life for the inhabitants of Srebrenica."[131] The *Satankunda* systematically targeted black civilians in Killalli.

The ICTY Appeals judgment in *Prosecutor v. Jelisić* argued that to extend the Genocide Treaty's definition of intent, there needs to be proof of specific intent or *dolis specialis.*[132] For example, in *Jelisić*, the Trial Chamber needed to provide "sufficient evidence allowing it to be established beyond all reasonable doubt that there existed a plan to destroy the Muslim group." No proof of a plan was available, making this a difficult case.

Proof of a *dolis specialis* by the ethnic Arab *Satanakunda* to target and kill African civilians in Killalli exists because of the gross and systematic attacks against civilian non-combatants, including women and children by the tens of thousands. Gratuitous killings without any military justification occurred repeatedly.

Just as in the *Bosnia v. Serbia*, towns were destroyed, and people were forced from their homes, the *Satankunda* of Notoria was involved in killings, rape, burning villages, and contaminating water supply. These acts listed above have indeed caused serious bodily harm and destruction of the life conditions of the inhabitants of Killalli. Killing members of a group does not only mean direct killings, but also indirectly causing environmental conditions that lead to the deaths of additional genocide victims in Killalli.

The *Satankunda* also deliberately inflicted on the group conditions of life calculated to bring about its physical destruction in whole or in part through the reported destruction of villages, displacement and/or killing large numbers of civilians. Under Article 2 of the Genocide Convention, no matter how large or small the casualties are, if there is an intended destruction of a group based on race, religion, and ethnicity, then genocide has indeed occurred. In this case, the

Killillians are of a different race from their ethnic Arab enemies, who attempt to end their existence in the region, primarily through murder.

In *Prosecutor v. Kristć*, Commander Kristć was sentenced for forty-six years for violating the Genocide Convention and for destroying part of the Muslim population to gain control over Srebrenica. This is evidence that the Muslim population of Bosnia was systematically targeted.[133] Notoria has also failed to prevent and punish genocide.

Under International Law, as well as the growing R2P norm, states are required to protect their citizens and are thus liable for any humanitarian crisis. Under the Genocide Convention, states that do nothing in the face of genocide commit the crime of omission. The crime of omission is equivalent to the act of commission to genocide: "there is in international law a general principle of law which states that . . . omission is normatively equivalent to action." For example, Serbia was found guilty and liable by the International Court of Justice for its omission, or failure to prevent genocide in another country, Bosnia. The International Law Commission has submitted the draft legal statement on the "Responsibility of States," which includes the responsibility to protect, as norms of customary international law.[134] Notoria posits that individuals should be charged for genocide, not states. This argument cannot stand due to growing Responsibility to Protect norms and ILC Drafts that hold states accountable. It is also argued by Notoria that civil war occurred, not genocide. Therefore, states (in this case Notoria) are not liable under the Genocide Convention. This also cannot be accepted as true since the legal issue is intent to destroy a group. Genocides usually occur in war; civil war is not a contradictory alternative to genocide and can occur at the same time.

Persons committing genocide shall be punished for failure to prevent and punish genocide occurring in a territory. Notoria supplied substantial material and other support to the *Satankunda,* who systematically killed ethnic African civilians in Killalli. The Government of Notoria has provided weapons, funding, logistical support, and other "encouragement" to the *Satanakunda* militia group, compelling evidence of a direct and special (*dolus directus* and *dolus especialis*) intent by the Notorian government to attack a protected group. Furthermore, the norm of command responsibility for the actions of agents has been clearly established under international criminal law in the ICC Statute. While there is ambiguity in the meaning of command responsibility, it is not necessary for the Court to determine the mental element of the principle regarding the desire for genocide. All that is necessary is that the principle, here the government of Notoria, had knowledge that the intent of the paramilitary agent was genocidal. It may also be true that the government shared this intent, but a court need not decide more than what is required under the circumstances. In addition, an objective test would seek to determine what a reasonable government would know about its paramilitary agents under the circumstances. A subjective test of the government's intent would permit innocent or malevolent denial of genocide to be used as a defense argument for failing to stop agents of the government from perpetrating genocide. Since there can be no doubt that a reasonable government would have and should have investigated reports of crimes against humanity, as well as possible genocide, it is reasonable to expect a government to know that genocide is occurring. In an affirmative investigation, then it would be incumbent for that government to undertake measures to prevent and punish genocide without any subjective excuse resulting from genocide denial. This Court is explicitly empowered to punish the failure of governments to prevent and punish genocide perpetrated by agents where the principle should have reasonably known that "crime of crimes" was being perpetrated in its name.

The government already knew that *its* paramilitary agents, who were both ethnic Arab Muslims, were committing eliminationist atrocities against the ethnic African Muslim population of Killalli. While this paramilitary was charged with fighting the rebels, it chose to attack non-combatant civilian villagers because they were Africans, not Arabs.

This Court does not yet accept that the R2P doctrine, which was cited by the prosecution, is relevant to whether or not a genocide has occurred. It is the basis for a remedy in the second part of this trial to be discussed below. The existence of a R2P situation does not automatically trigger the existence of genocide, as implied by the prosecution, because protection authorization by the UN Security Council can be applied to crimes against humanity or natural disasters. The Court regards the existing case law as setting a high bar for genocidal intent, as opposed to atrocity resulting from widespread or systematic attacks on civilian populations, as bad as they may be. Not just any atrocities against members of one of the four groups that occur during civil war, counter-insurgency, or counter-terrorism are tantamount to genocide. The journalistic term "ethnic cleansing" also is not automatically genocide. The key criterion for these military operations to rise to genocide is the consistent murder of protected persons, typically non-combatant civilians, under conditions where there is absolutely no legitimate military objective for such murders. A sweeping generalization that civilians are inconvenient is not enough. When civilians are murdered for territorial conquest, under detention, and of course for its own sake, these are acts that speak for themselves as genocidal intent. There is no legitimate military justification present.

In addition, the test of the mental element of genocide must be based on an objective test, what reasonable leaders of countries would understand the obligations of leadership require. In this case, a country's leaders are not permitted to believe that attacks on innocent village people are a necessary and proportionate military tactic. A subjective test, were this Court to accept such a legal standard for the mental element of genocide, would allow international criminal law to countenance atrocities as legal and justified any time a leader regarded such acts necessary to defeat a military opponent. There is a framework for examining such grotesque tactics as a necessity defense. The law cannot take such subjective beliefs of leaders into consideration of the mental element of genocidal intent. However, there must be evidence, in a necessity defense, again, that the criminal methods were in fact necessary to be committed. The necessity defense does not arise where the facts do not suggest that such measures were in fact, objectively, not subjectively believed, that such measures were necessary.

Finally, the number of people killed is not the exact test of genocidal intent or how large a part a group protected by the Genocide Convention must be destroyed to constitute genocide. As long as these attacks are gross and systematic, evidence of genocidal intent is clear. The part of the people killed cannot be minuscule, to be sure, but it does not have to rise to the majority of the population. The point about the Genocide Convention is preventive; it is supposed to stop genocides in their tracks before the part of the population killed rises to a third, a majority, two-thirds or whatever fraction makes the crime into an even worse genocide.

Civilians cannot be the targeted objects of combatants for no legitimate military purpose. It is clear here that the government of Notoria has used the ethnic Arab *Satanakunda* paramilitary because of its ethnic hatred of ethnic African Killallians. The gratuitous killings of villagers in order to induce their removal from the territory are each acts of genocide. These villagers are not insurgents or combatants. While the government may feel that the paramilitary must terrorize villagers in order to win this civil war and counter-insurgency, this Court must take an objective test of intent, not a subjective view of government intent that it does not believe that this is not a legitimate military objective. No reasonable observer can conclude that terrorizing and murdering villagers is intended by a reasonable government leader as a way to win a war. It is motivated by hatred and revenge, which are not legitimate motives and constitute part of the emotions that accompany genocidal hatred that impels some to take the next step to destroy part of a population.

Even though it is sometimes difficult to distinguish who are the combatants and who are the civilians, based on the facts, civilians were obviously targeted since entire villages were destroyed. Even though the *Satanakunda* were also attacking rebels and civilians in the region of Killalli, the *Satanakunda* killed civilians directly and deliberately. Genocide occurred because the killings were based on race, religion, nationality or ethnicity, not combat threats. Wald states that "genocide requires that the acts be committed against a racial, religious, national or ethnic group and be done with the specific intent of destroying the group in whole or in part as such."[135]

Notoria, therefore, is found guilty of the genocide by showing its intent to destroy ethnic African Killallian civilians, who were systematically targeted for elimination in the course of counter-insurgency operations. Based on an objective test, no leader could have believed these attacks, which resulted in the murder of innocent villagers, were motivated by military necessity. The leaders may have subjectively believed that they were necessary, but these were non-combatants who were terrorized for unacceptable motives of revenge, hatred and possible exterminationist or eliminationist desires against the ethnic African Killallians. Based on the definition of genocide, evidence was provided that there was (1) intent to destroy and (2) a group based on its race and ethnicity, which apply to this case, as well as religion and nationality, which do not. Under

Article 2 and Article 3(a) and (d) of the Genocide Convention, genocide occurred in Notoria. Notoria's subjective belief that genocide did not occur and deaths were only a result of on-going violence of the civil war in Notoria cannot be accepted, as governments have the obligation to behave reasonably and not attack civilians villagers through their agents or after learning what their agents are doing in the government's name. The precise number of ethnic Killallian, civilian non-combatants residing in villages is sufficient to constitute genocide since, as argued above, the Genocide Convention is meant to be preventive.

The Court hereby orders the government to pay $10,000 to the families of each of the victims of this genocide and to immediately desist in its counter-insurgency operations from violating the laws and customs of war. I call upon the Human Rights Council of the United Nations to appoint a special investigator to determine the exact number of civilians murdered by the paramilitary forces and to establish a process for identifying the families to receive the payments. In the meantime, the government of Notoria is ordered to pay $100 million into a UN escrow account to be reserved for the reparations to be paid as the families are identified.

PART TWO: Nolandia versus the United States of Idealia

Basis for the Court's Jurisdiction

This Court has jurisdiction for the second part of this trial for the same reasons as stated above in the first part. Both parties are states parties to the UN Genocide Convention, which in turn requires them to prevent and punish genocide and which also establishes jurisdiction in the International Court of Justice. As UN member states, both parties have standing in this Court, Notoria under binding jurisdiction and Idealia on a discretionary basis, which it has exercised.

Judgment

The second part of this case has been initiated by the plaintiff Nolandia, who argues that the defendant, the United States of Idealia, failed to prevent and punish the genocide in the Killalil region, where Idealia had helped to organize a Chapter VI, UNSC peacekeeping mission in this region. This Court must decide whether there is an obligation of Idealia, as a UN Security Council permanent member to try to prevent genocide, which was identified in part one of this case, and if so, what action must be attempted to satisfy the Genocide's requirements, given the possibility that threats to peace may be expanded to a responsibility to protect as a basis for UN Security Council or unilateral action. The type of actions needed to prevent and punish genocide is also a matter before this Court.

Article 5 of the Genocide Convention states,

> the Contracting Parties undertake to enact, in accordance with their respective Constitutions, the necessary legislation to give effect to the provisions of the present Convention, and, in particular, to provide effective penalties for persons guilty of genocide or any of the other acts enumerated in Article 3.

This means that Idealia had the responsibility to prevent, control, and punish the alleged genocide in Notoria. Since Idealia had knowledge that the humanitarian crisis was going on, under international law, the United States of Idealia was obligated to act to prevent, control, and punish the genocide. Because Idealia has ignored its responsibility to do so, by failing to publicly identifying the genocide, as the *de minimus* response, as well as lobbying publicly for either a coercive or voluntary diplomatic alternative through the UN Security Council, the Court holds that Idealia has not fulfilled its minimum obligations as a state party to the Genocide Convention. The Court also concludes that Idealia is not obligated to intervene unilaterally under either a humanitarian or R2P justification because those incipient legal norms are still not accepted under customary international law by major states, including Idealia itself. Until such time as that norm becomes legally binding, the Court does not have to decide whether or not state parties are obligated to intervene militarily in the absence of UN Security Council resolution authorizing forcible compliance to halt genocide.

The first legal question to be considered is what triggers a state's obligation to prevent and punish under the Genocide Convention? If that trigger is operative, what measures are required, if any? Is the test based on objective criteria? If it is based on subjective criteria, would these include the options from which a member state can choose to respond? Is a state party obligated to call a genocide "genocide" if it can be reasonably ascertained that a genocide has occurred, or are states allowed a measure of subjective dissent on this matter?

Legal Issues

The Court concludes that the existence of the genocide established in the first part of this case triggers obligations to prevent and punish genocide by the Convention's state parties. However, the obligation is not absolute and not based on obtaining the result of preventing genocide. Rather, the objective test that must be used on matters of such grave importance as genocide is what a reasonable leader of this country could do under the circumstances—even if it is not likely succeed. Not all situations are amenable to stopping genocide, and it is not at all remotely conceivable that some situations could cause more harm, in terms of lives lost, if military intervention ended the genocide, but then inspired a non-genocidal war that killed many more people. Therefore, the obligation is to call a genocide what it is, a genocide, and to take reasonable measures to attempt to halt it, without incurring endless obligations or costs in circumstances of political-military intervention. As a minimum, state parties must attempt to establish a peace, which is the best way to stop genocide. This could be promoted through coercive diplomacy, though it would be far preferable to induce peace talks without resorting to force, as envisioned by Article 2(4) of the UN Charter. It is not required by this Court to specify what Idealia should have undertaken, since rules should emerge gradually on the basis of a case-by-case analysis. What the Court can assert is its failing to explicitly proclaim genocide, as such, and to at least attempt to induce either peace talks or a UN Security Council resolution to halt the genocide. Then, the country in question would not meet the minimum requirements of a state party.

Idealia is in violation of Articles 5, 8, and 9 of the Genocide Convention which describes how third party states should intervene and punish other states that violate genocide. Since the Convention calls upon "able body members" to intervene, Idealia, who has the military resources, could conceivably be obligated to intervene militarily. However, in a world of limited options and unforeseen consequences, the Court cannot interpret the Genocide Convention as obligated forcible remedies that may prove ineffective, just because genocide is occurring. Indeed, such an order could violate Article 2(4) of the UN Charter, which remains the heart of the state sovereignty system on which international law is still based. However, the obligations of Idealia are not meaningless. It is indeed obligated under the Genocide Convention and permitted under customary international law to intervene in some fashion among legal, reasonable, and sensible alternatives.

For starters, Idealia is required, within reasonable limits to alleviate distress from genocide by asking the UN Security Council to take joint or separate action to provide humanitarian aid.[136] This means that Idealia is obligated to help assist by itself and other willing states if the UNSC is unwilling or unable to act, usually from being veto-deadlocked, or if it simply is uninterested. It is noteworthy that many states impose criminal penalties on those involved in genocide in order to punish it. For example, according to U.S. Code 50, those who have been involved in genocide, shall pay fines of no more than one million dollars.[137] International law also imposes similar obligation, such as Articles 55 and 56 of the UN Charter. Article 55 states are required to promote "universal respect for, and observance of, human rights and fundamental freedoms for all without distinction as to race, sex, language, or religion. Article 56 then obliges states to take "joint and separate action" to achieve these goals.

Cases in the past that have justified unilateral humanitarian intervention include the NATO intervention in Kosovo in 1999. Unilateral intervention can be justified if the cause for the intervention is for extreme humanitarian disasters.[138] Extreme loss of life due to ethnic cleansing can count as genocide and "can give rise to a right of military intervention." The international community increasingly accepts acting unilaterally as a way to deter and stop genocide, in the absence of UNSC authorization since genocide is a *jus cogens* norm that would preempt even Article 2(4) or any other treaty provision in unambiguous circumstances. That is, unilateral humanitarian intervention could be legal, despite its prohibition without UNSC sanction, if it were absolutely necessary and certain to succeed at limited cost in collateral or direct damages—and not be used primarily for other purposes or interests than genocide prevention, which cannot be used as a cover for other ulterior motives. Few cases would meet that criteria, and this Court cannot so assume it would in the present circumstances. Not any action intended to stop genocide is sufficient under the Convention.

Idealia argues that it would have acted illegally if it acted unilaterally because it would violate the UN Charter. This argument cannot stand because of the urgency of genocide. Genocide is an extreme humanitarian crime and if the obligation to prevent, control, and punish genocide is constantly breached, there would be no purpose of the Convention.

Notoria has forfeited its claims to sovereignty, should Idealia and/or the UNSC decide to intervene to stop the genocide because Notoria failed to halt and desist in its genocide against its own people. This gives other states permission to violate Notoria's sovereignty to stop the latter's genocide.

Idealia, however, is not responsible for the situation in Notoria becoming out of control.[139] Because of its neglect, all that can be concluded is that Idealia did not mitigate the effects of the genocide and thereby has violated its obligations to the Genocide Convention. If Idealia was hesitant about which actions to take, then it could have, as stated in Article 8 of that convention, "called upon the competent organs of the United Nations to take such action under the Charter of the United Nations." In particular, as a permanent member of the UNSC, Idealia could have appealed for the Council to authorize a forcible or a voluntary intervention that would have promoted a military or a negotiated solution to halt the war and with it, the genocide.

There has been very minimal and underdeveloped legislation regarding how to prevent genocide and who should do it. Currently, there exists no system in the UN and in the United States of Idealia that punishes the denial of genocide.[140] Because of this ambiguity and confusion, states have even more freedom to deny that a situation, such as that in Killalli, is genocide. State parties can more easily punish genocide through domestic prosecutions of genocide,[141] although Article 8 of the Convention says nothing about how to prevent genocide; we have many examples of leaders attempting to assert that treaty's aspirations in concrete situation. During the genocide in Darfur, then U.S. Secretary of State Colin Powell appealed to Article 8 of the Genocide Convention that urges "competent" contracting members to take action to prevent genocide.[142] Overall, because of the Convention's normative influence, it has become less acceptable for states to ignore genocide and to make excuses for lack of action.

Acting to prevent genocide is required, even if the content of the response remains undefined, but flexible. International norms such as Universal Jurisdiction and the R2P doctrine have strengthened the claim that sovereignty no longer must prohibit humanitarian action, including preventing genocide. The Genocide Convention internationalizes the matter of genocide and renders a claim of non-interference in the domestic affairs of a state null and void. The increased attention given in recent years to the R2P against atrocities and the reinforcement of the *ergo omnes* and *jus cogens* obligations further supports this proposition. According to Straus, just saying the word "genocide" triggers the need for intervention. Overall, what's more important than anything is simply "acting," i.e. doing something and anything in one's power to stop a genocide is sufficient to fulfill the idea of "acting to prevent" and failing to do so means to violate the Convention.[143] Thus, under these standards, the United States of Idealia has violated its obligation to the Convention.

Under Article 55 of the UN Charter, states are required to promote "universal respect for, and observance of, human rights and fundamental freedoms for all without distinction as to race, sex, language, or religion. Article 56 also obliges states to take "joint and separate action" to achieve these goals. Finally, under the *jus cogens* norm, all states have a responsibility to prevent genocide from occurring. This universal nature of the crime entitles all states, whether or not they have a direct interest in the situation, to take action to prevent the occurrence of genocide, even in the absence of the UNSC action. Under the Genocide Convention, states *may* receive permission from the UN Security Council, though, it is not required.

The Bosnian genocide provides an example of what states ought to do when genocide is recognized. Violence was targeted against Bosnian Muslims and the international community, recognizing the violence to be genocide intervened with NATO forces and cease-fire treaties. In this case, the United States did obtain UNSC authorization. In Kosovo in 1999, NATO, under US leadership, also forcibly intervened to stop the Bosnian genocide, without UNSC authorization. After the war ended eleven weeks later, the UNSC voted with a large majority that the intervention was not illegal and authorized NATO to implement the peace agreement under Chapter VII authority should force be necessary.

The ambiguity of the genocide concepts and terminology leads to great confusion, stalling, and irresponsibility when responding to genocide. This relates to Idealia's confusion on how it should have responded to the violence in Notoria. If a powerful actor or coalition does not emerge, or if the international community fails to act decisively, many more lives will be lost. Cassese highlights the urgency of "acting to prevent." He analyzes Article 3 of the Genocide Convention and argues that if a state has knowledge of genocide then "Article 3 obliges contracting states to take *any* possible measure designed to forestall acts of genocide." If the state ignores this knowledge and does not act, then the state then effectively becomes an accomplice in genocide.[144]

This Court is unwilling to charge Idealia with complicity to perpetrate genocide, even if it has committed a crime of omission. The United States of Idealia is guilty of breaching its responsibility to act to prevent, control, and punish genocide in Killalli, Notoria is not necessarily or consequently a threat to international peace, but it has forfeited any claims to trump state sovereignty if Idealia, acting alone, with a coalition of the willing, or through the UNSC, to effect an end to Notoria's violations of the Genocide Convention. The responsibility of states to *act*, sadly, must remain undefined, but is an absolute requirement under Articles 3, 8, and 9 of the Genocide Convention and under *jus cogens* norms.

Therefore, the Court orders Idealia to seek a peaceful or failing that, a forcible solution through the UNSC, and failing a good faith effort there, to consider other measures. The pacification and consequent mitigation or ending of this genocide presumably could be accomplished through established Chapter VII authority for the existing hybrid peacekeeping mission. Second, it orders Idealia to increase its humanitarian relief efforts under that same peacekeeping mission. Should those measures fail to prevent genocide, then it is incumbent that the United Nations becomes seized of the matter and both specifically in Nortoria, as well as in general, seeks to find new ways to combat genocide.

APPENDIX A: Examples of Judges' Questions and Lawyers' Answers from Student Moot Courts

Q: You stated the rebels were targeting groups based on ethnicity. Is it possible that they were targeted not on the basis of their ethnicity but because they were rebels fighting against the government?

A: The way that the rebels were targeted was not a way that can be considered as fighting back. The aerial strikes and the way of cutting off their commutation beforehand I would consider that to be evidence of a very immediate attack for which they would not have had time to respond or to fight back. It was a very aggressive manner in which to attack someone.

Q: Wouldn't cutting off their means of communication be a basic tenet of war? Respondent is claiming that what was occurring in the country was an ongoing civil war. During war cutting off the communication of the emery would be a primary tactic used, correct?

A: Yes but I don't see them retaliating in the same way, by cutting off communications of Respondent government forces. Moreover, most of the people affected by the attack were displaced and forced into refugee camps; many were still being attacked while in these camps.

Q: If that's the case would you concede that it was a civil war as opposed to the targeting a specific group? It was a war and you have aggressors on one side and the government is attacking a perceived threat. Could you say that the government's action does not demonstrate the intent to systematically destroy a group but merely intent to defend the country against a known aggressor? In other words, did the Respondent government demonstrate the intent to destroy a population on the basis of their ethnic, racial, religious or national identity?

A: I'm not sure what you're asking.

Q: You stated that the government was attacking a rebel group with the *Satanakunda* and you also stated that they were attacking a specific ethnic group. So are you claiming that they were being attacked because of their group identity and not because the country was at war?

A: Yes. It was a clash of Arabs and non-Arabs.

Q: Do you have anything to support that claim?

A: Yes. The majority of persons in the displacement camps were Arab.
Q: But isn't the majority of the country 70-75% Arab?
A: That was not in the statement of facts.
Q: The statement of facts did not include a breakdown of the population. I thought it would be helpful to include it here.
(space indicates a new topic)

Q: Was the paramilitary attacking on its own or were they acting in response to orders from a higher authority?
A: I argue that the government was essentially telling them what to do. They were acting as an agent of the government.
Q: The government had control of the actions of the paramilitary?
A: Yes they did. They were giving them orders. The *Satanakunda* paramilitary listened to the orders and acted.

Q: Can we have a finding of genocide without actually proving intent?
A: No you must have intent.
Q: So you concede that without intent you cannot have genocide?
A: Yes.

Q: Tell me how an attack against an armed militia by the *Satanakunda* can constitute genocide?
A: The *Satanakunda* was acting on the orders of the government to attack a group. Whether the victim group was armed or unarmed shouldn't manner.
Q: That seems a reasonable distinction. But what about the fact that the victim population many have been assisting the armed rebel militia by providing them food, supplies, logistics etc.?
A: Could you be more specific about the aid they were giving them?
Q: I'm saying perhaps they were not really civilians, but combatants who were providing logistical support to a rebel militia fighting the government.
A: I would say that everyone has a right to defend themselves particularly if they are being systematically targeted by a government.
Q: So you would admit that they're no longer civilians?
A: I would admit that yes.
Q: And if they're no longer civilians do they have the right to demand not to be shot?
A: Yes.
Q: Just because they killed these people does not mean that they intended to destroy the group in whole or in part. What is your proof that the killings were designed to completely get rid of this population as opposed to merely getting rid of the logistical support for the rebels?
A: I have a quote from the President.
Q: It was not in the facts.
A: It was not in the facts? Well if it was in the facts it would have shown that he intended to annihilate a group of people.

Q: Where is the evidence of annihilation from just killing people who were providing logistical support?
A: The killings occurred on a mass scale.
Q: The killings on a mass scale of people who were providing logistics are war crimes. They are also probably crimes against humanity because we're talking about a civilian population. The question is whether they constitute genocide. I'm not convinced by your presentation that war crimes and crimes against humanity, where you kill people for providing logistical support, is the same thing as destroying a part of a population. One doesn't not necessarily mean the other. So what in the facts leads you to say that they were motivated top destroy part of a population and not merely to get rid of logistical support for the rebels?
A: I would say that it's the individual perceptions of who was being targeted. The Arabs were targeting the African civilians.
Q: We know they were targeted but that makes it a crime against humanity.
A: But it was a separate and distinct group of people.
Q: A crime against humanity which targets a civilian population is bad. The question here is, is the state responsible for genocide? They say they were motivated to attack the population to get rid of the logistical support for the rebels, not because the group was a minority. Is it merely a coincidence that they were a minority group?
A: If another ethnic or religious group weren't involved, I would agree.
Q: You have two things that are correlated. Members of a minority group are being killed. But you cannot infer from that they were being killed because they were a minority. There is also a correlation because they were providing logistical support. Another person may infer causality because they were providing logistical support. Until you can show that the reason was they were a minority and the government wanted to get rid of them, I cannot be persuaded necessarily.
A: I guess I'll just have to restate that individual perception is very prevalent when you're dealing with one side or the other. Arabs were individually perceiving other black Africans as targets.
Q: They're shooting them not because their black. They're both black. One speaks Arabic; the other an African language. They're only shooting the group that speaks the African language because they're supporting the rebel group who also speaks the African language. They're part of the rebels, agents of the rebels and they provide logistical support for the rebels.
A: They don't speak the same language though.
Q: That's true. That could be a coincidence.
A: I don't believe so. We have two groups of people who don't speak the same language.
Q: But isn't it possible they are being killed because they provide logistical support as a means to deter others?
A: That could be possible, but I don't think that's going on here.

Q: Is it consistent with international law to have the human right to fight needed for survival?
A: No, it is not illegal if a country is to exercise its right to defend its sovereignty.
Q: Yet, if they were targeting males, does that imply that they are combatants? Wouldn't they target women and children too if it were genocide?
A: We need to shoot the militants and males because they are the enemy, not because we are trying to destroy them as a people.
Q: Genocide is an intent crime, the case falls on intent. Even if some have been killed and conditions led to deaths, then you need to infer intent from certain acts, otherwise if there is direct evidence no one would be convicted. These people don't leave incriminating evidence (viz., Hitler). So is there enough circumstantial evidence to infer intent?
A: The intended to flatten the capital city. That does not constitute intent to destroy all of the country.
Q: Yes, but its indiscriminate killing, so what is that—an unintended consequence or intending to target militants? Is the United States guilty of genocide in Japan after dropping two A-bombs, or was there no intent there? So as long as one can infer intent, can one find it in cases such as from WWII with Russians against Chechens?
A: There is no motive.
Q: What? They call all the rebels to be 'terrorists.'
A: Our leader said that he's open to diplomacy with those who want peace, and we cannot go fighting door-to-door without using a lot of resources.
Q: You stated that the state's responsibility to prevent genocide can only be determined after a genocide has taken place?
A: No I did not say that.

Q: Your statement is that because of the civil war, genocide could not have taken place.
A: I did not say that because of the civil war, genocide could not have taken place. I said that killings that were taking place were a consequence of the civil war. It was a conflict between two groups: the rebel group and the *Satanakunda*. So the group in question was not being attacked on the basis of their group identity. The population of Notoria is intermixed, Arabs and non-Arabs. Both groups were affected by the war, both were displaced from their homes.

Q: Is it possible to have elements of the crime of genocide during wartime?
A: Yes it is. As I mentioned in my argument there were killings of civilians and the burning down of homes and hospitals. It wasn't targeted towards a certain group of people but the entire population of the region.
Q: Although it was against the entire population is it not possible that the state's intention was to destroy a specific segment of the entire population?

A: The state had nothing to do with the militia group that attacked the population of Notoria. The state had no idea what was going on because of the geographical distance between the capital and the effected region.

Q: Was the paramilitary not supported by the government?
A: No they were not. There is no proof to show that the government had anything to do with the paramilitary.
Q: In the facts of the case it was stated that the *Satanakunda* were closely aligned with the government.
A: There is no proof of that. There were some individuals in the paramilitary who asked for assistance and the government gave it to them, but this does not mean that the government directed the paramilitary to attack.

Q: You're asserting that genocide could not have taken place because of the distance between the capital city and the effected region?
A: I'm not saying that genocide could not have taken place because of the geographical distance. I'm saying that the government was not alerted as to what was going on. The conflict in Notoria appeared to be a war between two rebel groups and the government had no idea of as to the scope of the violence.

Q: You stated earlier that the violence was due to a civil war. To have a civil war you need to have forces fighting against the government. Regardless of the distance between the capital city and the region, the orders to fight and defend the country must have come from the government?
A: No.
Q: So you have a civil war in the country without government interaction?
A: According to the Respondent, the government did not take sides in the conflict.
Q: In the facts it was stated that the army of the government was also involved in the conflict. Are you saying that Respondent Government has no control over its own military?
A: As the facts state in 2003 the rebels attacked a government airbase. So yes the government did respond. The government may have overreacted but it did not attack any group based on their group identity. The government only responded in retaliation.
Q: It doesn't matter whether the government was responding or not if their attacks constituted genocide, if the intent of the government was to commit genocide.
A: What I'm saying is that the government's response to the 2003 attack had nothing to do with the conflict between the rebel group and *Satanakunda* in Notoria, except to the extent to which the 2003 attacks made the rebel group in Notoria a scapegoat. In other words, the *Satanakunda* used the 2003 attack as a basis for their violent attacks in the Notoria region.

Q: You stated earlier that the government was naive as to what was going on. The government signed a peace accord with both groups in 2006. The parties promised not to engage in armed conflict with one another.

A: The peace agreement was three years after the war had started. The government did not know of the violence when it started. Later on the government knew and did what it could to stop it as demonstrated by the peace accord. The government does not call the violence that happened "genocide." The reason they are trying to end the violence is because it is a war. If what occurred was genocide the government would not have tried to achieve peace between the parties.

Q: Just to clarify, it is your contention that the government was unable to prevent the violence?

A: Yes because of the distance.

Q: Is it possible that the government just wasn't willing to stop it?

A: No because like I said if the government was not willing they wouldn't have tried to achieve peace. They would have just allowed the killings to continue in order to get rid of a troublesome group.

Q: The government only entered into the comprehensive peace agreement once high level officials began to be charged with acts of genocide and war crimes. It appears that the government was not so much unable as they were unwilling to engage in peace negotiations.

A: As I said if they were unwilling they would have never engaged in negotiations.

Q: Again it would appear that their willingness was a consequence of international pressure associated with the indictments of high level officials for crimes of genocide.

A: Is that a fact? As far as I know they were only charged with war crimes.

Q: They were charged with both. It was after the indictments for genocide that they actually agreed to sit down for peace negotiations, once they were charged with genocide.

A: Is that correct? Okay.

Q: No more questions.

Q: It is possible that ethnic cleansing took place? Can one infer from ethnic cleansing that genocide occurred? Can ethnic cleansing lead to genocide?

A: Okay what is ethnic cleansing?

Q: Ethnic cleansing was defined by the ICJ in the *Croatia* case as the mass expulsion of people from a region.

Judge Carey: That's not a crime it's just a concept.

Student Judge: I'm asking her if the commission of ethnic cleansing can lead to genocide.

A: Yes it can.

Q: But it also could not.

Q: The government stated when it signed the peace agreement that it had a responsibility to protect. That was one of the reasons why they signed the agreement. You stated that the government had no obligation to prevent genocide. If the government is a party to the treaty how can this be?
A: The government has no responsibility to protect through unilateral intervention.
Q: Don't all nations have a responsibility to prevent genocide?
A: Okay.
Q: Is it possible that someone could sign a peace agreement in order to get an amnesty?
A: It's possible.
Q: So it doesn't follow logically that signing a peace agreement means the individual is uninterested in obtaining an amnesty from prosecution? In other words, the fact that they signed a peace agreement could be a good sign, but it could also be a bad sign, correct?
A: Signing the agreement shows that the government is trying to bring peace.
Q: No it doesn't. Many peace agreements that get signed are ignored. The Syrian government signed a cease-fire with the UN six months ago and obviously had no intent to obey it.
A: Just because Syria did that does not mean that Respondent will.
Q: I agree with you. It could be that they have good faith. However, it could also be that they do not. You cannot make any logical conclusion from their behavior.
A: It shows that they are actually trying.
Q: No it doesn't. It shows that they signed a peace agreement. Their behavior could be insincere. Wouldn't you agree?
A: To a certain extent I do. To a certain extent I don't.
Q: Okay.

Q: The fact that the rebel groups in Notoria weren't attacked first doesn't logically require that there was no intent to commit genocide, because genocidal intent could result as a consequence of their (Respondent's) wanting revenge for the 2003 attack. Is that not right?
A: Can you say that one more time?
Q: The exact same type of question. The fact that there was a peace agreement, the very fact that the government was attacked first, doesn't logically prove anything.
A: Yes. Absolutely.
Q: Okay. So you concede that was well?
A: Yes.

Q: Does the fact that the government did have knowledge that the paramilitary was committing these atrocities does this demonstrate that the government might have had intent to commit genocide? Doesn't mean that they did but that

it's possible. And would you also concede that the paramilitary was an agent of the government?
A: No.
Q: They weren't an agent of the government?
A: The government fought its own battles for itself. The rebel forces and the *Satanakunda* forces fought their own battles.
Q: The *Satanakunda* was independent of the government? The government did not arm them? It said in the facts that the government was arming them.
A: The government did provide arms.
Q: If the government provided arms they were an agent weren't they?
A: To a certain extent yes.
Q: If the government armed them and has knowledge of the violence committed wouldn't this imply intent? I'm not saying that it does but that it's possible because the paramilitary is an agent of the government.
A: Yes.
Q: Okay so then the question comes down to intent. We've established that it's possible that the government may have intended for these arms to be used to destroy the rebel group and civilians. The question is did the government have the intent? The fact that the state has the responsibility to stop the violence as it is taking place implies that whether or not they originally had the intent, it's possible they could have gotten the intent after, once the fighting started. Would you concede that?
A: No.
Q: You wouldn't concede that genocidal intent could be established subsequent to previously having military intent? It's possible?
A: No.
Q: So therefore genocide is not possible ever.
A: No.
Q: So it's possible that they had genocidal intent after the fighting started, even if they didn't have it originally? So the fact that they were attacked first might mean that they became so angry that they decided to start attacking civilians. Now, it was established in earlier questioning that civilians may have engaged in illegal activities by providing logistical support for the rebels.
A: Absolutely.
Q: So if civilians provided logistical support they should have been arrested shouldn't they? Instead of being slaughtered?
A: They should have but the thing is it was not genocide if it was not committed against a certain ethnic group.
Q: Weren't the civilians all Africans? Weren't they a different ethnic group and a racial group? Not a racial group, they're both African but one speaks Arabic, the other African languages. Işn't that correct?
A: Yes, I'm African and I know in Africa that not everyone speaks the same language.

Q: But the fact is in this case that the majority of the population speaks Arabic which is a completely different family of languages from African languages.
A: But they don't.
Q: So we have an armed Arabic speaking group attacking unarmed civilians who may or may not have been supplying logistical support to a rebel group. They could have arrested them but the fact that they didn't arrest them implies that they were killing them to get rid of them. Is that right?
A: No.
Q: Why didn't they arrest them then?
A: I don't know
Q: if you want to prevent them from providing logistical support all you have to do is detain them.
A: Not provide them support, give them arms.
Q: They could have arrested the civilians for supporting the rebellion and instead they slaughtered them right?
A: My point is that for it to be genocide they have to be civilians.
Q: They were a different ethnic group. They were all Africans. Just because you speak a different language but are of the same race doesn't mean you're the same group. We have the same race but two separate ethnic groups here don't we?
A: No we don't.
Q: In Nigeria you have Ibos who are Christian . . .
A: I'm Nigerian and I know that.
Q: . . . and the Hausa who are Muslim, They are different ethnic groups aren't they?
A: Yes.
Q: Okay so if the Ibo were to commit genocide against the Hausa or vice versa as occurred in the Biafran war that would be genocide wouldn't it? The fact that you had a Muslim army slaughtering Christians was that not genocide? The Nigerian civil war that occurred in the late 1960s, and it was just a civil war like this one, was that not a case of genocide?
A: It was a case of genocide.
Q: So why is the slaughter by an Arabic speaking militia of African ethnic civilians who could have been arrested, not an attempt to destroy them? This is actually a bigger difference than the situation of Nigeria. There you have different religious groups but a similar family of languages. The ethnic differences in this case are even bigger because we have a different family of languages, correct?
A: Yes.
Q: So if you concede that what took place in Nigeria, with its smaller ethnic differences was genocide, why can you not concede that genocide happened in this case?
A: There wasn't the intent to destroy a group in whole or in part.
Q: Like there was in Biafra?

A: Right.

Q: What is the state's obligation to prevent genocide once genocide starts?
A: That's a good question. I think once it starts the only way to stop it is with the police and law enforcement.
Q: So the state did not take action in this case. Is it not possible that the state is in violation of the Genocide Convention?
A: Yes but is it the responsibility of the state or the region or the international community?
Q: The state here is not the only one responsible. But the state has a responsibility as per the Genocide Convention. If the facts suggest that the *Satanakunda* were committing genocide is the state not in violation of the Genocide Convention for failure to prevent once the actions of the *Satanakunda* became known to them?
A: Right.
Q: So you deny that the *Satanakunda* was motivated by genocide?
A: No they weren't motivated by genocide.
Q: The killing of civilians which almost always occurs during civil wars on a mass scale. The mass murder of civilian populations has been considered genocide in many cases, from your argument these were not genocides?
A: Just not in this case.
Q: What about Rwanda? There you had a civil war with Tutsis killed who were sympathetic to the Rwanda Patriotic Front.
A: That was genocide. This was not. This was a military rebellion.
Q: There was a military rebellion in Rwanda too. There was a Tutsi army and that army won the civil war. The Tutsi have been running the country ever since.
A: But the Arabs still are the ones in charge.
Q: So, the only difference is that in once case the minority rebels were victorious in Rwanda but they have lost so far in this country.
A: Yes.
Q: So what relevance is that? If it was mass murder in Rwanda by the government and the interahamwe militia why isn't the *Satanakunda* militia connected to this government?
A: The government in this case has not admitted to being on the side of the Arab militia. They didn't tell them who to go kill with their arms.
Q: Isn't giving them arms enough? The fact that they didn't have to tell doesn't prove that the *Satanakunda* didn't know who to kill. The fact that they didn't give orders doesn't prove there was an order either.
A: The Arabs could have killed each other.
Q: The Arabs could have killed each other?

APPENDIX B: Alterable Facts that Students and Faculty could Adopt to Change the Legal Arguments

1. The Republic of Notoria is or is not the largest country in Africa. Since 2003 the country has or has not been involved in an on-again, off-again conflict with three main rebels from the region of Killalli.
2. Killalli is close to or far from the capital of Notoria and the insurgent activity threatens secession or even the capital's security. The people of Killalli and the inhabitants of the North (including those who make up the *Satanakunda*) are or not of similar ethnic makeup as a consequence of years of intermarriage, which is or is not different from the ethnicity of the country's capital region. Most of the Arab and black residents of Notoria are or are not linked to the same religion, Islam.
3. Rebel groups do or do not exist in Killalli made up of members of the black Muslim population. As a consequence of rebel group activity in Killalli, the *Satanakunda* did or did not enter the region and destroyed villages in Killalli with thousands of residents of the region were displaced and/or killed in the process.
4. The *Satanakunda* is a militia group made up of members of the Arab Muslim population of northern Notoria and does or does not enjoy the support, moral and/or physical of the Arab Muslim population.
5. A UN Commission of Inquiry sent to the region concluded in 2004 that the violence that was being perpetrated against the inhabitants of Killalli was or was *not* yet genocide though evidence of genocidal intent was clear or unclear.
6. The Republic of Notoria and the United States of Idealia are or are not both state parties to the United Nations Convention on the Punishment and Prevention of the Crime of Genocide (Genocide Convention).
7. The President of Notoria was indicted by the International Criminal Court in 2010 for genocide in relation to the crimes perpetrated in the Killalli region, or the genocide case was referred by Idealia, also state party, or the case was referred by the UN Security Council.
8. The United States of Idealia is a developed Western country and a "leader of the free world," or it is merely a neighboring country with an interest in stability on its border and/or has ethnic ties to the ethnic group predominating in Killalli.
9. Idealia did or did not conclude that the violence in Killalli was or was not genocide through a declaration of its Foreign Minister and/or its national legislature to either effect.
10. Due to extensive inter-marriage and cohabitation the residents of Killalli do or do not constitute separate and distinguishable ethnic or racial groups from those residing in the North.
12. The *Satanakunda* are not an extremist Islamic militia or are merely secular forces fighting for the national sovereign borders of Notoria.

13. The Government of Notoria has or has no relationship with the *Satanakunda*, or it is a moral but not a monetary one. The Government of Notoria has or has no control over the actions of the *Satanakunda*.
14. Few, some or most attacks that did occur in Killalli were aimed at rebels or at citizens.
15. Rebels in the Killalli region have or have not frequently attacked civilians and/or government soldiers.
16. The Government of Notoria did or did not attempt to halt, restrict, or fostered the actions of the *Satanakunda* against Killallian civilians.
17. Because of the geographical distance separating Killalli from the capital of Notoria, the government did or did not have the capacity to inhibit any crimes of the *Satanakunda* far from the capital, only nearby.
18. The President of the Government of Notoria had or lacked knowledge of the actions perpetrated by the *Satanakunda*.
19. There was or was not any documentation or other hard evidence that demonstrates the Government of Notoria possessed the *dolus specialis* to destroy in whole or in part the black Muslin population of Killalli.
20. The deaths that have occurred in Killalli are or are not just an unfortunate by-product of the civil war between the Government of Notoria and the rebels of Killalli. The fact that a civil war is taking place in Killalli makes the distinction between civilians and rebels easy or difficult to discern.
21. Notoria is or is not using its own judicial process to investigate claims of Genocide. International inquiry is or is not necessary.
22. Idealia did or did not support a hybrid peacekeeping and humanitarian mission in Notoria to stop the killing or at least feed and help the needy.
23. The Responsibility to Protect norm as set forth by the United Nations World Summit 2005 and interpreted by scholars and or some powerful states does or does not recommend any other country intervene unilaterally to stop *jus cogens* violations or in any other country.

Here is an alternative version of the facts:

Darfur is a region located in the western part of Darfur, which is located in east Africa. Darfur covers over 190 square miles of Africa and has an estimated population of six million people. According to the United Nations Development Program's Human Development Index, Darfur is considered a Least Developed Country (LDC). Darfur is comprised of mainly tribal social environments, which can consist of up to 100 families.

A famine, which began in the 1980s, sent the region of Darfur into political turmoil and resulted in an armed conflict, with violence peaking in 2003 and continues to this day A year after the peak of the conflict, the UN considered the region of Darfur "in a state of ethnic cleansing." The main players in involved in the conflict where as follows: The Sudanese Armed Forces, the Janjaweed Rebel group and various other rebel movement groups. The groups involved in the conflict have used several violent tactics to systematically target civilians in the Rufrad region as severing telecommunication services in areas that were about to be attacked, aerial attacks followed by ground assaults on villages, targeting fleeing villagers, looting, slavery, rape, torture, kidnapping, and other human rights abuses.

Rufrad is considered a case study for genocide because of its large number of defenseless citizens, the lack of discipline inside the killing forces, the unstable government, and its overall underdeveloped infrastructure.

Several unsuccessful peace agreements have been signed in lieu of the conflict in particular the Darfur Peace Agreement between the Government Nadus and the Rufradi Rebel Groups, which was signed in 2006.

Or, alternatively:

On August 14th and 15th in 2006, Cheneystand invaded the country of Bidenland Country in August 2006 clear violation of Article 2(4) of the UN Charter. Bidenland has a GDP of 5000 US Dollars per capita. Cheneystand has a far more advanced and vast military force than Bidenland, Moreover, Cheneystand has nuclear capabilities. Over the past decade, the country has been increasingly threatened by a Cheneystand, which has its sights set on annexing Bidenland in an effort to gain control of the Bidenland's oil resources. The highest concentration of oil exists in a city of Bidenland called Butterport.

The Head of State of Bidenland, Hilary Clinton used chemical weapons in the Butterport area to defend her country against Cheneystand. Specifically, Bidenland used its chemical weapons on August 14th and 15th. Cheneystand ceased their attack after the chemical weapons were unleashed. Hilary Clinton, after the forces of Cheneystand retreated, ceased using the chemical weapons. Hilary Clinton made an effort to warn citizens. There was a 72-hour notice for the civilians to evacuate the area.

The total damages; 300 civilians, and 600 soldiers from the invading army died as a result of the attack and 1200-1500 suffer from various ailments. The property damages totaling 250,000 USD. Hilary Clinton made efforts to ensure for the well-being through the provision of medical assistance, after she knew their injuries. Time before any aid in the region arrived was 36 hours after the chemical attack.

The UN recognizes Bidenland's sovereignty. They are a party to statutes of ICC. The country of Bidenland is a signatory to the Convention on the Prohibition of the Development, Production, Stockpiling and Use of Chemical Weapons and on Their Destruction of 13 January 1993 (CWC). They are also a party to the Geneva Convention. And Article 7 and 8 of the Rome statute has also been ratified along with the UN Charter. Hilary Clinton is charged with violations of the War Crimes, and Crimes Against Humanity.

Notes

1. The case against Sudan was referred to the ICC by the UN Security Council. United Nations Security Council, Resolution 1593, S/RES/1593 (March 31, 2005).

2. Katherine Goldsmith, "The Issue of Intent in the Genocide Convention and its Effect on the Prevention and Punishment of the Crime of Genocide: a Knowledge-Based Approach," *Genocide Studies and Prevention*, 5, no. 3 (December 2010): 242.

3. Ahmad Muhammad Harun and Abdul Raheam Muhammad Hussein, Minister of Humanitarian Affairs and Minister of Defense respectively, were indicted by the ICC for war crimes and crimes against humanity. International Criminal Court, "Situations and Cases: Darfur," www.icc-cpi.int (accessed June 5, 2012).

4. Al-Bashir was charged with three counts of genocide per Articles 6(a)-(c) of the ICC Statute. Identical to Articles 2(a) through (c) of the United Nations Genocide Convention (paraphrasing) these include: killing group members; causing serious harm to group members (mental/physical) and deliberately inflicting on the group conditions intended to bring about their partial or total destruction. ICC, *Prosecutor v. Omar Hassan Ahmid Al Bashir*, Case No. ICC-02/05-01/09-05, Pre-Trial Chamber 1, Second Arrest Warrant (July 12, 2010).

5. More recent violent actions taken by the Khartoum government against the people in the Nuba mountains and the Ngok people in the Abeyi region demonstrate the urgency of bringing President Al-Bashir to justice. Eric Reeves, "In Sudan, Genocide Anew?," *Washington Post*, June 17, 2011, http//www.washingtonpost.com/opinions/in-sudan-genocide-anew/2011/06/17/AGcVLCVZH_story.html (accessed June 21, 2011).

6. Malcolm N. Shaw, *International Law*, 6th ed. (Cambridge, UK: Cambridge University Press, 2008), 1072.

7. On the dual genocide regime see Antonio Cassese, *International Criminal Law*, 2d edition, (Oxford: Oxford University Press, 2008), 129; also William Schabas, *Genocide in International Law: The Crime of Crimes*, 2d edition (Cambridge, UK: Cambridge University Press, 2009), 669.

8. ICTY, Prosecutor v. *Krstić*, Case No. IT-98-33-T, Judgment, (August 2, 2001), para. 562.

9. Shaw, *International Law*, 24-27; 49-54.

10. Cassese, *International Criminal Law*, 37.

11. Rome Statute of the International Criminal Court, UN Doc. A/CONF.183/9, Art. 21(1)(a)-(c) and (2).

12. These of course are not the only differences between common and civil law systems. In civil law systems judges take an active role in the investigatory process, and prosecutors are permitted to appeal an acquittal. Common law systems ("Anglo-American systems"), are far more adversarial. Prosecutors are the fact-finders, judges take on a more neutral role, and emphasis is placed on the rights of the accused. With respect to the latter, the ICC embraces some common law traditions (Rome Statute, Art 55), although compared to the ICTY and the ICTR its procedural rules are more inquisitorial. Gerhard Werle, *Principles of International Criminal Law*, 2d edition (The Hague: T-M-C-Asser Press, 2009), 47; Cassese, *International Criminal Law*, 369-374.

13. Statute of the International Court of Justice, Art. 38 (1945).

14. Convention on the Prevention and Punishment of the Crime of Genocide (UNGC), UN Doc. A/810, Art. 9 (1948).

15. UN Genocide Convention, Art. 3.

16. UN Genocide Convention 1, 8, 9.

17. Versus proper crimes of omission which are those in which the positive duty to act—to stop at a car accident, to make way for an ambulance—is usually one shared by society at large; it is an "inherent element" of the crime and a duty in which the capacity to act is shared by many. Proper crimes of omission on the international plane largely concern war crimes as laid out in the Geneva Conventions. Some of these obligations are "sweeping"; some more "qualified." Cassese, *International Criminal Law*, 234-235; also Michael Duttwiler, "Liability for Omission in International Criminal Law," 6 *Int'l Crim. L. Rev.* 1, 4-5; 8-11 (2006) and Gerhard Werle, *Principles of International Criminal Law*, 232-234.

18. Duttwiler, "Liability," 5-6.

19. As to treaty law referencing genocide, mention of commission by omission is indicated in Article 2 of the Convention on the Non-Applicability of Statutory Limitations to War Crimes and Crimes Against Humanity which does not establish criminal liability, but "refers to 'representatives' of a state who 'tolerate' the commission of war crimes, crimes against humanity or genocide." Duttwiler, "Liability," 14. As to customary international law there is very little *opinio juris* ("in opinion of law") on this issue; much of what has been decided on commission by omission has been decided by state courts in adherence with state laws. For his discussion regarding treaty and customary law see "Liability," 13-26.

20. Duttwiler, "Liability," 55.

21. Dutwiler suggests that the two current *ad hoc* Tribunals have assessed liability for omission generally by reference also to general legal principles. He bases this suggestion on certain features of the Tribunals' case law including their emphasis on the fact that a special duty and capacity are required for omission (which hints at commission by omission and logically excludes proper omission). Duttwiler here is referring to a number of cases. The short list includes: (regarding special duty) ICTR, *Prosecutor v. Musema*, Case No. ICTR-96-13-A, Judgment para. 123 (January 27, 2000), ICTY, *Prosecutor v. Blaskic*, Case No. IT-95-14-T, Judgment, para. 271 (March 3, 2000) and ICTR. *Prosecutor v. Ntagerura et. al.*, Case No. ICTR-97-63-T, Judgment, para. 659 (February 25, 2009); (regarding capacity to act); ICTR, *Prosecutor v. Bagambiki*, Case No. ICTR-97-63-T, Judgment, para. 659 (February 25, 2004). Dutwiler, "Liability," 46.

22. ICTY, *Prosecutor v. Mucić et. al.* Case No. IT-96-21-T, Judgment (November 16, 1998), ICTY, *Prosecutor v. Krnojelac*, Case No IT-97-25-T, Judgment (March 15, 2002), ICTY, *Prosecutor v. Aleksovski*, Case No. IT-95-14/1, Judgment (June 25, 1999). It should be noted with the latter case the defendant was acquitted. Duttwiler, "Liability," 52.

23. ICTY, *Prosecutor v. Blaškić*, Case No. IT-95-14-A, Judgment para. 668, 670 (July 29, 2004); see also "Statute of the International Tribunal for the Prosecution of Persons Responsible for Serious Violations of International Humanitarian Law Committed in the Territory of the Former Yugoslavia since 1992," Adopted by Security Council Res. 829 (1993), http://www.icty.org/sections/LegalLibrary/StatuteoftheTribunal (accessed July 31, 2011).

24. ICTR, *Prosecutor v. Mpambara*, Case No, ICTR-01-65-T, Judgment (September 11, 2006).

25. Rajat Rana, "*The Jean Mpambara Case*: Outlining 'Culpable Omissions' in International Criminal Law, 6 *Chinese J. Int'l L.* 439, 443 (2007); also *Mpambara*, Case No, ICTR-01-65-T, para. 27.

26. Rana, *Jean Mpambara*, 443; see specifically ICTR, *Prosecutor v. Rutaganira*, Case No. ICTR-95-1C-T, Judgment, paras. 81-84 (March 14, 2005).

27. *Application of the Convention on the Prevention and Punishment of the Crime of Genocide (Bosnia and Herzegovina v. Serbia and Montenegro) [Bosnia]*, 2007 ICJ 43 (February 26). For all judgments related to this case see the ICJ website http//www.icj-cij.org/docket/index.php?p1=3&p2=3&k=8d&case=91&code=bhy&p3=4.

28. Meaning the first in which a court was asked to interpret the UN Genocide Convention.

29. At issue here is the murder of approximately eight thousand Muslim men and by the Bosnian-Serb army in the summer of 1995.

30. *Bosnia*, Judgment, 2007 ICJ Reports at 221, para. 430; also 228-229, paras 448-50.

31. *Bosnia*, Judgment, 2007 ICJ Reports at 202-203, paras. 387-388; 214-215, paras. 413-415.

32. *Bosnia*, Judgment, 2007 ICJ Reports at 137-138, paras. 231-234; 155, para. 278; 166, para. 297; 202-203, paras. 387-88; 206-208, paras. 396-400; 214-215, paras. 413-415.

33. ICTR, *Prosecutor v. Akayesu*, Case No. ICTR-96-4-T, Judgment para. 498.

34. Schabas, *Genocide*, 270. Of course these components are found in Article 2 of the UN Genocide Convention; see UNTC.

35. Werle, *Principles*, 149.

36. Under international criminal law special intent is also required for terrorism, aggression, and for certain forms of crimes against humanity (e.g., persecution). Cassese, *International Criminal Law*, 140.

37. Cassese 141; Cherif Bassiouni makes a similar point in "Commentary on the International Law Commission's 1991 Draft Code of Crimes against Peace and the Security of Mankind," *Nouvelles Etudes Penales*, (1993), 233. Of course the practice of inferring intent from the facts of a case is common practice in domestic legal settings.

38. International jurisprudence on this latter issue has held that a plan is not necessary to demonstrate genocidal intent. Intent can be inferred from genocidal acts. Nevertheless as Cassese suggests rarely do genocidal acts in and of themselves occur randomly and in isolation from one another. As such widespread and systematic acts of murder, bodily harm etc. presuppose a larger plan of destruction. However, they "remain nevertheless factual events, not provided for or required by the relevant treaty or customary rules." Cassese, *International Criminal Law*, 140.

39. As a note to instructors it will be extremely useful for students to become familiar with the UN Genocide Convention as it is referred to throughout this text.

40. Robert Weiner, "The Law of Genocide," in *The International Studies Encyclopedia*, ed. Robert A. Denemark (Blackwell Publishing, 2010), www.isacompendium.com/subscriber/tocnode?id=g9781444336597_chunk_g978144433659712_ss1-6> (accessed November 15, 2010).

41. Larry May, *Genocide: A Normative Account* (Cambridge: Cambridge University Press, 2010), 40-58. May bases his argument for group identity on the conclusions about identity reached by the UN Commission of Inquiry in their 2005 report on Darfur.

42. Cassese, *International Criminal Law*, 138-140.

43. ICTR, *Prosecutor v. Rutaganda*, Case No. ICTR-63-3-T, Judgment, para. 55 (December 6, 1999).

44. UN Genocide Convention, Articles 1, 8-9.

45. The U.S. response (or more accurately lack of response) to these and other cases of genocide are thoroughly examined in Samantha Power's noteworthy contribution, *A Problem From Hell: America and the Age of Genocide* (New York: Harper Perennial, 2003).

46. Cassese, *International Criminal Law*, 130.

47. United Nations, 2005 World Summit Outcome, Resolution Adopted by the General Assembly, A/60/L.1, September 15, 2005, http://daccess-dds-ny.un.org/doc/UNDOC/GEN/N05/487/60/PDF/N0548760.pdf?OpenElement (accessed November 10, 2010), 30.

48. The most obvious one of these can be found in Article 8 wherein "Any Contracting Party *may* [emphasis added] call upon the competent organs of the United Nations to take such action under the Charter of the United Nations . . . for the prevention and suppression of acts of genocide." Schabas, Genocide, 669. For his fuller discussion about Article 8 see *Genocide*, 533-539. Idealia's arguments are in large part a consequence of the various ambiguities or loopholes in the Genocide Convention, which have permitted states to argue that they do not have mandated responsibilities to prevent genocide. The position of the United States has changed from avoiding the "G-word" in Rwanda and Bosnia under President Clinton, to using the word once under Bush, to Obama's officials claiming that any responsibility in the Convention involves only genocide occurring inside the same state. Legal scholars argue that the responsibility to protect is most clearly activated for a genocide in any state party if not everywhere, though it remains a discretionary right in law. See Chip Carey, "Syria's Civil War has become a Genocide," http://www.worldpolicy.org/blog/2013/09/16/syrias-civil-war-has-become-genocide.

49. Luke Glanville, "Ellery Stowell and the Enduring Dilemmas of Humanitarian Intervention," *International Studies Review*, 15 (2011): 251.

50. John Bolton, quoted in Glanville, "Ellery Stowell," 251.

51. UNGC, Doc. A/810 (1948).

52. UNGC, Art. 9.

53. UNGC, Art. 2.

54. Antonio Cassese, *International Criminal Law*, 2d edition, (Oxford: Oxford University Press, 2008), 139, referring to ICTR, *Prosecutor v. Akayesu*, Case No. ICTR-96-4-T, Judgment, para. 511 (September 2, 1998); also *Prosecutor v. Rutaganda*, Case No. ICTR-96-3-T, Judgment, para. 55 (December 6, 1999).

55. ICTY, *Prosecutor v. Jelisić*, Case No. IT-95-10-T, Judgment, para. 70; also paras. 71-72 (December 14, 1999); see also ICTY, *Prosecutor v. Krstić*, Case No. IT-98-33-T, Judgment, paras. 556-560 (August 2, 2001). For an earlier perspective on group identity see, for example, *Akayesu*, Trial Judgment, paras. 511, 516, 702.

56. UNGC, Art. 1

57. UNGC, Art. 3.

58. This was affirmed by the ICTR in *Prosecutor v. Akayesu*, Trial Judgment, paras. 497, 544; *Prosecutor v. Rutaganda*, Trial Judgment, para 59; and ICTR, *Prosecutor v. Musema*, Case No. ICTR-96-13-T, Judgment, para. 164 (January, 27 2000).

59. ICTY, *Prosecutor v. Stakić*, Case No. IT-97-24-T, Motion for Judgment of Acquittal (October 31, 2002).

60. ICTY, *Prosecutor v. Jelisić*, Case No. IT-95-10-A, Judgment, para. 47 (July 5, 2001). See also ICTR, *Prosecutor v. Rutaganda*, Case No. ICTR-3-3-A, Judgment, para. 528 (May 26, 2003) and *Prosecutor v. Mpambara*, Case No. ICTR-01-65-T, Judgment, para. 8 (September 11, 2006).

61. ICTR, *Akayesu*, Trial Judgment, para. 523.

62. International Law Commission (ILC), Draft Articles on Responsibility of States for Internationally Wrongful Acts, *Official Records of the General Assembly, Fifty-sixth session, Supplement No. 10*, UN Doc. A/56/10, (November 2001). http://www.ilsa.org/jessup/jessup06/basicmats2/DASR.pdf.

63. ILC, Draft Articles, Art. 2.

64. ILC, Draft Articles, Art. 12.

65. In this case the military would more correctly be acting as a direct organ of the state pursuant to Article 4 of the ILC Draft Articles.

66. ILC, Draft Articles, Art. 7.

67. United Nations, 2005 World Summit Outcome, Resolution Adopted by the General Assembly, UN Doc. A/60/L.1, paras. 138-139 (September 15, 2005).

68. *Application of the Convention on the Prevention and Punishment of the Crime of Genocide (Bosnia and Herzegovina v. Serbia and Montenegro) [Bosnia], Judgment of February 26, 2007*, 2007 ICJ Reports 43 (2007).

69. *Bosnia*, 2007 ICJ Rep at 201, para. 382.

70. *Bosnia*, 2007 ICJ Rep, at 220, para. 427.

71. *Bosnia*, 2007 ICJ Rep, at 221, para. 430.

72. *Bosnia*, 2007 ICJ Rep, at 221, para. 430.

73. *Bosnia*, 2007 ICJ Rep, at 222, para. 431.

74. *Bosnia*, 2007 ICJ Rep, at 225-226, para. 438.

75. *Bosnia*, 2007 ICJ Rep, at 218, para. 421.

76. *Bosnia*, 2007 ICJ Rep, at 230, para. 453 referring to *Application of the Convention on the Prevention and Punishment of the Crime of Genocide (Bosnia and Herzegovina v. Yugoslavia [Serbia and Montenegro]), Provisional Measures, Order of April 8, 1993*, 1993 ICJ Reports 3 at 24, para. 52.

77. Genocide Convention, "Preamble."

78. *Reservations to the Convention on the Prevention and Punishment of the Crime of Genocide, Advisory Opinion of May 8, 1951*, 1951 ICJ Reports 15 (1951) at 23.

79. United Nations, "A More Secure World: Our Shared Responsibility: Report of the Secretary-General's High-Level Panel on Threats, Challenges, and Change," UN Doc. A/59/565 (December 2, 2004), http://www.un.org/secureworld/report.pdf.

80. United Nations, 2005 World Summit Outcome.

81. Center for International Human Rights, Northwestern University School of Law & Responsibility to Protect, *The Responsibility to Protect and the International Criminal Court*, Conference Report (March 2008), 11.

82. Adam Roberts and Richard Guelff, *Documents on the Laws of War*, 2d ed. (Oxford: Clarendon Press; New York: Oxford Univ. Press, 1989), 137.

83. *Application of the Convention on the Prevention and Punishment of the Crime of Genocide (Bosnia and Herzegovina v. Yugoslavia [Serbia and Montenegro]), Provisional Measures, Order of September 13 1993, Separate Opinion of Judge Elihu Lauterpacht*, 1993 ICJ Reports 407, at 440.

84. *Reservations to the Convention on Genocide, Advisory Opinion*, 1951 ICJ Reports 15 (1951) at 24.

85. Security Council Resolution 1161, S/RES/1161 (April 8, 1998), 2.

86. *Barcelona Traction, Light and Power Company, Limited, Judgment of February 5, 1970*, 1970 ICJ Reports 3 at 32, paras. 33-34.

87. *Barcelona Traction*, ICJ Rep. 1970 at 32, para. 33.

88. Stephen Toope, "Does International Law Impose a Duty upon the United Nations to Prevent Genocide?," 46 *McGill L. J.* 187, 193 (2002).

89. United Nations Charter, Art. 55 (June 26, 1945).

90. United Nations Charter, Art. 56

91. Christopher C. Joyne, "'The Responsibility to Protect': Humanitarian Concern and the Lawfulness of Armed Intervention" 47 *Va. J. Int'l. L.* 693 (2007).

92. Scott Shackelford, "Holding States Accountable for the Ultimate Human Right Abuse: A Review of the International Court of Justice's Bosnian Genocide Case," 14, no. 3, *Human Rights Brief* 21 (2007).

93. *Bosnia*, ICJ Rep 2007, at 233, para. 461.

94. Joyne, "'Responsibility to Protect,'" 707, citing International Commission on Intervention and State Sovereignty, *The Responsibility to Protect: Report of the International Commission on Intervention and State Sovereignty* (2001), 17.

95. Joyne, "'Responsibility to Protect,'" 705, citing to Kofi Annan, "'We the Peoples': The Role of the United Nations in the 21st Century," U.N. Sales No. E.00.I.16 (2000), http://www.un.org/millennium/sg/report/full.htm.

96. Joyne, "'The Responsibility to Protect,'" 712-713.

97. Independent International Commission on Kosovo, *The Kosovo Report: Conflict, International Response, Lessons Learned* (Oxford: Oxford University Press, 2000), 289.

98. William Schabas, *Genocide in International Law* (Cambridge: Cambridge Univ. Press, 2000), 495.

99. UN Charter, Art. 1(3) which articulates as a principal goal of the UN, "promoting and encouraging respect for human rights and for fundamental freedoms"; see also UN Charter, Arts. 55-56.

100. Ingrid Detter, *The Law of War*, 2d ed, (Cambridge, Cambridge University Press, 2000), 34.

101. Rosalyn Higgins, *The Development of International Law through the Political Organs of the United Nations* (London: Oxford University Press, 1963), 58; Louis Sohn and Thomas Buergenthal, *International Protection of Human Rights* (Indianapolis: Bobbs Merrill, 1973), 556.

102. Security Council Resolution 1674, S/RES/1674 (April 28, 2006).

103. UNGC, Doc. A/810 (1948).

104. UN Charter, Art. 2 (1945).

105. UNGC, Article 8; also United Nations, 2005 World Summit Outcome, Resolution Adopted by the General Assembly, A/60/L.1, para. 139 (September 15, 2005).

106. UNGC, Art. 4.

107. *Application of the Convention on the Prevention and Punishment of the Crime of Genocide (Bosnia and Herzegovina v. Serbia and Montenegro), [Bosnia], Judgment of February 26, 2007, Separate Opinion of Judge Owada,* 2007 ICJ Reports 285 at 298, para. 44.

108. Hirad Abtahi and Philippa Webb, *The Genocide Convention: The Travaux Préparatoires* (Netherlands: Brill Publishers, 2009).

109. Application of the Convention on the Prevention and Punishment of the Crime of Genocide (Bosnia and Herzegovina v. Serbia and Montenegro), [Bosnia], Judgment of February 26, 2007, Joint Declaration of Judges Shi and Koroma 2007 ICJ Reports at 279, para. 1, quote cited from Territorial Dispute (Libyan Arab Jamahiriya/Chad), Judgment of February 3, 1994, ICJ Reports 1994 6 (1994) at 22, para. 41.

110. Vienna Convention on the Law of Treaties, Art. 31, (1969).

111. International Military Tribunal, Judgment of the International Military Tribunal, Trial of Major War Criminals, 1947, Vol. 1, 223, cited in *Bosnia, Judgment of February 26, 2007, Separate Opinion of Judge Owada,* 2007 ICJ Reports at 300, para. 50.

112. *Bosnia, Judgment of 26 February, 2007, Joint Declaration of Judges Shi and Koroma*, 2007 ICJ Reports 279, para. 1.

113. Hersh Lauterpacht, *International Law and Human Rights* (Archon Books, London, 1950), 44; quoted in *Bosnia, Judgment of February 26, 2007, Joint Declaration of Judges Shi and Koroma* 2007 ICJ Reports at 281, para. 4.

114. *Application of the Convention on the Prevention and Punishment of the Crime of Genocide (Bosnia and Herzegovina v. Serbia and Montenegro), [Bosnia], Judgment of February 26, 2007*, 2007 ICJ Reports, 43 at 221, para 431 (2007).

115. *Bosnia*, 2007 ICJ Reports at 222, para. 431.

116. UNGC, Art. 2.

117. *Bosnia*, 2007 ICJ Reports at 221, para. 430.

118. *Bosnia*, 2007 ICJ Reports at 221, para. 430.

119. *Bosnia*, 2007, ICJ Reports at 126, para.198.

120. Allan A. Ryan, "Genocide: What Do We Want It to Be?," *New England Journal of Public Policy* 19, no. 2 (2005).

121. *Bosnia*, 2007, ICJ Reports at 122, para. 189.

122. Benedict Anderson, *Imagined Communities* (London: Verso, 1983).

123. As quoted in Ilias Bantekas, *International Criminal Law*, 4th ed. (Portland, OR: Hart Publishing, 2010), 211.

124. Bantekas, *International Criminal Law*, 211.

125. UN Charter, Art. 2(7).

126. UN Charter, Art. 2(4).

127. UN, 2005 World Summit Outcome, para. 139.

128. International Court of Justice. *Jurisdiction*, http://www.icj-cij.org/jurisdiction/index.php?p1=5 (Aug.30, 2013).

129. Gerhard Werle et al., *Principles of International Criminal Law* (TMC Asser Press, 2005), 225.

130. Appeals Judgment Summary for Ante Gotovina and Malden Markać, *Bosnia and Herzegovina v. Serbia and Montenegro*, www.icty.org (Sep.1, 2013).

131. Katherine G. Southwick, "Srebrenica as Genocide-The Krstić Decision and the Language of the Unspeakable." *Yale Hu,am Rights and Development Journal Law Journal* 8 (2005): 188.

132. *Prosecutor v. Goran Jelisić (Trial Judgment)*, IT-95-10-T, International Criminal Tribunal for the Former Yugoslavia (ICTY), 14 December 1999, available at: http://www.refworld.org/docid/4147fe474.html [accessed 2 September 2013].

133. Appeals Chamber Judgment, *Prosecutor v. Kristć*, Judgment Summary, www.icty.org/x/cases/krstic/acjug/en/040419_Krsti_summary_en.pdf (Sep.1, 2013).

134. Marko Milanovic, "State Responsibility for Genocide." *The European Journal of International Law* 17, no. 3 (2006): 553–604.

135. Patricia M. Wald, "Genocide and Crimes against Humanity," *Wash. U. Global Stud. L. Rev.* 6 (2007): 621.

136. Customary and International Humanitarian Law, http://www.icrc.org/eng/war-and-law/treaties-customary-law/customary-law/index.jsp

137. United States Code; Chapter 50A - Section § 1091. Genocide. Aug.30, 2013.

138. Robert Kolb, "Current Issues and Comments: Note on Humanitarian Intervention," http://www.icrc.org/eng/assets/files/other/irrc_849_kolb.pdf (March 2003).

139. Cornell University, "Res Ipsa Loquitor," Legal Information Institute, http://www.law.cornell.edu/wex/res_ipsa_loquitur (Sep. 1, 2013).

140. David Luban, "Calling Genocide by Its Rightful Name: Lemkin's Word, Darfur, and the UN Report,, *Chicago Journal of International Law*, 7(1) (2006).

141. Christopher C. Joyner, "United States: Genocide Convention Implementation Act of *International Legal Materials*," Vol. 28, No. 3 (May 1989), 754-785.

142. Jamal Jafari, "'Never Again' Again: Darfur, the Genocide Convention, and the Duty to Prevent Genocide." *Human Rights. Br.* 12 (2004): 8-46.

143. Scott Straus, "Darfur and the genocide debate." *Foreign Affairs* (2005): 123-133.

144. Antonio Cassese, "On the Use of Criminal Law Notions in Determining State Responsibility for Genocide." *Journal of International Criminal Justice* 5, no. 4 (2007): 875-887.

Chapter 4

Responsibility to Protect: Prosecutor versus Marmyan President

With Becky Sims

"Disaster" has been defined as "'a calamitous event or series of events resulting in widespread loss of life, great human suffering and distress, or large-scale material or environmental damage, thereby seriously disrupting the functioning of society.'"[1] As students will soon discover the factual circumstances of the case in this chapter are strikingly similar—if not nearly identical—to those which occurred in the country of Myanmar (formerly Burma) in 2008.

The Government of Myanmar—ruled by a military junta—actively prevented international aid efforts following the country's devastation by Cyclone Nargis in May 2008. In addition to the destruction of several towns, the cyclone killed over eighty-five thousand persons and more than fifty-three thousand went missing.[2] As Ford discusses:

> Most of the initial deaths were caused by the storm surge, which sent a twelve-foot-high wave sweeping across parts of the Irrawaddy Delta and submerging many villages.[. . .]The storm surge destroyed housing,[. . .] polluted water sources,[. . .] and contaminated or destroyed food stocks.[. . .] Many areas remained underwater for days or weeks after the cyclone.[. . .] The widespread devastation caused by the cyclone created the potential for a massive secondary humanitarian crisis [associated with lack of materials necessary for human sur-

> vival and the possible spread of disease].[. . .] Moreover, the geography of the Irrawaddy Delta made the delivery of humanitarian aid very difficult.[3]

The military junta in command of the government initially refused aid from Western countries out of a fear of a "seaborn invasion by Western powers."[4] As a consequence the offers and attempts by France, the United States, and other countries to deliver aid were rejected and the junta made United Nations (UN) access especially difficult. Although eventually they permitted greater foreign aid, including Western aid, into the country their initial mishandling of the situation was characterized as a "shocking [mistake]."[5] Thousands of lives could have been saved which were not due to the regime's grave miscalculations; demonstrated by, among other things, its lack of concern for the victims of the cyclone, its lack of internal resources with which to handle the crisis, its refusal to permit foreign access to the hard-hit Irrawaddy Delta, and its stubborn insistence on controlling the receipt and distribution of humanitarian aid.[6] Adding insult to injury in the days that followed the military junta began forcibly displacing survivors "from camps and shelters and sending them back to their home villages even if their homes no longer existed."[7]

The present case also concerns the efforts by ruling elites to prevent a humanitarian relief mission. As discussed below, however, the humanitarian relief mission in the hypothetical case of Marmyan was sanctioned by the United Nations Security Council (UNSC), with the mandate to provide aid to segments of the population in response to a natural catastrophe of horrendous proportions, *as well as* to protect international peace and security pursuant to Chapter VII, Article 42 of the UN Charter. In the case of Myanmar, by contrast, the change in the regime's position was a consequence of a deal reached between UN Secretary-General Ban Ki-Moon and the leadership of the junta to permit foreign aid workers greater access.[8] Moreover, unlike the Myanmar example, international criminal charges were filed against the leader of the government and controversies regarding the Responsibility to Protect (R2P) norm—introduced in the previous section—come to the fore.

The first legal issue is the leader's defiance of the UNSC, which is presumptively illegal, as a UN Charter violation of Article 48, but is not necessarily a crime. The prosecutors argue that R2P has become part of customary international law, permitting even unilateral intervention to save lives, as well as justification for the UNSC to sanction an intervention to save lives, even against a sovereign government because it has forfeited its sovereignty by failing to protect the lives of its own citizens. The defense would naturally argue Chapter VII actions do not extend to natural disasters, because they do not threaten the peace. Prosecutors would argue that UNSC resolutions are legally binding. This allegedly illegal act may or may not be evidence of other crimes. One must consider when human rights violations can come to be considered crimes by judges in past legal cases that influence interpretations of binding, customary international law.

Second, sovereignty, based on Article 2(4) of the UN Charter might be a defense against the legally binding, UNSC decision if there were no doctrine of responsibility to protect, which would expand the UN Charter basis for UNSC sanctioned intervention if there is not, under Article 39, a credible finding of a threat to international peace, a breach of the peace, or an act of aggression. Is the leader criminally responsible for the war crime of depriving citizens of their means of survival? Is withholding aid tantamount to a "widespread or systematic attack on a civilian population," a crime against humanity in other words? The strongest criminal case is an Article 8 war crime because there are explicit rules on humanitarian relief.

Facts of the Case

The Republic of Marmyan is an underdeveloped country that has been ruled since 2001 by a military junta. The junta, led by President and General Xavier Marbur, obtained power via coup following the death of Marbur's predecessor. Once in power the junta dissolved the National Assembly, centralized the economy, and suspended the country's Constitution. There is a nascent opposition movement in Marmyan. Called the "United Front for Democracy" (UDF) the movement has gained momentum in the countryside through its appeals for a return to rule of law and economic stability. The UDF has gained the tacit support of a number of powerful Western countries and more tangible support, including military aid, from neighboring countries. The UDF is perceived by the military junta, led by President General Xavier Marbur to be a threat to the stability of the country. UDF are organized as an umbrella organization; factions of which exercise de facto control of rural areas; particularly those in the Northern region of Marmyan.

Making matter worse Marmyan was devastated by a massive earthquake in June 2009 that destroyed villages and killed many of Marmyanic civilians; particularly those residing in a rural area in the Northern region of the country. In the immediate aftermath of the earthquake access to food, electrical power, medicine, and clean water was incredibly difficult for most of the population to obtain. Moreover government promises to provide the necessary goods and services to the earthquake's victims were severely hampered by a lack of financial and other resources. The plight of the country of Marmyan became a concern to the international community, in particular the Western countries, Western NGOs, regional and international organizations. Marmyan experienced widespread famine and disease, including an outbreak of Cholera and Dysentery in the Northern region of the country. Although these dismal conditions affected many in the country, they heavily impacted an ethnic minority in the Northeast who happened to constitute the primary membership of the UDF.

International efforts to assist the people of Marmyan were rejected by the military government. Per government policy foreign aid permitted into the country was to be distributed by Marmyan government and military personnel. Growing concern regarding the government's response compelled the UNSC to authorize—under Chapter VII of the UN Charter (furthered justified on the basis of the R2P norm)—a humanitarian relief mission which included the use of peacekeeping force to help maintain order and deliver the aid; this taking place over the objections of the Marmyan government. Consequently, several members of the UN relief mission were arrested and detained by armed local security forces upon the orders of President Marbur shortly after their arrival in Marmyan. President Xavier Marbur was eventually arrested by a faction of the UN peacekeeping force and sent to the International Criminal Court at The Hague to stand trial for crimes against humanity, war crimes, and genocide. The UNSC resolution invoked Chapter VII, and stated that the UNSC had the R2P based on a threat to international peace and security to justify a threat to international peace. The judge has to decide if the UNSC has that prerogative. Marbur was convicted on all counts. The briefs included in this section have to do with Marbur's appeal of his conviction in 2010.

Students and/or faculty are free to, indeed are encouraged to, come up with their own sets of facts, in order to generate different legal arguments and briefs, as well as a different legal judgment. There is no issue as to whether or not the UNSC has the authority to violate sovereignty, since that is authorized in the Charter and universally accepted. The barrier to the UNSC is not Article 2(4), but Articles 39 and 51. However, if one were to entertain an argument that Article 2(4) could prevent the UNSC from authorizing a humanitarian mission, then one would have to address not only the humanitarian interventions authorized by the UNSC such as Somalia in 1992 and Haiti in 1994, but also the forcible interventions authorized by Chapter VII, such as Iraq in 1991.

Some potential variations on the facts scenarios could include: A humanitarian relief mission that is coordinated by the UN Coordinator for Humanitarian Affairs, without the UN Security Council invoking Chapter VII in order to make the mission legally binding. The extent of government resistance to relief could vary, from arresting aid workers to merely failure to cooperate. If the UNSC is to refer the case to the ICC, one can also wonder if there is an actual criminal charge, based on a political vote. Charges of genocide via starvation, for example, might be the basis of referral by the UNSC. The government might blame the deaths on the original natural disaster. So, in an ICC referral, one would need to state what the specific criminal charge is from the ICC statute, even if it is not a literal application of the law. Students would also need to state, for the factual record, the relief efforts. In this case the UNSC has authorized the humanitarian mission. In alternative versions of the facts, students could have the mission occur unilaterally by a powerful country and not legally sanctioned by the UNSC, in which case legal issues concerning human rights treaties, especially the International Covenant on Civil and PoliticalRights, as well as soft, influential, but not technically binding law, such as coercive intervention to protect human rights, the R2P doctrine. Also, the legal argument for criminal charges would be weaker since the ICC statute does not specify R2P. Also, you would have to investigate the legislative history, as well as the text of the R2P doctrine to see if criminal liability was envisioned, since the focus of that World Summit Outcome Resolution in 2005 was to authorize the UN Security Council to authorize intervention in instances in which one of the four crimes—genocide, ethnic cleansing, war crimes, crimes against humanity—is perpetrated.

Legal Matters and Other Issues for Discussion

Appellant Marbur's brief focuses in large part on the behavior of the UNSC, and by extension the international community as a whole; specifically their right to intervene in Marmyan on the basis of the R2P doctrine. Marbur contends that the actions of the UNSC—under the guise of the newly emerging R2P norm—violated the principles of sovereignty and non-intervention as set forth under the Article 2 of the UN Charter.[9] As the Appellant argues in his brief his decision to distribute foreign aid with the use of domestic personnel did not constitute a threat to international peace and security and consequently did not warrant action by the UNSC. This of course raises interesting questions about what constitutes a threat to international peace and security. Moreover does the mere violation of a UNSC resolution constitute a crime that is prosecutable by the ICC?

Even more interesting is his argument that R2P, as a suggested norm of international law, is in fact only a theory; "a new international law plaything" concocted and advocated by members of the International Commission on Intervention and State Sovereignty (ICISS) and contested by legal scholars.[10]

Adopted via UN General Assembly Resolution in 2005 R2P is defined as, "the responsibility (of each state) to protect its populations from genocide, war crimes, ethnic cleansing and crimes against humanity."[11] It is a responsibility that extends to the international community as a whole. In the event an individual state cannot or will not protect its population R2P requires that appropriate action be taken through the UNSC. If peaceful means fail, R2P calls for: "collective action, in a timely and decisive manner, through the UNSC, in accordance with the Charter, including Chapter VII, on a case-by-case basis."[12] Recent examples of the application of R2P as justification for humanitarian intervention include NATO enforcement of the UNSC sanctioned no-fly zone over Libya.[13] Of course appeals for action on the basis of R2P must "[bear] in mind the principles of the [UN] Charter and international law."[14]

As Glanville and others contend the notion of an international responsibility to protect is not a new concept but one that has firm foundations in the work of past scholars such as Ellary Stowell. Working in the early twentieth century Stowell wrote that the notion that sovereignty was not necessarily absolute; that there appeared to be limits on non-intervention under the "'universally recognized principles of decency and humanity.'"[15] Yet although he believed states had an obligation to intervene Stowell recognized that this obligation was unenforceable. Glanville suggests that, since Stowell's time, international opinion has certainly changed on the matter of intervention. As the 2005 UN Summit indicates, there is a greater willingness on the part of the international community to acknowledge their "collective responsibility to act to protect populations in instances where states fail to do so," due to the emergence of an international criminal law regime, as well as certain "socio-political developments" (some of which concern the political fallout endured by those states who fail to intervene.)[16]

At the same time limitations placed on use of R2P curtail its effectiveness as a tool for effective humanitarian response. As Heath discusses, states are not individually obligated by the 2005 Summit Resolution to intervene. This is contrary to what the 2001 ICISS report suggested.[17] Rather per section 139 of the Summit Resolution action can only be taken via UNSC authorization. Secondly, the types of events to which the international community—through the UNSC—can respond are limited to: "genocide, war crimes, ethnic cleansing, and crimes against humanity";[18] raising immediate questions with respect to crises "less than" the four outlined above but which also produce large-scale death and destruction. This is not to say that situations less than crimes against humanity for example obviate the responsibility of the affected state to accept humanitarian aid or more generally to provide and care for its population. Quite the contrary.

As Heath contends R2P is grounded in international law, particularly that which pertains to the fundamental rights citizens have to life,[19] an adequate standard of living,[20] as well as the obligation of states to cooperate to ensure for "higher standards of living," and "universal respect for, and observance of, human rights and fundamental freedoms for all," among others.[21] Moreover the obligation of states to facilitate and/or seek disaster relief specifically has made some progress as an emerging—albeit weak—aspect of customary international law as per, for example, the guidelines set forth by the International Federation of the Red Cross and Red Crescent Societies,[22] the *Bruges Resolution*,[23] and international humanitarian treaty law (IHL).[24] Unfortunately because much of these state obligations are associated with IHL, they become more difficult to apply/enforce during peacetime. Heath argues in support of the idea of strengthening international law to ensure that states meet their obligations while still respecting "the power of states to make informed and reasonable choices regarding relief operations on their territory," (subjecting them to shaming, and possibly criminal prosecution and UNSC intervention if their refusal appears arbitrary and unjustified).[25]

It is hoped that greater clarity regarding the rules for intervention would assuage those that remain critical of the R2P doctrine. Ford for one suggests: "it seems futile to rely on the state to prevent crimes that it is committing, and encouragement by the international community [as in the case of Myanmar] is unlikely to be of much use either."[26] Others have argued that R2P will be used to justify humanitarian interventions in response to state actions that may *not* lead to crimes against humanity. Questions have been raised over its possible application to situations of environmental degradation in Haiti, for example.[27] There is also the possibility that R2P could be utilized by states as a means to justify unilateral military intervention where such intervention is *not* warranted or violates international law (a point raised by the Applicant).[28] Moreover critics of the application of R2P to the case of Libya, for example, suggest that its use is both limited and selective. What about Yemen, Bahrain, and the Democratic Republic of the Congo for instance?[29]

Indeed R2P, as Hall and others suggest, will likely require a reconceptualization of the concepts of national sovereignty and human security.[30] Heath suggests that a distinction should be made between internal and external sovereignty. Internal sovereignty derives from external sovereignty and pertains to the obligations leaders owe to their citizenry. R2P therefore does not violate sovereignty as sovereignty is commonly understood (e.g., as external sovereignty).[31] Moreover, by signing treaties and joining international and regional organizations for example, states are placing limitations on their sovereignty. Seen in this light, R2P is just an extension of this trend.

Unlike the case in the preceding section the President of the country is being held individually responsible for war crimes, crimes against humanity, and genocide under international criminal law; specifically the Rome Statute. It is advisable for instructors to once again point out to students the differences between the sources of law utilized by the ICC and ICJ; making it clear to them that in the ICC lawyers and judges look to the Rome Statute "in the first place" when assessing the mental, material, and contextual elements of these crimes.[32] Of course in situations in which the Statute is not clear, student lawyers will also need to consult case law, customary law, and so forth. All of the crimes included throughout this text have a strong basis in both treaty and customary law.

The accused was charged with and convicted of the following crimes in violation of Articles 6 through 8 of the ICC Statute: crimes against humanity: extermination,[33] persecution,[34] murder,[35] other inhumane acts ("intentionally causing great suffering, or serious injury to body or to mental or physical health"):[36] acts of genocide;[37] and war crimes: intentionally directing attacks against humanitarian personnel (for international conflicts only),[38] and using starvation of the civilian population as a means of warfare which includes "willfully impeding relief supplies."[39] Many of these crimes are crimes of proper omission, in other words, crimes in which the duty bearer has a positive duty to act.[40] Some, such as the genocide charges, are crimes of culpable omission or commission by omission.

Similar to the other ICC cases included in this book, the Prosecutor *must* demonstrate that the material, mental, and contextual elements of the crimes in question were met by the accused "beyond a reasonable doubt."[41] The contextual element differs for the three crimes. For crimes against humanity the context in question is a "widespread or systematic attack" on a civilian population. According to the jurisprudence of the two *ad hoc* Tribunals—the International Criminal Tribunal for the Former Yugoslavia (ICTY), the International Criminal Tribunal for Rwanda (ICTR)—crimes against humanity do not require a connection to armed conflict,[42] and the attack can be either widespread *or* systematic.[43] In *Kunarac et. al.*, the ICTY Appeals Chamber ruled that an attack against "any" civilian population requires an attack, the acts of the perpetrator to be part of this attack which must also be directed against a civilian population, as well as being either widespread or systematic; lastly the perpetrator must know that his actions contribute to or are part of the larger crime (e.g., the widespread or systematic etc.).[44]

Per the ICC Statute "attack" does not necessarily entail the use of arms (as is the case with war crimes) but refers to the logical consequences of the behavior of the accused.[45] Those representing the defendants of course will seek to reinterpret "attack" to mean forcible attack only, in other words a crime of commission *not* omission. Of course the ICTY has held that attacks as crimes against humanity can also include non-violent behavior.[46] This ruling becomes especially important for the crime of persecution (discussed below). Moreover the ICTR Trial Chamber in *Akayesu* ruled that attacks can even include "exerting pressure on the population to act in a particular manner . . . if orchestrated on a massive scale or in a systematic manner."[47]

Another aspect that's relevant to the context of crimes against humanity is the question of who counts as members of a "civilian population"? Does it matter if members of a rebel group or opposing army are inter-mixed with the civilians; does this alter the status of the civilian population targeted? As stated above, the prosecution contends that the members of the political opposition movement resided in the hardest hit area of the country. International jurisprudence is clear on the fact that the presence of non-civilians within a mostly civilian group does not deprive the targeted population of their civilian status.[48] In other words whether or not members of the UDF were present in the area (regardless of the "threat" the posed to the regime) their presence should not negatively impact the status of the residents of the Northern region; their ability to receive food, medicine, and other humanitarian aid.[49]

As the prosecution's brief demonstrates, the contextual element of the crimes against humanity charge is stronger than the material element, especially when it comes to the crime of persecution as opposed to extermination which includes "deprivation of access to food and medicine."[50]

The context for war crimes is simply an armed conflict, either international or internal.[51] "Armed conflict" can also include occupation. The case in this section demonstrates some of the difficulties surrounding the application of armed conflict to the situation at hand. Instructors and students should discuss whether or not deprivation of food aid has occurred within the context of armed conflict.

Moreover if it cannot be determined that the situation was an armed conflict then other applicable crimes listed under Article 8 of the ICC Statute with which the Defendant is charged would be inapplicable.[52] To address these questions both sides will need to look beyond the ICC Statute to other sources of law. As will be demonstrated the material element of the war crimes charge in this case is far stronger then the contextual.

The mental element of the crime has to do with the perpetrator's intent and knowledge of his/her conduct as spelled out by Article 30 of the Rome Statute.[53] Instructors should make students aware of the various types of "knowledge" associated with intent under international criminal law.[54] Cassese describes these as "knowledge as part of intent" or in other words knowledge that one's conduct is targeting persons protected by international law; "knowledge of consequences" or awareness that one's conduct will produce consequences prohibited under international law (e.g., mass death); and "knowledge of a broader purpose" or that one's conduct is part of a widespread or systematic attack or a plan of elimination (when we're talking about persecution [a crime against humanity] and genocide; both of which require *dolus specialis*).[55]

The subjective test of intent pertains to the mindset of the accused. In this case, for example, did President Marbur decide to prevent international aid from reaching the population with knowledge that it would amount to "widespread or systematic plan" to harm the civilian population; or worse still did he act with the knowledge that his actions were part of a plan focused on towards the elimination of a specific group? The subjective dimension of intent has usually been determined on a case-by-case basis. However, intent is also determined objectivelly, in other words, what would a *reasonable* person do under similar circumstances? In this case can Marbur's actions reasonably be categorized as possessing the intent and knowledge required by the ICC Statute for the various crimes? These are questions with which student lawyers will have to contend in this and other cases in this text.

On a separate but related note it is also advisable for instructors to clearly explain to students the other lesser forms of intent, emphasizing the distinction between *dolus directus* (described above), recklessness (*dolus eventualis*), and culpable negligence (*culpa gravis*). Recklessness is different from culpable negligence. With recklessness one knowingly acts in disregard of a rule prohibiting his/her conduct on the belief that the prohibited outcome is only probable, not certain. The assumption of risk is different with culpable negligence in that the actor knowingly violates a set of rules and "is aware of [the] risk but believes that it will not occur, and in addition takes a conduct that is blatantly at odds with the prescribed conduct."[56] Instructors can ask students whether or not any of these other forms of intent are applicable to this case. For example for certain war crimes (e.g., "attacking or bombarding . . . towns, villages, dwellings or buildings which are undefended and which are not military objectives"[57]) would recklessness be appropriate? Cassese indicates a number of courts have decided on the applicability of recklessness on a case-by-case basis and that recklessness may be interpreted as being encompassed in Article 30 of the ICC Statute.[58]

The material element (or objective element of the crime) refers to the conduct in question. The material elements are described by Werle as "all conditions that determine the external appearance of the act" and include, context under which the act occurred and the consequences of the act (e.g., starvation, mass death etc.).[59] The acts President Marbur is being held responsible for have in large part to do with omission; in this case his failure to provide necessary aid for his population (a proper crime of omission). As Ford discusses the crime of extermination may be "proved by evidence that the victims were intentionally subjected to conditions that contributed to their deaths, such as the deprivation of food and medicine."[60] The ICTY concluded in *Kristić* that to prove extermination: "in addition to the general requirements for a crime against humanity, there must be evidence that a part of the population was targeted and that its members were killed or otherwise subjected to conditions of life calculated to bring about the destruction of a numerically significant part of the population."[61] While this makes extermination sound nearly identical to the crime of genocide, it differs "by the very fact that the targeted population does not necessarily have any common national, ethnical, racial or religious characteristics."[62]

Additionally Marbur is being charged with persecution. Persecution, like genocide, requires a *dolus specialis* on the part of the perpetrator; a "discriminatory intent."[63] Absent this intent the crimes become other types of crimes against humanity. On this point the ICTY has ruled: "With regard to the crime of persecution, a particular intent is required, in addition to the *specific intent* (to commit the act and produce its consequences) and the *general intent* (objective knowledge of the context in which the accused acted). This . . . discriminatory intent . . . is what sets the crime of persecution apart from other . . . crimes of humanity."[64] It becomes a unique form of special intent in that it seeks "'to cause injury to a human being because he belongs to a particular community or group'."[65] Unlike other crimes against humanity, mere knowledge of the widespread or systematic attack is not enough.[66]

Persecution can encompass a variety of acts the effect of which is cumulative.[67] These acts which violate the fundamental rights of their victims, include the forced transfers of civilians, beatings, murders, and destruction of property not justified by military necessity.[68] In determining whether acts committed by the accused were in fact persecutory the Trial Chamber in *Kupreškić et, al.* utilized a four-part test. Specifically the Court stated persecution is "the gross or blatant denial, on discriminatory grounds, of a fundamental right, laid down in international customary or treaty law, reaching the same level of gravity as the other acts prohibited in Article 5 [of the Court's Statute]."[69]

Before assigning this case for review instructors should discuss the ambiguities of this crime. For instance could persecution apply to the population of the entire country? The question becomes: was it the president's intention to persecute everyone in the country because of their identity? In which case we may be talking about the persecution of a national group to which the accused himself belongs. Absent this intent was it merely the will of the President to harm his population? Was he acting in reckless disregard of the well-being of his population? Given the fact that Marbur's actions targeted a national ethnic minority group in the country it may be advisable to limit the charges of persecution to this group alone. However, for more ambitious students broadening the target group may be worth it as this will certainly challenge extant notions of the typical targets of persecution and/or genocide.

As the above paragraphs indicate, challenges will be made by the accused on the basis of the contextual, material, and mental elements of the crime. The prosecution must overcome these challenges and demonstrate that each element has been met by the accused. Although not raised by the Appellant it is possible for the accused to declare immunity from prosecution. As stated in the introduction to this text this defense is *inapplicable* to civilian heads of state, politicians, and forth. The question remains, however, whether or not it applies to heads of state who are not elected. Article 27 of the ICC Statute does not include military leaders. Students should be asked to consider whether this means that leaders of military juntas are "off the hook" for grave offenses. In light of a lack of specificity in the Rome Statute, is there any customary law that could overcome this particular obstacle? This becomes a jurisdictional issue, in other words a question of whether or not the ICC has the authority to try the accused at all. In all cases the Prosecutor must first demonstrate the ICC has jurisdiction over the matter at hand. Otherwise it's a dead issue.

Also the defense raises certain due process issues associated with his first trial in the ICC. Students will likely be familiar with much of what constitutes due process protections as per the Bill of Rights to the U.S. Constitution for example. For the ICC these protections are enshrined in Articles 55, 66, and 67 of the Rome Statute.[70] More generally, rights of the accused are found throughout the entire treaty. Instructors should also make students cognizant of other conventions that address these rights; in particular the ICCPR.

Lastly, for individual criminal responsibility to attach under international law there is an additional requirement: that there are no "circumstances . . . that exclude individual responsibility on the part of the perpetrator."[71] It is useful here to distinguish between two broad categories of defenses: justification and excuses.[72] As Cassese writes, the former concerns a generally prohibited act that is deemed lawful given the circumstances (e.g., killing in self-defense); the latter, factors that contribute to a lack of *mens rea* (intent) on the part of the offender such that he/she is not punished for the unlawful act he/she committed. These factors include intoxication, mental defect etc. (or as Cassese categorizes them "Excuses based on lack of individual autonomy"), and following superior orders, necessity/duress etc. (or those deriving from "external circumstances").[73] All of these defenses are conditional on the facts of the case, as will become clear in other briefs included in this text. For the present case, the Appellant is not raising any of these defenses for reasons which will become clear in his brief.

The Prosecution/Respondent's brief is especially instructive as a means of understanding the legal basis for the R2P doctrine (at the very least) per the ICC Statute. Respondent suggests the actions of the president should be interpreted consistently with the purposes outlined in the ICC's Preamble, specifically the protection of the "well-being of the world," as well as state practice, and *opinio juris*. Interestingly, the notion of actions taken on behalf of the "well-being of the world" brings in the concept of substantive justice or the notion that "the legal order must primarily aim at prohibiting and punishing any conduct that is socially harmful or causes danger to society, whether or not that conduct has already been legally criminalized at the moment it is taken."[74] Substantive justice addresses issues of equity and fairness; what is morally right for society as a whole. This is an important concept that was, for example, used by the International Military Tribunal at Nuremberg to get around the *nullum crimen sine lege* problems associated with crimes against peace.[75]

LEGAL BRIEF OF APPELLANTS

THE QUESTION

The International Criminal Court (ICC) is asked to determine whether the Appellant Xavier Marbur is guilty of crimes against humanity, genocide, and war crimes under the Rome Treaty.

ISSUES

The following issues will be addressed in this memorial (I) the legality of UN and foreign intervention in the domestic affairs of Marmyan; (II) the applicability of Chapter VII, Articles 39 and 42 of the UN Charter to domestic relief operations; (III) the Prosecution's failure to demonstrate the contextual, material, and mental elements of the crimes of genocide, crimes against humanity, and war crimes; (IV) Appellant Xavier Marbur was denied due process by the Trial Chamber in violation of Articles 55 and 67 of the Rome Treaty.

SUMMARY OF ARGUMENTS

Appellant President of Marmyan Xavier Marbur submits that the UN relief mission authorized by the UN Security Council impaired the ability of the Government of Marmyan to control and conduct relief operations in the country. This intrusion was a clear violation of international law, specifically Article 2 of the United Nations Charter. The UN Security Council did not possess the legal authority to authorize a relief mission to be conducted with the use of UN peacekeepers. The manner in which the Appellant Xavier Marbur chose to orchestrate disaster relief operations in Marmyan, including efforts to deliver the foreign aid with the use of domestic aid workers, in no way constituted a threat to international peace and security. Hence it did not warrant forcible UN intervention. Appellant's conviction by the Trial Chamber of the ICC for acts of omission rising to the level of genocide and crimes against humanity has no basis in international law. Moreover the actions of Appellant, in arresting some members of the UN relief mission for their misbehavior in no way constituted an act of war or a threat to international peace and security. Consequently Appellant Xavier Marbur's conviction by the Trial Chamber of the ICC for war crimes also has no legal merit. Additionally, the Appellant was denied due process. President Xavier Marbur was denied adequate time to prepare for trial, the opportunity to confront his accusers, and access to an interpreter during the trial proceedings.

THE PROSECUTION'S CASE

The Prosecution based much of its case on the argument that a head of state has a responsibility to ensure the well-being of his or her population, which includes adequate provision of disaster relief. The failure of a head of state to adequately care for his or her population is a matter of international concern which rises to the level of an international threat to peace and security warranting military intervention by the international community through the United Nations if it is determined that the head of state's failure to provide aid was intentional on his or her part. Integral to the Prosecution's case is the argument that actions by the Appellant Xavier Marbur are intentional acts of omission making him culpable under international criminal law. Specifically the Prosecution contends that these acts of omission on the part of Appellant amounted to genocide and crimes against humanity.

According to Article 66(3) of the Rome Statute, "In order to convict the accused, the Court must be convinced of the guilt of the accused beyond reasonable doubt." The burden therefore rests with the Prosecution to demonstrate this guilt which requires the Prosecution to demonstrate the contextual, material, and mental elements of each of the crimes with which a defendant is accused. Imminent international legal scholar Gerhard Werle has remarked that the "first step" towards demonstrating individual liability under international criminal law is demonstrating that the material elements of the crime have been met, by which he means the "conduct, consequence, and any other accompanying circumstances contained in the definition of the crime under international law."[76] Secondly, the mental element of the crime must be demonstrated.[77]

The Prosecution contends that it met the objective and subjective criteria for each of the crimes with which the Appellant Xavier Marbur was charged per Articles 6 through 8 and Article 30 of the Rome Treaty.

Appellant was charged and convicted by the Trial Chamber of the ICC for the crime of genocide pursuant to Articles 6(a), 6(b), and 6(c) of the Rome Statute. Article 6(a) is "Killing members of the group"; 6(b) "Causing serious bodily or mental harm to members of the group"; and Article 6(c) "Imposing measures intended to prevent births within the group."

The Prosecution based the charge for these crimes chiefly on the contention that President Xavier Marbur (a) withheld domestic relief aid and (b) prevented the UN relief mission from disembarking and delivering aid to the population because his contention was to "destroy, in whole or in part," a segment of his population; specifically those residing in the Northern part of the country wherein members of an opposition rebel group—the United Democratic Front—operate and reside. Members of the UDF are members of a distinct ethnic minority. However, the allegations did not stop there. The Prosecution also extended the genocide argument to cover the *entire* population of the country; that is to say a national group.

The Appellant was also charged and convicted by the Trial Chamber of the ICC for four counts of crimes against humanity: Article 7 (1)(a) murder; 7(1)(b) extermination; 7(1)(h) persecution; and 7(1)(k) which covers "Other inhumane acts of a similar character intentionally causing great suffering, or serious bodily injury to body or to mental or physical health."

The Prosecution based these charges on the contention that President Xavier Marbur (a) withheld domestic relief aid and (b) prevented the UN relief mission from disembarking and delivering aid to the population as part of a widespread and/or systematic plan to harm the civilian population of Marmyan, including, but not limited to, the residents of the Northern region of the country. Moreover the Prosecution argues that Marbur acted with the intent and knowledge of the consequences as required by Article 30 of the Rome Statute. The Prosecution demonstrated the "knowledge" requirement by the argument that Appellant "should have known" the consequences that would ensue for the population of Marmyan should he prevent the UN relief mission from achieving its mandate.

Lastly the Appellant was charged and convicted by the Trial Chamber of the ICC of two counts of war crimes pursuant to Article 8 of the Rome Statute: the first under Article 8(2)(b)(iii) "Intentionally directing attacks against personnel, installations, material, units or vehicles involved in a humanitarian assistance or peacekeeping mission in accordance with the Charter of the United Nations, as long as they are entitled to the protection given to civilians or civilian objects under the international law of armed conflict."

The Prosecution based these charges on the contention that the actions of President Xavier Marbur—his alleged refusal to permit UN relief workers to disembark on Marmyan soil, his arrest and detention of some of these workers—constituted an international attack. The Prosecution argued that international humanitarian law applies to UN workers as protected persons and that an attack can take place on these workers with or without the use of force.

The Appellant was also charged and convicted of "Intentionally using starvation of civilians as a method of warfare by depriving them of objects indispensable to their survival, including willfully impeding relief supplies as provided for under the Geneva Convention" pursuant to Article 8(2)(b)(xxv) of the Rome Treaty.

With the exception of the first of the war crimes charges (a crime of commission), the Prosecution argued that the evidence showed that Appellant Xavier Marbur is criminally responsible for crimes of omission in that his intentional failure to deliver aid to the victims of the 2009 earthquake was an attack on the civilian population, as well as an effort to destroy part of the population of Marmyan.

THE LEGALITY OF UN INTERVENTION

Foreigners May Not Intrude in a Country's Local Relief Efforts

It should go without saying that the basic premise of harmonious international relations is mutual respect for other nations' sovereignty. As legitimated by the *Treaty of Westphalia* in 1648, the sovereign nation-state exists as the building block of a peaceful world. On this point it has been stated that "the obligation not to intervene in the affairs of any other State is an essential condition to ensure that nations live together in peace with one another."[78] Without government restraint in their dealings with one another the world would descend into chaos. This means, *inter alia*, that neither single states nor groups of states may presume to meddle in the internal matters of other states, even if they differ with one another on matters of policy, such as how best to provide relief for their citizens following natural disasters.

The *Bruges Resolution* to which the Prosecution frequently refers states in Article 3(1) that following natural disasters it is the *affected* state that "has . . . the primary responsibility in the organization, provision, and distribution of humanitarian aid."[79] Despite the "Responsibility to Protect" doctrine to which the Prosecution also repeatedly refers, the holder of the primary duty of providing assistance and ensuring the well-being of a population in the wake of a natural disaster is still the government that rules over that population.

This has also been the position of the United Nations. Section 4 of the "Guiding Principles" of the General Assembly's 1991 resolution regarding humanitarian assistance, for example, states that "the affected State has the primary role in the initiation, organization, coordination, and implementation of humanitarian assistance within its territory."[80] Moreover Section 5 of the "Guiding Principles" states that, in the event that humanitarian aid is sought from the international community by the affected state, "such cooperation should be provided in accordance with international and national laws."[81]

Moreover states affected by natural disasters have a right to reject an offer of humanitarian assistance that is not *bona fide*; that is an offer made with some sort of ulterior motive on the part of the offering state or states. Such offers are illegal under international law. The International Court of Justice ruled as such in *Nicaragua* case. In this instance the ICJ determined that much of US aid to the *contras* rebel group in Nicaragua was given with the purpose "to coerce Nicaragua in respect of matters in which each State is permitted to decide freely."[82] For humanitarian aid to be legitimate the ICJ ruled that "it must be limited to the purposes hallowed in the practice of the Red Cross, and above all be given without discrimination."[83] Although we are not certain as to what the motives were for the intervention in our internal affairs by the United Nations and UN Security Council, we can only surmise that the resort to the use of force was intended to achieve some other unknown objective.

The United Nations May Not Intervene in Essentially Domestic Matters

A basic rule of conduct for nations, as well as for the international community in the form of the United Nations, is embodied in its Charter, Article 2(7).[84] This fundamental principle forbids foreign intervention "in matters which are essentially within the jurisdiction of any state." The only exception is "the application of enforcement measures under Chapter VII," which has no relevance here.

Article 2(7) is perhaps the most widely respected and adhered to rule of the entire UN Charter, or even of the whole corpus of international law. To casually disregard it, as the UN Security Council and the ICC Prosecutor have done, is to court judicial disaster and turn back the clock on orderly relations among nations.

THE SECURITY COUNCIL MAY NOT AUTHORIZE FORCE UNLESS PEACE AND SECURITY ARE BREACHED

The basic Chapter VII mandate of the UN Security Council, as plainly written in Article 39 of the UN Charter, is to "make recommendations, or decide what measures shall be taken in accordance with Articles 41 and 42, to maintain or restore international peace and security."

There was no threat to international peace and security resulting from Appellant's direction that foreign relief supplies received from abroad be distributed within Marmyan by domestic aid personnel, who know the terrain and where the greatest needs are, far better than any outsiders. It bears repeating that disaster relief is the chief prerogative of the affected state. The use of military force to deliver aid is therefore an illegitimate endeavor. Even the UN's own Special Rappoteur for the International Law Commission's disaster relief project has stated that: "nothing can be clearer than the fact that forced intervention is illegal under international law absent a justifiable claim of self-defense or action by the Security-Council."[85] As discussed above the UN Security Council's conclusion that the manner in which disaster aid is distributed by an affected state constitutes a threat to international peace and security warranting the use of force has no legitimate basis whatsoever.

And besides, what national leader would not be expected by his people to protect the sovereign rights and privileges of his citizens rather than letting in untold numbers of foreigners, whose motives cannot be adequately known? Consider the outrageous record of UN peacekeepers in various parts of the world where they have sexually abused innocent children and women. A chilling example is provided by the behavior of members of the UN peacekeeping mission in the Democratic Republic of Congo who are responsible for the rape of

Congolese women and girls.[86] Why should our President, a moral man determined to protect the honor of his vulnerable people, betray them by casually inflicting rapacious foreigners on them when there is no need?

Lastly Appellant finds it curious that the Prosecution's argument relies on the example of Myanmar and the response of the Government of Myanmar to the international community's offer of aid. In this case, despite international criticism of the government's aid distribution policies, no action was taken on the part of the UN Security Council to force the Government of Myanmar to accept foreign aid. Instead the choice was left to the domestic leadership of the Government of Myanmar. The question becomes: why then was aid forced on the Republic of Marmyan?

Responsibility to Protect (R2P) Is Only a Theory, Not Established Law

A few years ago, before the fad known as "R2P" faded from memory in the turmoil of widespread battle and financial catastrophe, certain law school professors fancied they had found a new international law plaything. It came from the dreams of twelve mostly non-government individuals styling themselves as an "International Commission on Intervention and State Sovereignty." It has made no long-term dent in the time-honored concept of sovereignty, and in fact was ridiculed by President of the American Society of International Law, José Alvarez who suggested that, because of its potential for misinterpretation and misapplication, "We should be cautious about turning [R2P] . . . from political tool to legal principle."[87]

To put it politely, this phantom concept is nowhere near to becoming an established and generally accepted principle of customary international law, and has no place as a basis for charging or convicting an outstanding public servant striving only to protect the welfare of his people.

Moreover it is worth pointing out that the UN World Summit Outcome Resolution was in existence at the time of the 2008 natural disaster in Myanmar, yet the international community did not respond in the same manner to which it did with the earthquake in Marmyan. The question becomes again: why was aid forced on the Republic of Marmyan by the UN Security Council? It is highly doubtful that international interest and concern has changed that much since 2008. Critics of R2P have suggested that has been applied selectively and often for political reasons. Appellant argues that this is exactly what has occurred in this case.

However even if the Applicant *were* to concede to the existence of Responsibility to Protect as a valid international norm, per section 139 of the 2005 UN World Summit Outcome Resolution the only instances in which the international community can take collective action through the UN Security Council pursuant to this "norm" are in instances in which crimes against humanity, genocide, ethnic cleansing or war crimes have occurred.[88] Appellant Xavier Marbur strongly contends that the Prosecution has failed to demonstrate the material, contextual and mental criteria for these crimes.

FAILURE OF THE PROSECUTION TO DEMONSTRATE THE CONTEXTUAL, MENTAL, AND MATERIAL ELEMENTS

In every legal system around the world, a clear distinction regarding criminal responsibility is made between acts of commission and acts of omission. The latter are only charged as crimes in extreme cases of parental neglect of children or the elderly. There is good reason for this, and Your Honorable Court should, in keeping with that world-wide distinction, refrain from extending the judicial wisdom of the ages into uncharted territory.

The fact is that President Marbur is chiefly charged with acts of proper omission, in other words crimes in which Appellant had a duty to act inherent in the particular laws in question. Many of these apply to the crimes against humanity charges. Moreover Appellant has also been charged with culpable omission in association with the genocide charges. Culpable omission requires a special duty and capacity to act.[89] All of these charges are without substance. It is a point of fact that foreign suppliers of material assistance refused to unload their life-saving goods at Marmyan's seaports or airports. They refused to permit the Government of Marmyan to control the distribution of the aid and as a consequence many people died. Appellant agrees that he possessed the duty to act as head of state to care for his population after a natural disaster, however his capacity to act was curtailed by the actions of the UN relief mission and peacekeeping force. It is the foreigners, acting through the auspices of the UN and under the guise of the "R2P norm," not the Appellant, who should be standing before you charged and convicted of serious crimes. The Appellant Xavier Marbur pleaded with the UN mission to unload their supplies in order to save the people of Marmyan.

Genocide

For the crime of genocide (an act of commission), the Prosecution must demonstrate that Appellant possessed the *dolus specialis* to destroy a group on the basis of that group's identity. As the International Criminal Tribunal for Rwanda (ICTR) held in *Akayesu*, and international courts have held since, this special intent is the fundamental element of the crime of genocide.[90] This special intent is interwoven with the material and contextual elements of the crime. As Werle indicates the circumstances under which the conduct in question occurred and is closely linked to the mental and material requirements, often forming an essential part of these requirements. This is particularly the case for genocide, in which the context—"the destruction of a protected group, is included in the mental element of the crime."[91]

The courts have also ruled in *Akayesu* and in many other cases,[92] and the Prosecution has argued that, in the absence of a "smoking gun," intent can be inferred from the actions of the perpetrator (e.g., "from the facts and circumstances of a case"[93]). In this case Appellant's alleged refusal to permit UN relief workers from completing their mandate to deliver aid to the population of Marmyan was taken as evidence of his intent to "destroy, in whole or in part" both a segment of his population (i.e., members of an ethnic minority in Marmyan residing in the Northern region), and his population as a whole.

The ICTR in *Akayesu* also held that "the seriousness of the charges brought against the accused makes it all the more necessary to examine scrupulously and meticulously all the inculpatory and exonerating evidence, in the context of a fair trial and in full respect of the rights of the Accused."[94] The Appellant Xavier Marbur contends that the Trial Chamber committed errors of fact and law; misinterpreting Appellant's rightful efforts to control the distribution of aid in his country as evidence of a "genocidal intent." However nothing in the actions taken by Appellant in the wake of the 2009 earthquake demonstrate this intent.

Crimes against Humanity

With respect to the four counts of crimes against humanity with which the Appellant Xavier Marbur was charged he maintains that the Trial Chamber's conclusion that Appellant is individually criminally responsible for murder, extermination, persecution, and other inhumane acts is also legally incorrect and based on an erroneous interpretation of the facts at hand.

As the ICTY ruled in *Kunarac* the Prosecution must demonstrate that Appellant Xavier Marbur actually attacked the civilian population; that the attack was widespread or systematic; and that Appellant had knowledge that his acts would constitute part of the widespread or systematic attack.[95] As a point of fact Appellant reiterates that his executive decision as head of the Government of Marmyan to control the distribution of the aid as is his prerogative in no way constituted a widespread or systematic attack. Although the failure of the distribution of aid to the people of Marmyan had "widespread" consequences, these are a result of the refusal of UN relief mission workers to permit Appellant Xavier Marbur from exercising his executive authority.

Moreover although the courts have ruled that a "pre-existing plan" is not a requirement for the systematic element of the contextual aspect of crimes against humanity in *Blaškić* the Appellate Chamber of the ICTY held that such a plan "may be evidentially relevant in proving that an attack was directed against a civilian population and that it was widespread or systematic."[96] In this instance, Appellant did not have in place any systematic plan to attack his civilian population in a widespread or systematic manner. To the contrary Appellant tried to assist the population of his country and his efforts were impaired by the international community.

If there was no widespread and systematic attack, the knowledge and intent requirement per Article 30 of the Rome Treaty is therefore moot. Consequently the charges of murder, extermination, and other inhumane acts have no basis in fact or law. The Trial Chamber therefore erred in its decision to convict the Appellant Xavier Marbur for these offenses.

With respect to the charge of persecution it requires a special intent similar to the crime of genocide. The international courts have ruled that this distinguishes the crime of persecution from other crimes against humanity.[97] Per Article 7(1)(h) of the Rome Treaty the accused must intentionally target an "identifiable group or collectivity on political, racial, national, ethnic, cultural, religious, gender, . . . or other grounds that are universally recognized as impermissible under international law, in connection with any . . . crime within the jurisdiction of the Court."

This *dolus specialis* is similar to that required for genocide and, as stated above, the defendant did not possess this intent. Moreover as the ICTY has ruled in *Vasilijević*, the intent for persecution cannot be inferred from the facts of the case, but must "relate to the specific act charged."[98] The Prosecution has failed to demonstrate that the attempt of the Appellant to distribute aid in his country without foreign interference demonstrates this special intent. This finding is similar to that associated with the failure of the Prosecution to demonstrate that the actions of the Appellant were in fact crimes against humanity more broadly understood. The Trial Chamber therefore erred in its decision to convict the Appellant of these crimes.

War Crimes

With respect to the first charge, intentionally directing attacks against UN personnel, the basis of this charge is that the UN relief mission were "protected persons" in an international armed conflict. Appellant contends that an international conflict was not taking place. Absent the context, the acts for which Appellant has been charged become moot.

Appellant concedes the fact that foreigners intruded into the domestic affairs of the Government of Marmyan. However, the refusal of the UN relief mission to permit Appellant to control the distribution of aid did not take place in the context of an international armed conflict. Consequently the government's lawful arrest and detention of a few UN relief workers for their unlawful behavior certainly did not constitute a war crime against a protected group as there was no war.

DENIAL OF DUE PROCESS

The Appellant President Xavier Marbur was denied the due process guarantees to be granted to all defendants. These guarantees are enshrined in Articles 55, and 67 of the Rome Treaty. The behavior of the Prosecution during the pretrial and trial phases is contrary to the principles of international justice which are the bedrock of the International Criminal Court, not to mention the international criminal justice regime.

The Appellant was Denied Access to Legal Counsel

The Appellant Xavier Marbur was denied access to counsel of his choosing in violation of Articles 55(2)(c) and 67(1)(d).[99] Appellant was provided with a limited choice of attorneys, none of whom spoke his language. This problem could have been avoided had the Appellant been provided with an interpreter pursuant to Articles 55(1)(c) and 67(1)(f) of the Rome Treaty. This was not done. Therefore Appellant was left with no other alternative but to defend himself in the pre-trial and trial proceedings.

The Appellant was Denied Adequate Time to Prepare for Trial

The Appellant was also denied adequate time to prepare for his trial in violation of Article 67(1)(b). The time between his arrest in 2009 and trial in 2010 left the Appellant with inadequate time to prepare his case; specifically the opportunity to gather and interview witnesses on his behalf, this in violation of Article 67(1)(d) of the Rome Treaty.

The Appellant was Refused the Opportunity to Confront his Accusers

Likewise the Appellant was denied the ability to confront his accusers which is also a protection that is guaranteed by Article 67(1)(d) of the Rome Treaty. Many of the witnesses for the Prosecution were kept from the Appellant. The Prosecution based this action on the need to "protect the security of victims and witnesses." The Prosecution's assumption that the Appellant Xavier Marbur would threaten or harm any of his accusers is ludicrous and without merit. Secondly the Prosecution's power to control which witnesses the Appellant has access to, creates an un-level playing field to the detriment of the Appellant, not to mention any other defendant that comes before the ICC.

The Trial Chamber of the ICC displayed what can only be characterized as indicia of prejudice against the accused. In short, this Court must not condone what happened at trial, or the future of international courts in general will be in jeopardy

CONCLUSION

The Appellant strongly contends that the Trial Chamber of the ICC erred in its conviction of Appellant on genocide, crimes against humanity, and genocide. The presumption of innocence to which Appellant is due under Article 66 of the Rome Treaty was nonexistent; this evidenced by the denial of due process afforded the Appellant. Additionally the Prosecution failed to demonstrate the contextual, mental, and material elements required for each of the crimes with which the Appellant was charged. The Prosecution bases much of its argument on the notion that the Appellant—in his efforts to control the distribution of aid in his country—is somehow for war crimes, genocide, and crimes against humanity because people died as a consequence of lack of access to disaster relief. What the Prosecution chooses to ignore is the fact that Appellant, as sovereign head of the country of Marmyan, was merely exercising his prerogative to handle disaster relief operations internally; a prerogative that is his due as stated by the UN, the *Bruges Resolution*, and other international resolutions. The actions taken by the UN Security Council, specifically its efforts to control the distribution of aid in Marmyan in the name of international peace and security, is a violation of the UN Charter and the principle of sovereignty.

This is a new Court. Its experience has been brief. One and only one other defendant has been in its custody. One other Head of State is under the threat of arrest. But the case of President Marbur is the case that will make or break this Court. Therefore, the whole world is watching to see whether the outcome here will build towards a future of international law and order, or to a lawless jungle of injustice and fear. It is up to you, the Honorable Appellate Chamber of the International Criminal Court.

LEGAL BRIEF OF RESPONDENTS

THE QUESTION

The International Criminal Court (ICC) is asked to determine whether or not the Trial Chamber of this Court erred in its judgment that General Xavier Marbur is guilty for crimes against humanity, genocide, and war crimes under the Rome Treaty.

THE ISSUES

The following issues will be addressed in this brief (I) the legality of the UNSC authorization of the UN relief mission and peacekeeping force; (II) the fact that the Prosecution successfully demonstrated the contextual, material, and mental elements of the crimes of genocide, crimes against humanity, and war crimes; and (III) Appellant President and General Xavier Marbur was afforded all due process guarantees under the Rome Treaty.

SUMMARY OF ARGUMENTS

President Xavier Marbur perpetrated violations of international law which necessitated the action of the international community. The UNSC was legally authorized to act pursuant to Chapter VII of the UN Charter. The actions of the international community, acting through the UNSC, is an example of the strength of the Responsibility to Protect (R2P) norm; a norm that continues to gain strength as a means with which to constrain the ability of regime leaders to violate the fundamental rights of their citizenry. The purpose of the UN relief mission was to deliver humanitarian aid to the population of Marmyan in response to a natural disaster. Per customary international law states have an obligation to facilitate and/or seek humanitarian assistance following a natural disaster. President Marbur's dereliction of his duty to provide and permit humanitarian assistance following a natural disaster and his attacks on UN relief personnel are crimes under international criminal law for which the Appellant bears individual responsibility. The Prosecution will show that the conviction of the Appellant, by the Trial Chamber of the ICC for war crimes, genocide, and crimes against humanity was legally justified. There were no errors of law or violations of due process.

THE LEGALITY OF UN INTERVENTION IN DISASTER RELIEF OPERATIONS

One of the primary issues of contention raised by the Appellant is that the contextual element of each of the above-mentioned crimes is absent. The contextual elements of these crimes must be interpreted pursuant to the Preamble of the Rome Statute which holds that crimes against humanity, genocide, and war crimes "threaten the peace, security, and well-being of the world." The Preamble also requires states to "refrain from the threat or use of force . . . in any manner inconsistent with the Purposes of the United Nations."

The Appellant perpetrated violations of international law which necessitated the action of the international community. The UNSC was legally authorized to act pursuant to Chapter VII of the UN Charter, Article 39 of which mandates that the "Security Council shall determine the existence of any threat to the peace, breach of the peace, . . . or decide what measures shall be taken in accordance with Articles 41 and 42, to maintain or restore international peace and security."[100] The UN relief mission is further authorized under Article 51 of the UN Charter, as well as customary law. Moreover pursuant to Article 25 of the UN Charter, Security Council resolutions are binding upon all member states.[101]

The justification for UNSC intervention in disaster relief is further strengthened by the 2005 UN World Summit Outcome Resolution, section 139 of which holds that, in cases in which a state fails to prevent crimes against humanity, genocide, or war crimes, collective action by the international community of states "through the UNSC, in accordance with the Charter, including Chapter VII," is called for.[102] The international norm, referred to as the "Responsibility to Protect," (R2P) suggests that states have a duty to ensure the well-being of their populations. It is not a recent development or a "conspiracy" cooked up by the international community, contrary to what the Appellant contends. Scholars have traced this responsibility as far back as the work of Hugo Grotius who suggested in the seventeenth century that, "'[t]he final and most wide-reaching cause for undertaking wars on behalf of others is the mutual tie of kinship among men, which itself affords sufficient ground for rendering assistance.'"[103]

The Prosecution wishes to make clear that, in the case of Marmyan, the action by the UNSC was by no means warlike. Rather the relief mission authorized by the UNSC was a peaceful and necessary response to a humanitarian disaster which was in and of itself a threat to international peace and security. The volatile human rights situation in Marmyan, the government's unwillingness to care for its population, threatened to destabilize the region.

The right to declare that a humanitarian emergency is a threat to international peace has been firmly established under customary international law. An important precedent is the response of the UNSC pursuant to Chapter VII of the UN Charter authorizing the use of force in response to human rights violations occurring in Haiti in 1994, which destabilized the region, as well as undermined a UN authorized and monitored election.[104] Similar UNSC Resolutions have been issued in countries such as Rwanda, the Democratic Republic of Congo, and the Sudan in response to human rights violations perpetrated against civilians.[105]

The purpose of the relief mission to Marmyan was to deliver humanitarian aid to the population of Marmyan in response to a natural disaster. Per customary international law states have an obligation to facilitate and/or seek humanitarian assistance following a natural disaster. As the International Law Commission (ILC) stated in Article 9(1) of its 2010 Draft Articles: "The affected State, by virtue of its sovereignty, has the duty to ensure the protection of persons and provisions of disaster relief and assistance on its territory."[106] Similar obligations or duties are included in the 2003 *Bruges Resolution*. Appellant refers to this document but fails to acknowledge Article 3(3) which asserts that states that are unable to provide humanitarian assistance to their population have a *duty* to "seek assistance from competent international organizations."[107] Per Article 7 of the resolution states have a duty to facilitate humanitarian assistance including permitting relief workers access to victims of natural disasters.[108] Article 8 contends that states have a duty not to "arbitrarily reject" offers of humanitarian assistance made by outside parties, particularly if this rejection has a detrimental impact on their population, in which case outside states "may call on the United Nations bodies dealing with humanitarian issues . . . to consider taking appropriate measures";[109] lastly Article 9 states that humanitarian personnel involved in relief missions cannot be attacked.[110] Appellant fails to address these provisions in his argument. He suggests instead that the interference by UN relief workers hampered his ability—duty and capacity—to deliver aid to his population. Moreover Appellant also neglects to address the human rights situation in Marmyan more broadly which is of no great surprise considering the fact that agents of his regime are responsible for the regular commission of human rights violations in his name.

The arrest of UN relief workers by the President of Marmyan, Xavier Marbur is illegal under international law. The actions of the humanitarian relief mission, authorized by UNSC, did not violate Article 2(7) of the United Nations Charter as the Appellant contends. Rather per customary law General Marbur had a duty to cooperate with the Security Council relief mission.

Appellant's attack on UN relief workers and his efforts towards preventing them from fulfilling their mandate constitute war crimes. Appellant's dereliction of his duty to provide and permit humanitarian assistance following a natural disaster amounts to crimes against humanity and genocide for which the Appellant bears individual responsibility under international criminal law. These are *jus cogens* violations that "shock the conscience of all mankind." Individual responsibility for such crimes is firmly rooted in international law, stretching back to the post-World War II *ad hoc* tribunals, the International Military Tribunal (IMT) and the International Military Tribunal for the Far East (IMFTE). As imminent international jurist and legal scholar Antonio Cassese has stated: "in modern criminal law the notion of collective responsibility is no longer acceptable."[111] The basis for individual responsibility rests with the notion that "the individual is normally endowed with free will and the independent capacity to choose his conduct."[112]

Moreover as international legal scholar Gerhard Werle contends, systematic violations of human rights inside a country are a threat to international peace of the type that the ICC seeks to prosecute; specifically; "a threat to *world* peace can be presumed even as a result of massive violations of human rights within one state. In the Preamble of the ICC Statute, the well-being of the world appears as a separate object of protection next to peace and security; . . . the allocation of the necessities of life is included as an additional guideline for the application and interpretation of the Statute."[113] International treaty law, customary, and domestic law require prosecution of *jus cogens* offences such as genocide and crimes against humanity perpetrated by individuals, including political leaders. If, as in this case, the affected state is not willing or able to prosecute the offender or offenders, the ICC has jurisdiction per Article 17 of the Court's Statute pertaining to Issues of Admissibility.

CONTEXTUAL, MENTAL, AND MATERIAL OF GENOCIDE, CRIMES AGAINST HUMANITY, AND WAR CRIMES

In terms of applicable law Werle and Theodor Meron have argued, in conflicts between sovereignty and human rights: "international criminal law intervenes on the side of humanity. In this war it supplements and safeguards."[114] The ICC statute is not the exclusive source of prosecutable law and procedures to be used in this Court, as the Statute itself states in Article 21(b): "In the second place, where applicable treaties and the principles and rules of international law, including the established principles of the international law of armed conflict; (c) Failing that, general principles of law derived by the Court from national laws of legal systems of the world." More directly, Article 22(3) holds that the statute holds that conduct can be "as criminal under international law independently of this Statute." As Werle discusses this not only means that criminal behavior can come from sources like treaties, customary international law, principles of international law, domestic jurisprudence, but also that such rules are fluid, as international is meant to develop progressively; this prohibiting a rigid interpretation of the Statute's terms.[115]

The mental elements of each of the crimes with which the Appellant was convicted are laid out in Article 30 of the ICC Statute: "a person shall be criminally responsible and liable for punishment for a crime within the jurisdiction of the Court only if the material elements are committed with intent and knowledge." Moreover intent is shown if: "that person means to engage in conduct," he or she "means to cause the consequence or is aware that it will occur in the ordinary course of events"; and lastly "knowledge" is defined by the Court as "awareness that a circumstance exists or a consequence will occur in the ordinary course of events." For many of these crimes, as Werle discusses the circumstances under which the conduct in question occurred and is closely linked to the mental and material requirements, often forming an essential part of these requirements.[116]

Genocide

Applicant President Xavier Marbur is responsible for the perpetration of genocide pursuant to Article 6(a) through (c).

Contextual Elements

The context for the crime of genocide is identical to the mental element of the crime; in other words "any of the following acts committed with the intent to destroy, in whole or in part, a national, ethnical, racial, or religious group as such."[117] To demonstrate the contextual element of the crime of genocide, the Prosecution must prove the perpetrator possessed the *dolus specialis* to destroy a protected group; in other words a group defined by its nationality, etc., in whole or in part.[118] In this case, the Prosecution maintains that there was such intent to destroy a part of a national group. There are two groups concerned: a national minority (constituting members of or those affiliated with the United Democratic Front), as well as the national majority as a whole.

When addressing the crime of genocide of a national group international jurisprudence has focused on the destruction of national groups by foreign states. Yet the destruction of a national group by that group's head of state is not without precedence. The massacre of Cambodian nationals by the Khmer Rouge is now widely considered by genocide scholars and the international community as a genocide.[119] The Cambodian Genocide Program at Yale University laid the evidentiary basis for the Extraordinary Chambers of the Cambodian Courts (ECCC) and also played a key role in the international advocacy necessary for the tribunal's creation. The ECCC includes genocide as a crime under its jurisdiction.[120] As international lawyer and legal scholar William Schabas has pointed out domestic courts are now also starting to prosecute political elites accused of perpetrating genocide against members of their own national group; current examples trials in Argentina, and Mexico.[121] Article 6 of the ICC Statute does not exclude targeting members of one's own national, ethnic, racial, or religious group. What matters is that genocide is committed with the intent is to destroy a designated group either in whole or in part. Genocide is therefore present in this case.

Material Elements

The deliberate withholding of aid directly contributed to the mass starvation of the national groups and minorities and destroyed a significant part of their physical and social existence. This amounts to a crime of culpable omission on the part of the President Xavier Marbur; in other words the omission is normatively equivalent to commission and requires a duty and capacity to act. The ICTY ruled as such in *Mucić et. al., Krnojelac, Aleksovski.*[122] The Appellant's contention that he lacked the capacity to act due to the actions of the UN relief mission and peacekeeping force are without merit. The Appellant always possessed the capacity to cooperate with international efforts to deliver the badly needed aid.

Mental Elements

As Cassese states "normally to prove the existence of genocidal intent one has to infer such intent from factual circumstances;"[123] this in the absence of a direct confession from the perpetrator for example. For genocide the special intent required can be inferred "a certain number of presumptions of fact," which can include "the scale of atrocities committed, their general nature . . . or furthermore the fact of deliberately and systematically targeting victims on account of their membership in a group."[124] Therefore the President's deliberate withholding of aid meant for the victims of the June 2008 earthquake, which caused mass starvation and disease, is evidence that he intended at the very least the partial destruction of a national group. As the ICTY held in *Krstić*, the intent to kill a certain number of a protected population indicates the intent to destroy that population.[125]

Crimes against Humanity

Applicant President Xavier Marbur has been held responsible for crimes against humanity in violation of Article 7(1)(a), (b), (h) and (k).

Contextual Elements

Per Article 7 of the ICC Statute and international jurisprudence more generally, crimes against humanity occur as part of a "widespread or systematic attack directed against any civilian population." In determining whether or not a crime meets this contextual element, the jurisprudence of the *ad hoc* international tribunals is especially helpful.

The International Criminal Tribunal of the Former Yugoslavia (ICTY) and the International Criminal Tribunal for Rwanda (ICTR) have held that the context of crimes against humanity can be determined by the presence of either a widespread *or* systematic attack.[126] In *Akayesu* the Trial Chamber of the ICTR defined "widespread" as "massive, frequent, large scale action, carried out collectively with considerable seriousness and directed against a multiplicity of victims."[127] "Systematic" has been defined by the ICTY as being non-random, repeated. and conducted on the basis of an organized common policy.[128] which may or may not necessitate a formalized government policy or plan.[129] In any event the fact that an attack is widespread is usually an indication that it is also systematic;[130] at the very least the widespread element generally requires some sort of planning.[131]

Werle argues that if "peace, security and well-being" is threatened or harmed, then the contextual requirement for crimes against humanity would occur from the "systematic or widespread violation of the fundamental rights of the civilian population," because acts of omission can attack the well-being of a civilian population as disastrously as armed attacks can.[132] In the present case the Prosecution contends that the actions of President General Xavier Marbur constitute both a widespread and a systematic attack in that his omission of aid to the victims of the June 2008 earthquake—both in Northern region and throughout the entire country—effected a "multiplicity of victims" and was certainly a "large scale action" that reflected a policy on the part of the military junta of which Appellant was in charge to willfully refuse foreign aid, as well as to maintain exclusive control over the distribution of all aid to the earthquake victims.

Material Elements

Additionally "attack" can include a variety of acts both violent and non-violent which in this case is clearly demonstrated by the refusal of Appellant to provide aid to and adequately care for his population. The *ad hoc* Tribunals have held that the civilian population is the primary target of the attack,[133] which has a collectivized nature,[134] which can include persons of the same nationality as the perpetrator,[135] as well as non-civilians.[136]

Article 7(2)(a) of the ICC Statute defines "Attack directed against any civilian population" as "a course of conduct involving the multiple commission of acts referred to in paragraph 1 against any civilian population, pursuant to or in furtherance of a State or organizational policy to commit such attack." Appellant Marbur has been convicted by the Trial Chamber of a multitude of crimes under Article 7 of the ICC Statute including murder, persecution, extermination, and "Other inhumane acts of a similar character intentionally causing great suffering, or serious injury to body or to mental or physical health"; the latter of which under Article 7(1)(k) of the ICC Statute. "Extermination" is defined by the Article 7(2)(h) as including "the deprivation of access to food and medicine, calculated to bring about the destruction of part of a population" (also a crime of culpable omission). The actions of Appellant Xavier Marbur in withholding aid from the victims of the 2009 earthquake constitute a crime of omission that clearly meets the material elements of murder, extermination, and other inhumane acts spelled out in the Court's Statute in that their result was the massive death and physical suffering and serious injury of a large segment of the country's population.

The crime of "persecution" is defined by Article 7(2)(g) of the Rome Statute as "the intentional and severe deprivation of fundamental rights contrary to international law by reason of the identity of the group or collectivity." The ICTY has ruled that "persecution can take numerous forms, so as long as the common element of discrimination in regard to the enjoyment of a basic fundamental right is present."[137] These "fundamental rights" are spelled out in international human rights law and include the right to life, and a right to "an adequate standard of living . . . including adequate food, clothing, and housing," and the right to the highest attainable standard of physical and mental health' regardless of group identity including "national or social origin."[138] These rights are to be guaranteed by governments.

The crime of persecution under Article 7(1)(h) of the Rome Statute requires connection with other crimes enumerated in the Court's Statute. As indicated above, the deprivation of materials necessary for human survival (a "gross and blatant denial"),[139] and their disastrous results amount to extermination, murder, and inhumane acts. By withholding aid in violation of the fundamental rights of his citizenry on the basis of their group identity the material element for persecution has been met. The mental element of persecution is linked to the material and is discussed in further detail below.

Mental Elements

As per Article 30 of the ICC Statute the mental element for most crimes against humanity requires the perpetrator have both intent *and* knowledge of consequences of the act and its circumstances. With respect to knowledge Cassese describes it as "knowledge as part of intent" or in other words knowledge that one's conduct is targeting persons protected by international law; "knowledge of consequences" or awareness that one's conduct will produce consequences prohibited under international law (e.g., mass death), and "knowledge of a broader purpose" or that one's conduct is part of a widespread or systematic attack.[140] Similar to genocide the intent of the perpetrator can also be inferred from the facts of the case, the scope and gravity of the crime etc. Moreover for murder, other inhumane acts, and extermination, the intent of the perpetrators does not necessarily have to be direct. As Stuart Ford has discussed with respect to the Myanmar case, international courts have held that indirect intent or (*dolus eventaualis*) is acceptable if it can be shown that the perpetrators: "were aware that . . . death was a probable consequence of their acts or omissions, they act or omit to act anyway, and the death does occur."[141] The Prosecution meets the mental element of these crimes against humanity if it can be demonstrated that the omissions of President Xavier Marbur were perpetrated with the direct or indirect intent to cause the consequences that ensued (e.g., murder, massive death, and physical suffering or injury). Even if the Court finds that direct intent is absent, given the scale of the natural disaster the president had to have known, as leader of the Republic of Marmyan, that the withholding of food, medicine, and other aid would produce disastrous consequences for the Marmyanic population. The president could have easily reversed his decision at any moment, as the Government of Myanmar eventually did.

The crime of persecution necessitates a different mental element in addition to the other mental elements required. Similar to genocide, persecution requires a *dolus specialis* on the part of the perpetrator(s). This is unlike other crimes against humanity in which courts have ruled that a discriminatory intent is *not* required.[142] To demonstrate the crime of persecution the Prosecutor has to demonstrate that the accused consciously intended to discriminate and acted in a discriminatory fashion; otherwise the acts committed could be categorized as other types of crimes against humanity.[143] With respect to the targeted group what matters is how they are defined by the perpetrator.[144] The action of Appellant Marbur demonstrated an intent above and beyond the general intent for crimes against humanity to destroy a part of his population on the basis of their group identity; in this instance national identity. As per emerging customary international law, it is illegal for political leaders to members of their own nationality.

War Crimes

President Xavier Marbur is guilty of war crimes by preventing the distribution of humanitarian relief authorized by the UN Security Council by force, This activity constitutes a crime under Article 8(2)(b)(iii) of the ICC Statute. Appellant was also convicted of "Intentionally using starvation of civilians as a method of warfare by depriving them of objects indispensable to their survival, including willfully impeding relief supplies as provided for under the Geneva Convention" pursuant to Article 8(2)(b)(xxv) of the Rome Statute.

Contextual Elements

The contextual requirement for war crimes is an armed conflict of an international or national character. As Cassese writes on this issue the nexus between the offense and armed conflict has been restated numerous times, in particular by the ICTY, ICTR in cases including *Tadić*, *Musema*, and *Kayishema and Ruzindana* among others.[145]

The conflict in question is an international armed conflict because of the involvement of the United Nations. As Werle discusses international armed conflict exists "if international organizations such as the United Nations participate in them, and humanitarian law is applicable."[146] Furthermore, there are times in which "international humanitarian law . . . [is] applicable although no use of force has actually occurred. This could be the case where a declaration of war is not followed by acts of war."[147] In other words, "The magnitude of the use of force is irrelevant; international humanitarian law, and thus also the law of war crimes, is applicable even to minor skirmishes ('first shot'). It is not necessary for the parties to the conflict to see it as, or to call it, a war. A state that employs armed force cannot prevent the application of international humanitarian law by referring to its use of armed force as a police action."[148]

The actions of the Appellant Marbur meet the contextual requirement for war crimes. By forbidding the UN humanitarian relief mission, authorized by the UN Security Council resolution to enter the country by force, President Xavier Marbur declared war and created an armed conflict between the UN Security Council, its agent—the humanitarian relief mission—and Marmyan.

Material Elements

The types of offenses that constitute war crimes are many. As Cassese states under international humanitarian law (IHL) they make up six groups: "Crimes committed *against persons not taking part, or no longer taking part, in armed hostilities*; Crimes against enemy combatants or civilians, committed by resorting to *prohibited methods of warfare*; Crimes against enemy combatants and civilians, involving the use of *prohibited means of warfare*; Crimes *against specifically protected persons and objects* . . . ; Crimes consisting of *improperly using protected signs and emblems* . . . ; and Conscripting or enlisting children under the age of fifteen years or using them to participate actively in hostilities."[149]

Forcibly preventing the UN relief mission from conducting its work—delivering aid and care to the Marmyanic population—constituted an attack against a protected group. The protection of medical personnel, relief workers and other who render assistance during times of conflict is deeply rooted in international customary and treaty law; in particular the Geneva Conventions and their Additional Protocols.[150] The arrest of some of the relief workers and the forcible prevention of the entire mission from disembarking on Marmyan soil meets the material requirement for a war crime as defined by Article 8(2)(b)(iii) of the ICC Statute which prohibits "Intentionally directing attacks against personnel, installations, material, units or vehicles involved in a humanitarian assistance or peacekeeping mission in accordance with the Charter of the United Nations."

Intentionally depriving the civilian population of Marmyan from receiving aid vital and necessary to their survival led to the starvation of tens of thousands, all of whom are protected persons under international humanitarian law. The Prosecution maintains that this is also a war crime in that it constituted a prohibited means of warfare.

Mental Elements

The mental requirement for the war crime with which the Applicant was tried and convicted is the intention per Article 30(2)(a) "to engage in the conduct," which in this instance refers to attacking the UN humanitarian relief mission by way of the arrest and forcible prevention of the mission from delivering aid necessary for the survival of the Marmyanic population, as well as the starving his population. The president had knowledge of the circumstances in which his conduct took place. Moreover there exists no requirement for awareness by the perpetrator of the facts that established the character of the conflict as international or non-international. Rather there is only a requirement for the awareness of the factual circumstances that established the existence of an armed conflict that is implicit in the terms "took place in the context of" and "was associated with."

DENIAL OF DUE PROCESS

Appellant argues that he was denied due process in his first trial. His accusation that he was denied legal counsel is ludicrous. Appellant Xavier Marbur was provided a list of attorneys from which to choose pursuant to the Rome Treaty. Some of those on the list spoke the language of the Appellant and also understood English, French, and other languages spoken at the Court. However Appellant was offered an interpreter to aid in his defense. What Appellant neglects to mention is the fact that he rejected the offer of an interpreter. Appellant President Marbur was afforded every opportunity to obtain legal counsel during his trial before the ICC, but insisted on representing himself. The Prosecution nevertheless made secondary counsel available to the Applicant, another fact which he neglects to mention.

Respondent reiterates that Applicant was offered every available due process protection to which he was entitled. Despite the fact that the Prosecution was still conducting its investigation into the crimes to which Marbur was accused, pursuant to Article 56(1)(b) the Pre-Trial Chamber made every effort to "ensure the efficiency and integrity of the proceedings, . . . to protect the rights of the accused." Appellant was provided with adequate time to prepare for trial.

The Appellant was granted the ability to confront his accusers pursuant to Article 67 of the ICC Statute. However certain witnesses could not be openly questioned by the defense for security reasons, pursuant to Article 68 of the ICC. Statute Marbur is the head of a military junta, agents of which are rumored to have targeted witnesses for the prosecution with harassment and threats to their personal safety. Although several of these witnesses testified *en camera* during the trial proceedings, their testimony was made available to the Appellant. Every effort was taken by the Prosecution to ensure that the rights of the Appellant were not prejudiced in any way.

CONCLUSION

The Prosecution has clearly demonstrated the contextual, mental and material necessary to convict the Applicant, President of the Republic of Marmyan Xavier Marbur, of war crimes, genocide, and crimes against humanity.

The UN relief mission, authorized by the UN Security Council, was legally permitted to enter the country of Marmyan to distribute aid to the population following the devastating earthquake that struck the country in June 2008. As a consequence of the natural disaster President Marbur had a duty to render aid and assistance to his population, whether this aid was the result of domestic or international sources. His willful disregard of this duty constituted a humanitarian crisis of epic proportions. This crisis was correctly determined by the UN Security Council as a threat to international peace and security. The fundamental human rights of the citizens of Marmyan were being grossly violated by the president. President Marbur's insistence on forcibly preventing the UN relief mission from conducting its duties was an act of war. Marbur was bound by the dictates of international humanitarian law to provide safe passage to relief workers in the country; a provision he intentionally ignored. Moreover pursuant to Article 25 of the UN Charter, the UNSC's resolutions are binding upon all member states. The consequences of President Marbur's actions and inactions were disastrous. Tens of thousands were killed. The crimes for which the Applicant was convicted are *jus cogens* violations and deserving of international prosecution. The Applicant's claims regarding lack of due process have no merit.

JUDGMENT

INTRODUCTION

The Appeals Chamber of the International Criminal Moot Court is addressing an appeal from the written Judgment rendered by the Trial Chamber in the case of *Prosecutor v. President Xavier Marbur, President of the Republic of Marmyan* ("Trial Judgment") finding him guilty of crimes against humanity (murder, extermination, persecution and other inhumane acts), genocide, and war crimes under the Rome Statute. Appellant appeals all convictions.

STATEMENT OF JURISDICTION

Marmyan is a signatory to the 1998 Rome Statute of the International Criminal Court (Rome Statute) and has accepted its jurisdiction.[151] The United Nations Security Council acting pursuant to United Nations Charter Chapter VII referred the situation to the International Moot Trial Court Prosecutor pursuant to the ICC Statute Art. 13(b).

The hearing, assessing, and weighing of evidence presented at trial is left primarily to the Trial Chamber, and only where the evidence relied on by that Chamber could not have been accepted by any reasonable tribunal of fact or where the evaluation of the evidence is "wholly erroneous" may the Appeals Chamber substitute its own finding for that of the Trial Chamber.[152]

LEGAL ISSUES RAISED ON APPEAL

The following legal issues are before the Appeals Chamber: A). Whether Appellant was denied due process by the Trial Chamber in violation of Articles 55 and 67 of the Rome Treaty; B). The legality of Appellant's arrest and United Nations (UN) intervention in the domestic affairs of Marmyan under the UN Charter; C). The applicability of United Nations Charter, Chapter VII to domestic relief operations; and D). Whether the Prosecution failed to demonstrate facts supporting the contextual, material, and mental elements of the crimes of genocide, crimes against humanity, and war crimes.

LEGAL ISSUES

A. Due Process

The Appellant contends that he was denied adequate time to prepare for trial, the opportunity to confront witnesses, and access to an interpreter during the trial proceedings. The Appellant was provided a list of attorneys pursuant to Art. 55 Section 2 (c) of the Rome Statute and he chose to act *Pro Se*. Where one chooses to represent oneself, an objection to counsel is waived. The Appellant was offered an interpreter from a list including some who spoke his language pursuant to Art. 67 Sec.1 (a) of the Statute. A party may not raise a matter which was apparent during the trial for the first time on appeal.[153]

The Appellant was granted the opportunity to confront witnesses pursuant to Article 67 of the Statute. Some witnesses were questioned *en camera* pursuant to Art. 68 of the Statute for their safety, but Appellant was allowed access to their testimony. There is no evidence the Appellant preserved this objection at trial. *Pro Se* defense is no excuse for failure to raise an issue. Trial Chambers afford *pro se* defendants every benefit of the doubt generally and the Trial Chamber in this case had an obligation to comply with Art. 67, Sec.1 of the Statute requiring "a fair hearing conducted impartially."[154] The time frame from arrest to trial was adequate for preparation. The Appeals Chamber finds that no material due process errors occurred at the trial.

B and C. Legality of Arrest and Applicability of Chapter VII to Domestic Relief Operations

The Appellant argues that: 1) his arrest was illegal and the intrusion of the UN and world aid workers in Marmyan was a violation of UN Charter, Art. 2; 2) the Trial Chamber erred in finding that his country was blocking foreign aid: aid could have been unloaded at Marmyan airports and seaports, and distribution by domestic personnel did not create a threat to international peace or security; 3) the Trial Chamber should have found that the UN Security Council (UNSC) was conspiring with other countries for invasion of Marmyan based on the Responsibility to Protect (R2P), an illegal concept under international law; and 4) he was protecting national sovereignty from invading forces.

The Prosecutor argues: 1) the Appellant continuously perpetrated violations of international law for nine years prior to the earthquake and humanitarian disaster of June 2009, including denial of human rights, arbitrary arrest and detention of civilians, denial of due process to citizens, extrajudicial killings, the use of torture, and specific persecution of the UDF movement which includes a large membership of an ethnic minority; 2) the Appellant intentionally failed to facilitate or seek aid after the earthquake in violation of a duty to his citizenry, seriously magnifying the extent of a humanitarian crisis of starvation and disease that developed particularly in the northern part of Marmyan where previous military and UDF conflict had occurred; 3) UNSC intervention and Appellant's arrest were legally justified, because the Appellant's omission of action for his own people under the circumstances was a violation of international law amounting to criminal conduct for which he is legally responsible; and 4) the Appellant's acts in arresting UN aid workers indicate his intent and are also against international law.

(1) The United Nations Charter Requirements

The legality of UN intervention and subsequent arrest of President Marbur and Chapter VII application of the Charter are related legal issues and so will be discussed together.

A complex and deplorable situation has long prevailed in Marmyan. There has been much suffering by the local population and destabilization of the region exacerbated by the earthquake and affecting neighboring States. The task of the Trial Chamber and the Appeals Chamber on review is to respond on the basis of international law to the particular legal issues before it. Sources of law such as binding resolutions, recent developments in international humanitarian law, and decisions adopted by organs of international organizations are persuasive but not binding on the Court.[155] We find no wholly erroneous interpretation of law or fact by the Trial Chamber in legal issues B and C. Our discussion follows.

UNSC security decisions under Chapter VII are binding.[156] The Appeals Chamber has no general power to review Council resolutions adopted under Chapter VII.[157] However, the UNSC is not *legibus solutes* (unbound by law)."[158] The General Assembly can recommend measures in *any* situation and under UN

Charter Art. 14 may make recommendations to the UNSC. The UNSC is bound by the requirements of Chapter VII of the Charter (peacekeeping). The General Assembly did not become involved in this case, so there is a presumption that it agreed with the UNSC action taken. At the time the UNSC made its decision to send peacekeepers and aid workers to Marmyan, direct use of force was not contemplated by the Peacekeepers although the scenario was considered a humanitarian disaster and one where conflict could begin again thus a threat to regional peace. Peacekeepers were sent pursuant to Chapter VII to facilitate delivery of aid and maintain order. The Trial Chamber found that the UNSC action in Marmyan was a Chapter VII action.

Sovereignty, codified in the UN Charter, is a customary legal norm[159] in practice since 1648. Variance from protection of sovereignty is strictly interpreted by courts leaving no room for discretion.[160] UN Charter Art. 2 Sec. 1, 4, and 7 make clear that sovereignty is a fundamental principle of the UN, but that enforcement actions under Chapter VII (peacekeeping) are not prohibited by sovereignty. UN Charter Art. 2 Sec. 7 provides the SC a safety valve.

The language of the UN Charter taken as a whole affirms UN support for international human rights and humanitarian efforts as means to avoid aggression and humanitarian disaster. The Preamble of the Charter provides that the organization is "to reaffirm faith in fundamental human rights . . . to establish conditions under which justice and respect for the obligations arising from treaties and other sources of international law can be maintained, and to promote social progress and better standards of life in larger freedom." Member states agree in Chapter 1, Art. 1 "to employ international machinery for the promotion of the economic and social advancement of all peoples," have an obligation "to maintain international peace and security," and "to achieve international cooperation in solving international problems of . . . or humanitarian character, and in promoting and encouraging respect for human rights." The UN and its member states are obligated in Chapter IX Art. 1 to "promote . . . solutions of international economic, social, health, and related problems . . . and universal respect for, and observance of, human rights." In Art. 25, Members "agree to accept and carry out the decisions of the Security Council in accordance with the present Charter," and in Art. 24 (1), the Security Council has "primary responsibility for maintenance of international peace and security" and that "in carrying out its duties under this responsibility the Security Council acts on their behalf."

Once UN Peacekeepers were duly authorized by vote of the UNSC, the government of Marmyan was obligated under the UN Charter Art. 104, and 104 (1) and (2) to allow them to conduct their mission. When the Peacekeeper Mission of the UNSC was proper under UN Chapter VII or by virtue of the Responsibility to Protect, President Marbur violated the UN Charter, Geneva Additional Protocol II, and the ICC Statute by impeding work of the peacekeepers and aid workers who were authorized by the UNSC.[161] Whether or not causing arrests was criminal will be discussed below.

The arrest of President Marbur was legally justifiable through the UNSC Resolution creating the Marmyan Peacekeeping force. One of the issues troubling international peacekeeping efforts through the UN is the lack of enforcement authority given to peacekeepers. Peacekeepers have no general enforcement power absent authorization pursuant to UNSC resolution. After the instant case, in 2013, specific language was included in the UN resolution creating a peacekeeping force in Democratic Republic of the Congo authorizing power to arrest.[162] The Congo resolution is viewed as being a historic step forward in capacity for UN peacekeeping efforts,[163] but is case specific and subsequent to the Marmyan case and therefore not applicable. Generally accepted national common law authorizes warrantless arrest when evidence supports probable cause that a crime has been committed and there is no reasonable time or immediate source from which to obtain a warrant. "Peacekeeping personnel . . . must be able to recognize human rights violations or abuse, and be prepared to respond appropriately *within the limits of their mandate and their competence.*"[164] Peacekeepers "may use force at the tactical level, with the authorization of the SC, to defend themselves and their mandate, particularly in situations where the State is unable to provide security and maintain public order."[165] Furthermore, the "operation must have the political and analytical skills, the personal resources, and the will to manage situations where there is an absence or breakdown of local consent . . . in some cases this may require, as a last resort, the use of force."[166] We uphold some of the Trial Chamber convictions of Appellant under the ICC Statute, agreeing with its findings on the legality of Appellant's arrest.

(2) Was There a Threat to International Peace?

UN Charter Chapter VII allows the Security Council to choose what measures shall be taken to maintain or restore international peace and security once it first makes an affirmative finding of a "threat to the peace, breach of the peace, or act of aggression." The R2P doctrine also requires a threat to international peace, outlining four specific crimes for which the responsibility arises. "Threat to Peace" will be discussed for both purposes in this section.

"Peacekeeping" by the UN is soft law as peace enforcement (as opposed to military intervention) operations under Chapter VII. It has been accepted as authority since the 1960s and the *Expenses Cases.*[167] This Chamber has only to determine whether any reasonable trier of fact could conclude that there was a threat to international peace and security in Marmyan at the time in question.[168]

The lines between peacekeeping, peace enforcement, and peace building have become blurred in recent years in practice.[169] Intrastate conflict and non-military sources of instability in the economic, humanitarian and ecological fields may become a threat to peace and security[170]and have in recent years. A massive humanitarian crisis existed in Marmyan with potential expansion of human rights violations beyond the Marmyan border and regional instability for additional thousands of people. The facts illustrate the transparency of President Marbur's weak attempt to get aid to the Northern part of Marmyan, home to the dissident group his Junta had been in conflict with for eight years. A reasonable person would conclude that starvation and disease would be immediate and inevitable for the entire region under the circumstances and would question President Marbur's motives. We agree. Customary international practice supports a definition of "threat to peace" which includes large scale humanitarian disaster.[171]

The International Commission on Intervention and State Sovereignty (ICISS) report, which became the basis for R2P, provides persuasive moral guidelines for intervention by the international community to avoid human catastrophe such as mass murder and starvation.[172] Humanitarian intervention must be for a just cause and follow certain principles. "Just cause" included interventions to prevent (1) "large scale loss of life" or (2) "large scale 'ethnic cleansing,'" and the precautionary principles were (1) right intention, meaning for the purpose of halting human suffering; (2) last resort, meaning only after every nonmilitary option had been explored; (3) proportional means, meaning that the "scale, duration and intensity of the . . . intervention should be the minimum necessary to secure the defined human protection objective"; and (4) reasonable prospects, meaning that there "must be a reasonable chance of success in halting or averting the suffering." The Commission cited such developments in international law as the proliferation of human rights accords, changing state practice, and the responsibility of the Security Council for the maintenance of international peace.[173] Peacekeepers in Marmyan operated well within these guidelines.

Haiti is comparable to Marmyan but also distinguishable. Haiti involved peacebuilding as much as peacekeeping.[174] In that case, the UNSC held that internal chaos constituted a threat to international peace and security in Haiti in 2004,[175] but the peacekeeping effort began in 1993, prior to the ICISS guidelines and R2P and has a unique history. Unlike Marmyan, the Haitian effort was actually initiated by letter dated October 15, 1993, from Haitian democratically-elected President Aristide requesting the Security Council to call on Member States to take the "necessary measures to strengthen the provisions of resolution 873 (1993)."[176] The next day, the SC, by resolution 875 (1993), called upon Member States to ensure implementation of an embargo against Haiti, and to halt and inspect ships travelling towards Haiti to verify cargoes and destinations. The UNSC was prepared to consider further measures to ensure full compliance with the provisions of its resolutions.[177] The UNSC was unable due to noncooperation of the Haitian military authorities to fully carry out its mandate.[178] Haitian de facto authorities "delivered to the Executive Director of MICIVIH in Port-au-Prince a decree of the "provisional President" declaring the international staff of MICIVIH "undesirable" and giving them forty-eight hours to leave Haitian territory.[179] As a result, UNSC Resolution 940 was adopted by the UNSC on July 31, 1994[180] wherein the UNSC authorized a 20,000 strong multi-national force to "facilitate the prompt return of the legitimate Haitian authorities, maintain a secure and stable environment in the country, and promote the rule of law." In the Haitian case there was a breakdown of government, chaos and crimes, and a request by a democratically elected president as compared to the "provisional" usurper for world help. In the Marmyan example the president did not want help and the government was fully functioning, although repressively so.

We find that the Haitian example is unique and that it does not set a precedent under international law for humanitarian intervention generally. The criteria of the ICISS above provide guidelines for determinations of appropriate internal intervention by the UNSC under Chapter VII assuming a finding of threat to peace and armed conflict, and each case must be evaluated on an individual basis. Internal intervention is still not fully accepted in positive law but has been justified by its success and is accepted widely as customary international law[181] which is permissible under the limited circumstance of Chapter VII and R2P.

This Chamber finds that delayed aid to Marmyan increased human catastrophe for the entire region amounting to a threat to peace, particularly in consideration of ongoing internal conflict. Disasters may affect not only individual States but also several States or entire regions, and are matters of concern for the international community as a whole.[182] Starvation as a tool of armed conflict even in non-international situations is prohibited by international law.[183] The UNSC has tried to respond more rapidly to human catastrophe in the last twenty years in order to be effective, and its authority is legally exercised to prevent increased humanitarian suffering where it can be said that a threat to the peace exists or a crime against humanity exists.[184]

Armed Conflict

Marmyan was engaged in an ongoing conflict with the UDF but no outside state was involved.[185] The threshold for intervention is higher for non-international conflicts, only applying where the armed forces of a High Contracting Party are in conflict with "dissident armed forces or other organized armed groups which, under responsible command, exercise such control over a part of the territory as to enable them to carry out sustained and concerted military operations."[186] The evidence rises above the threshold of "isolated and sporadic acts of violence" of an "internal disturbance" and amounts to armed conflict. President Marbur was not initially arrested and peacekeepers offered only assistance, meeting international criteria for intervention in the sovereignty of another state.[187] The Appeals Chamber finds the decision of the Security Council to send Peacekeepers and aid workers to Marmyan was legal as a response to a "threat to peace" under the UN Charter and Chapter VII specifically.

(3) Responsibility to Protect

Is the Responsibility to Protect legal under international law as applied to this case? The Appeals Chamber finds that it is. Although the doctrine of R2P is an area of disagreement for international legal scholars,[188] "sovereignty as responsibility . . . has always encompassed legal obligations,"[189] and the R2P doctrine is accepted generally as a means of defining appropriate legal intervention in the domestic affairs of a state. As discussed above, under threats to international peace and mass humanitarian crisis, sovereignty may be challenged by the international community on a limited basis.

"Responsibility to Protect" was adopted by 2005 UN Resolution A/60/1. The concept continues to gain general acceptance based on moral obligations and international humanitarian law to prevent mass human disaster.[190] The UN Resolution was based upon the 2005 United Nations World Summit Outcome Resolution[191] and the previous 2001 ICISS Study,[192] the ICISS having been specifically created to resolve the conflict in international law between decision-makers faced with humanitarian disasters and the international norm of non-interference in the internal affairs of states. The general principles of R2P date back to post World War II world self-examination of what might have been done to prevent the Holocaust. The Doctrine accepted by UN Resolution specifically affirms a case-by-case analysis as opposed to a general legal rule.[193]

The international community may only intervene in 1) cases where the state is failing to adequately meet its responsibility to prevent genocide, war crimes, ethnic cleansing or crimes against humanity either intentionally or due to lack of capacity; and 2) when diplomatic, humanitarian, and peaceful means pursuant to UN Charter Chapters VI and VIII have been considered where appropriate; and 3) only for protection of populations against genocide, war crimes, ethnic cleansing and crimes against humanity. The responsibility is to react to and also to prevent human catastrophe.[194] No established criteria exist by which to determine exactly when the responsibility contemplated shifts from the state to the international community.[195] In the Haiti example, the Haitian government requested assistance.[196]

It is clear that the analysis of a potential R2P situation normally includes analysis of UN Charter Chapters 6 and 8. The parties must seek solutions by various means of peaceful settlement of their own choice, but the UNSC has authority to investigate any dispute or situation which might lead to endangerment of international peace and security, and if the parties fail to resolve the situation, the UNSC under Art. 34-37 may recommend appropriate action. R2P only becomes involved if the UNSC acts. Application of Chapters VI and VIII is not before this Chamber on Appeal and so will not be addressed here.

In this case, the threshold question is whether original failure to supply aid to the UDF/Northern region amounted to one or more of the crimes set out in the R2P. Was there a duty, and then a violation of that duty with the requisite intent, and all the elements for the crime alleged? The SC action was legally based upon facts before it at the time the decision was made to send a mission to Marmyan. Sufficient facts existed at that time and R2P did apply. Our explanation follows.

a. President Marbur had a Duty to Distribute Aid Regardless of the Presence of the UDF

International law *implies* a duty and non-binding international norms find such a duty. Marmyan is party to the UN Charter agreement and is responsible for and impliedly obligated to cooperate with the UNSC in solving humanitarian problems pursuant to UN Charter Ch. I, Art. 1, Ch. 9, Art. 55, Art. 25, and Art.

104. The Bruges Resolution specifically states that a primary responsibility of states affected in a disaster is a duty to take care of victims within its territory, and, when unable to do so, to "seek assistance from competent international organizations and/or from third States" and to "not arbitrarily and unjustifiably" "reject a *bona fide* offer exclusively intended to provide humanitarian assistance or to refuse access to the victims."[197] "Humanitarian assistance must be provided in accordance with the principles of humanity, neutrality and impartiality.[198] Humanitarian law applies in war and peace and obligations on States are based on "certain general and well-recognized principles, namely: elementary considerations of humanity, more exacting in peace than in war."[199] UN General Assembly Resolution 46/182 (1991) by Annex set out principles for strengthening coordination of humanitarian emergency assistance of the United Nations. Each state has a primary responsibility to take care of victims of natural disasters including a primary role in the initiation, organization, coordination and implementation of humanitarian assistance within its territory. International cooperation "should be provided." High level officials have a responsibility to actively facilitate "the access by operational organizations to emergency areas for the rapid provision of emergency assistance by obtaining the consent of all parties concerned."[200] A State that is not capable of addressing the consequences of a disaster sufficiently is still obliged to cooperate. "The duty to cooperate not only provides a basis for the requirement of consent, but further underlines that treaty law implies a duty *not to withhold consent arbitrarily.*"[201] A growing body of emerging customary international law exists on this topic.

The UDF were primarily in the north of Marmyan and civilian noncombatants were also in that region. Civilian noncombatants are protected regardless of armed groups that may be in their midst.[202] The Appellant unreasonably failed to ask for aid, did not supply appropriate aid, unreasonably refused aid, and refused access to victims. The Appellant's refusal to cooperate with the UN peacekeepers is illegal. We affirm the Trial Chamber finding that Appellant had a duty, failed to meet it, and withheld consent to assistance arbitrarily, resulting in thousands of deaths.

b. Was Omission of That Duty a Crime Under These Facts?

The Bruges Resolution notes special rules of international humanitarian law applicable in armed conflict, but does not itself define crimes against humanity thus causing legal reasoning to revert to the Statute for this Chamber which does define crimes against humanity.

D. Elements of the Crimes of Genocide, Crimes against Humanity, and War Crimes

(1) Genocide

Article 6 of the Rome Statute defines "genocide." The intent requirement for genocide under the Statute is not the same as that for the other crimes in this case, providing that criminal intent must include commission of the material elements with specific intent and knowledge. The group element of genocide is determinative, however, so the Appeals Chamber does not discuss the intent requirement.

This Chamber reverses the Trial Chamber and acquits Appellant on the genocide conviction. The previous evaluation of the evidence and application of the law thereto was wholly erroneous as to element 3 of the offense. The facts are clear that Appellant had intent to destroy at least a part of the Northern people of his country, but there is insufficient evidence for a reasonable man to determine that a national or ethnic group contemplated by the Statute was targeted specifically beyond a reasonable doubt in that region nor was a national, religious or racial group alleged. The Trial Chamber previously accepted unchallenged as a "group" the Bosnian Muslims[203] but there is no such identification in evidence here. Furthermore, "intent to destroy" "in part" must include a substantial part of the group. There is no way to know in this case if "part" is enough to have a significant impact on the group as a whole as required.[204] One must show a "substantial part" relative to the entire group.[205]

The UDF are a political movement made up of people in a region. Labeling them mere citizens of a region without other distinguishing characteristics alters the intent of the statute. Identity of a group becomes meaningless and response to any people in the state could be interpreted as genocide, rather than crime control, civil war or response to protest, for example. Article 22 (2) of the Statute requires that definitions of crimes be strictly construed and not extended by analogy. Where ambiguity exists, the definition is interpreted in favor of the person charged[206] and the standard of proof is beyond a reasonable doubt.[207] There is no reasonable doubt as to the group element of the offense of Genocide.

(2) Crimes against Humanity

Appellant was convicted of crimes against humanity pursuant to Article 7(1)(a) murder, (b) extermination, (h) persecution, and (k) other inhumane acts of a similar character. Prerequisite elements of all of these offenses include finding each was committed as part of a "widespread or systematic attack directed against any civilian population, with knowledge of the attack.[208] Additional elements of each crime except murder are defined in the statute.[209]

Widespread or Systematic Attack

Proof under Article 7 may be of widespread or systematic attack. Both are not required. "Widespread" refers to the large-scale nature of the attack and the number of targeted persons while "systematic" refers to the organized nature of the acts of violence and the improbability of their random occurrence. Patterns of crimes, in the sense of the non-accidental repetition of similar criminal conduct on a regular basis, are expression of such systematic occurrence. Only the attack, not the individual acts of the accused, must be widespread or systematic."[210] "Attack" is not limited to the conduct of hostilities but may also encompass situations of mistreatment of persons taking no active part in hostilities. The Court may consider the means and method used in the course of the attack, the status of the victims, their number, the nature of the crimes committed, the extent to which the attacking force attempted to comply with the laws of war, and the extent to which the crimes against humanity were committed."[211] An "attack" within the meaning of the Statute and International Law is not the same as "armed conflict." Under customary international law "the attack could precede, outlast, or continue during the armed conflict, but it need not be a part of it." A crime committed before or after the main attack against the civilian population may be connected to or part of the attack if the crime is not an isolated act.[212] The attack in the context of a crime against humanity is not limited to the use of armed force; it encompasses any mistreatment of the civilian population and a plan or policy may be relevant but is not a required element of the crime.[213]

Act or Omission and Intent

An attack may involve the commission or omission of acts. In *Prosecutor v. Kunarac,* the Appeals Chamber found for the offense of torture under the same statutory requirements in the ICC Statute as the alleged crimes in this case, the elements could be established by an act or omission so long as the act was intentionally committed or participated in and the accused knew that it would have a certain effect.[214] Where an accused orders an act or omission with the awareness of the substantial likelihood that a crime will be committed in the execution of that order, he is said to have the requisite *mens rea* for liability.[215] A mere possibility that a crime will occur as a result of the conduct is not sufficient for criminal responsibility.

Against Civilian Population

"Directed against" means that the primary object of the attack is the civilian population.[216] The entire population of the geographical area need not have been subject to the attack so long as the attack was against some civilians.[217] Article 50 of Additional Protocol I to the Geneva Conventions defines civilians and civilian populations.[218] A civilian is any person who is not a member of the armed forces or a militia or a volunteer corps. If there is doubt about status, then the person shall be considered a civilian.[219] In determining whether the presence of soldiers/militia within a civilian population deprives the population of its civilian character, the number of soldiers, as well as whether they are on leave must be examined.[220] In this case there is no evidence of numbers of alleged UDF forces in the northern region of Marmyan. The nexus between the acts of the accused and the attack is the requirement of knowledge on the part of the accused that there is an attack on the civilian population and that his act is part of the attack.[221] and the accused must have known of the wider context in which his acts occurred and that his acts were part of that context of attack.[222]

The Appeals Chamber agrees with the Trial Chamber and considers the entire context of conditions in Marmyan at the time that the earthquake struck the country. Any reasonable person would have concluded a substantial likelihood existed that mass starvation and disease would strike a widespread portion of the civilian population and that food and medicine were immediately necessary to stem the tide of disaster to those people. Marmyan civilians were under a widespread "attack" within the meaning of the ICC Statute. The fact that the UDF were interspersed with the civilian population in the northern region of the country does not absolve the accused of responsibility for an omission to act with dire consequences to civilians in that section of the country. The Appeals Chamber affirms the Trial Chamber's finding that President Marbur intentionally committed an omission with clear substantial likelihood of resulting widespread mass starvation and disease to thousands of civilians. The facts in this case presented far more than a mere possibility of a crime happening. The immediate and irreversible results of failure to act were obvious. Appellant had a duty to act and his failure to do so rose to the level of criminal *mens rea*.

a. Elements of the Offense of Murder

Elements of the offense of murder are not defined in the ICC Statute, therefore customary international law applies. "When the accused has the requisite intent to commit the underlying offence with which he is charged and he knows that there is an attack on the civilian population and also knows that his acts comprise part of that attack"[223] then the Appeals Chamber considers that the *mens rea* of a crime against humanity is satisfied. The Trial Chamber finding of indirect intent (*dolus eventualis)* for murder is affirmed. Thousands died due to Appellant's omission to act, a result substantially likely and clearly predictable. The threat of mass murder in Marmyan due to withholding aid existed at the time the UNSC considered intervention and justified the UNSC decision to implement the R2P Doctrine. The Appeals Chamber confirms his conviction of murder.

b. Elements of Extermination

The Prosecutor had to prove the "intentional infliction of conditions of life, inter alia, the deprivation of access to food and medicine, calculated to bring about the destruction of part of a population."[224] Specific intent is not required. Intent as contemplated in the common elements of crimes against humanity is sufficient. Destruction of a part of the population did occur as a direct result of Appellant's intentional failure to act. This element was proved and the Appeals Chamber affirms Appellant's conviction by the Trial Chamber.

c. Elements of Persecution

Persecution requires proof of "intentional and severe deprivation of fundamental rights contrary to international law by reason of the identity of the group or collectivity"[225] thus a specific *mens rea (dolus specialis)* directed toward a specific group. This Chamber does not find the group sufficiently identified for the same reasons as set out in the discussion on the charge of genocide, and so does not find specific intent beyond a reasonable doubt. The Appeals Chamber reverses the conviction for persecution.

d. Other Inhumane Acts

Proof of "acts of a similar character intentionally causing great suffering, or serious injury to body or to mental or physical health"[226] is required for the crime of other inhumane acts.President Marbur's acts causing the starvation of civilians could be considered inhumane acts as lesser included offenses to murder and extermination, however the Prosecution failed to specify starvation as a specific inhumane act so the Appeals Chamber reverses this conviction.

(3) War Crimes

The *Tadić* Case[227] expanded the concept of war crimes to internal armed conflicts and the ICC Statute specifically includes internal armed conflict in the categories of War Crimes. The elements of this offense include a plan or policy or large-scale commission of such crimes, and grave breaches of the Geneva Conventions, including for this case: willful killing or willfully causing great suffering, or serious injury to body or health.[228] The context in this case includes years of extra-judicial killings, torture, and deprivation of due process rights prior to the earthquake. Events after the earthquake must be considered in context. The arrest of peacekeepers was illegal under customary international law, but those arrests do not qualify as war crimes since they were not large scale and did not themselves cause great suffering and serious injury to body or health of the peacekeepers or amount to any of the other statutory war crimes offenses. The acts of Appellant contributed to a large scale commission of a crime and willfully caused great suffering, serious injury to body and health, and death. The elements of this offense are met beyond a reasonable doubt and the Appeals Chamber finds no actionable error. The Appeals Chamber affirms Appellant's convictions for Murder, Extermination and War Crimes, and reverses the convictions for Genocide, Persecution and Inhumane Acts.

SENTENCING

The offenses of Murder, Extermination and War Crimes are all based upon the same facts. Cumulative charging might have been an issue,[229] but the Appellant has not asked for a review of sentence in this case and so the Appeals Chamber will not.

DISPOSITION

The formal orders made by the Appeals Chamber in the Disposition section of the judgment are as follows:

In relation to Counts 1 (Genocide), 4 (Persecution), and 5 (Inhumane Acts) of the Indictment, the Appeals Chamber ALLOWS Appellant's appeal and QUASHES the verdict of the Trial Chamber accordingly, and it enters a verdict that Xavier Marbur is NOT GUILTY upon the Genocide count, the Persecution count and the Inhumane Acts count. In relation to Counts 2 (Murder), 3 (Extermination), and 6 (War Crimes) the Appeals Chamber QUASHES Appellant's grounds for appeal and AFFIRMS his convictions on each count. The crimes upheld are no less grave in nature than those reversed. Many of the deaths of 90,000 Marmyans would have been averted if international aid had been allowed. With no Trial Court showing of allocation of weight as between the convictions, the Appeals Chamber finds the Trial Chamber sentence of fifteen years imprisonment remains reasonable, and so affirms.

APPENDIX A: Examples of Judges' Questions and Lawyers' Answers from Student Moot Courts

Q: You define "attack" as being both violent and non-violent. Can the potentially unintended consequences of the president's act be considered a non-violent attack? In other words, can an attack be unintended?

A: Sure. I believe that an attack can be unintended but in this particular case there was intent because a president of a country should have greater than average skills and he should be held to a higher responsibility. A reasonable person would have to assume that withholding aid would have disastrous consequences especially if people are dying and there is no food, water or any type of aid.

(space indicates a new topic)

Q: Considering the argument that President Marbur did not allow aid, by arresting and detaining foreign aid workers in order to protect state sovereignty, would he have been able to prevent aid without the use of force?

A: I believe so. I believe if he had accepted the aid when they first offered it to him, he would not have had to deal with the Chapter VII UN Security Council sanction by force. He is party to the UN Charter therefore he should be held responsible for his noncompliance with the Charter.

Q: Was there a legitimate reason to force humanitarian aid on the country of Marbur? Did the UN have any regard for the domestic laws of Marbur?

A: We believe that the Chapter VII UN sanction was legitimate because there was an international concern being that no one was receiving any type of aid. We believe that international law superseded domestic law. Therefore since the UN sanction was carried out legally, we believe that the president should have complied with that and allowed the aid workers to come in to the country.

Q: Beginning with genocide, where is the intent to destroy a group "as such"? Where is the evidence in your facts that there was any intent whatsoever?
A: We believe that there was an intent, as such because there had been conflicts in the country between the UDF and government forces and because the region where the UDF lives was the hardest hit region. I know he could not control the earthquake . . .
Q: Why isn't that just a coincidence?
A: It's not . . . I think he saw it as an opportunity to destroy a troublesome group.
Q: Is there any evidence to support that?
A: No, I don't have any evidence.
Q: Was this an authoritarian regime that just didn't want outside people coming in during the referendum?
A: The Prosecution doesn't believe so because nobody was getting aid, there was nothing being done.
Q: Nobody was getting aid in the entire country. Why does this mean he was targeting one population?
A: We're saying that he was targeting the ethnic group associated with the UDF. If the Court feels that that is not enough we argue that he was targeting the entire population.
Q: I've never heard of that concept. In Cambodia the entire country was affected, but scholars and prosecutors say that the genocide pertained to only a few ethnic minority groups. The majority population is not considered, they were a political group.
A: The reason I brought up Cambodia was the fact that international jurisprudence has shown that it's a national group being destroyed by a foreign state.
Q: It wasn't a foreign state.
A: I know that's why I brought it up. In Cambodia the people were being destroyed by their own state.
Q: I know but it wasn't genocide. Why don't you just stick with the minority group in your case.
A: Okay.

Q: Let's turn to crimes against humanity. You very brilliantly provided us with legal language as to why it was widespread and systematic. You demonstrated the widespread and the systematic but you didn't show us the attack. I don't see any attack. Where is the attack? Not doing something is an attack?
A: The scholar said that you don't have to directly physically harm these people. If you know that the consequences of your actions will cause death then

the scholar believes that that constitutes an attack. The president had to have known that by not delivering aid people would die.
Q: Do you have any case law to back that up?
A: I don't have any.
Q: Let's talk about the case law you cited as to the material element of the crimes against humanity charges. What were the facts of the cases?
A: I don't know.
Q: Let me help you. The Akayesu case was a violent attack involving rape, the Tadić case involved a psychopathic killer and torture in a prison camp. These were all direct acts, none of them indirect. You're citing to acts of omission.
A: The reason why I brought up the Tadic case was to define systematic. The Akayesu case the same thing but to define widespread.
Q: I didn't hear a single case associating acts of omission with a widespread or systematic attack.
A: I haven't . . .
Q: So you're just relying on that scholar?
A: Yes.

Q: Finally on war crimes, the mental element concerns me. Where is the evidence that the president, in trying to protect the national sovereignty of the country and in arguing that the state should provide aid to its people, intended to harm his people?
A: I find it hard to believe that the president would not know that a denial of aid would result in deaths, that that could be perceived as an attack.
Q: Okay. Doesn't the president have the right to distribute the aid himself? Does the UN Security Council have the right to ignore the rights of a president?
A: I'm sure the president does have the right, but to me that sounds factual and I'm not supposed to be arguing the facts.
Q: Does the president have the right to distribute the aid assuming the facts are that he indicated a willingness to distribute aid?
A: Yes, but . . .
Q: He does have a right?
A: He has the right to do anything he wants, but . . .
Q: Does he have the right to tell the UN Security Council to stay out of his country?
A: No, because that's legally binding.
Q: What was the threat to international peace that the UN Security Council invoked in order to invade the country?
A: The fact that these people were dying.
Q: How does that threaten international peace and security or citizens of other countries?
A: I don't know what to say to that.

Q: Last question. if the mental element was satisfied in all three cases and the president actually intended to kill this minority group, why would he do it when the international community is watching?
A: I don't know him. Sure it's implausible that he would do this while the world is watching. It's also implausible that he would deny aid.
Q: I'm talking about his intent to kill. If he intended to kill them surely he wouldn't do it while the whole world was watching?
A: I don't have any response to that.

Q (question asked in rebuttal): With respect to the charges of genocide, can you please tell us why this is a group? I'm not sure this is a group. I don't see any intent to destroy the group. The withholding of aid affected many groups. Secondly "in whole or in part," "in part" implies a large part.
A: From my interpretation of the facts, to answer your first question, even though they were part of the UDF they still served as a minority.
Q: Well where's the intent?
A: Because of their opposition towards the Marbur regime.
Q: Would withholding aid only antagonize them? As I asked earlier why do it now when the whole world is watching? In the long run withholding aid will only increase their will to resist.
A: Well I can only say that he tried to legitimate his means by only withholding aid in the northern region.
Q: No he arrested aid workers and aid was withheld from the entire country. The aid workers came into the capital not into a particular region necessarily.
A: Okay.

Q: The deliberate withholding of aid is an act of omission that is the basis for all three charges and yet when we think of murder we don't think of it as an act of omission. Can you give me any example of extermination or mass murder that resulted from an act of omission? Inhumane acts may be a stronger case. It seems there was no intent for murder. Extermination also not intent. You could say other inhumane acts apply to the withholding of aid, except for the fact that he asked for the aid and they wouldn't give it to him.
A: Are you asking what was the inhuman act, or are you asking me was it murder?
Q: I'm asking was the inhumane act committed by the President or by the UN Security Council?
A: I would say it was the president by not allowing the relief mission in.
Q: Compared to other options it wasn't as though he threatened to kill people. He was saying "this is our country. We don't want you in our country. We want to distribute the aid ourselves." Why isn't that a valid argument?

A: He can say he'll distribute the aid, but you also have to consider his motives. Will he really distribute the aid? Will he go back on his word? I see that as a way to follow up on his actions. Freedom House shows that the country's ratings are going down. You have to take that into consideration.

Q: First regarding Article 6 genocide isn't it true that acts of omission can lead to consequences that can constitute the material element of genocide?
A: Well you have to have all three elements don't you?
Q: Let's just take them one at a time. With regards to the material element isn't possible there was the destruction of a minority group. You say they're a political group. His political opponent is the UDF but the people who were killed were not all members of the UDF but an ethnic minority group. They were killed as an act of omission.
A: Right but the UDF is a group that contains mostly this ethnic group but not all of the ethnic group belong to the UDF.
Q: The denial of aid distinguished between members of the UDF and other members of this same ethnic minority.
A: The denial of aid did not distinguish between any groups within the country.

Q: Let's talk about the mental element. Given that the president knew that members of the ethnic group who make up the UDF would be particularly harmed with the denial of aid, wouldn't a reasonable person by an objective test assume that the president should have known that the denial of aid would result in the killing and dying of this minority group?
A: Well the president couldn't control where this earthquake struck and it happened to strike in the area inhabited by the UDF and this minority ethnic group. By denying aid to the entire country.
Q: Wouldn't a reasonable person know as president that members of that minority group would be the ones who died?
A: Yes but that doesn't prove that he intended to destroy them. It just happened to be a consequence.
Q: A reasonable person would know that they would be the ones who were killed.
A: Yes but the entire country was suffering as well. The ethnic minority just happened to be suffering more because they were in the region where the earthquake struck. This doesn't necessarily imply the intent to destroy that ethnic group.
Q: Even though the large majority of victims were from that group?
A: Yes.

Q: On Article 7 crimes against humanity you critique the argument that it was a widespread or systematic attack. What about the argument that it was not a literal attack but an attack by acts of omission? It is well established in international humanitarian law that acts of omission can constitute an attack, that they constitute war crimes. The lack of case law refers to the fact that the ICTY and ICTR address cases that took place during traditional conflicts. This particular example, acts of omission which is at the heart of this case, is a fundamentally unprecedented case.

A: So there is no precedent in place. In this case I would read the statute literally where it says "attack," and take that to mean violent attack.

Q: But doesn't that mean that any time you have acts of omission the law won't be able to respond? That anyone can just use national sovereignty as an excuse to evade the law? Is that the kind of rule that you want to come out of this case? International human rights law is founded on the premise that there are limits to national sovereignty.

A: Well traditionally national sovereignty has trumped almost everything.

Q: It did, but not since the UN Charter . . .

A: But the UN Charter has nothing in it with respect to this R2P doctrine. R2P is a fairly new idea. Like I said it was created by a small number of individuals and not all nations ascribe to it.

Q: Not all nations, but the large majority did by acclamation in the 2005 World Summit. There's the Bosnia example where the UN Security Council said you can have a legally binding Chapter VII situation where there is no clear threat to international peace and security and it's mostly domestic human rights violations occurring. Certainly the Haiti example underscores that more than Bosnia which is more of an international situation.

A: Not from a natural disaster like an earthquake though.

Q: Right. But what was the threat to international peace? The Security Council didn't have the authority to order an invasion of Haiti?

A: There were armed groups fighting in Haiti. I'm not very familiar with the Haiti case. There was a possibility for a spillover in violence. In this case there was no violence in Marmyan in the first place. In this case there were no armed groups fighting in the country.

Q: What about the UDF?

A: They were just an opposition group. They were not a guerilla group.

Q: Okay finally on war crimes, Article 8(2) (b) (3) refers to intentionally directing attacks against a peacekeeping force; that seems pretty clear. They were arrested. Are you saying that arrest does not constitute an attack because these aren't civilians? Some of those arrested were civilians.

A: No I'm saying that the Government of Marmyan does not have to allow aid if they cannot be reasonably assured of their control.

Q: But doesn't the ordinary language, "potentially directing attacks on a peacekeeping mission."

A: No, I'm referring to Article 23 of the Geneva Convention.

Q: Well the indictment is 8(2) (b) (3).

A: Right. I'm sorry what's your point?

Q: The point is this is a charge, the ordinary language of the Statute says "potentially directing attacks on a peacekeeping mission." That was legally there. Are you saying that any country can claim national sovereignty against the UN Security Council and Chapter VII missions?
A: They have a right to self-defense. It's stated in the UN Charter.

Q (questions asked in rebuttal): What about the president's argument that his intent was to protect the civilian population against a foreign invasion and that his intent was to get the aid to them faster and more efficiently?
A: Exactly, exactly. His offered to accept the aid himself, the food, medicine, and water. He didn't want any international aid workers distributing the aid. The Security Council rejected this out of hand.
Q: The actions of the Security Council were not for arbitrary reasons, but because of Marbur's human rights record no?
A: Of course, but you're still trumping national sovereignty out of speculation of what he might do. The speculation might be grounded in past history but it is still speculation.
Q: This R2P doctrine did not come out of nowhere. The majority of countries theoretically support it under some circumstances. This is about as good a situation as any. Natural disasters kill many more people than armed conflicts each year. Don't governments have a responsibility to protect their own populations with disaster relief provided by the international community? Why doesn't Marbur have an obligation to let the aid workers in? They're not coming in trying to take over his country. They just want to save lives and leave.
A: Well obviously they're interested in regime change because the president has been convicted of all of these charges.
Q: No one has arrested the president.
A: Well he has been convicted by the ICC.
Q: The point is whether there is regime change or not, doesn't the international community have the right to say "your sovereignty is not being threatened. We just want to deliver aid."
A: No because the national government of a country has the final say as to who is allowed into the country and how aid is distributed.
Q: Anytime you submit to a human rights treaty you're giving up a little bit of sovereignty. They didn't have to ratify the UN Charter, they chose to.
A: Yes, but I don't think international aid for a natural disaster is the same thing as say genocide or something like that. I don't think it's the same circumstances as specifically targeting a population . . .
Q: What would have happened if for example the UN Security Council had not authorized the aid mission, would the president have been in violation of international law by not saving his own people with aid that was offered him?
A: Offered as in giving the supplies or sending international aid workers?
Q: Giving the supplies.
A: Yes. If he didn't accept the supplies he would have been in violation of international law.

Q: So what's the problem with aid workers coming in temporarily?

A: The international community does not have the right to mandate people coming in to help. The president has the right to distribute aid as he sees fit. He was ready and willing to accept aid and supplies from the international community. He just didn't want any foreign nationals coming in to his country.

Q: So you think it's irrelevant that an objective test might hold that a reasonable person would have concluded that the Security Council had a valid basis for its lack of faith in the president?

A: I think it's a subjective test really. I don't see it as an objective test.

Q: What's the legal basis for a subjective test?

A: I don't have that information. I can say that you're purely speculating. I mean you can base it off of past actions.

Q: The Security Council was not acting arbitrarily. They had objective evidence from the reports submitted by human rights organizations about conditions in the country which stated that Marbur did not care about his people's welfare.

A: The Prosecution has this evidence? That he had failed to provide aid in the past? Okay I might have missed that. I didn't see anything . . . that there was something that said the president and his government refused to provide aid to the country.

Q: Is it possible for a reasonable person to conclude that if there was murder and torture of the UDF, that when this earthquake happened the president would not come to the aid of the minority group associated with the UDF? So therefore the Security Council felt there was a reasonable basis for ordering aid workers be sent in instead of relying on the president's word that he would distribute the aid?

A: I suppose it might be reasonable to assume that he might not distribute the aid equally. I still don't think that necessitates the breach of national sovereignty.

Q: Why?

A: Because I've never heard of the UN Security Council authorizing the invasion of a country in response to a natural disaster.

Q: That's true there's no precedent. This is a new situation. It hasn't happened before.

A: My opinion is that national sovereignty would trump any sort of international intervention like this.

Q: But what is the legal argument? I understand the political argument.

A: I don't have any specific cases. There's Article 2 of the UN Charter.

Q: And the counterargument is that Chapter VII basically overcomes it.

Q: Finally, this argument about indirect intent and acts of omission. Death was assumed to be a likely consequence. If that were to be assumed, wouldn't indirect intent be a reasonable basis?

A: Well I haven't seen any precedent for indirect intent. The only precedent I've seen is for direct intent.

Q: Are you saying that the Court should never accept an expansion of the doctrine of indirect intent in a situation where there was no doubt that there was no capacity to distribute the aid domestically?
A: If there was absolutely no doubt that the president could not or would not distribute the aid then I might concede to an expansion of this doctrine. That did not happen in this case.

Q: I didn't see in the facts that the attack was directed against the rebellious region. The attack was directed against an invading army. You are inferring from the facts that the president wanted to attack a rebellious region, but the facts are that the chemical attack was to stop an invading army. That's the heart of the case. So you're making an inference are you not?
A: Yes.
Q: Well that's not an issue before the appellate court. You're making an inference that that was the motive for the attack. You're introducing a new argument here.
A: We are trying to show the appellants willingness to attack a region knowing what effect the attack would have. We are not trying to say the attack was directed at a rebellious population but was directed at a rebellious region.
Q: Now that we've clarified that the attack was directed against the invading army, you state the objective test is what a reasonable person would have done. There is an argument that the law is subjective, that what matters is the mindset of the president not that of an objective person. But let's start with the objective test. Is it not reasonable for the president of a country to use chemical weapons against an invading army that means to take over the country?
A: It was not the intention of the invading army to capture the entire country which is evident since they stopped their invasion once they had occupied their intended target. They remain close to the boarder and occupied an ethnically similar region to their own country. IF they had continued perhaps the attack would have been warranted.
Q: Isn't it also a fact of the case that the country did not have a conventional army at its disposal?
A: They had a conventional army just not to the scale of the invading army, although it is not as if the invading army invaded with their entire force. This invasion was limited to a small region along the border of the invading state.
Q: I want to talk about the necessity issue. How is it that you argue that conventional weapons couldn't have stopped the invading army and that chemical weapons weren't necessary?
A: The president should have made an attempt to petition the UN Security Council or to seek assistance from another international source or ally? They could have attempted an alternative or provided evacuation for the surrounding population. If chemical weapons were the only source then a better effort to protect the citizens would be required.

Q: But that's a separate question. That's a question as to whether it's legal or not. I'm asking you whether it's necessary.

A: I don't think it was necessary.

Q: Given that conventional weapons could not have stop the invasion?

A: The country being invaded could have attempted to negotiate with the invading army or petition the international community before resorting to chemical weapons.

Q: But the country was invaded. The negotiations failed because of the invasion not because of the president's use of chemical weapons. I'm asking you why, when conventional weapons weren't an option, the use of chemical weapons was not a necessity?

A: No just because a country has a small army does not allow them to do atrocious things to "protect their country." The head of state is claiming the only option was to repel the invaders was to poison her own population.. There was no attempt at anything else besides to most extreme method to remove the invaders which is not necessary.

Q: What you're saying is that it was necessary but the necessity has to be proportionate?

A: No it was not necessary and it definitely was not proportionate.

Q: You're admitting that it was necessary.

A: No.

Q: You say that it's an objective test, what a reasonable person might do. What's your source of law for that?

A: I looked it up online.

Q: Please tell us what it said from memory. Just the general argument you don't have to quote it. Why is a subjective test not necessary, but an objective test is? Why must a president be reasonable as opposed to just sincere? You're conceding that the president was sincere but not reasonable?

A: No, I'm saying he was neither.

Q: You're saying the president failed both tests? If the Court were to rule that a subjective test applies you'll have to address that. If the Court rules that an objective test applies you're going to have to say why you think an objective test is the better test; why the law says it must be a reasonable person test rather than a subjective test. You can address this in closing statements.

A: A reasonable person is a hypothetical . . .

Q: That's the definition of a reasonable person, not why it must be an objective test. You can address this in closing statements.

Q: A widespread or systematic attack against a civilian population is the contextual element of crimes against humanity which is covered in Article 7 of the Rome Statute. How is the contextual element met when the president did not intend to attack a civilian population?

A: The long term damage to the region and its population constitutes a crime against humanity. Even if Clinton claims to have not intended to attack civilians she did with the knowledge of the detrimental nature of Chemical X.

Q: Are you arguing that the attack was not on an invading army?

A: No, it intended to halt the invading army. However, its long term effect constitutes an attack on civilians as defined by the ICTR cases. (refer to argument)

Q: Does the UN Charter have a time limit for notification of the Security Council?

A: Under Article 51 of the UN Charter, it states that they don't have to be notified before action is taken but should be made aware as soon as possible.

Q: What is the legal basis for this? There are cases of countries notifying the Security Council that they're acting in self-defense. You can't expect the president, in the midst of an attack, to know every facet of the law can you?

A: His country is signatory to various international treaties that ban the use of Chemical weapons. Ignorance is no excuse.

Q: The Charter says that it is also an "inherent right to self-defense." So that would imply that notification of the Security Council is not absolutely necessary. Isn't that right?

A: What does notifying the UNSC of an armed conflict have to do with breaking the law by employing illegal substances into a region?

Q: So it's just a detail, a formality, informing the Security Council. Is that right?

A: They should be informed so that they may act as a mediator and also provide solutions and aid. Clinton however will never know what resolutions they would have come up with now will she?

Q: With respect to the war crimes charge, Article 8(2) addresses willful killing of the civilian population which implies intent. Is there any evidence that the president intended to kill the civilian population?

A: Her choice to withhold vital information constitutes intent.

Q: But that's negligence, not willfulness. Are you saying that negligence is the legal intent requirement and not intent itself?

A: Can you clarify the question?

Q: So you're saying that the president intended to kill her own civilians?

A: Yes.

Q: So you're not saying that the president used chemical weapons to save her population?

A: No saving them would mean that she acted in a responsible way to insure their safety. She did more harm than good.

Q: Later on I want you to address negligence as opposed to willfulness and objective versus subjective tests.

A: Ok.

Q: (asked in rebuttal): Why is the objective test appropriate?

A: The subjective isn't appropriate for our argument. We will not just take her word. When it comes to the danger to the civilian population the reasonable person test is best. That's why I think an objective test should be used in this case. Does that suffice?

Q: Well you really want the advice of case law on this.

A: Yes

Q (asked in rebuttal): I just have one question, is it reasonable for the president to have evacuated the region ahead of time? Wouldn't that give notice to the invading army of the president's plans to use chemical weapons? Would it not be a valid defense that they needed to keep that a secret?
A: No, the president's main obligation is to protect her civilian population. In this scenario she failed to do this. There are other ways in which the president could have evacuated the region without the invading army knowing about it.

APPENDIX B: Alterable Facts that Students and Faculty Could Adopt to Change the Legal Arguments

Students and faculty can alter the facts so that different legal issues are raised from those presented in this chapter. Were the president's actions intended to interfere with the humanitarian relief or to prevent foreign political monitoring or other interference? Could not the Security Council have handed over the aid, and therefore the violation of sovereignty failed strict scrutiny tests of the least intrusive involvement possible? Was there an intent to destroy part of the population that might have been part of the opposition? Does the government have the capacity to arrest and put opponents into detention camps? Did the government deliberately kill people or seek to destroy them? Were motives or facts of revenge, hatred, the fog of war, and military uncertainty as relevant as claims to an international necessity to protect the population from human and natural disasters?

Factual changes could include:

1. The military junta, led by President and General Xavier Marbur, is an authoritarian regime that assumed power extra-constitutionally, or he is a democratically elected leader whose congress has authorized him commander-in-chief powers.
2. Civil liberties and political rights are available or not protected. Political parties and civic associations are or are not banned. The country has continually scored a "7" ("not free") on the Freedom House scale of political rights and civil liberties, or it has scored a 1 or 2 ('free').
3. Rule of law is weak-to-nonexistent or strong in Marmyan. A culture of impunity exists for those agents of the government who perpetrate human rights violation in Marmyan, or there is occasional accountability of democratic leaders for illegal or criminal acts.
4. The regime represses or tolerates the opposition, United Democratic Front. The conflict can or can does not reflect ethnic differences that are a large or complete base of opposing support for these two political forces. Human rights violations might include, but are not limited to,

arbitrary arrests and detention, extrajudicial killings, and the use of torture. President Marbur has or has not being indicted domestically or internationally for any of these offenses.
5. Human rights conditions in Marmyan result or do not result from a growing political conflict between the UDF and government forces, and the different ethnic groups that form the base of support for each. The conflict has or has not prevented humanitarian aid from reaching the hardest hit area of Marmyan, the Northern region, where a substantial part of the population consists of members of the UDF and the corresponding ethnic groups reside in large or exclusive numbers.
6. The President of Marmyan, Xavier Marbur did or did not obstruct foreign aid from entering the country and did or did not arrest foreign aid workers. That aid was absolutely or partly necessary for the survival of the victims of the 2009 earthquake and was or was not authorized for delivery by foreign aid workers by the United Nations Security Council.
7. The President of Marmyan, Xavier Marbur legally or illegally arrested some or all of the foreign aid workers and forcibly prevented the aid mission from disembarking on Marmyan and delivering the humanitarian aid. Force was or was not used in response to resistance to arrest by the peacekeepers who accompanied the foreign aid mission.
8. President of Marmyan, Xavier Marbur, deliberately withheld extant aid from reaching the hardest hit area of Marmyan, the Northern region, or he attempted to deliver aid to that region, but with little or large success, causing or not causing the deaths or illnesses of small or large parts of the population consists of members of the UDF.
9. In total over ten-thousand, ninety-thousand, or one million Marmyanic civilians died from starvation and disease as a consequence of the lack of access to humanitarian aid, as well as the deaths from the natural disaster initially.
10. The UN Security Council did or did not invoke the Responsibility to Protect norm in its resolution authorizing the foreign aid mission and did or did not invoke Chapter VII authority because of a declared "threat to international peace," and did or did not authorize peacekeeping troops accompanying the aid workers to use "all means necessary" to assure the distribution of humanitarian relief.
11. The humanitarian relief mission authorized by the UNSC pursuant to Chapter VII would or would not have had the capability to save many lives, given their weak or strong or uncertain logistical capabilities and limited or extensive knowledge of the country.
12. The arrest of several members of the UN humanitarian relief mission by armed security forces on the orders of the President of Marmyan, Xavier Marbur occurred before or after the arrival of the UNSC relief mission and was taken in response or not in response to

the mission's refusal to hand over the aid to the Marmyan government, which planned to distribute the aid itself.

13. The President of Marmyan, Xavier Marbur, was or was not accorded all available due process guarantees pursuant to the Rules of Procedure of the Rome Treaty of the International Criminal Court.

Faculty and Students could also modify the facts, such as the following scenario:

1. In October 2011, the nation of Sierra Leone was devastated by a natural disaster. An earthquake affected a large geographical area of the country, with a subsequent tsunami destroying the coastal regions. Following the natural disasters, it was determined that the current President and Vice President were missing. Along with the President and Vice President, 100,000-150,000 citizens of Sierra Leone were reported missing or dead. Immediately following the disaster, the UNSC deployed its first round of aid efforts, comprised of international volunteers.

2. Speaker of Parliament, Abel Stronge, assumed the role of the presidency as the next in the line of succession. Stronge is a known representative of the National Party which is localized on the Northern Coast of Sierra Leone.

3. Determining that the initial efforts would not be enough to fulfill the demands of the suffering citizens of Sierra Leone, the UNSC authorized a larger relief effort to be led by peacekeeping forces. Through an act of force on the part of Abel Stronge, the UNSC aid efforts, which had been ordered and authorized by the UNSC, were forcibly removed from Sierra Leone by armed officers under Stronge's command. As requested by Stronge, the peacekeeping forces left the country leaving the physical aid supplied by the UNSC.

4. In the months following President Stronge's orders to remove the peacekeeping forces, the deaths of Sierra Leone grew to 600,000. A significant amount of these deaths were reported in the Southern region of Sierra Leone, the known residence of supporters for the People's Party of Sierra Leone, opposition to President Stronge.

Notes

1. UN International Law Commission, Protection of Persons in the Event of Disasters: Text of Draft Articles, 1, 2, 3, 4, and 5 as Provisionally Adopted by the Drafting Committee, UN Doc. A/CN.4/L.758 (July 24, 2009), as quoted in J. Benton Heath, "Disasters, Relief, and Neglect: The Duty to Accept Humanitarian Assistance and the Work of the International Law Commission," 43 *NYU J. Int'l L. & Pol.* 419, 424 (2010-2011).

2. "Myanmar: Cyclone Nargis 2008 Facts and Figures," *ReliefWeb*, http://www.reliefweb.int/node/399732 (accessed June 21, 2011).

3. Stuart Ford, "Is the Failure to Respond Appropriately to a Natural Disaster a Crime against Humanity: The Responsibility to Protect and Individual Criminal Responsibility in the Aftermath of Cyclone Nargis," 38 *Denv. J. Int'l L. & Pol'y* 227, 227-228 (2009-2010). Much of Ford's article contains an excellent accounting of the disaster and response of the Myanmar government and international community to the devastation. A great deal of the facts surrounding the crisis Ford gathered from the extensive reporting on the crisis by *New York Times* reporters, in particular, Seth Mydans. See Ford, "Failure," 227-233.

4. "Cyclone Nargis," *New York Times website*, (updated April 30, 2009), http://topics.nytimes.com/topics/news/international/countriesandterritories/myanmar/cyclone_nargis/indes/html (accessed June 21, 2011).

5. "Cyclone Nargis" *New York Times website*. Some of the junta's behavior has been attributed to the criticism leveled against the Myanmar government by President Georgia W. Bush; in particular his focus on the undemocratic nature of the government was believed by some to be "counterproductive." See Seth Mydans and Helene Cooper, "Aid for Myanmar Mobilizes, Mixed with Criticism," *New York Times* (May 7, 2008), www.nytimes.com/2008/05/07/world/asia/07Myanmar.html?ref=cyclonenargis (accessed June 21, 2011).

6. Ford, "Failure," 230-231.

7. Ford, "Failure," 233.

8. Ford, "Failure," 232-233. As Ford discusses the idea for a UNSC Resolution for a humanitarian aid mission was dropped due to the objections of China. "Failure," 233-234.

9. Charter of the United Nations (UN Charter), Art. 2(1) and 2(7) (1945).

10. For the ICISS' position on R2P see ICISS, *The Responsibility to Protect* (Ottawa: International Development Research Center, 2001).

11. United Nations, 2005 World Summit Outcome, Resolution Adopted by the General Assembly, A/60/L.1, September 15, 2005, http://daccess-dds-ny.un.org/doc/UNDOC/GEN/N05/487/60/PDF/N0548760.pdf?OpenElement (accessed November 10, 2010), 30.

12. United Nations, 2005 World Summit Outcome, 30.

13. Jayshree Bajoria, "Libya and the Responsibility to Protect," *Analysis Brief*, Council on Foreign Relations, http://www.cfr.org/libya/libya-responsibility-protect/p24480 (accessed March 24, 2011). The no-fly zone was imposed by UNSC Resolution 1973.

14. United Nations, 2005 World Summit Outcome, 30.

15. Ellary Stowell, *Intervention in International Law*, (Washington, DC: John Bryne & Co., 1921), 51-52, quoted in Luke Glanville, "Ellery Stowell and the Enduring Dilemmas of Humanitarian Intervention," *International Studies Review*, 15 (2011): 242.

16. Glanville, "Ellary Stowell," 249-255; see also Heath on this point, "Disasters," 421-422. Glanville concludes however that, even with these developments, states still face the same dilemmas when it comes intervention. The "imperfect obligation" referred to by Stowell still exists. Only now states tend to cloak their unwillingness to act in the terms of the current R2P discourse. "Ellary Stowell," 255-256.

17. Heath, "Disasters," 430-431; also ICISS, *Responsibility*, §2.29. Glanville, "Ellary Stowell," 251.

18. Heath, "Disasters," 431.

19. *International Convenant on Civil and Political Rights* (ICCPR), Art. 6(1) (966).

20. International Covenant on Economic, Social and Cultural Rights (ICESCR), Arts. 11-12 (1966).

21. *UN Charter*, Arts. 55-56. For his full discussion on other international documents and treaties that concern the obligations of states to care for their populations, see Heath, "Disasters," 437-442.

22. This is the "bottom-up" approach referred to by Heath, "Disaster," 445-446; see also International Federation of Red Cross and Red Crescent Societies, Guidelines for the Domestic Facilitation and Regulation of International Disaster Relief and Initial Recovery Assistance, 30th International Conference, IFRC 301C/07/R4 Annex (November 30, 2007).

23. Institute de Driot International, Annuaire de l'Institute de Droit International 262 (2004) (Bruges Resolution); Heath, "Disaster," 454-455.

24. See for example the Fourth Geneva Convention. Convention (IV) relative to the Protection of Civilian Persons in Time of War, Geneva, August 12, 1949, http://www.icrc.org/ihl.nsf/FULL/380?OpenDocument (accessed June 30, 2011); Heath, "Disaster," 452-458.

25. "Disasters," 469; also 469-477.

26. Ford, "Failure," 265.

27. Malone is clear on the fact that the UN and the UNSC (at this point at least) do not include environmental degradation as falling under the R2P doctrine. However if conditions in a country deteriorate such that they do in fact become a threat to peace and security, this would justify action on the basis of R2P. See Linda A. Malone, "The Responsibility to Protect Haiti," *ASIL Insight* 14, no. 7 (March 10, 2010), http://www.asil.org/insights100310.cfm (accessed November 13, 2010).

28. This has been the response to the argument made by Russian officials that Russian military operations in Georgia in 2008 where conducted in adherence to the R2P doctrine. International Coalition for the Responsibility to Protect, "The Georgia-Russia Crisis and the Responsibility to Protect: Background Note," http://www.globalr2p.org/pdf/related/GeorgiaRussia.pdf (accessed March 24, 2011). For responses to these and other criticisms about R2P, see Evans, Gareth, *Responsibility to Protect: Ending Mass Atrocity Crimes Once and for All* (Washington, DC: Brookings Institution Press, 2008), 55-76.

29. See Bajoria, "Libya."

30. For a thorough discussion of these and other issues related to R2P see B. Welling Hall, ,"International Law and the Responsibility to Protect," in *The International Studies Encyclopedia*, ed. Robert A. Denemark (Blackwell Publishing, 2010), http://www.isacompendium.com/subscriber/tocnode?id=g9781444336597 (accessed November 15, 2010); also Evans, *Responsibility to Protect*.

31. Heath, "Disasters," 434-436.

32. Rome Statute of the International Criminal Court, UN Coc. A/CONF.183/9, Art. 21(a).

33. Rome Statute, Art. 7(1)(b).

34. Rome Statute, Art. 7(1)(h).

35. Rome Statute, Art. 7(1)(a).

36. Rome Statute, Art. 7(1)(k).

37. Rome Statute, Art. 6.

38. Rome Statute, Art. 8(2)(b)(iii).

39. Rome Statute, Art. 8(2)(b)(xxv).

40. Michael Duttwiler, "Liability for Omission in International Criminal Law," 6 *Int'l Crim. L. Rev.* 1, 4-5(2006).

41. Rome Statute, Art. 66(3).

42. This was especially significant for the ICTY in that Art. 5 of the Tribunal's Statute mandated a connection between the crimes against humanity outlined and the Yugoslavian wars of secession. See for example ICTY, *Prosecutor v Tadić,* Case No. IT-94-1-A, Judgment, paras. 249, 251 (July 15, 1999); ICTY, *Prosecutor v. Krnojelac*, Case No. IT-97-25-T, Judgment, para. 53 (March 15, 2002).

43. ICTY, *Prosecutor v Tadić,* Case No. IT-94-1-T, Opinion and Judgment, para.644 (May 7, 1997).

44. ICTY, *Prosecutor v Kunarac et. al.*, Case No. IT-96-23/1-A, Judgment, para. 85 (June 12, 2002).

45. Rome Statute, Art. 7(2)(a).

46. ICTY, *Prosecutor v. Kunarac et. al.*, Case No. IT-96-23-T; IT-96-23-/1-T, para. 416 (February 22, 2001) .

47. ICTR, *Prosecutor v. Akayesu*, Case No. ICTR-96-4-T, Judgment, para. 581 (September 2, 1998) ; see also ICTR, *Prosecutor v. Kayishema*, Case No. ICTR-95-1-T, Judgment, para. 122 (May 21, 1999).

48. ICTR, *Prosecutor v. Rutaganda*, Case No. ICTR-96-3-T, Judgment, para. 72 (December 6, 1999); ICTR, *Kayishema, Trial Judgment*, para 128; see also ICTY, Prosecutor v. *Blaškić*, Case No. IT-95-14-T, Judgment, para. 214 (March 3, 2000).

49. Ford's discussion regarding the applicability of crimes against humanity to Myanmar is also informative. Ford, "Failure," 241-261.

50. Rome Statute, Art. 7(2)(b).

51. Rome Statute, Art. 2(b) and 2(c),(e).

52. See Rome Statute, Art. 8(2)(b)(iii) which is applicable to international conflicts and (2)(e)(iii) which applies to intrastate conflicts. Of course issues arise in this case as to whether or not the arrest of aid workers constitutes an "attack" in the first place; moreover if it is found to be the case that an armed conflict did not occur, whether or not the aid workers had protected status.

53. Rome Statute, Art. 30.

54. Although in Article 30(3) of the Rome Statute, "knowledge" refers to types one and two described above.

55. For his full discussion see Antonio Cassese, *International Criminal Law*, 2d ed. (Oxford: Oxford University Press, 2008), 61-65.

56. Cassese, *International Criminal Law*, 70.

57. Rome Statute, Art. 8(2)(b)(v).

58. Cassese, *International Criminal Law*, 73-74; 93-94. For an opposing view see Werle, *Principles*, 153-155.

59. Werle, *Principles*, 143-146.

60. Ford, "Failure," 246.

61. ICTY, *Prosecutor v. Kristić*, Case No, IT-98-33-T, Judgment, para. 503 (August 2, 2001).

62. ICTY, *Kristić,* Trial Judgment, para. 500.

63. As the Appeals Court ruled in *Tadić*: this discriminatory intent is "an indispensible legal ingredient . . . with regard to . . . various types of persecution"). ICTY, *Prosecutor v Tadić,* Appeals Judgment, para. 305 (July 15, 1999); see also *Blaškić*, Trial Judgment, para 235; ICTY, *Prosecutor v. Kordić and Čerkez,* Case No. IT-95-14/2-T, Judgment, para. 212 (February 26, 2001); ICTY, *Prosecutor v. Stakić*, Case No. IT-97-24-T, Judgment, para. 737 (July 31, 2003).

64. ICTY, *Kordić and Čerkez,* Trial Judgment, para. 212.

65. ICTY, *Kordić and Čerkez,* Trial Judgment, para. 212; see also ICTY, *Prosecutor v. Krnojelac*, Case No IT-97-25-T, Judgment, para. 435 (March 15, 2002).

66. ICTY, *Blaškić*, Trial Judgment, para 244; *Kordić and Čerkez*, Trial Judgment, para. 212.

67. ICTY, *Kupreškić et. al.* Case No. IT-95-16-T, Judgment, paras. 615, 622; ICTY, ICTY, *Prosecutor v. Krnojelac*, Case No IT-97-25-T, Judgmemt, para. 434 (March 15, 2002).

68. ICTY, *Tadić*, Trial Judgment, para. 717; ICTY, *Blaškić*, Trial Judgment para. 234.

69. ICTY, *Kupreškić et. al.*, Trial Judgment, para. 621.

70. Rome Statute, Articles 55, 67. More generally rights of the accused are found throughout the entire treaty. Instructors should also make students cognizant of other conventions that address these rights; in particular the ICCPR.

71. Werle, *Principles*, 142.

72. This is a distinction made by Cassese in *International Criminal Law*, 255.

73. Cassese, *International Criminal Law*, 255-301; also Werle, *Principles*, 197-227.

74. Cassese, *International Criminal Law*, 36.

75. And only crimes against peace. On this point see Cassese, *International Criminal Law*, 105.

76. Gerhard Werle, *Principles of International Criminal Law*, 2d edition (The Hague: T-M-C-Asser Press, 2009), 142.

77 Werle, *Principles*, 142.

78. "Preamble," The Declaration on Principles of International Law Concerning Friendly Relations and Co-operation among States in Accordance with the Charter of the United Nations, Resolution adopted by the General Assembly, 26/25 XXV, October 24. 1970.

79. L'Institute de Driot International, Annuaire de l'Institute de Droit International 262 (2004) (*Bruges Resolution*).

80. "Guiding Principles," Strengthening of the Coordination of Humanitarian Emergency Assistance of the United Nations, §4, 78th plenary meeting, UN Doc. A/RES/46/182 (December 19, 1991); this notion of primary state responsibility is also enshrined in International Federation of the Red Cross and Red Crescent Societies, *Guidelines for the Domestic facilitation and Regulation of International Disaster Relief and Initial Recovery* Assistance, 30th International Conference, IFRC 301C/07/R4 (November 30, 2007).

81. "Guiding Principles," §5.

82. *Military and Paramilitary Activities in and Against Nicaragua (Nicaragua v. United States of America)* 1986 ICJ 14 §242; see also J. Benton Heath discussion of *Nicaragua* in "Disasters, Relief, and Neglect: The Duty to Accept Humanitarian Assistance and the Work of the International Law Commission," *New York University Journal of International Law and Politics*, 43 (2010-2011): 465-466.

83. *Nicaragua v. the United States*, §242.

84. Charter of the United Nations (UN Charter), Art. 2(1) and 2(7) (1945), http://treaties.un.org/doc/Publication/CTC/uncharter-all-lang.pdf (accessed August 15, 2011).

85. Eduardo Valencia-Ospina, Special Rapporteur on Protection of Persons in the Event of Disasters, "Speech to the International Law Commission" (July 10, 2009); see also Heath p. 423.

86 Human Rights Watch, "MONUC: A Case for Peacekeeping Reform," February 28, 2005, http://www.hrw.org/en/news/2005/02/28/Monuc_case_peacekeeping_reform (accessed August 13, 2011).

87. José. E. Alvarez, "The Schizophrenias of R2P," *ASIL Newsletter: Notes from the President*, 23, no. 3 (Summer 2007), www.asil.org/newsletter/president/pres070927.html (accessed August 13, 2011).

88. United Nations, 2005 World Summit Outcome, Resolution, A/60/L.1, September 15, 2005.

89. Michael Duttwiler, "Liability for Omission in International Criminal Law," *International Criminal Law Review*, 6 (2006): 4-5.

90. International Criminal Tribunal for Rwanda, *Prosecutor v. Akayesu*, Case No, ICTR-96-4-T (September 2, 1998) Judgment, para. 498.

91. Werle, *Principles*, 141.

92. International Criminal Tribunal for Rwanda (ICTR), *Akayesu*, paras. 123-128; also the recent decision in *Prosecutor v. Seromba*, ICTR-01-66-A, Judgment, para 176 (March 12, 2008) and ICTR-01-66-T, Judgment, para 320 (December 13, 2006); see also ICTR judgments in *Prosecutor v. Nahima et al.*, Case No. ICTR-99-52-A, para 524 (November 28, 2007); *Prosecutor v. Rutaganda*, Case No, ICTR-96-3-A, Judgment, para 525 (May 26, 2003). For similar opinions expressed by the International Criminal Tribunal for the Former Yugoslavia (ICTY), see *Prosecutor v. Kristić*, Case No, IT-98-33-A, Judgment, para 34 (April 19, 2004) and *Prosecutor v. Jelisíć*, Case No, IT-95-10-A, Judgment para 47 (July 5, 2001).

93. ICTR, *Seromba*, para. 176.

94. ICTR, *Akayesu*, para. 129; for a similar opinion see ICTY, *Kristić*, para 37.

95. ICTY, *Prosecutor v. Kunarac*, Case No. IT-96-23/1-A, Judgment, para. 99 (June 12, 2002).

96. ICTY, Prosecutor v. *Blaškić*, Case No. IT-95-14-A, Judgment, para. 120 (July 29, 2004).

97. ICTY, Prosecutor v. *Blaškić*, Case No. IT-95-14-T, Judgment para. 244 (March 3, 2000); *Prosecutor v. Kordić and Čerkez*, Case No. IT-95-14/2-T, Judgment, paras. 212, 217 (February 26, 2001).

98. ICTY, *Prosecutor v. Vasilijević*, Case No. IT-98-32-T Judgment para. 249 (November 29, 2002).

99. See also "Rule 21 Assignment of Legal Counsel," Rules of Procedure and Evidence, ICC—ASP/1/3, Adopted by the Assembly of States Parties, First session, New York, September 3-10, 2002.

100. Charter of the United Nations (UN Charter), Art. 39, San Francisco, June 26, 1945.

101. UN Charter, Art. 25.

102. United Nations, 2005 World Summit Outcome Resolution, Adopted by the General Assembly, A/60/L.1, September 15, 2005.

103. J. Benton Heath, "Disasters, Relief, and Neglect: The Duty to Accept Humanitarian Assistance and the Work of the International Law Commission," 43 *NYU J. Int'l L. & Pol.* 419, 465 (2010-2011) quoting Hugo Grotius, *De Jure Belli Ac Pagis Libre Tres*, James Brown Scott ed., Francis Kelsey translator (Carnegie Endowment for International Peace, 1925), 582.

104. UN Security Council (UNSC), "On Authorization to form a Multilateral Force under Unified Command and Control to Restore the Legitimately elected President and Authorities of the Government of Haiti and Extension of the Mandate of the UN Mission in Haiti," S/RES.940 (July 31, 1994).

105. UNSC, "On the Adjustment of the Mandate of the UN Assistance Mission for Rwanda due to the Current Situation in Rwanda and Settlement of the Rwandan Conflict," S/RES/912 (April 21, 1994); UNSC, "The Situation Concerning the Democratic

Republic of the Congo," S/RES/1925 (May 28, 2010); UNSC, "Extension of Mandate for African Union-United Nations Hybrid Operations in Darfur (UNAMID)," S/RES/2003 (July 29, 2011). All of these resolutions build on earlier UNSC resolutions.

106.· International Law Commission, Draft Articles 6, 7, 8, and 9 Provisionally Adopted by the Drafting Committee on 6, 7 and 8 July 2010, A/CN.4/L.776 (accessed August 15, 2011).

107.· L'Institute de Driot International, Annuaire de l'Institute de Droit International, Article 3(1), (2004) (*Bruges Resolution*).

108.· *Bruges Resolution*, Art. 7.

109.· *Bruges Resolution*, Art. 8

110. *Bruges Resolution*, Art. 9.

111. Antonio Cassese, *International Criminal Law*, 2d ed. (Oxford: Oxford University Press, 2008), 33.

112. Cassese, International Criminal Law, 33.

113. Gerhard Werle, *Principles of International Criminal Law* (The Hague: TMC/Asser Press, 2009), 31; see also on this point Otto Triffterer, "Preamble," in *Commentary of the Rome Statute of the International Court*, ed. Otto Triffterer, 2d ed. (Oxford: Hart Publishing, 2008).

114. Werle, *Principles*, 46; see also Theodor Meron, *War Crimes Law Comes of Age: Essays* (Oxford University Press, 1999).

115. For his full discussion see Werle, *Principles*, 48-62.

116. Werle, *Principles*, 141.

117. Convention on the Prevention and Punishment of the Crime of Genocide (UNGC), (1948), tp://treaties.un.org/doc/Treaties/1951/01/19510112%2008-12%20PM /Ch_IV_1p.pdf.

118. William Schabas, *Genocide in International Law: The Crime of Crimes*, 2d edition (Cambridge, UK: Cambridge University Press, 2009), 270. Of course these components are found in Article 2 of the UNGC.

119. Samuel Totten and William S. Parsons eds., *Century of Genocide: Critical Essays and Eyewitness Accounts*, 3d ed. (New York: Routledge, 2009); Robert Melson, *Revolution and Genocide: On the Origins of the Armenian Genocide and the Holocaust*, (Chicago: Chicago University Press, 1992); Craig Etheson, *After the Killing Fields: Lessons from the Cambodian Genocide* (Praeger, 2005). Samantha Power, *A Problem from Hell: America and the Age of Genocide* (New York: HarperPerennial 2003), pp. 88, 90. See Susan E. Cook, *Genocide in Cambodia and Rwanda: New Perspectives* (Transaction Publishers, 2005); H. Jarvis and T. Fawthrop, *Getting Away with Genocide: Cambodia's Long Struggle against the Khmer Rouge* (London; Ann Arbor, MI: Pluto Press, 2004).

120. Law on the Establishment of the Extraordinary Chambers in the Courts of Cambodia for the Prosecution of Crimes Committed During the Period of Democratic Kampuchea, available at http://www.eccc.gov.kh.

121. Schabas, *Genocide*, 424-425; also Werle, *Principles*, 261, 263-264.

122. ICTY, *Prosecutor v. Mucić et al* (IT-96-21), Judgment (November 16, 1998), ICTY, *Prosecutor v. Krnojelac*, Case No IT-97-25-T, Judgment (March 15, 2002), ICTY, *Prosecutor v. Aleksovski*, Case No. IT-95-14/1), Judgment (June 25, 1999).

123.· Cassese, *International Criminal Law*, 141.

124. International Criminal Tribunal for Rwanda (ICTR), *Prosecutor v. Akayesu*, Case No, ICTR-96-4-T, Judgment, para. 523 (September 28, 1998).

125. ICTY, *Prosecutor v. Kristić*, Case No IT-98-33-T, Judgment, paras. 593-7 (August 2, 2001) as cited in Cassese *International Criminal Law*, 142.

126. ICTY, *Prosecutor v Tadić*, Case No. IT-94-1-T, Opinion and Judgment, paras 646-48 (May 7, 1997) and Appeals Judgment, para. 248 (July 15, 1999); ICTY, *Prosecutor v. Kunarac*, Case No. IT-96-23/1-A, Judgment, para. 93 (June 12, 2002).

127. ICTR, *Akayesu*, Trial Judgment, para 580.

128. ICTY, *Tadić*, Trial Judgment, para. 648.

129. ICTY, *Tadić*, Trial Judgment, paras. 653, also ICTY, *Prosecutor v. Kupreškić et al.* Case No. IT-95-16-T, Judgment, paras. 551 (January 14, 2000).

130. ICTY, *Prosecutor v. Jelisíć*, Case No, IT-95-10-T, Judgment, para. 53 (December 14, 1999).

131. ICTY, Prosecutor v. *Blaškić*, Case No. IT-95-14-T, Judgment, para. 207, (March 3, 2000). See also Werle on this point, *Principles*, 299.

132. Werle, *Principles*, 29.

133. ICTY, *Kunarac et al.*, Appellate Judgment, paras. 85, 92.

134. ICTY, *Jelisíć*, Trial Judgment, para. 54.

135. ICTY, *Tadić*, Trial Judgment, para 643.

136. ICTY, *Tadić*, Trial Judgment, para 643; ICTR, *Prosecutor v. Rutaganda*, Case No ICTR-96-3-T, Judgment, para. 73 (December 6, 1999); *Akayesu*, Trial Judgment, paras 582.

137. ICTY, *Tadić*, Trial Judgment paras. 694, 704.

138. International Covenant on Economic, Social and Cultural Rights (ICESCR), December 16, 1966, http://treaties.un.org/doc/Treaties/1976/01/19760103%2009-57%20PM/Ch_IV_03.pdf (accessed August 3, 2011); see also *International Convenanon Civil and Political* Rights (ICCPR), Art. 6(1), New York, December 16, 1966, http://treaties.un.org/doc/Treaties/1976/03/19760323%2006-17%20AM/Ch_IV_4p.pdf (accessed July 6, 2011).

139. ICTY, *Kupreškić et. al.* Trial Judgment, para 621.

140. For his full discussion see Cassese, *International Criminal Law*, 61-65.

141. Stuart Ford, "Is the Failure to Respond Appropriately to a Natural Disaster a Crime against Humanity: The Responsibility to Protect and Individual Criminal Responsibility in the Aftermath of Cyclone Nargis," 38 *Denv. J. Int'l L. & Pol'y* 227, 245 (2009-2010); for Ford's full in-depth discussion on extermination and inhumane acts see "Failure," 246-250.

142. ICTY, *Prosecutor v Tadić*, Case No. IT-94-1-A, Judgment, para. 305 (July 15, 1999); see also ICTY, *Prosecutor v. Blaškić*, Case No. IT-95-14-T, Judgment, para. 244 (March 3, 2000); ICTY, *Prosecutor v. Kordić and Čerkez*, Case No. IT-95-14/2-T, Judgment, para 212 (February 26, 2001).

143. ICTY, *Prosecutor v. Krnojelac*, Case No IT-97-25-T, Judgment, para. 435 (March 15, 2002): *Kordić and Čerkez*, Trial Judgment, para 217.

144. ICTY, *Prosecutor* v *Naletilić & Martinović*, Case No IT-98-34-T, Judgment, para. 636 (March 31, 2003).

145. Cassese *International Criminal Law*, 82-83.

146. Werle, *Principles of International Law*, 1st ed. (The Hague: T-M-C Asser Press, 2005), 291. Werle is citing to Knut Ipsen in Knut Ipsen, *Völkerrecht*, 5th ed. (2004), Section 67, marginal 5.

147. Werle, *Principles*, 1st ed., 290. He notes that this applied to Latin American states during World War II, which declared war on the Axis powers, but were not involved in hostilities.

148. Werle, *Principles*, 1st ed., 287-288.

149. Cassese, *International Criminal Law*, 88-92.

150. Convention (I) for the Amelioration of the Condition of the Wounded and Sick in Armed Forces in the Field, Geneva, August 12,1949, http://www.icrc.org; Convention (II) for the Amelioration of the Condition of Wounded, Sick and Shipwrecked Members of Armed Forces at Sea, Geneva, August 12, 1949, http://www.icrc.org; Convention (III) relative to the Treatment of Prisoners of War. Geneva, August 12, 1949, http://www.icrc.org/ihl.nsf/FULL/375?OpenDocument; Convention (IV) relative to the Protection of Civilian Persons in Time of War, Geneva, August 12, 1949, http://www.icrc.org/ihl.nsf/FULL/380?OpenDocument; Protocol Additional to the Geneva Conventions of 12 August 1949, and relating to the Protection of Victims of International Armed Conflicts (Protocol I), Geneva, June 8, 1977, http://www.icrc .org/ihl.nsf/FULL/470?OpenDocument; Protocol Additional to the Geneva Conventions of 12 August 1949, and relating to the Protection of Victims of Non-International Armed Conflicts (Protocol II), Art. 4(2), June 8, 1977, http://www.icrc.org/ihl.nsf/FULL /475?OpenDocument.

151. 1998 Rome Statute of the ICC (Rome Statute), Art. 12 (1).

152. ICTY, *Prosecutor v. Thomer Blaškić,* Case No. IT-95-14-A, Appeals Judgment.

153. ICTY, *Prosecutor v. Mucić*, Note 640. IT-96-21-A.

154. 1998 Rome Statute.

155. Statute of the International Court of Justice, Art. 38(1).

156. ASIL. http://www.asil.org/insight128.cfm.

157. ICTY, *Prosecutor v. Tadic*, IT-94-1, Note 262.

158. ICTY, *Tadic,* Trial judgment, 43.

159. J. Crawford and M. Koskenniemi ed., *The Cambridge Companion to International Law,* (2012). New York: Cambridge University Press, p. 132.

160. Crawford and Koskenniemi, Citing *Oil Platforms,* ICJ Reports 2003, 161, Para. 73.

161. UN S/Res/2098, April, 2013.

162. http://amicc.blogspot.com/2013/04/new-un-security-council-resolution.html.

163. "The Evolution of UN Peacekeeping" http://pbpu.unlb.org.

164. "Evolution," 19.

165. "Evolution," 33.

166. Susan V. Scott, *International Law in World Politics: An Introduction* (CO: Lynne Rienner Publishers, 2010), 33.

167. Scott; *Mucić*; and Rome Statute.

168. "Evolution."

169. L. A. Malone, "Green Helmets: A Conceptual Framework for Security Council Authority in Environmental Emergencies,"17 *Mich. J. Int'l L* 515, 522 (1996). Citing Szasz, Paul C., "Restructuring the International Organizational Framework in Environmental Change and International Law."

170. UNSC Res. 1529 (2004, Haiti, and successive resolutions for the next six years) and UNSC Res. 733 (1992, Somalia, and successive resolutions for the next twenty years).

171. Int'l Comm'n on Intervention and State Sovereignty (ICISS).

172. ICISS. See also W. Magnusson, 43 *Vand. J. Transnati'l L.* 255, 273 (2010).

173. "The Evolution."

174. MINUSTAH: UN Stabilization Mission in Haiti. http://www.un.org.

175. http://www.un.org/en/peacekeeping/missions/past/unmihbackgr2.html#three.

176. http://www.un.org/en/peacekeeping/missions/past/unmihbackgr2.html#three.

177. http://www.un.org/en/peacekeeping/missions/past/unmihbackgr2.html#three, 1.

178. http://www.un.org/en/peacekeeping/missions/past/unmihbackgr2.html#three.

179. S/RES/940 (1994).

180. Jean-Pierre Fonteyne, "The Customary International Law Doctrine of Humanitarian Intervention: Its Current Validity under the UN Charter."4 *Cal.W.Int'L.J.* 203, 204 (1974).

181. Bruges Resolution, 2003.

182. Geneva Conventions Additional Protocol II, Art. 14; ICRC.

183. UNSC Res. 1529 (2004, Haiti, and successive resolutions for the next six years) and UNSC Res. 733 (1992, Somalia, and successive resolutions for the next twenty years).

184. IIHL Manual on the Law of Non-international Armed Conflict with Commentary Ch. 1.1.1.a.

185. IIHL Manual Ch.1.1.1.b.4

186. The Secretary-General, Report of the Security-General's High-level Panel on Threats, Challenges and Change, A More Secure World: Our Shared Responsibility, pp. 2-3, delivered to the General Assembly, UN Doc. A/59/565 (Dec. 2, 2004), available at http://www.un.org/secureworld/report2.pdf.

187. Scott (2010).

188. M. Payandeh, "With Great Power Comes Great Responsibility? The Concept of the Responsibility To Protect Within the Process of International Lawmaking," 35 *Yale J. Int'l L.* 469,(2010), Citing the 1970 Friendly Relations Declaration of the G.A. and G.A. Res. 2625 (XXV), UN Doc; and A/RES/8082 (Oct. 24, 1970).

189. See also ICISS.

190. UN, 2005 World Summit Outcome Resolution, Adopted by the General Assembly, A/60/L.1, September 15, 2005.

191. ICISS, "The Commission's Report." http://responsibilitytoprotect.org (2001).

192. U.N., G.A. A/60/1.

193. ICISS (2001), "The Commission's Report."

194. M. Payandeh (2010), p. 498.

195. UN S/Res/2098, April, 2013.

196. Bruges Resolution 2003 III (1) and (3).

197. A/64/84-E/2009/87 para. 23, Report of UN Secretary-General.

198. *Corfu Channel Case*, Corfu Channel Case/United Kingdom and Northern Ireland v. Albania, Judgment of 9 April 1949, ICJ Reports 1949, p.2.

199. U. N.G.A. Res. 46/182 with Annex attached (1991).

200. UN International Law Commission, Fourth Report on the protection of persons in the event of disasters by Valencia-Ospina, Eduardo, Special Rapporteur (2011).

201. ICTY, *Prosecutor v. Blaskic,* Case No. IT-95-14-T, Judgment of 3 March 2000, §180.

202. ICTY *Prosecutor v. Krstić*, IT-98-33-A.

203. *Krstić.*

204. *Krstić.*

205. Rome Statute.

206. Rome Statute.

207. Rome Statute.

208. Rome Statute, Art. 7.

209. *Blaškic,* Appeals Judgment, Para. 101.

210. *Blaškic.*

211. ICTY, *Prosecutor v. Dragoljub Kunarac, Radomir Kova, and Zoran Vukovi,* Case No. IT-96-23 & IT-96-23/1A, 12 June 2002.

212. *Blaškić*, Note 66, at Para. 101.
213. *Blaškić*, Appeals Judgment.
214. *Blaškić*.
215. *Blaškić*.
216. *Kunarac*, Appeals Judgment.
217. *Blaškić*, Para. 110-113.
218. *Blaškić*.
219. *Blaškić* Note 15.
220. *Blaškić*.
221. *Blaškić*, Para. 105. *Kunarac*, Appeals Judgment.
222. *Blaškić*, Para. 124-126.
223. Rome Statute, Art. 7(2)(b).
224. Rome Statute, Art. 7(2)(g).
225. *Blaškić*, Para. 163-166.
226. Rome Statute, Art. 7(1)(k).
227. Antonio Cassese, *International Criminal Law, 2d Ed.* (Oxford: Oxford University Press, 2008).
228. Rome Statute, Art. 8(1); (2)(a)(i) and (2)(a)(iii).
229. Cassese, *International Criminal Law*.

Chapter 5

The Necessity Defense to the Criminal Use of Chemical Weapons: Prosecutor versus the Head of State, Post-War Country

With Stephanie Wolfe, Dave Benjamin, and Rick Crawford

The case addressed in this section is a hypothetical case before the International Criminal Court (ICC) involving the use of chemical weapons by the Head of State of a post-war country. Although this case does not specifically address the Responsibility to Protect (R2P) doctrine, the actions of the Head of State in this case would certainly warrant its application. The topic discussed in this section is relevant to any scenario where leaders allegedly utilize illegal weapons of mass destruction, perhaps under the "fog of war," or aggressively, such as Bashir al-Assad's alleged chemical attacks on civilians, or Saddam Hussein's purportedly defensive use of chemical weapons against the Kurdish population of Iraq in response to rebellious activity in the Kurdish region of the country. The al-Anfal campaign, which also included deportations and disappearances, resulted in the deaths of tens of thousands of Kurds.[1] The accused—a group which included former Iraqi President Saddam Hussein—were tried by the Iraqi High Tribunal between 2006 and 2007. Schabas writes: "The judgment, issued on 24 June 2007, confirmed that genocide was committed in Iraq by Saddam Hussein and his colleagues. Three of the six defendants [Saddam Hussein was not included as he had by now been executed] were sentenced to death for genocide, two others to life imprisonment, and one was acquitted."[2] Of course it is important to remember that the scenario depicted in the third case is not hypothetical. Saddam Hussein used these weapons as the Iranian army approached Iraq in war between the two countries. On August 21, 2013, the Government of Syria attacked and killed over a thousand civilians in a Damascus suburb in a civil war with armed support from Iran and Russia to the regime and covert U.S. and Saudi support to the armed opposition, along with al-Qaeda linked groups. These two perpetrators regarded themselves as under siege from foreign elements.

The defense would argue that any chemical weapons attack was against the invading army, not the civilians; that their use was necessary; and that it was both proportionate and discriminatory enough to be legal. The prosecution would reject the necessity defense but, if the Court were to accept it, then it would also argue that the chemical weapons were used indiscriminately and disproportionately, killing many more civilians and soldiers than necessary to stop the illegal invasion. The normal burden of proof is on the prosecution, but the burden of proof shifts to the defendant if he invokes necessity. The facts of the case are ambiguous enough to allow counter-factual speculations about whether or not the invasion, which was stopped, could have been halted using conventional defensive techniques.

Regarding proportionality, the Head of State may or may not have used too many chemical weapons. The judge must decide whether an objective test of the mental element is legally required, and, if so whether it would have been reasonable for the Head of State to know this was excessive in its short and long-term impacts. Prosecutors would cite the need for an objective legal test in deciding what would be reasonable. Since a crime has allegedly been committed, there would not be the deference for administrative decisions that accompany a subjective test of intention. With a subjective test, the Head of State merely has to show that his intent was sincere. The Head of State is arguably responsible in the short term for not providing warning and aid in anticipation of the use of chemical weapons and could be indicted in the long run for not continuing to provide care and concern for the affected population. The judge could rule on appeal that the conviction is struck down in part but not in whole. The necessity defense could be sustained, but the judge could find that the level of chemical weapons used was excessive (more were used than were needed to repel the attack) or that they were used without taking reasonable steps to protect civilians and soldiers by providing them ways to safety.

Facts of the Case

The Post-War Country is a small developing country with an annual per capita Gross Domestic Product of 1,280 U.S. dollars. The Post-War Country's chief source of revenue is natural gas. Over the past decade the country has been increasingly threatened by a neighboring country which has its sights set on annexing the Post-War Country in an effort to gain control of the latter's natural gas resources. The Neighboring Country therefore clearly posed a national security threat to the well-being of the Post-War Country. After a failed series of negotiations between the two countries, the army of the Neighboring Country invaded the country of the Post-War Country in August 2006, a clear violation of Article 2(4) of the UN Charter.[3]

The Head of State's choice to use chemical weapons was as a last resort intended to resolve a national security problem. The difference between this case and the Iraqi case rests chiefly with the fact that in the latter, prohibited weapons were used as a means to destroy, or at the very least, severely weaken an ethnic group. The national security threat in the present case was an invading army that was threatening resources crucial to the economic survival of an already impoverished country. It is worth noting that these resources *did not* include water.

The Head of State contends that he did not anticipate substantial injury to the civilian population as a consequence of the use of these weapons. The chemical material he employed for the attack was a poisonous herbicide banned by the Convention on the Prohibition of the Development, Production, Stockpiling and Use of Chemical Weapons and on Their Destruction of 13 January 1993 (CWC) and widely known for its long-term negative impact on both humans and plant-life, particularly when spread through the air. The means by which the herbicide was deployed was military aircraft. The weapon was delivered over the area specifically occupied by the invading army from Neighboring Country.

The use of chemical weapons against the Neighboring Country ended once the Head of State achieved his military objective: retreat of the invading forces. The use of chemical weapons was therefore isolated and limited; they were used between August 14 and 15, 2006. The defendant Head of State contends that he had no knowledge of the harm that would be caused by the herbicide. Therefore, civilians were not forewarned of the impending attack. It is important to point out here that the population of the region in question has a long history of government opposition. As a consequence of the use of the chemical weapons in question, thousands were killed. Thousands more were forced from their homes with many unable to return as a consequence of the damage done to the ecosystem by the weapons used.

Students will discover that another issue concerns the Head of State's efforts (or lack thereof) to prevent civilians from re-entering the effected region after the attack. However, the Head of State did make efforts to ensure for their well-being through the provision of medical assistance after their injuries became known to him. These injuries immediately included loss of consciousness, skin maladies, general physical weakness, and lethargy. If left untreated exposure to the herbicide could lead to organ failure, sterilization, and death.

Moreover, the use of the herbicide by the Government of the Post-War Country seriously damaged crop land and livestock in the affected areas. These areas included the initial target location and soon extended to other portions of the country. The effected land was deemed unfit for crop production until 2012. This consequently had a deleterious impact on the country's ability to feed its population.

Lastly, the Post-War Country is a party to the CWC, as well as a State Party to the Rome Statute of the ICC.

The use of chemical weapons by the Head of State was deemed unnecessary and disproportionate to the threat posed by the invading army of the Neighboring State. The Head of State was convicted by the Trial Chamber of this Moot International Criminal Court of crimes against humanity and war crimes pursuant to Articles 7 and 8 of the Rome Statute; specifically Articles 7(1)(a) ("murder") and 7(1)(k) ("inhumane acts"); and Articles 8(2)(a)(iii) ("Willfully causing great suffering"); 8(2)(a)(iv) ("Extensive destruction . . . of property, not justified by military necessity"); 8(2)(b)(i) ("Intentionally directing attacks against the civilian population"); 8(2)(b)(iv) ("Intentionally launching an attack in the knowledge that such attack will cause incidental loss of life or injury to civilians or damage to civilian objects or widespread, long-term and severe damage to the natural environment"); 8(2)(b)(v) ("Attacking or bombarding . . . towns, villages, dwellings or buildings which are undefended and which are not military objectives"); and 8(2)(b)(xviii) ("Employing asphyxiating, poisonous or other gases, and all analogous liquids, materials or devices").

Legal Matters and Other Issues for Discussion

The case in question is an international armed conflict, not an intrastate war. If they so decide, students may change the present case to an intrastate conflict, along the lines of the Iraq example mentioned above. It will be useful for instructors to discuss with their students the international law applicable to intrastate conflicts, including Common Article 3 of the four Geneva Conventions of 1949 and, of course, the ICC Statute Articles 8(c) through (f).[4] Moreover, students should be made aware of the problems associated with Article 8 of the ICC Statute covering internal conflicts. For instance, to fall under the jurisdiction of the ICC must internal conflicts always be "protracted"? How long does a conflict have to persist before it can be categorized as "protracted"?[5] In any event, in the present case the contextual element of the war crimes charges is not debated by the parties. Everyone acknowledges that conflict occurred during the period in question.

The prohibition of the use of chemical weapons will introduce students to prohibitions regarding the means of warfare, which include the use of biological weapons, poisons, bacterial weapons, and so forth. An interesting topic for debate and discussion in the classroom is whether or not the ban on chemical weapons falls under the jurisdiction of the ICC in the first place; in particular once Articles 8(2)(b)(xviii) (with which the Defendant is charged) and 8(2)(b)(xx) are taken into account.[6] Is this a valid point that can be raised by the Head of State? To address the vagueness of the ICC on this issue, Werle suggests a two-step approach: first "examine whether a prohibition exists in . . . customary international law or an international treaty" and secondly determine "whether the violation of such a prohibition is criminal under customary law."[7]

The point has been made by legal scholars that the ban on chemical weapons is deeply embedded in customary international law, including the Geneva Protocol of 1925 and the Chemical Weapons Convention.[8] As Werle states: "there is no doubt as to the validity of [this] primary norm [step one]"[9] on prohibition, or for that matter, the second issue of criminal liability. Moreover, students should be aware that Article 8(2)(b) of the ICC Statute provides for the prohibition of "other serious violations of the laws and customs applicable in international armed conflict, within the established framework of international law,"[10] which, of course, includes customary law.

Moreover, chemical weapons are by their very nature indiscriminate in their application. They can harm a population directly or indirectly by their harm to the environment. Protection of civilians and soldiers during armed conflict is derived from international humanitarian law treaties, including all four 1949 Geneva Conventions and their two 1977 Protocols, and the Hague Conventions of 1899 and 1907.[11] In demonstrating the material element of the war crimes charges, the Prosecution/Applicant argues that the Defendant used prohibited means of warfare in violation of a number provisions of Article 8, including "Intentionally launching an attack in the knowledge that such attack will cause incidental loss of life or injury attacks against civilian objects," and "Willfully causing great suffering or serious injury to body or health."[12] Violations of Article 8(1)(a) of the ICC Statute are those which constitute "grave breaches" of the four Geneva Conventions.[13]

One of the primary challenges with which the prosecution will have to contend is the mental requirement of "intent and knowledge" laid out in Article 30(2) of the ICC Statute: "For the purposes of this article, a person has intent where: (a) In relation to conduct, that person means to engage in the conduct; (b) In relation to a consequence, that person means to cause that consequence or is aware that it will occur in the ordinary course of events."[14]

Instructors should use this case to discuss issues associated with "knowledge."[15] Must the perpetrator have had full knowledge of the consequences of the act? In other words, did the Head of State of the Post-War Country realize the short and long-term impact the government's use of chemical weapons would have on the civilian population? Students can discuss whether or not it is reasonable to conclude that the Head of State, as head of a country that is a signatory to the CWC, would *not know* that his use of chemical weapons—no matter how isolated—would have a deleterious impact on the people of his country? Or for that matter, whether or not he knew or should have known that the weapons would also target persons protected by international humanitarian law, not to mention Article 8(2)(a) of the ICC Statute? An objective test of knowledge would be based on what a "reasonable person" or a "reasonable Head of State" would have or should have known. However, the law is ambiguous, and a case can be argued that the mental element should be understood from a subjective legal test: what the defendant actually knew. If the latter argument prevails, all that has to be shown is that the defendant did not know and did not willfully avoid knowing. Does time frame make a difference? In other words, both sides need to argue if the law states that it matters *if*, *when*, and *how* the Head of State acquired knowledge of the consequences in relation to the attack. An objective test, if shown to be legally required, would inquire whether or not a reasonable person has this knowledge. If it is shown that the he did *not* have knowledge of the consequences of his use of chemical weapons, does this in fact strengthen or worsen his case? In other words, does this damage his necessity defense (see below)? Did he in fact intend to target the civilian population? Questions such as these challenge the mental requirement for the crimes in question. Moreover, with respect to intent, students can discuss whether the lesser standard of recklessness is appropriate; if not for these crimes, which crimes? Is recklessness synonymous with "willful," a term used in some of the crimes outlined in Article 8(a) for example?[16] What does case law say about willfulness?

In this case the prosecution is also alleging that the Head of State is guilty of crimes against humanity. Similar to the war crimes accusations, the prosecution faces the challenge of making sure that the contextual, material, and mental elements are met. Perhaps the biggest challenge will concern the contextual aspect of the crime, in other words, whether the use of chemical weapons constituted "a widespread or systematic attack directed against any civilian population."[17] Of course the prosecution does not have to demonstrate *both* "widespread" and "systematic," but problems with their application are immediately raised by the Head of State; specifically, does his isolated use of chemical weapons meet either of the contextual criteria for crimes against humanity, especially when the definition of "attack," included in Article 7(2)(a) of the ICC Statute, is taken into account? Based on the facts outlined above, was this in fact an attack on the civilian population or an unfortunate consequence of the legitimate defense of a country? It would be useful at this point for instructors to discuss with students other current examples of state "misbehavior" towards civilians (e.g., Syria, Sri Lanka) and whether or not these government attacks meet the criteria for either of the contextual elements of crimes against humanity. This would be an excellent way to pinpoint the differences between "widespread" and "systematic" as they apply to actual cases.[18]

As to the material element the prosecution argues that Respondent/Defendant Head of State's use of chemical weapons was consistent with Article 7(1)(a) ("murder")[19] and 7(1)(k) of the ICC Statute, which prohibits "inhumane acts of a similar character intentionally causing great suffering, or serious injury to body or to mental or physical health."[20] As the facts about the injuries sustained by the population indicate, the material element of these charges is fairly straightforward. However, students may wish to consider other crimes against humanity including extermination and forcible transfer of a population. The prosecution can claim, even if a necessity defense is accepted on the material elements of criminality, that the manner in which the illegal chemical weapons were used is a separate source of criminality. Specifically, even if chemicals weapons were necessary as the only means available to stop an aggressive invasion, these weapons were still, given the facts in this case or others stipulated by students, violate *jus in bello*, the means of war inconsistent with IHL. *Jus in bellum* questions include proportionality (only minimum force may be used against combatants consistent with legitimate military objectives) and discrimination (only targeting legitimate military targets and minimizing any harm to civilians and their property.) Similar to other cases discussed in this text, the Defendant Head of State is also responsible for a crime of omission, specifically his failure to forewarn the population of the impending attack. This touches again on the question of knowledge, with the prosecution alleging that Defendant Head of State had full knowledge of the consequences of his act and the Head of State making the opposite contention. Students can discuss the issue of whether or not intent to harm the civilian population can be derived from the Head of State's failure to take adequate precautions for their safety. Given the nature of these weapons, does the Head of State's "lack of knowledge" argument hold any water at all, or, for that matter the prosecution's contention that the Defendant intended the harm to his own population to be *equal* to that inflicted on the invading military? Moreover, could one argue that the civilians were responsible in any way for their own fate? Was their failure to flee the invaded area intentional in any way; thus a question of "voluntary exposure"? Can intention to harm the population be derived from the Head of State's failure to protect his population? The arguments offered by both sides provide another excellent example of differing interpretations of fundamental concepts, including the meaning of "protect" and/or "defend."

Among the defenses offered by the Head of State are self-defense and necessity/duress. The former is raised pursuant to Article 51 of the Charter of the United Nations, which specifically holds: "Nothing in this Charter shall impair the inherent right of individual or collective self-defense if an armed attack occurs against a Member of the United Nations, until the Security Council has taken measures necessary to maintain international peace and security."[21] Moreover, as the International Court of Justice held in *Nicaragua*, self-defense is an inherent right grounded in customary international law.[22] State self-defense is different from self-defense claimed by an individual in that a state's right to self-defense justifies the use of force in a defensive campaign.[23]

To determine whether or not self-defense can be used as a justification by a state, the state is required to meet various criteria. Self-defense in this regard is closely linked with the defenses of duress and necessity[24] in terms of the conditions required for its use: the violation of international criminal law (in this case the use of banned weaponry) must be reasonable in relation to the threat posed or action perpetrated by the belligerent force;[25] it must be proportionate to the action/threat facing the country; and it must be unavoidable.[26] The threat to the state *must* be imminent or actual in other words.[27] With regard to the "unavoidable" criterion, it is incumbent on the Prosecutor to demonstrate to the Court that there were in fact other options available to the Defendant which the Defendant, in this case the Head of State, deliberately ignored.

The defense of necessity/duress marks another distinction between civil or code based legal systems and common law systems. With respect to the latter, these excuses are taken into account to mitigate punishment of the offender not to necessarily to assess his/her guilt or innocence.[28]

On a separate but related note, when making similar arguments in their own moot courts, students should make sure to avoid straying into a *tu quoque* type of defense; which is to say an argument in which one side justifies their behavior strictly on the illegality of their opponent's behavior.[29]

To defend the criminal use of banned weapons, in addition to large-scale destruction of civilian property and life prohibited by Article 8(2)(a)(iv) of the ICC Statue, military necessity is a last-resort legal option.[30] A necessity defense is specifically in the ICC Statute in Article 8(2)(a)(iv) and especially Article 31(1)(c), which exonerates a defendant if:

> The person acts reasonably to defend himself or herself or another person or, in the case of war crimes, property which is essential for the survival of the person or another person or property which is essential for accomplishing a military mission, against an imminent and unlawful use of force in a manner proportionate to the degree of danger to the person or the other person or property protected. The fact that the person was involved in a defensive operation conducted by forces shall not in itself constitute a ground for excluding criminal responsibility under this subparagraph.

Necessity may also be derived from Article 31(3) which permits the Court to consider other grounds "for excluding criminal responsibility" as per the additional sources of applicable law.[31] Students will find that military necessity is grounded in international humanitarian law, including the Geneva Conventions. Similar to self-defense, duress, and so forth, its use is also restricted to situations of "last resort."[32] Discussions of military necessity invite debate over the term itself. How do you measure "military necessity"?[33] Does "military necessity" in this case justify the use of weapons that can have long-term deleterious effects on a population?

Finally, was the use of chemical weapons absolutely the *last* resort available to the Respondent? Establishing necessity depends on speculation about imagined policy options and then dismissing them. One would be to fight without chemical weapons. Using an objective test, would a reasonable person have concluded that military self-defense without chemical weapons would have been a failure? Offensive invasions are rarely conducted when a power thinks they are likely to lose. The necessity defense for the My Lai Massacre was, after all, dismissed on the grounds that Lieutenant William Calley went back to the village to look for people, and thus was involved in revenge, not self-defense. Also, per Article 51 of the UN Charter, could the Head of State have relied instead on the United Nations Security Council (UNSC) to restore peace and eliminate the existing threat? Even if the use of some type of chemical weapons is justified, the means used must still be a proportionate response under international humanitarian law, as well as Article 31 of the Court's Statute. The means used requires a subjective and objective "balancing of interests" on the part of the actor.[34] An objective test, or a combination of objective and subjective mental factors, is the legal norm. However, subjective elements are sometimes legally accepted. Occasionally, a subjective test is legislated, such as in the Rodney King verdict in 1992 in California. Here police officers were statutorily protected for their decision, made in good faith, to use force that, while objectively necessary, was also objectively excessive. Top leaders are often granted subjective deference through judicial discretion. When a leader knows an action is wrong and unnecessary, even a subjective test is inadequate.

Were chemical weapons indeed the "lesser of two evils"? Students should be encouraged to become familiar with other sources of international humanitarian law on this issue; in particular the requirements that armed forces avoid "collateral damage" to civilian populations and structures.[35]

Ultimately the judge can consider factors that are not provided by either side in addition to the necessity defense, which is provided by the ICC statute. The third source of international law, principles from domestic legal systems, can supplement the defense's claim of necessity or provide skepticism for the prosecution's case. If the other defenses were not accepted as an alternative the defense could ask the judges to accept the alleged facts as meeting the material element of crime, but also to accept that the defendant had no other course of action but to break the law. As with debates over subjective and objective mental elements of crime, necessity can be interpreted using either the objective, reasonable person criteria or on the more lenient subjective standard that the defendant genuinely thought that the crime was necessary to achieve the greater good of protecting his country from military takeover, and notwithstanding all the other negative consequences that would thereby ensue.

Students should study writings on self-defense in general, especially derived from UN Charter Article 51 as well as in individual criminal cases in international and domestic law, especially military cases (though the government and military are reluctant to punish these kinds of claims). Special attention on how to frame objective and subjective tests of perceived alternatives will be debated by both sides in an area of ambiguous law.

LEGAL BRIEF OF APPELLANTS

THE QUESTION

The Moot International Criminal Court is asked to determine the legality of the Head of State's conviction for crimes against humanity and war crimes.

THE ISSUES

The following issues will be addressed in this brief: (I) the Prosecution's failure to demonstrate the material and mental elements of war crimes; (II) the Prosecution's failure to demonstrate the contextual, mental, and material elements of crimes against humanity; and (III) whether or not Appellant's use of chemical weapons to halt an invading army was justified and/or excused under Articles 31(c) and (d) of the Rome Statute, respectively, as well as Article 51 of the UN Charter.

SUMMARY OF ARGUMENTS

Appellant Head of State submits that his decision to use chemical weapons, in response to the unlawful invasion of his country by the armed forces of the Neighboring State, was reached after a careful consideration of all of the options available to him. In order to protect his country from a worse fate, the Head of State strongly contends that he had no viable option *other than* launching the chemical weapons attack. The Appellant Head of State in no way denies that he exercised command responsibility over those directly responsible for the launching of the chemical weapons attack (his military officers) and is responsible for their actions. However, Appellant's actions were justified as a means of self-defense pursuant to Article 51 of the UN Charter and Article 31 of this Moot Court's Statute. Appellant Head of State sincerely believed at the time his decision was made that the chemical weapons attack was proportional to the threat posed by the invading army of the Neighboring State. The Appellant Head of State also submits that his choice to use chemical weapons is excused by the conditions of duress he was experiencing as a result of external and internal circumstances beyond his control. The Appellant Head of State lacked adequate knowledge about the extent of the harm that would result from the weapons attack. He in no way intended to harm any members of his own population. Once the degree of injuries sustained by his population became known to him, Appellant evacuated the northeast region and provided the injured with medical treatment. Given the facts of the case, the Head of State submits that his actions cannot be considered war crimes or crimes against humanity. The Prosecution has failed to demonstrate the material and mental elements of war crimes and the contextual, mental, and material elements of crimes against humanity.

PROSECUTION'S CASE

The Head of State was charged with and convicted of crimes against humanity in violation of Articles 7(1)(a) (murder) and 7(1)(k) ("other inhumane acts of a similar character intentionally causing great suffering or serious injury to body or to mental and physical health") of the Rome Statute of this Moot International Criminal Court.

The Prosecution bases this charge on the notion that chemical agents were used by Appellant precisely because they are indiscriminate weapons. The Prosecution argues that Appellant Head of State purposefully neglected to warn his civilian population about the impending use of chemical agents. Moreover, the Prosecution contends that, after the weapons were launched and the extent of the harm became known to the Appellant, medical care was offered only in hindsight to mitigate unfavorable circumstances.

The Trial Chamber of this Moot International Criminal Court also convicted the Head of State with violating Articles 8(2)(a)(iii) ("Willfully causing great suffering, or serious injury to body or health"); 8(2)(a)(iv) ("Extensive destruction and appropriation of property, not justified by military necessity and carried out unlawfully and wantonly"; 8(2)(b)(i) ("Intentionally directing attacks against the civilian population as such or against individuals civilians not taking direct part in hostilities"); 8(2)(b)(iv) ("Intentionally launching an attack in the knowledge that such attack will cause incidental loss of life or injury to civilians or damage to civilian objects or widespread, long-term and severe damage to the natural environment"); 8(2)(b)(v) ("Attacking or bombarding, by whatever means, towns, villages, dwellings or buildings which are undefended and which are not military objectives"); and 8(2)(b)(xviii) ("Employing asphyxiating, poisonous or other gases, and all analogous liquids, materials or devices").

The Prosecution contends that Appellant knowingly deployed chemical weapons in the battlefield with intent to force the withdrawal of the invading forces of the Neighboring State. The Prosecution argues that chemical agents were used as a *first* rather than last resort by Appellant. Moreover, the Prosecution maintains that the use of chemical agents was a violation of the norm of proportionality in international humanitarian law. Proportionality also goes to the heart of the matter of intent. The Prosecution contends that the intent of the Head of State was to bring hostilities to an end as soon as possible. He was therefore prepared to deploy weapons of mass destruction to achieve that objective, the end result of which was to inflict the maximum amount of suffering possible on the invading forces and his own civilian population.

The Prosecution argues that Appellant's failure to do all that was possible and necessary to destroy his stockpile of chemical weapons, and his use of same on the battlefield to halt the invasion of the Neighboring State, is a clear violation of the CWC, to which Appellant's country is a signatory. Specifically Article 1 of the treaty declares that signatory states undertake to never (a) use chemical weapons or to (b) engage in any kind of military preparations to use chemical weapons.

The Prosecution argues that Appellant is responsible for war crimes and crimes against humanity in failing to protect his population from the short and long term damaging effects of toxic chemical agents. The actions of the Head of State, the Prosecution argues, violate the principle of proportionality. In presenting this point, the Prosecution cites two examples: the Ogoni case before the African Commission on Human and People's Rights and the use of Agent Orange by the United States in Vietnam in the late 1960s and early 1970s.

The Prosecution argues that Appellant failed in his primary responsibility to protect the civilian population of his country, and authorized a course of action that resulted in the deaths of untold numbers of civilians, as well as military personnel from the invading state. According to the Prosecution/Appellant has acted in violation of Article 30(2) of the Rome Statute in his intent to cause maximum damage to invading forces, even to the detriment of his own population as collateral damage.

FAILURE OF THE PROSECUTION TO DEMONSTRATE THE CONTEXTUAL, MENTAL, AND MATERIAL ELEMENTS

The burden of proof rests with the Prosecution who, according to Article 66(3) of the Rome Statute, must convince this Moot Court of "the guilt of the accused beyond reasonable doubt." This requires the Prosecution to fully demonstrate the contextual, material, and mental elements of each of the crimes with which the accused is charged.

Appellant contends that the elements of crimes under Articles 7 and 8 of the Rome Statute have *not* been proven by the Prosecution. Appellant contends further that negligence or recklessness do not satisfy the requirement that Appellant act with intent and knowledge under Article 30.

Crimes against Humanity

Appellant argues that the Prosecution failed to demonstrate to the Trial Chamber of this Moot International Criminal Court Appellant's responsibility for crimes against humanity beyond a reasonable doubt. *Actus reus* did not support *mens rea* in this case.

The Head of State contends that the contextual, material, and mental elements required to demonstrate crimes against humanity pursuant to Article 7 of the Rome Statute were not met by the Prosecution. First, neither systematic nor widespread attacks on a civilian population occurred. "Attack" is defined by Article 7(2)(a) of the Rome Statute as one "involving the multiple commission of acts referred to in paragraph 1 against any civilian population, pursuant to or in furtherance of a State or organizational policy to commit such attack." This criteria is absent in the present case as "multiple acts" did not in fact take place.

This is consistent with this Court's finding in the *Harun* case. In *Harun* this Court found that the standard of Article 7 had been met in that the Sudan Armed Forces, in conjunction with a militia, conducted hundreds of attacks on towns and villages. Moreover, the ICC Pre-Trial Chamber I in that case concluded:

> there are reasonable grounds to believe that, in his public speeches, Ahmad Harun not only demonstrated knowledge of the methods used by the Militia/Janjaweed, which attacked civilians and pillaged villages, but also personally encouraged the commission of such illegal acts, which he considered "justified or excusable."[36]

The Pre-Trial Chamber affirmed a conviction based on *mens rea* as established by Harun's leadership of a conspiracy to cause mass murder and his knowledge of every facet of operations having brought together state and non-state paramilitary forces for the purpose of killing of civilians.

In the present case the *Harun* standard has not been met. Appellant did *not* use state resources (in this case ordering the military to launch a chemical weapons attack on an invading military) with the direct or indirect intention of also targeting members of his own population for harm. Consistent with international jurisprudence, and Article 30 of this Court's Statute, knowledge is inextricably linked with intent; that is the perpetrator of a crime against humanity must know that his acts constitute part of a widespread and systematic attack on a civilian population.[37] Appellant did not have knowledge of the full impact the use of chemical weapons would have on members of his own population. He did not know the high probability of death or injury. Consequently, he did not feel it necessary to evacuate the area or warn the population prior to the attack.

The Head of State acknowledges that the population harmed by the chemical attack resides in a region known for its opposition to the ruling party. Although the Prosecution charged Appellant with systematic and widespread acts of murder in violation of 7(1)(a) and "other inhumane acts" in violation of 7(1)(k) of the Rome Treaty, the Prosecution's argument would seem to suggest that Appellant, by his failure to warn the population of the target region of the impending attack, was actually intending to *persecute* members of an opposing group. Nothing could be further from the truth. For the crime of persecution what is required over and above regular intent is the *dolus specialis* associated with extreme *jus cogens* violations, such as genocide.[38] Such as showing is lacking in this case. There was no deliberate attempt to target civilians *of any group* in the Head of State's country for destruction or harm.

Appellant maintains that there were no acts of omission under Article 7(1) of the Rome Statute. His actions may have been inhumane and even negligent, but he did not murder civilians with chemical weapons. Chemical weapons were used only to deter an invading force only. The standard of the mental element in the *Harun* case is not applicable to this case.

Appellant acted purely in self-defense and out of military necessity. The use of chemical agents was not part of a widespread and/or systematic attack, and the civilian population was *not* the primary target of the attack.[39] Appellant's use of chemical weapons conformed to the standard of military necessity. Appellant ordered evacuation of the affected area and provided medical assistance to civilians when knowledge of the impact of the deployment of chemical agents became known to him. Consequently, the dangerous effects of these weapons were mitigated to the extent possible. Unfortunately, in violation of Appellant's evacuation order, some civilians refused to leave the area and/or returned before the area was made safe; this in violation of the Head of State's evacuation order. This Moot International Criminal Court should know that Appellant made *every* attempt to ensure that the area was vacated. Consequently, he cannot be held at fault for the failure of some civilians to exercise due diligence.

War Crimes

Appellant concedes that the contextual element contained in Article 8 of the Rome Statute was present in this case as there was in fact an armed conflict of an international character. However the mental and material elements of the war crimes charges are absent. Appellant did not anticipate the collateral damage which resulted from his use of chemical weapons. Article 8(2) therefore cannot not be applied because civilians were neither willfully nor intentionally targeted.

Appellant argues that the *mens rea* element required to sustain a charge of war crimes was not met in this case. Jefferson D. Reynolds lays out four individual elements to meet the standard of *mens rea*:[40]

1. The perpetrator launched an attack.
2. The attack was such that it would cause incidental death or injury to civilians, damage civilian objects or cause widespread, long-term and severe damage to the natural environment
3. The perpetrator knew that the attack would result in excessive collateral damage.
4. The attack was such that the extent of the collateral damage would be clearly excessive in relation to the concrete and direct overall military advantage anticipated.

According to Reynolds,

> A defendant would not be criminally liable if an attack was executed under the personal belief that any collateral damage was not excessive compared to the military objective achieved. Under this interpretation, a defendant's culpability

> depends entirely and exclusively on that individual's own value judgment. If the defendant believed the collateral damage was not excessive, then there could not be a finding of guilt. The court's own evaluation of the defendant's value judgment as to the excessive character of the damage is irrelevant.[41]

Therefore, the Prosecution failed to prove *mens rea* as required in order to support a conviction.

THE USE OF CHEMICAL WEAPONS IN SELF-DEFENSE AND AS A MATTER OF DURESS

As a signatory to the CWC, Appellant realizes the importance of limiting or prohibiting the use of chemical weapons as a means of warfare. Appellant contends, however, that the use of chemical weapons was justified in this case by the circumstances that prevailed at the time. Appellant reminds this Moot Court that the use of chemical weapons may or *may not* fall within the jurisdiction of this Court given that they are not specifically included in the Rome Treaty. Article 8(2)(b)(viii), with which Appellant was charged and convicted, applies only to "asphyxiating, poisonous or other gases." Chemical weapons, like other weapons of mass destruction, could perhaps fall under the general rubric of Article 8(2)(b)(xx) of this Court's Statute, which prohibits the use of weapons that "cause superfluous injury or unnecessary suffering or which are inherently indiscriminate." However, this provision has not yet entered into force subject to the requirements of Articles 121 and 123.[42]

The Head of State argues that his actions were justified by Article 51 of the UN Charter, which permits member countries of the United Nations to exercise their "inherent right of individual or collective self-defense if an armed attack occurs . . . until the Security Council has taken measures necessary to maintain international peace and security."[43] Given the immediate threat posed by the invading army to the well-being and security of the Head of State's country, he had no other choice but to use whatever means necessary to protect his people.

Moreover, the Head of State contends that his actions were justified by Article 31(1)(c) of the Rome Statute. His decision to use chemical weapons was a lawful response to "an imminent and unlawful use of force." The invasion of Appellant's country by Neighboring State was a clear violation of Article 2(4) of the UN Charter.

Moreover, Article 31(1)(c) of the Rome Statute requires that actions in self-defense be "proportionate to the degree of danger" faced by the target, which in this case was the Head of State's country. Proportionality was clear in this instance in that the consequences that would have resulted from the conquest and occupation of the Head of State's country by the Neighboring State would have been far worse. The Neighboring State sought to seize control of natural resources in the Head of State's country that are essential to the survival of the population of his country. This would have resulted in the deaths of untold numbers of civilians of the Head of State's country, a number that would have *far surpassed* the number of civilians killed in the chemical attack.

Therefore, pursuant to Article 31(1)(c), the Head of State acted "reasonably to defend himself . . . or another person or, in the case of war crimes, property which is essential for the survival of the person or another person or property which is essential for accomplishing a military objective." In this case, the alleged war crime was committed with the intent to protect access to vital resources. Using chemical weapons was the only reasonable course of action to deter enemy combatants and secure the state's vital resources.

The Trial Chamber of the International Criminal Tribunal for the Former Yugoslavia (ICTY) ruled in *Kordić and Čerkez* that "[t]he notion of 'self-defence' may be broadly defined as providing a defence to a person who acts to defend or protect himself or his property (or another person or person's property) against attack, provided that the acts constitute a reasonable, necessary and proportionate reaction to the attack."[44] This is further supported by the *Willi Tressmann et al.* case after World War II, in which the Court found self-defense an acceptable defense "only in the last resort."[45] Werle notes that either self-defense or duress gave legitimate defense for exclusion of responsibility.[46] Thus, defensive measures are permitted for "imminent and unlawful use of force against certain protected interests."[47]

The Head of State did not intentionally target the civilian population to punish members of a group opposed to his government, his decision-making was nevertheless affected by the "increasing number of demonstrations against the government" conducted by persons from the affected region in the sense that these actions exacerbated an already dire set of circumstances. The existing context therefore placed the Head of State under duress and, when combined with the military necessity of repelling invading forces, influenced him to authorize deployment of chemical weapons. Pursuant to Article 31(1)(d) the Head of State acted out of necessity and did not "intend to cause a greater harm than the one sought to be avoided."

DEFENSE CONCLUSION

The Head of State argues that he could not have been expected to react otherwise in response to the attack by the Neighboring State. The Head of State was faced by an unanticipated set of circumstances and was forced to take immediate action in defense of his country. The facts do not support the standard of *mens rea*. There was no evidence that the Head of State intended to engage in widespread or systematic killing of civilians/military personnel. He deployed chemical agents out of military necessity and in a proportionate manner.

LEGAL BRIEF OF RESPONDENTS

THE QUESTION

This Moot International Criminal Court is asked to determine whether or not the Trial Chamber of this Court erred in its judgment that the Head of State is guilty of crimes against humanity and war crimes under the Rome Treaty.

THE ISSUES

The following issues will be addressed in this brief: (I) illegality of the use of chemical weapons as a matter of treaty and customary law; (II) whether or not the Head of State is personally responsible for crimes against humanity and war crimes; (III) that the Prosecution successfully demonstrated to the Trial Chamber of this Moot International Criminal Court the contextual, mental, and material elements of the war crimes and crimes against humanity charges; and (IV) that the actions by the Head of State failed to meet the criteria for self-defense, as well as duress under Article 31 of the Rome Treaty.

SUMMARY OF ARGUMENTS

Prohibitions of the use of chemical and biological weapons have a strong foundation in international law. The Head of State's decision to use chemical weapons to halt the invading forces of the Neighboring State was a clear breach of Article 1 of the CWC, to which the country of the Head of State is a party. The deliberate failure of the Head of State to warn his population of the impending dangers of the chemical attack constituted a crime against humanity in violation of Article 7 of the Rome Treaty in that its effects were both widespread and systematic and targeted a civilian population. Moreover, the actions of the Head of State were also in violation of a number of provisions of Article 8(2) of the Rome Treaty, including 8(2)(b)(xviii) ("Employing asphyxiating, poisonous or other gases, and all analogous liquids, materials or devices"). The use of chemical weapons by the military of the Head of State's country meets the contextual, mental, and material elements of crimes against humanity and war crimes. The Head of State failed in his duty to protect his population. Moreover, the use of chemical weapons violated the norms of necessity and proportionality.

ILLEGALITY OF CHEMICAL WEAPONS AS A MATTER OF INTERNATIONAL LAW

The ban on the use of chemical weapons is deeply embedded in customary international law. The Geneva Protocol of 1925, for instance, forbids "the use in war of asphyxiating, poisonous or other gases, and . . . all analogous liquids materials or devices."[48] Although chemical weapons are not specifically mentioned in the 1925 Protocol, noted legal scholar Gerhard Werle has noted that its "uncontroversial broad interpretation . . . [does] not permit the exclusion of modern weapons."[49]

The concern about the deleterious impact of chemical agents further intensified during and after the years of the Cold War. The CWC, which affirms the basic principles of the 1925 Geneva Protocol, states in its Preamble that the States Parties to the Convention are "[d]etermined for the sake of all mankind, to exclude completely the possibility of the use of chemical weapons"; that they "[undertake] never under any circumstances: (a) To develop, produce, otherwise acquire, stockpile or retain chemical weapons, or transfer, directly or indirectly, chemical weapons to anyone; (b) To use chemical weapons; (c) To engage in any military preparations to use chemical weapons."[50]

It is widely acknowledged that the use of chemical weapons can have devastating long-term effects on vegetation including food supply; this violating the principle of proportionality. The extensive use of Agent Orange during the Vietnam War, for example, resulted in sustained and prolonged toxicity to the vegetation, topography, and population of that country. Cathy Scott-Clark and Adrian Levy have noted that:

> New scientific research . . . confirms what the Vietnamese have been claiming for years. It also portrays the U.S. government as one that has illicitly used weapons of mass destruction, stymied all independent efforts to assess the impact of their deployment, failed to acknowledge cold, hard evidence of maiming and slaughter, and pursued a policy of evasion and deception.
>
> Teams of international scientists working in Vietnam have now discovered that Agent Orange contains one of the most virulent poisons known to man, a strain of dioxin called TCCD which, 28 years after the fighting ended, remains in the soil, continuing to destroy the lives of those exposed to it. Evidence has also emerged that the U.S. government not only knew that Agent Orange was contaminated, but was fully aware of the killing power of its contaminant dioxin, and yet still continued to use the herbicide in Vietnam for 10 years of the war and in concentrations that exceeded its own guidelines by 25 times. As well as spraying the North Vietnamese, the U.S. doused its own troops stationed in the jungle, rather than lose tactical advantage by having them withdraw.[51]

More recently, the use of chemicals and oil spills in Ogoniland, Nigeria by the Shell oil company over a number of years was finally resolved in early August 2011 when Shell admitted that it had caused long-term environmental damage in and to the region.[52] This followed a ruling in 2001 by the African Commission on Human and People's Rights that supported claims made by the Ogoni people. The Commission further found that the government and oil companies had engaged in "terrorizations and killings" and that "the pollution and environmental degradation to a level humanly unacceptable has made living in [Ogoniland] a nightmare."[53]

Moreover, Coomans has pointed out that, in the Ogoni case, the Government of Nigeria:

> was actively involved in the pollution, the contamination of the environment and related health problems of the Ogoni people, by condoning and facilitating the activities of the oil companies through the placing of the state's legal and military powers at the disposal of the oil companies. Furthermore, the government also kept the Ogoni communities uninformed about the damages created by the activities of the oil companies. It also failed to produce basic health and environment impact studies, nor asked the oil companies to do so. In other words, the government has not taken care to protect the inhabitants of Ogoni Land against the harmful activities of the oil companies.[54]

Long-term damage caused by chemical agents in battle goes to the heart of proportionality. Proportionality is a principle of the Laws of War "which [seek] to establish criteria for limiting the use of force."[55] On this point Roberts and Guelff note that "[t]he principle can refer to (1) the proportionality of a military action taken in response to a grievance—in which sense it is a link between *jus ad bellum* and *jus in bello*; and (2) proportionality in the conduct of armed hostilities (*jus in bello*)."[56]

The second qualification refers to the proportionality of the steps taken by a state that has been attacked by use of force; in short, its military response to the use of force. Derived ultimately from the Oxford Laws of War 1880, the purpose of the principle of proportionality is the prevention of military responses that are more catastrophic in their objectives and consequences then containment or repulsion of forces of the enemy state. The use of chemical weapons clearly violates the principle of proportionality.

Moreover, and contrary to the argument of the Head of State, the destruction of life, property, and livelihood caused by the deliberate use of chemicals and other toxins is clearly forbidden by Articles 8(2)(b)(xvii) and (xviii) of the Rome Statute of this Moot International Criminal Court.[57] Legal scholars such as Gerhard Werle conclude that "the clear wording of Article 8(2)(b)(viii) of the ICC Statute and the uncontroversial broad interpretation of the underlying Poison Gas Protocol of 1925 do not permit the exclusion of modern weapons," including chemical weapons.[58]

The use of chemical agents was also in violation of Article 147 of the Fourth Geneva Convention (crimes committed against persons or property). The intent of the Head of State was, clearly, to cause great suffering, while little was done to protect property. The failure of the Head of State to protect civilians and their property, both of which are protected by the Fourth Geneva Convention and the Rome Statute, demonstrated his intent.

CONTEXTUAL, MENTAL, AND MATERIAL OF CRIMES AGAINST HUMANITY AND WAR CRIMES

The elements of crimes are central to this case. Although the Rome Statute provides for prosecution of three categories of crimes: genocide, crimes against humanity, and war crimes, three essential conditions must be met for the Court to be satisfied by the merits thereof. For example, Cassese points out that,

> murder as a crime against humanity requires (i) the objective element of murder (causing the death of another person) as well as a mental element (intent to bring about by one's action the death of another person); plus (ii) a broader objective context (the existence of a widespread or systematic attack on the civilian population, whether in time of armed conflict or in any time of peace) and a mental element: awareness of the existence such broader context.[59]

These elements of crimes are fundamental to international criminal law in that they lay down an objective standard by which an individual may be prosecuted for genocide, crimes against humanity, or war crimes.

The material element is the fact of a crime having been committed. This includes "all conditions that determine the external appearance of the act."[60] Largely descriptive, the material element is concerned with the imperative of ascertaining the facts. Article 30(2) of the Rome Statute distinguishes three material elements: a) the conduct of the person; b) the consequences of the conduct; c) and the act itself. A successful prosecution requires that "a person shall be criminally responsible and liable for punishment for a crime within the jurisdiction of the Court only if the material elements are committed with intent and knowledge."[61] Cassese considers notable "that . . . conduct is either (a) linked to an international or internal armed conflict or, absent of such a conflict, (b) has a political or ideological dimension, or is somehow linked or otherwise connected to (instigated, influenced, tolerated, or acquiesced in) the behavior of state authorities or organized non-state groups or entities."[62] Thus, an essential characteristic of conduct is that it occurs either on behalf of the state or is "somehow connected with a state policy or at any rate with 'system criminality.'"[63] The material element is consequently "fundamental in presenting a case to this Court,"[64] in that the material element refers to matters of functional value.[65]

The contextual element refers to the circumstances in which a crime is deemed to have occurred.[66] Such circumstances are "any objective or subjective facts, qualities or motives with regard to the subject of the crime (such as the perpetrator and any accomplices), the object of the crime (such as the victim or other impaired interests) or any other modalities of the crime (such as means or time and place of commission)."[67] Broader questions of fact may come into play, such as whether there were mitigating circumstances in which an act occurred including necessity or duress.

The mental element (*mens rea*) is crucial in that, according to Article 30(1) of the Rome Statute, "a person shall be criminally responsible and liable for punishment for a crime within the jurisdiction of the Court only if the material elements are committed with intent and knowledge." Intent and knowledge are the two operative words in Article 30(1) to the extent that they qualify Articles 6, 7, and 8 of the Rome Statute. The three categories of crimes addressed by the Rome Statute pertain to the intent to kill or harm populations. In the case of crimes against humanity this takes the form of a "a widespread or systematic attack directed against any civilian population, with knowledge of the attack"; in reference to war crimes "grave breaches of the Geneva Conventions," including "willful killing," "willfully causing great suffering, or serious injury to body or health," "compelling a prisoner of war or other protected person to serve in the forces of a hostile power," "willfully depriving a prisoner of war or other protected person of the rights of fair and regular trial," and so on.

Mens rea is qualified in Article 30(2) of the Rome Statute in two respects: a) "the person means to engage in the conduct," and b) "that person means to cause that consequence or is aware that it will occur in the ordinary course of events." Intent includes acts of commission and omission (*actus reus*).[68] The very fact that an act is wrong is a matter of knowledge. According to Badar, "Generally, the prosecution must prove that the defendant had knowledge of facts which would make the conduct illegal, but ordinarily is not required to prove the defendant's awareness of the legal consequences of the conduct (e.g., that the conduct was illegal)."[69] There is, consequently, no requirement that the individual committing the act knows that the specific act is illegal; the fact of having committed an act is sufficient to prosecute an international crime. In short, *mens rea* implies guilt. As Lord Goddard put it, "the court should not find a man guilty of an offence against the criminal law unless he has a guilty mind."[70]

Mens rea has become a cardinal consideration in international criminal law in the last two decades. It presumes a root intent to do harm to others, irrespective of such harm being classified as international crime. William Schabas points out, for example, that "from their very decisions, the judges of the ICTY have simply assumed that *mens rea* is an essential element of the offences within their jurisdiction," despite the norm not being written into the rules of procedure of the Tribunal:[71]

> the issue was central to the first conviction, that of Erdemovic, because the availability of the defense of duress had been raised. Erdemovic had confessed to killing a large number of defenseless prisoners at Srebrenica, but when asked to explain his actions he said he had been compelled to do so. This defense of duress amounts to a claim that the accused lacked a guilty mind, because the compulsion under which he acted amounted to something irresistible, leaving him no moral choice in the matter. . . . All of the judges of the Appeals Cham-

ber, in their 1997 ruling rejecting the admissibility of a defense of duress, approached the issue as one of the presence or absence of *mens rea.*[72]

The intent to commit harm is not new in international criminal law; it goes back to the Nuremberg Tribunal. As per IMT precedent state leaders are held to a higher standard than others in that they are deemed responsible for the safety, security, and well-being of their peoples. Departure from this standard is construed not merely as dereliction of duty, but as a punishable offence in international criminal law. Furthermore, those who represent the state have access to and utilize the resources of the state, including to commit crimes against humanity such as genocide and war crimes. Therefore, they purport to act on behalf of and in the service of the state, making the state responsible for their actions.

Integral to the Prosecution's case is the idea that idea that the responsibilities of state leaders supersede and transcend the laws of their countries. In rendering judgment in the *Goering* trial, for example, the IMT asserted that "[c]rimes against international law are committed by men, not by abstract entities, and only by punishing individuals who commit such crimes can the provisions of international law be enforced."[73] In so doing, the IMT affirmed that leaders act on behalf of the state, and based on some sort of plan put together in the service of the state. As Schabas notes, "Essentially all prosecutions have involved offenders acting on behalf of a state and in accordance with state policy, or those acting on behalf of an organization that was state-like in its attempts to exercise control over territory and seize political power."[74] Their culpability is consequently synonymous with that of the state, and they are to be held accountable in law for their deeds and misdeeds as the final decision-makers in the apparatus of the state.

Crimes against Humanity

The Head of State has been held responsible for crimes against humanity in violation of Article 7(1)(a) and (k) of the Rome Statute.

The Prosecution has met the contextual and material criteria for crimes against humanity in this case. Article 7 of the Statute of this Court defines crimes against humanity as those "committed as part of a widespread or systematic attack directed against any civilian population, with knowledge of the attack." International jurisprudence demonstrates that crimes against humanity require the presence of either a widespread or systematic attack which may or may not be part of a formal government plan.[75]

The Prosecution successfully demonstrated to the Trial Chamber of this Court that the Head of State's decision to deploy chemical weapons in his country—specifically his failure to warn his population of the impending dangers—constituted an act that was both widespread, in that it impacted a substantial number of civilians, and systematic, in that required the use of extensive public resources.

The Prosecution has also met the mental criterion for crimes against humanity pursuant to Article 30(2)(b) of this Court's Statute. The Prosecution successfully demonstrated to the Trial Chamber of this Moot International Criminal Court that the omissions of the Head of State—his failure to warn and evacuate the population of the target area—were made with knowledge of the likely consequences that would ensue from his deployment of chemical weapons in the target region. As a signatory to the CWC, the Head of State in fact possessed sufficient understanding of the harmful short-term and long-term effects that chemical agents have on a population. Indirect intent or *dolus eventualis* does not suffice; rather, the mental criterion for the use of prohibited weaponry—*dolus directus*—was established by the Prosecution.

War Crimes

The Head of State was charged and convicted of war crimes pursuant to several provisions of Article 8 of the Rome Treaty.

There is no dispute between the Head of State and the Prosecution with regard to context. The facts seem to show that the Head of State was responding to an armed incursion by forces of a neighboring state after a period of escalating tension. The incursion was unprovoked and, therefore, a violation of Article 2(4) of the Charter of the United Nations (UN Charter), as a consequence of which the Head of State was within his right in invoking Article 51 of the UN Charter that affirms the right of a state to self-defense.

At the same time chemical agents were used within the borders of the violated state. Whereas invading troops were the military target, civilians were also impacted causing illness, loss of life, and damage to property, all within the borders of the state that had been invaded.

The facts meet the requirements of Article 30 of the Rome Statute in both *mens rea* and *actus reus*. The Head of State intended to inflict maximum harm and damage to the invading forces of the Neighboring State and so opted to utilize chemical agents. In so doing he committed an act that he knew to be a crime; a violation of Article 8(2)(b)(viii). He did so in the knowledge that chemical agents would, by being dispersed, cover a wide area and inflict injury and suffering effectively. It mattered not whether the Head of State possessed technical knowledge about the types of chemicals used and their effects. He used chemical agents with intent and with knowledge of their devastating impact.

The use of chemical agents clearly affected the domestic population, hence the government offered medical care to nationals who had suffered injuries. Whether the government anticipated and calculated collateral damage is not material. Rather, the use of chemical agents, which would normally be classified as a weapon of mass destruction because of their indiscriminate impact, was a war crime under Article 8(2)(b)(i) of the Rome Treaty to the extent they were directed "against the civilian population as such or against individuals civilians not taking direct part in hostilities"; Article 8(2)(b)(iv) of the Rome Statute to the extent that the government intentionally directed an attack in the knowledge that the attack was going to cause "cause incidental loss of life or injury to civilians or damage to civilian objects or widespread, long-term and severe damage to the natural environment." The use of chemical agents was also a violation of Article 8(2)(b)(v) of the Rome Statute in that a village, dwellings and buildings which were *not* military targets were clearly targeted.

The offer of medical assistance once knowledge of the impact of chemical agents on the civilian population became known to the Head of State, notwithstanding their use by the government, was an act of both commission and of omission.

As an act of commission, the attack violated Article 30 of the Rome Statute in *mens rea* was evident. The failure of the Government to do all possible to protect the civilian population, including preventing or calling off the order to use chemical weapons, was a violation of Article 57 of the Additional Protocol I to the Geneva Conventions of 1949.[76] Article 57(1) affirms that "[i]n the conduct of military operations, constant care shall be taken to spare the civilian population, civilians and civilian objects." The Head of State failed to observe this critical rule of international criminal and humanitarian law and, consequently, knowingly exposed his population to the immediate and long-term effects of a weapon of mass destruction.

The government had a duty to minimize civilian casualties and ensure that they were removed from the theater of military operations. Martin et al. point out that "[t]he law of armed conflict requires that military forces protect civilians and minimize loss of life and property."[77] Elsewhere, Francisco Forrest Martin notes that, in an age of highly technological warfare and military operations, there is an even greater onus on the state to minimize injury and death to civilian populations and damage to property.[78] In *Prosecutor v. Kordić and Čerkez*, the Appeals Chamber of the ICTY ruled that a lower form of intent is established when "a person who orders an act or omission with the awareness of the substantial likelihood that a crime will be committed in the execution of that order, has the requisite *mens rea* for establishing responsibility under Article 7(1) of the Statute pursuant to ordering. Ordering with such awareness has to be regarded as accepting that crime."[79]

If the Head of State failed to take all necessary steps to protect the civilian population from injury, death, and damage to property including long-term damage, then there is culpability under the principle of omission. Consequently, the Head of State is liable as per Articles 8(2)(a)(iii) and 8(2)(a)(iv) of this Court's Statute.

INAPPLICABILITY OF SELF-DEFENSE AND DURESS

Proportionality

To successfully make the case for self-defense under Article 31(1)(c) of the Rome Treaty, one must demonstrate that his/her unlawful use of force was "proportionate to the degree of danger" present. This requirement is only magnified in cases involving chemical, biological, and other poisonous weaponry.

The statutory underpinning of the principle of proportionality lies in Article 51 of the Additional Protocol I (1977) to the Geneva Conventions, which asserts that "[t]he civilian population and individual civilians shall enjoy general protection against dangers arising from military operations. To give effect to this protection, the following rules, which are additional to other applicable rules of international law, shall be observed in all circumstances."[80] Article 51 specifically prohibits indiscriminate acts, which are defined as:

> (a) those which are not directed at a specific military objective; (b) those which employ a method or means of combat which cannot be directed at a specific military objective; or (c) those which employ a method or means of combat the effects of which cannot be limited as required by this Protocol; and consequently, in each such case, are of a nature to strike military objectives and civilians or civilian objects without distinction.

The principle is also contained in Protocol II to the Geneva Conventions and the Amended Protocol II to the Convention on Certain Conventional Weapons,[81] as well as, of course, Article 8(2)(b) of the Rome Statute, which specifically prohibits indiscriminate attacks against civilian populations, including those that result in damage to the natural environment that is "clearly excessive in relation to the concrete and direct overall military advantage anticipated."[82]

This is consistent with Article 57 of Additional Protocol I, which offers precautions that can be taken to protect civilians during conflict, including verification of military objectives, "all feasible precautions in the choice of means and methods of attack with a view to avoiding, and in any event to minimizing, incidental loss or civilian life, injury to civilians and damage to civilian objects," and refraining from "deciding to launch any attack which may be expected to cause incidental loss of civilian life, injury to civilians, damage to civilian objects, or a combination thereof, which would be excessive in relation to the concrete and direct military advantage anticipated." Article 57 further affirms that an attack can be cancelled or suspended "if it becomes apparent that the objective is not a military one or is subject to special protection or that the attack may be expected to cause incidental loss of civilian life, injury to civilians, damage to civilian objects, or a combination thereof, which would be excessive in relation to the concrete and direct military advantage anticipated."[83]

Although proportionality is not a total ban on military actions, it represents an effort to protect civilians from the scourge of conflict, incidental loss of life, long-term suffering, and damage to property. As Gary Solis notes, "Proportionality is a necessary consideration in attacks on civilians, not on combatants."[84]

However, as Solis notes, proportionality cannot be reasonably applied in the theater of operations where combatants are targets. In citing the sinking of the Argentine ship *General Belgrano* by HMS *Conqueror* during the Falklands-Malvinas conflict in 1982, for instance, Solis notes that the *Belgrano* was a legitimate target because it was transporting combatants. Hence, "[p]roportionality employs a different standard in a civilian law enforcement context, where human rights-related law prevails' rather than the laws of armed conflict."[85] Cassese concurs with this assessment, noting that, in the use of countermeasures, "[w]hat is exacted by international law is that countermeasures be not grossly disproportionate in gravity and magnitude."[86] Thus, Roberts and Guelff note three customary principles on which the principle of proportionality rests: (1) necessity; (2) humanity; and (3) chivalry.[87] In short the proportionality rule seeks to protect civilians from deliberate or incidental loss of life, long-term suffering, and damage to property as a consequence of the use of excessive force in armed conflict.

Thomas Franck points out that, in *Nicaragua v. United States* (1986) the International Court of Justice held that the mining of Nicaragua's harbors by the United States in retaliation for Nicaragua's support for revolutionaries in El Salvador was *not* proportionate to the actions of the Nicaraguans. He notes that "even in the event of a demonstrable transborder armed attack, one warranting a military response, the Court may review whether the level of countermeasures deployed is permitted by law: whether it is proportionate to the attack itself and to the needs of self-defense."[88] Nicaragua, a relatively small state in Central America had not declared war against the United States and had not violated U.S. territorial integrity. Yet, agents of the U.S. government mined the harbors of Nicaragua, deterring commercial shipping and humanitarian assistance. The International Court of Justice (ICJ) ruled that the mining of Nicaragua's harbors was disproportionate to the conflict between the states.

Proportionality is germane to this matter. The use of chemical agents in a peripheral village within one's borders may have been intended to repel the attack, but it was disproportionate to the scale of military operations and placed the lives, property, and livelihood of civilians in jeopardy. The use of chemical agents was a violation of Articles 51 and 57 of the Additional Protocol to the Geneva Conventions of 1949 in that (a) it endangered civilians through the use of an indiscriminate weapon and (b) no effort was made to exercise restraint or call off the attack.

The willingness of the government to offer medical assistance to civilians *after* the attack indicated that, with forethought, there was knowledge of the impending catastrophe. However, no effort was made to protect civilians in advance of the use of chemical agents. Thus the Head of State was willing and able to make the health and well-being of his nationals in the effected region of secondary importance at best.

The government did not warn the resident population of its intent to disperse chemicals in the region. The population was therefore unable to seek shelter or any effective means of avoiding exposure to the chemicals. No effort was made by the military to avoid exposure of the population to these chemicals. Consequently the Head of State is not exempt from the charge of failure to adhere to the principle of proportionality, even when Article 31(1)(c) of the Rome Statute is applied.

Necessity and Duress

The final questions to be considered pertain to military necessity and duress. Chemical agents in this instance caused "incidental loss of life or injury to civilians or damage to civilian objects or widespread, long-term and severe damage to the natural environment" that was "excessive in relation to the concrete and direct overall military advantage anticipated" as prohibited by Article 8(2)(b)(iv) of the Rome Treaty. Chemical agents were used as a weapon in violation of Article 1 of the Chemical Weapons Convention, which prohibits stockpiling and use of chemical weapons, although the state was party to the CWC. Furthermore, Article 9 of the Chemical Weapons Convention prohibits use of "the toxic properties of chemicals" for military purposes. The Head of State clearly engaged in an act that violated Article 8(2)(b)(i) of the Rome Statute, in that the attack was intentionally directed against civilians who were not taking part in the hostilities and who were not military objects.

Necessity or duress "may be urged as a defense when a person, acting under a threat of severe and irreparable harm to his life or limb, or to life and limb or another person, perpetrates an international crime."[89] Cassese notes an important distinction between necessity and duress, in that the latter occurs when a third party imposes its will on the person deemed to have committed the crime, so that duress "is commonly raised in conjunction with superior orders."[90]

The Head of State is not subordinate to any superior who gave him an order to disperse chemical weapons. In *Prosecutor v. Erdemovic,* Justice Cassese noted in his dissenting opinion that for duress to be offered as an acceptable excuse, it must emanate from a subordinate, *not* an individual who holds ultimate authority. Moreover it requires involvement of a third person "that is, the person threatening the agent."[91] In this case the Head of State was the agent and there was no superior person.

CONCLUSIONS

The case against the Head of State is based on four principles of international criminal law: the elements of crimes, especially the mental and contextual elements; acts of commission and omission; proportionality; and necessity. The preponderance of the evidence, when weighed against current standards in international criminal and humanitarian law, demonstrates that the Head of State was intent on causing the maximum harm and damage possible, knowing the catastrophic immediate and long-term effects of chemical agents; failed to do all possible and necessary to protect his population; pursued a course of action that was a significant departure from the rule of proportionality; and did not conform to any standard of military necessity. The Prosecution has met the burden of proof required by Article 66 of this Court's Statute. We therefore urge the Appeals Chamber of this Moot International Criminal Court to uphold the decision of the Trial Chamber.

JUDGMENT

REFERRAL AND INDICTMENT

The instant case resulted from a referral to the Prosecutor by the Security Council of the United Nations pursuant to Article 13(b). Subsequent to an investigation, Appellant was indicted for the following offenses constituting crimes against humanity: Article 7(1)(a) murder and Article 7(1)(k) inhumane acts intentionally causing great suffering or serious injury. Appellant was also indicted for the following offenses constituting war crimes: Article 8(2)(a)(iii) willfully causing great suffering or serious injury; Article 8(2)(a)(iv) extensive destruction of property not justified by military necessity; Article 8(2)(b)(i) intentionally attacking civilians; Article 8(2)(b)(iv) intentionally launching an attack knowing it would impact civilians; Article 8(2)(b)(v) attacking undefended civilian targets that are not military objectives; and Article 8(2)(b)(xviii) employing poisonous or asphyxiating gases or analogous materials.

Appellant was found guilty of all counts by the Trial Chamber, and this appeal results. We shall discuss each of the charges in turn.

WAR CRIMES

Historically, responsibility for violations of the rules of armed conflict was ascribed to the states involved. Over time this line of thinking shifted dramatically, particularly with the Nuremberg and Tokyo Tribunals in the aftermath of World War II, so as to allow for the individuals involved to be held individually responsible for their actions. Ultimately, this approach culminated in the adoption of the Rome Statute and the establishment of this Court.[92]

Here Appellant was convicted by the Trial Chamber of the following:

> Article 8(2). For the purpose of this Statute, "war crimes" means:
> (a) Grave breaches of the Geneva Conventions of 12 August 1949, namely, any of the following acts against persons or property protected under the provisions of the relevant Geneva Convention:
> (iii) Willfully causing great suffering, or serious injury to body or health;
> (iv) Extensive destruction and appropriation of property, not justified by military necessity and carried out unlawfully and wantonly.
> (b) Other serious violations of the laws and customs applicable in international armed conflict, within the established framework of international law, namely, any of the following acts:

(i) Intentionally directing attacks against the civilian population as such or against individual civilians not taking direct part in hostilities;
(iv) Intentionally launching an attack in the knowledge that such attack will cause incidental loss of life or injury to civilians or damage to civilian objects or widespread, long-term and severe damage to the natural environment which would be clearly excessive in relation to the concrete and direct overall military advantage anticipated;
(v) Attacking or bombarding, by whatever means, towns, villages, dwellings or buildings which are undefended and which are not military objectives;
(xviii) Employing asphyxiating, poisonous or other gases, and all analogous liquids, materials or devices.

The Appellant concedes that the contextual element of these offenses has been met, in that the events took place during an international armed conflict, but contends that the Prosecutor failed to meet his Article 66 burden of proof beyond a reasonable doubt as to the material and mental elements of the offenses. More specifically, Appellant's primary contention is that there was insufficient proof of intent. Appellant argues that intent must be determined on a subjective rather than an objective basis. In other words, Appellant argues that he cannot be convicted absent proof that he intended to cause the harms that resulted from the ordered use of the chemical agent. He contends this is not possible, as he neither intended for harm to result nor knew that it would result. At most, then, the Prosecution can show either negligence or recklessness on his part, neither of which is sufficient to support a conviction.

Of course, the Prosecution takes a different view. Essentially, the Prosecution points to the sheer extent of the resulting harm in support of its contention that Appellant did actually intend to cause the harm or, alternatively, that he at least knew such harm would result but decided to use the chemical agent regardless. Per the Prosecution's argument, either is sufficient to support the conviction.

Before turning to a more detailed examination of these competing contentions, it is useful to first consider further the nature of the offenses charged. Cassese identifies two categories of crimes: those of conduct and those of result. Crimes of conduct include "offences consisting in the breach of an international rule that imposes a specific behaviour; there, it is irrelevant whether or not this breach brings about any harm or injury to prospective victims."[93] Crimes of result, on the other hand, "confine themselves to imposing the achievement of a certain end, regardless of the modalities for the realization of that end."[94]

Thus, per their statutory definitions, three of the Article 8 offenses charged do not require the achievement of any harm. These are 8(2)(b)(i) attacking civilians as such; 8(2)(b)(v) attacking undefended targets that are not military objectives; and 8(2)(b)(xviii) use of chemical weapons. The Record in this case is clear in that the military action ordered by Appellant was directed at the invading army of Neighboring Country and was carried out only in the area occupied by the invading army. Therefore, we now rule that the Prosecution failed to carry its burden of proof as to the material element with regard to subparagraphs (i) and (v), in that there is no proof that Appellant targeted the impacted civilians as such or that the area impacted was not a military objective.

Conversely, we also rule that there is perhaps no better illustration of a crime of conduct than the use of chemical weapons, an issue with an international history now extending more than three centuries. International efforts to eliminate the use of chemical weapons can be traced at least to a 1675 treaty between France and Germany forbidding the use of poison bullets. Even though far more expansive international efforts followed, more than 100,000 fatalities resulted from the rampant use of chemical weapons during World War I. This generated renewed international efforts, including the 1925 Geneva Protocol for the Prohibition of the Use of Asphyxiating, Poisonous or Other Gases, and Bacteriological Methods of Warfare.[95]

Significantly, the Geneva Protocol was directed only at the *use* of such weapons. International efforts ultimately resulted in the adoption of the Chemical Weapons Convention (CWC), which took effect in April 1997 and is far more comprehensive. The Preamble to the CWC includes the following:

> Determined for the sake of all mankind, to exclude completely the possibility of the use of chemical weapons, through the implementation of the provisions of this Convention, thereby complementing the obligations assumed under the Geneva Protocol of 1925[.]

Further, Article I provides as follows:

> 1. Each State Party to this Convention undertakes never under any circumstances:
> (a) To develop, produce, otherwise acquire, stockpile or retain chemical weapons, or transfer, directly or indirectly, chemical weapons to anyone;
> (b) To use chemical weapons;
> (c) To engage in any military preparations to use chemical weapons;
> (d) To assist, encourage or induce, in any way, anyone to engage in any activity prohibited to a State Party under this Convention.
> 2. Each State Party undertakes to destroy chemical weapons it owns or possesses, or that are located in any place under its jurisdiction or control, in accordance with the provisions of this Convention.

Here, Appellant admits ordering the military use of a substance known by him to be prohibited by the CWC. As made plain by these excerpts from the text, it is a violation of the CWC even for Post-War Country to fail to destroy its holdings of the substance. One hundred and eighty nine nations, representing 98 percent of the world's population, are now States Parties to the CWC. It is obvious, then, that the instant case raises very grave matters of great concern to the international community.

Nonetheless, Appellant does not appear before this Court charged with violations of the CWC. Appellant appears before this Court ascribing error to the judgment of the Trial Chamber in finding him guilty of violating Article

8(2)(b)(xviii). The Record in this case is clear that Appellant chose to launch a military attack using a chemical agent known by him to be prohibited by the CWC, an international understanding so firmly and widely established as to be embraced by all but a small handful of States. Appellant asserts that he cannot be convicted because he neither intended for the resulting harm to occur nor knew that it would result. However, as discussed above, whether Appellant intended for the resulting harm to occur, or even whether there was any such harm, is irrelevant to the ultimate conclusion. To the extent to which Appellant may seek to avoid this conclusion by contending that the material element is not satisfied because the chemical agent used is not specifically prohibited by Article 8, we find this contention to be without merit. The nearly universal acceptance of the CWC is more than sufficient to establish Appellant's conduct as a "serious violation of the laws and customs applicable in international armed conflict, within the established framework of international law." In addition, the language in question is certainly broad enough to include a prohibition of modern weapons.[96] Therefore, Appellant's conviction on Article 8(2)(b)(xviii) must stand.

The remaining Article 8 charges are 8(2)(a)(iii) willfully causing great suffering; 8(2)(a)(iv) extensive destruction of property; and 8(2)(b)(iv) launching an attack in the knowledge of civilian or environmental impact. As there is no question that Appellant intended to launch the attack using a prohibited chemical agent, the real issue here is whether or not the Prosecution met its burden of proof in demonstrating that Appellant intended to cause the harm identified by the statute.

As discussed above, Appellant contends this cannot be the case because he neither intended to cause the resulting harm nor did he know it would result. The Prosecution contends that the magnitude of the harm is sufficient to demonstrate that Appellant did intend to cause the harm or, alternatively, that he at least knew the harm would result but proceeded with the attack regardless.

Issues of intent and knowledge are governed by Article 30, which provides as follows:

> 1. Unless otherwise provided, a person shall be criminally responsible and liable for punishment for a crime within the jurisdiction of the Court only if the material elements are committed with intent and knowledge.
> 2. For the purposes of this article, a person has intent where:
> (a) In relation to conduct, that person means to engage in the conduct;
> (b) In relation to a consequence, that person means to cause that consequence or is aware that it will occur in the ordinary course of events.
> 3. For the purposes of this article, "knowledge" means awareness that a circumstance exists or a consequence will occur in the ordinary course of events. "Know" and "knowingly" shall be construed accordingly.

The plain language of Article 30, especially the language describing knowledge that a consequence will occur in the ordinary course of events,[97] appears to support the Prosecution's view. This alone is not sufficient to resolve the matter, however, in light of Appellant's adamant contention that he was unaware that the resulting harm would occur. It must also be said that the Prosecution's only real response to this contention, that the sheer magnitude of the resulting harm must mean at least that Appellant knew such harm would occur, is less than compelling. We believe the key to this inquiry lies in Appellant's status as a Head of State. While it is undisputed that Post-War Country is a small, developing state, meaning that Appellant certainly lacks the resources and support available to the Head of State of a developed country, he is nonetheless a Head of State. This means he has at his disposal resources and support beyond those available to ordinary persons. While he may lack highly technical knowledge, it is undisputed that he was aware of the CWC and knew that the substance used was prohibited by it. This leads us to conclude that, at a minimum, Appellant had an awareness of the dangerous nature of the substance and of the kind of harm that would likely result from a chemical attack. Nonetheless, he decided to proceed with the attack regardless and did so without making any attempt to warn or evacuate the civilian population of the affected area. Since this is sufficient to satisfy the Article 30 definition of intent, Appellant's convictions as to these offenses must stand.

CRIMES AGAINST HUMANITY

International efforts at addressing crimes against humanity originated in 1915 through the response of France, Russia, and Great Britain to the mass killing of civilians by the Ottoman government.[98] Little of permanent international significance was accomplished by these efforts, in part due to objections raised by the United States that the "law of humanity" was too vague and amorphous to serve as the basis for prosecution. Progress resulted from the Nuremberg Tribunal, which was created to address German atrocities during World War II. However, this progress was limited by the linking of crimes against humanity to war conduct. Subsequent to the Nuremberg trials the United Nations General Assembly adopted a resolution in support of the principles of the Nuremberg Charter, an event considered by Cassese to be a significant step in the establishment of crimes against humanity as a part of customary international law.[99] In the years following World War II, the linkage between prohibited conduct and war was gradually dropped. Presently the Rome Statute contains no such requirement.

Turning now to consideration of the specific offenses involved here, the Trial Chamber convicted Appellant of the following:

> Article 7(1). For the purpose of this Statute, "crime against humanity" means any of the following acts when committed as part of a widespread or systematic attack directed against any civilian population, with knowledge of the attack:
> (a) Murder;

(k) Other inhumane acts of a similar character intentionally causing great suffering, or serious injury to body or to mental or physical health.

Article 7 further provides as follows:

7(2). For the purpose of paragraph 1:
(a) "Attack directed against any civilian population" means a course of conduct involving the multiple commission of acts referred to in paragraph 1, against any civilian population, pursuant to or in furtherance of a State or organizational policy to commit such attack.

The primary challenge that must be addressed by the Court lies in determining whether or not the material element has been sufficiently proven; that is, whether or not Appellant's decision to launch the chemical attack constitutes conduct prohibited by the language of the statute. Under the circumstances of this case, the most crucial element is that the attack must have been committed as part of a widespread or systematic attack on the civilian population. Appellant characterizes the attack as an isolated incident designed solely to repel an invading army and not targeted against the civilian population at all. The Prosecution relies on the magnitude of civilian impact, the failure to warn the civilian population of the impending attack, and the history of political unrest in the region directed toward Appellant's regime as indicative of something much broader.

Indeed, the breadth of conduct involved is crucial. "Normally, the very nature of crimes against humanity involves violations against civilians on a mass scale and not merely sporadic, isolated incidents."[100] "However, an offence under this particular Article may be committed against even one person, provided it is connected with a systematic or widespread attack against any civilian population. It is the attack which must be widespread or systematic, not the acts of the perpetrator."[101] Thus, the conduct in question must be "part of a pattern of misconduct. Subsequent case law has consistently borne out that this is a major feature of the crimes."[102] "Isolated inhumane acts of this nature may constitute grave infringements of human rights or, depending on the circumstances, war crimes, but fall short of the stigma attaching to crimes against humanity."[103]

What, then, is meant by the term systematic? "The word 'systematic' refers to the actual preparation, planning, strategy and the ultimate execution of those plans; in other words, the overall organizational skills attached to the particular operation."[104] Because nothing about the attack in question here appears consistent with such parameters, we conclude that the attack authorized by Appellant was not systematic.

However, the language of the statute can still be satisfied if the attack is determined to be sufficiently widespread, as it requires *either* widespread or systematic, not both. "It is not always an easy task to determine whether the attack was widespread. Factors to be considered include the actual numerical size of the group, the area in which the population lives, and the grave consequences that resulted from the attack on a particular group."[105] The Prosecution relies on the raw civilian casualty figures in support of its case. While we recognize the tragic nature of the human suffering reflected in these figures, we cannot conclude that, without more, the attack authorized by Appellant rose to a level that can be construed as widespread within the meaning of the statute. Given the typical population of even a very small state, the casualties that resulted here cannot include but a very small percentage of the civilian population. Furthermore, the record is devoid of any evidence to indicate that the attack was carried out anywhere but the geographic area actually occupied by the invading army. Thus, there is insufficient evidence to support a contention that the civilian population was targeted as such.

Therefore, we see no conclusion to be reached other than that the Prosecution failed to present sufficient evidence to prove the material element of the Article 7 offenses beyond a reasonable doubt as required by Article 66. Accordingly, the decision of the Trial Chamber as to these offenses must be reversed.

NECESSITY DEFENSE

Given the confusion that often arises among courts and commentators on these topics, we believe it would be useful to briefly explore the theoretical underpinnings of the concepts of justification and excuse before turning to their application to the instant case. "A justification is a circumstance that makes the accused's conduct preferable to even worse alternatives, such as self-defense; an excuse, such as duress, involves an action that, while voluntary, nevertheless was produced by an impairment of a person's autonomy to such a degree as to negate their blameworthiness."[106] Because these concepts are applicable only under extraordinary circumstances, they "are therefore relatively underdeveloped in international criminal jurisprudence and have not always been scrupulously distinguished from each other in the cases where they have arisen."[107] The basic distinction is that a justification results in conduct that would ordinarily be considered criminal being considered non-criminal, while an excuse still views the conduct as criminal but recognizes that the circumstances make it inappropriate to punish the perpetrator.[108]

This brief conceptual review is useful in that Appellant's Brief appears to raise both necessity and duress as defenses. Necessity is considered a justification, while duress is considered an excuse.[109] While necessity and duress are presented separately in Article 31, they are lumped together in one rule; the statute does not distinguish between them.[110]

Unfortunately, this lumping together of distinct concepts is also problematic of what appears to be the most recent major international case on the issue, certainly the one that is most discussed, *Prosecutor v. Erdemovic*.[111] Erdemovic was an ethnic Croat member of the Bosnian Serb army who, along with other members of his unit, participated in the firing squad execution of more than 1,000 unarmed Muslim men. Charged with crimes against humanity, Erdemovic admitted his role in the killings and entered a guilty plea but asserted that when he protested he was threatened with execution himself if he did not comply with the orders. Thus, the victims would have been killed regardless of whether or not he participated in the executions; he could not have saved any of them by sacrificing himself.

The Trial Chamber accepted Erdemovic's guilty plea but concluded that duress did not apply.[112] Following a lengthy review of various international and domestic legal contexts a bare majority of the Appeals Chamber ruled that duress cannot be asserted as a defense in settings involving the killing of unarmed innocent civilians. The court's conclusion appears to have been driven by the policy concern that the victim's life cannot be said to be outweighed by the defendant's. Such reasoning is found in a number of the world's legal systems. It is not new and can be traced to seminal cases such as *Dudley and Stephens*,[113] in which two shipwrecked sailors killed and ate the cabin boy when they had no other food.

Nonetheless, the *Erdemovic* court's reasoning appears inconsistent with a precise consideration of the concepts involved, a perspective shared by Luis E. Chisea.[114] Chisea argues that *Erdemovic* was wrongly decided because the Appeals Chamber failed to properly distinguish between duress as a justification and duress as an excuse. More specifically, improperly treating duress as a justification led the majority to incorrectly base its reasoning on a choice of evils analysis. This makes it all but impossible for a defendant to assert such a defense in a crimes against humanity context, as any harm to the individual defendant would be virtually assured of being outweighed by the sheer gravity of the harm involved in such an offense, whereas a correct approach would have avoided such a trap and led to duress being available as an excuse. Thus, the proper resolution would have been to maintain Erdemovic's conduct as unlawful but to recognize that he should not be punished for his unlawful conduct because in choosing it his will was overcome by the duress of the direct threats to his own life.

Regardless of whether *Erdemovic* was correctly decided, however, any contention that a necessity defense is inapplicable in the instant case due to the war crimes context is without merit. This becomes quite clear from a review of the history of Article 31,[115] adopted subsequent to the *Erdemovic* decision. The drafting committee received and considered a number of proposals with regard to defenses, many of which prohibited the defences from being applied to charges of murder.[116] The exclusion for murder charges continued through subsequent revisions but was ultimately dropped from the draft submitted by the working group's first report,[117] and obviously does not appear in the final version of Article 31 as adopted. This clearly indicates that the drafters of the statute seriously considered excluding applicability of the defenses to charges of murder but ultimately decided against such an exclusion. Therefore, we conclude that Article 31 defenses, subject to the court's discretion, are available to be raised in all cases prosecuted under the Rome Statute, thus effectively foreclosing any contentions to the contrary based on *jus cogens* considerations.

Having reached this conclusion, we now turn to a consideration of specific issues regarding the applicability of these defenses in the instant case. Article 31 provides in relevant part as follows:

> 31(1). In addition to other grounds for excluding criminal responsibility provided for in this Statute, a person shall not be criminally responsible if, at the time of that person's conduct:
> (c) The person acts reasonably to defend himself or herself or another person or, in the case of war crimes, property which is essential for the survival of the person or another person or property which is essential for accomplishing a military mission, against an imminent and unlawful use of force in a manner proportionate to the degree of danger to the person or the other person or property protected. The fact that the person was involved in a defensive operation conducted by forces shall not in itself constitute a ground for excluding criminal responsibility under this subparagraph;
> (d) The conduct which is alleged to constitute a crime within the jurisdiction of the Court has been caused by duress resulting from a threat of imminent death or of continuing or imminent serious bodily harm against that person or another person, and the person acts necessarily and reasonably to avoid this threat, provided that the person does not intend to cause a greater harm than the one sought to be avoided. Such a threat may either be:
> (i) Made by other persons; or
> (ii) Constituted by other circumstances beyond that person's control.

It is immediately apparent that the language of Article 31 fails to maintain the clarity we have sought to establish with regard to these important concepts. Eser also recognizes this and contends that this in artful blending of distinct concepts arose from the need for compromise in order to secure sufficient votes to assure passage of the statute.[118] While we are certainly appreciative of the practical need to pursue compromise in a legislative setting, such a course inescapably complicates the task of courts subsequently faced with the challenge of somehow applying a degree of certainty and specificity to the deliberate vagueness that results.

Although they are not expressly identified, it is apparent that 31(1)(d) addresses duress and 31(1)(c) addresses necessity. Turning first to duress, we recognize that the language of subparagraph (d) is quite broad and arguably supports a broader application of the defense than discussed above. However, we conclude that the statutory language is not so broad as to negate the fundamental concept that the defense properly applies to situations in which a crime is committed only because the will of the perpetrator is overpowered by a serious and specific threat or by circumstances beyond his control. Indeed, *Erdemovic* presents perhaps the prototypical scenario for duress. In this case there is no evidence that Appellant's will in choosing his conduct was overcome by a specific threat or by the circumstances in question. We are not unmindful of the grave nature of the situation in which Appellant acted, but such circumstances, their urgent nature notwithstanding, are not unlike those that high officials such as heads of state must sometimes face and are simply too indirect to support a defense of duress.

In addressing the applicability of the defense of necessity, we believe it is appropriate to first emphasize the last sentence of subparagraph (c):

> The fact that the person was involved in a defensive operation conducted by forces shall not in itself constitute a ground for excluding criminal responsibility under this subparagraph[.]

Unlike much of the language of Article 31, this language is more than sufficiently clear to dispel any contention that necessity automatically applies simply because Appellant's conduct occurred within the context of acting to repel the illegal invasion of his country. This does not mean that necessity cannot apply here; it simply means that we must examine the evidence to determine whether or not the conditions regarding the applicability of the defense have been satisfied.

In this regard, the Record clearly indicates that Appellant's country was the object of an illegal invasion by military forces of Neighboring State; that the war was going poorly for Appellant's country; that the invading forces were on the verge of seizing control of the natural gas resources that are the economic life blood of Appellant's country; and that significant civilian casualties had already resulted from the actions of the invading forces. The Prosecutor's response to Appellant's assertion of necessity is essentially limited to the conclusory contention that the invasion could have been repelled without resorting to the use of chemical weapons; however, no specific factual evidence (troop counts, relative levels of armaments between the two states, etc.) was presented in support of this contention.

Since the facts of the case are largely undisputed, the crucial question is whether the circumstances thus established satisfy the statutory conditions for necessity to apply. Because Appellant acted in the context of seeking to repel an illegal invasion of his country that had already resulted in significant civilian casualties and threatened control of vital resources, the essence of this inquiry is whether or not the use of chemical weapons was proportionate to the degree of danger created by the invasion. The requirement that a response be proportionate is not at all unusual and is found in the criminal law of a number of major legal systems, including those of the United States,[119] France,[120] and Germany.[121]

Before the question of proportionality can be answered, however, we must first determine whether the inquiry is to be made using an objective or a subjective perspective. Unfortunately, the in-artful drafting that blurred together the distinct concepts of necessity and duress also blurred together the subjective and objective perspectives. Eser[122] contends that both the subjective duress issue (whether the person's will was overcome by the threat) and the objective necessity issue (whether the Defendant actually chose the lesser of evils) disappear in the language of Article 31; they are replaced by an in-between standard that requires more than that required by the subjective/duress standard but less than that required by the objective/necessity standard. Thus, under this approach, what ultimately matters is not whether Appellant's conduct actually did accomplish the lesser evil but whether the conduct was chosen with the intent to do so.

While we understand the reasoning behind Eser's position, we tend to share Scaliotti's criticism that such a standard is "both difficult to be conceived in theory and concretely applied."[123] Given the very great gravity of the offenses prosecuted in this Court, we conclude that a proper analysis cannot lose sight of whether or not another person placed in Appellant's circumstances would choose the same conduct in pursuit of the lesser evil. We believe such an approach is both easier to apply in practice and more reflective of the ultimate policy goal, which is to extend to accused persons the opportunity to evade punishment for very grave offenses only under extraordinary circumstances. This important goal would be undermined by a focus on the subjective perspective of the perpetrator. Finally, we find that an objective approach is directly supported by the language of Article 31(1)(c) stating that "[t]he person acts *reasonably* to defend himself" (emphasis added).

In this case we see Appellant's position as offering a choice between watching his country be conquered by invading forces and resorting to the use of chemical weapons in an effort to repel the invasion. While, as discussed previously, turning to chemical weapons is an extreme measure by any standard, the relevant question is whether or not someone else placed in Appellant's circumstances would view it as a lesser evil than the alternative. We cannot say that the answer is other than yes. This is especially so in light of the fact that Appellant used the chemical agent only once; used it only in the geographic area occupied by the invading forces; and terminated its use immediately upon the retreat of the invading forces. We are mindful of the Prosecutor's contention that the loss of 2,000 civilians demonstrates the inherently excessive nature of Appellant's actions, but how can anyone know with reasonable certainty that fewer would have been lost had the invasion continued unabated?

In addition, this point serves to emphasize that the Prosecutor failed to offer any specific evidence to rebut Appellant's assertion of necessity. To be clear, to the extent that Appellant contends that he bears no burden of presenting evidence with regard to Article 31 defenses, we find such a contention to be without merit. While Article 66 makes it clear that the Prosecution bears the burden of proving guilt, both it and Article 31 are silent as to the burden of proof for asserting an Article 31 defenses. However, the Rules of Procedure and Evidence of the Rome Statute include the following:

> Rule 79
> Disclosure by the defence
> 1. The defence shall notify the Prosecutor of its intent to:
> (b) Raise a ground for excluding criminal responsibility provided for in article 31, paragraph 1, in which case the notification shall specify the names of witnesses and any other evidence upon which the accused intends to rely to establish the ground.

Paragraph 2 of Rule 79 goes on to provide that the Prosecutor is to have an opportunity to respond, including, where necessary, the right to a delay in the proceedings in order to prepare a response. Therefore, it is apparent that the language of Rule 79 places the burden of submitting sufficient evidence to demonstrate the applicability of the asserted defense on the Defendant, with the opportunity to respond being extended to the Prosecutor.[124] While the Prosecutor is thus under no obligation to present evidence in contravention of asserted defenses, failing to do so leaves the defense at issue where, as here, the facts in evidence are sufficient to indicate that the defense is properly before the court.

Finally, we trust that our analysis of these very significant issues of first impression in this Court will be of use to practitioners and others with an interest in these matters. We recognize that there exist a variety of reported decisions on similar issues, particularly in Post-World War II decisions and those of the various *ad hoc* tribunals. That we do not discuss more of them reflects no disrespect for the tribunals or their decisions but rather our desire to establish a jurisprudence of this Court based on a permanent statutory scheme for addressing these pressing international matters. In this regard, our decision in this case should not be taken in any way to suggest that the use of chemical weapons, under any set of circumstances, is anything other than one of the gravest situations that could confront the international community. Rather, our decision simply reflects the confluence of Appellant's very dire circumstances and the Prosecutor's ineffective response to Appellant's assertion of the necessity defense.

CONCLUSION

For the foregoing reasons, the decision of the Trial Chamber is hereby REVERSED. Furthermore, because the language of Article 31 specifies that "a person shall not be criminally responsible" where one of the defences applies, the sentence imposed on Appellant by the Trial Chamber is hereby vacated.

APPENDIX A: Examples of Judges' Questions and Lawyers' Answers from Student Moot Courts

Q: What is considered a "reasonable person" in this case?

A: A reasonable person is defined by criminal law in this case as a person who under normal circumstances would make reasonable judgments or arguments. In this instance a reasonable person would have prior knowledge of the consequences of an action and would take these into account when making his or her decision.

(space indicates a new topic)

Q: How do you know that the Head of State acted with intent?
A: As I said earlier on, the key words here are "rebellious region." The Head of State intended to kill or cause great harm to these rebellious civilians. Furthermore, the president did not inform or warn the rebellious civilians of the impending danger. Thirdly the president had the opportunity to evacuate the region before deploying the chemical weapons but did not. Lastly, the president violated Article 51 of the UN Charter by not informing the UN Security Council of the invasion of the country.

Q: I didn't see in the facts that the attack was directed against the region under rebellion. The attack was directed against an invading army. You are inferring from the facts that the Head of State wanted to attack a rebellious region, but the facts are that the chemical attack was to stop an invading army. That's the heart of the case. So you're making an inference are you not?
A: Yes.
Q: Well that's not an issue before the appellate court. You're making an inference that that was the motive for the attack. You're introducing a new argument here.
A: That was one of the Head of State's motives; attacking the invading army was the main motive.

Q: Now that we've clarified that the attack was directed against the invading army, you state the objective test is what a reasonable person would have done. There is an argument that the law is subjective, that what matters is the mindset of the Head of State, not that of an objective person. But let's start with the objective test. Is it not reasonable for the Head of State of a country to use chemical weapons against an invading army that means to take over the country?
A: I don't think the invading army would have been able to capture control of the country.
Q: Isn't it also a fact of the case that the country did not have a conventional army at its disposal?
A: It is also in the facts of the case that the Head of State wanted to protect natural resources.
Q: I want to talk about the necessity issue. How is it that you argue that conventional weapons couldn't have stopped the invading army and that chemical weapons weren't necessary?
A: The Head of State could not have used chemical weapons because he is a party to the Chemical Weapons Convention (CWC) and should not . . .
Q: But that's a separate question. That's a question as to whether it's legal or not. I'm asking you whether it's necessary.
A: I don't think it was necessary.
Q: Given that conventional weapons could not have stop the invasion?
A: Well then I think that she could have tried to negotiate with the invading country rather than deploying chemical weapons . . .

Q: But the country was invaded. The negotiations failed because of the invasion, not because of the Head of State's use of chemical weapons. I'm asking you why, when conventional weapons weren't an option, the use of chemical weapons was not a necessity?
A: I think that as a party to the CWC, which I know you say is a separate question. The Head of State should not have used chemical weapons. I think there were other means to stop the invasion. At the very least the Head of State should have evacuated the region beforehand or provided enough medical support needed for the population. The Head of State should have made efforts to protect the civilian population.
Q: What you're saying is that it was necessary but the necessity has to be proportionate?
A: Yes and it wasn't proportionate.
Q: You're admitting that it was necessary.
A: I do not want to agree that it was necessary. I'm not agreeing that it was necessary.

Q: You say that it's an objective test, what a reasonable person might do. What's your source of law for that?
A: I looked it up on www.law.com.
Q: Please tell us what it said from memory. Just the general argument; you don't have to quote it. Why is a subjective test not necessary, but an objective test is? Why must a president be reasonable as opposed to just sincere? You're conceding that the Head of State was sincere but not reasonable?
A: I'm saying the Head of State wasn't sincere and he was not reasonable.
Q: You're saying the Head of State failed both tests? If the Court were to rule that a subjective test applies, you'll have to address that. If the Court rules that an objective test applies, you're going to have to say why you think an objective test is the better test; why the law says it must be a reasonable person test rather than a subjective test. You can address this in closing statements.
A: A reasonable person is a hypothetical . . .
Q: That's the definition of a reasonable person, not why it must be an objective test. You can address this in closing statements.

Q: A widespread or systematic attack against a civilian population is the contextual element of crimes against humanity which is covered in Article 7 of the Rome Statute. How is the contextual element met when the Head of State did not intend to attack a civilian population?
A: Because of the long-term damage to the region from the president's use of chemical weapons.
Q: Are you arguing that the attack was not on an invading army?
A: Well, obviously he intended to stop the invasion but actually the magnitude of the attack was felt by the civilian population. The long-term damage to the civilian population was greater.

Q: Does the UN Charter have a time limit for notification of the Security Council?
A: I don't think so. I think it has to be right away.
Q: What is the legal basis for this? There are cases of countries notifying the Security Council that they're acting in self-defense. You can't expect the Head of State, in the midst of an attack, to know every facet of the law can you?
A: This is why the president has other people on command to be sure that he does what is expected of him as a Head of State. So I would assume that someone would inform him of the law. I assume that the Head of State cannot act by instinct but must be rational. This is another reason why the objective test is used.
Q: The Charter says that it is also an "inherent right to self-defense." So that would imply that notification of the Security Council is not absolutely necessary. Isn't that right?
A: Well, that is right, but also being party to the CWC . . .
Q: So it's just a detail, a formality, informing the Security Council. Is that right?
A: Well, it is a formality, but I think that the Security Council makes the ultimate call. One of its goals is to prevent wars and chaos and to continue peace between the neighboring states. They should have to be informed right away because they could offer substantial help.

Q: With respect to the war crimes charge . . . Article 8(2) addresses willful killing of the civilian population which implies intent. Is there any evidence that the Head of State intended to kill the civilian population?
A: As I argued before the Head of State chose not to inform civilians of the danger . . .
Q: But that's negligence, not willfulness. Are you saying that negligence is the legal intent requirement and not intent itself?
A: I think intent is the main requirement.
Q: So you're saying that the Head of State intended to kill her own civilians?
A: Yes.
Q: So you're not saying that the Head of State used chemical weapons to save her population?
A: No, it was an excuse to attack a rebellious population.
Q: Later on I want you to address negligence as opposed to willfulness and objective versus subjective tests.

Q (asked in rebuttal): Why is the objective test appropriate?
A: Well, because in this case we cannot use subjective. We cannot just take her word as Head of State as correct. Rather we have to compare and contrast if a reasonable person would be able to foresee the harm or the danger to

the civilian population. That's why I think an objective test should be used in this case. Does that suffice?
Q: Well, you really want the advice of case law on this.

Q (asked in rebuttal): I just have one question: is it reasonable for the Head of State to have evacuated the region ahead of time? Wouldn't that give notice to the invading army of the Head of State's plans to use chemical weapons? Would it not be a valid defense that they needed to keep that a secret?
A: One of the Head of State's main obligations is to protect her civilian population. In this scenario he failed to do this. There are other ways in which the Head of State could have evacuated the region without the invading army knowing about it.

Q: At what point is an attack proportional?
A: The criteria used are that it is proportionate to the degree of danger faced by the nation. In this case the Head of State did have to make a choice between sacrificing the lives a few to save the remaining ninety eight percent of the population. We argue that the attack was proportionate. Also if you want to address the damage to natural resources, the attack only affected one region and the damage lasts only for a few years. In terms of the criteria it was proportionate. And if the invading country had taken over the Head of State would have had no land at all so it was proportionate.

Q: I have another question. Let's say this class was being attacked by a mob and we were stuck inside this classroom. We can't escape and the only weapon we have to protect ourselves is a grenade. We know that if we launch this grenade it will kill the mob outside plus innocent persons. So in that instance would you launch the grenade in self-defense?
A: Under the circumstances first I would consider what other options I had. I would want to have exhausted those options first. The attack is legal under the necessity defense if it is a last resort. My options in that case would be to scream, call for assistance, or try to negotiate with the mob outside. If the grenade was my last resort, yes I would use it. If this were a country, under Article 51 of the UN Charter, we do have an inherent right to self-defense.

Q: Your co-counsel said that the term "widespread and systematic attack," the contextual element of crimes against humanity, was very ambiguous. However you appear to provide a more precise definition. Could you explain this discrepancy?
A: Yes, it's ambiguous in the general term, but we provided case law . . .
Q: No, you didn't. You cited Gerhard Werle on this matter. Why should we listen to him?
A: He's a renowned scholar.
Q: It's just his opinion though isn't it?

A: Well he quotes a lot of case law in his book. One of the cases he quotes is the one I mentioned: *Prosecutor v. Kunarać*. We relied on that source to argue that it was systematic. Also, with regards to that case the defendants in that case were clearly isolating women and then attacking them. We argue in this case that the same criteria are not inapplicable. The Head of State did not isolate any one, he acted on the basis of a threat.
Q: So that case is not even relevant. In that case the set of facts states that they intended to harm the population whereas in your case the Head of State didn't. Why rely on that case?
A: Because in that case defendants acted in a discriminatory nature. In our case the Head of State didn't.
Q: So indiscriminate attacks are legal? That case was discriminate; yours is indiscriminate.
A: Well, what I'm saying is that in that case it seems that there was discrimination. In this case there wasn't. The Trial Chamber in *Kunarać* held that since it was discriminatory it was systematic. We're just using it to contrast with our case and our facts. In our case it wasn't discriminatory, therefore it was not systematic.

Q: Please tell me why you think the subjective test should replace the objective test? Secondly if the Court does not accept your argument about the subjective test tell me why the objective test would follow the criteria of reasonableness that you have presented which is that a percentage of the population was killed for crimes against humanity and more importantly in war crimes that the killing avoided the standard of negligence which the prosecutor said would apply?
A: Can we address the issue of recklessness or negligence in our rebuttal?
Q: All right. Why do you think the subjective test should replace the objective test?
A: I do not know what to say to that. The reasoning of using the subjective test is based on the principle of natural law, self-determination. So in the case the country has the right to self-defense.
Q: That's not natural law. It's in the UN Charter.
A: But that is another criteria that Werle mentions in his commentary.
Q: I'm asking why should we rely on the subjective test when the test is the mind of the person not the test of a reasonable person?
A: Because we are dealing with a specific set of circumstances.
Q: What about the law? What set of legal sources do you have?
A: I do not have any legal sources.
Q: If you could address that in your rebuttal that would be great.

Q: In defining self-defense the Prosecution argued that it has to be construed narrowly. Self-defense has never been a broad doctrine. Among the requirements for self-defense is that, not only does it have to be proportionate, but the notion of reactive self-defense or instantaneousness. The use of chemical weapons did occur after the invasion but what is your evidence that it was an instant reaction as opposed to something that was not done with forethought and premeditation?

A: What we're arguing is that he did not have the predetermination . . . that he only chose to use chemical weapons after he had exhausted all of her options.

Q: Your definition of necessity, which you provided from the Statute, do you have any case law on that? It clearly needs some case law to flesh out the application.

A: The author (Werle) said that it was used in the Nuremberg trials.

Q: For what Nazi war crime?

A: I don't have a specific answer for that.

Q: If you think that negligence and recklessness are not the criteria for the mental element for either war crimes or crimes against humanity, I would appreciate some case law saying that it's only intent and knowledge in your final remarks, as well as some case law saying the consequences of the attack on the invading army is not the same thing as a widespread or systematic attack on a civilian population.

Q: Collateral damage requires some advance analysis, according to some cases, that is it is only okay to have collateral damage against civilians if you considered it beforehand. The Prosecution says that this was not considered at all. There is no evidence from the set of facts given that there was any evaluation of the consequences of an attack to the civilian population. Although 1.7 percent deaths sounds like a low number, we're talking about higher numbers of injured over the long run. It seems unreasonable to expect there not to be cancers and some of the other diseases that show up as a consequence of the use of chemical weapons.

A: As I mentioned he did not know the full extent of the damage. We will concede that he didn't know beforehand the full extent of the damage.

Q: Did he evaluate at all . . .

A: Well, when he was deciding to use the weapons he probably evaluated that the deaths of the 1.7 percent of the population were the necessary means to stop an invasion, to protect the other 98.3 percent of the population.

Q: He didn't know it would be 1.7 percent or 100 percent or zero percent.

A: He didn't anticipate the excessive collateral damage.

Q: Okay and a reasonable person would have?

A: Well, we're considering the subjective test.

Q: You're arguing that a reasonable person would not have known that either?

A: I don't see how a reasonable person would not have known that.

Q: Now given that these are illegal weapons why didn't the country inform the Security Council immediately that this was their last resort?

A: Because they were under attack and did not have time.

Q: You don't have to ask for permission you just have to notify the Security Council. Don't you think that a reasonable person would have notified the Council? It would have strengthened their case, that this was a last resort.
A: A person might, but countries are not people; they are distracted states attempting to survive in a hostile environment.
Q: Now, the Prosecution argues that the use of chemical weapons was disproportionate. You're arguing that it was proportionate to the military objectives. Why is the criteria the military's objectives and not something like national security which would be considered a political objective? And if this population was rebelling, they may be rebelling because they don't want to be in the country, or because that they don't care about the national security of the country and they feel the objective of national security is really the political objective of the Head of State.
A: The facts of the case did not really state why these people were rebelling. We used proportional standards in regard to military objectives because they were attacking a country, its essential national resources. If she did not kill every single one of the invading army it would have been a threat to their natural resources. If he hadn't acted he would have lost her country, her sovereignty.

Q: You said you cannot provide us with a source of law for the objective versus subjective tests, but how about a source of law for the mental element, which is the question of why recklessness and/or negligence are not the test?
A: As far as this case goes, I don't have it. There are many cases in the International Tribunal for the former Yugoslavia that address the issue of recklessness and in most of those cases that I read neither negligence nor recklessness amounts to intent.
Q: So you're saying that if there was a mass murder that happened as a result of negligence that could not be a war crime?
A: Well as far as war crimes go you have to have intent to murder to a civilian population . . .
Q: For murder, but it could be manslaughter.
A: Right, well as far as recklessness goes perhaps the Head of State was reckless in the amount of chemical weapons that were used because these weapons had not been used before . . . .
Q: You're admitting to a crime?
A: Being reckless?
Q: Well what you're saying is that recklessness not a requirement?
A: Right.
Q: And the reason is you've read these cases in the ICTY?
A: Right.
Q: If recklessness and negligence were to apply do you have any argument to say that Head of State was not negligent or reckless? If the Court were to find that a lower mental standard were applicable could you argue the facts to say that the Head of State was not reckless or negligent? You seem to be saying that the Head of State was reckless.

A: I didn't say that he was reckless. I said possibly. He might be construed as having been reckless.
Q: You might say that there is no proof beyond a reasonable doubt that the Head of State was reckless or negligent?
A: Right.
Q: Why would you say that?
A: Because in order to be negligent you need to have a conscious or unconscious deviation from the standard of care which causes a result prohibited by criminal law.
Q: Is there any precedent for chemical weapons where it's legal because of necessity?
A: Unfortunately, no. I haven't found any precedent.
Q: How about for recklessness? Is there any analogy? If the Germans had used chemical weapons to defend themselves from the Allies would that have been legal?
A: I would say, prior to the CWC, yes. During WWII, that was prior to the Geneva Conventions which prohibit asphyxiating gasses as well, so I would say yes.
Q: Actually, there were prior Geneva Conventions that addressed that.
A: Well, in World War I, they used chlorine gas offensively. The Geneva Conventions resulted from that because it proved to be indiscriminate and unfair.

Q (question asked in rebuttal): The Prosecution argues that there was a duty of care to mitigate the consequences of the chemical attack. What is your explanation for the delay in response?
A: Well, unfortunately under a fog of war there is so much information coming in to a Head of State that a lot of times things go not according to plan or unforeseen circumstances arise. In this case the unforeseen circumstance was that the chemical weapons transferred from the battlefield to the civilian areas. It as an unintended result. Plus, it took time to protect the people. It takes time to equip the first responders.
Q: What about the Prosecution's argument that the only responsible response would have been to announce an evacuation?
A: Well, announcing an evacuation in an area under political turmoil would have foiled the military's objective.
Q: Why?
A: Because the civilian population could have possibly sympathized with those invaders or there could have been informants that the invading army placed in that region knowing that that is an area of political turmoil. It would have been a perfect area for the enemy to go in and infiltrate. As I said before, this was not a direct attack on the civilian population. It was an attack on a battlefield that was near the civilian population.

Q: Wouldn't the knowledge that you're about to use chemical weapons have stopped them from invading? Would it not have been preferable to say that we're willing to use chemical weapons?
A: That would have been preferable but unfortunately . . . if invading country is party to the CWC then neither of these countries should have had access to chemical weapons. But being that invading country's invasion was unlawful under Article 2 of the UN Charter . . . like I said under the fog of war many things happen. Invading country had already walked away from the peace agreements. They were unwilling to negotiate. If they were intent upon invading and taking over the natural resources, I believe they would have done so regardless of whether the Head of State used chemical weapons or said he was going to use chemical weapons or not. They could have just called her bluff.

APPENDIX B: Alterable Facts that Students and Faculty Could Adopt to Change the Legal Arguments

Students and faculty can alter the facts so that different legal issues are raised from those presented in this chapter. One might want to increase the relevance of the fog of war, causing lack of real-time knowledge as well as the tendency of warring sides to lie, to themselves and to others. There are blue walls of silence. People do not always report things accurately from the battlefield. In the Head of State's office they also lie and they are not going to concede anything. Democracies do not always prosecute their own. Dictatorships prosecute even fewer than democracies do, which is almost none. Would it be reasonable for a judge to assume that the defense is holding back information and that there might even be proof beyond a reasonable doubt that the Head of State knew these other consequences that might deny the necessity defense on grounds of distinction? Should the facts make the necessity defense ambiguous, where the "more likely than not" standard is unclear in real time? Could the Head of State have called up all these extra divisions and used weapons more effectively?

Factual changes could include:

1. In 2006 the Neighboring State invaded the territory of the Head of State's country in violation of Article 2(4) of the United Nations Charter, possibly or definitely committing the crime of aggression and did or did not claim that the motive was in anticipatory or preventive self-defense because of past disputes between the two countries. The invasion by the Neighboring State threatened the oil resources of the Head of State's country, as both countries have or have not had a boundary dispute over the ownership of these resources for several decades. The Head of State had or had not attempted to have the International Court of Justice resolve this boundary dispute.

2. The tactics by the invading army of the Neighboring State were or were not intended to cause incidental deaths and/or injuries to civilians, damage to civilian properties, and widespread, long-term damage to the environment, or were the result of recklessness or negligence. Additionally the invading army did or did not threaten other resources of the Head of State's country.
3. The Head of State did or did not order the use of banned chemical weapons on August 14, 2006. The country is or is not a state party to the Convention on the Prohibition of the Development, Production, Stockpiling and Use of Chemical Weapons and on Their Destruction, to the Rome Statute of the International Criminal Court, and to the United Nations.
4. The chemical weapons were used outside or inside the borders of the Head of State's country and were or were not limited to the extent that they halted the attacks of the invading army or were or were not to retaliate or to deter additional attacks.
5. Approximately 400 to 500 or 40,000 to 50,000 national combatants were killed in action, in addition to 1,600 to 2,000 or 100,000 to 125,000 civilian deaths and 4,000 or 400,000 injuries. Long-term effects in the region did or did not include a rise in birth defects, widespread disease, crop devastation, and damage to the environment.
6. Prior to 2006, there was or was not a period of unrest in the region where chemical weapons were deployed, which did or did not include members of the opposition and/or ethnic minorities in small or large percentages. During the unrest, a low or high percentage of the civilians engaged in anti-governmental protests. The chemical weapons were deployed in the areas with the highest concentration of unrest.
7. Efforts were or were not made to warn the civilian population *before* or after the commencement of hostilities.
8. The government did or did not discover civilian health problems, which did or did not prompt the government to evacuate the areas where chemical weapons were used. The government did or did not provide health care to those injured, including or not including foreign soldiers captured. Civilians were or were not warned to keep away from the battlefield before or after the chemical weapons were used.
9. There was or was not evidence of the chemical weapons attack which did or did not implicate the civilians or minority groups. The invading soldiers did or did not have reason to suspect that chemical weapons might be used against them and did or did not take precautions against that possibility.
10. The United Nations had or had not negotiated a peace treaty between the two countries two years prior to the invasion and the invasion was or was not response to an alleged or actual, grave breach of that treaty by the Head of State's country. Escalating tensions did or did not lead to additional negotiations occurring during the attack or ending be-

forehand in failure. After the invasion, the Head of State did or did not report to the UN Security Council that it was taking defensive actions permitted under the legal doctrine of necessity. Conventional defensive methods using artillery and combat soldiers would or would not have repelled the invading forces, or there was substantial uncertainty over what might occur. The UN Security Council did or did not respond to the information of the defensive actions in a timely manner.

11. The long-term impact on natural resources and livestock in the Head of State's country was or was not wonton as the chemical weapons did or did not produce widespread destruction of said resources and the Head of State did or did not attempt to protect said resources.

12. The Head of State did have or lacked knowledge of the likely consequences the use of chemical weapons would have on his population. He did or did not believe that the use of chemical weapons to halt the invading army of the Neighboring State was proportional to the threat.

13. The alleged war crimes were or were not intended to protect the country's access to raw materials it did or did not actually need for survival. If the country had waited, the resources would, might have, or would not have fallen into its enemies hands and/or risked the potential of being destroyed during the conflict. Given the time constraints, potential for disaster, and limited national defense resources, the Head of State had or did not have other military options then to deploy the chemical weapons.

14. The region in which the chemical weapons were deployed had a long history of rebellious activity, some or none of it stimulated by covert activity and arms provision by the neighboring country.

15. The Head of State's attitude about the safety and well-being of civilians residing in the target region was or as not influenced by anti-government demonstrations conducted by some or many members of this civilian population, representing the goals irredentist goals of the neighboring country. These protests did or did not induce the Head of State to refrain from warning the civilian population of the impending chemical weapons attack, or his failure to warn them reflected negligence or just oversight based on ignorance of the consequences.

Faculty and students could consider a different scenario, such as:

In August of 2010 the north-east region of Asialand was the scene of an international armed conflict. Two years prior its outbreak, the Security Council of the United Nations had negotiated a peace treaty between the two sovereign States of Asialand, where Defendant Sue Young was President, and Punkistan, country of the invading army. Despite the peace treaty, Punkistan, in August of 2010, invaded the north-east territory of Asialand, which constituted a violation of Article 2(4) of the United Nations Charter. The Trial Chamber of this Moot-ICC considered it noteworthy to indicate that, prior to 2010, there was a period of unrest and anti-government protests in that north-east region of Asialand. The chemical weapons were used within the borders of Asialand in the areas with the highest concentration of unrest, although there were no issues of direct chemical weapons attack on civilians or minority groups. The deployment was limited to the extent that it halted the attacks of the invading army of Punkistan. When civilian health problems were identified, the government evacuated the area and promptly provided medical assistance to the injured civilians.

On August 14, 2010, in response to the invasion of the army of Punkistan, the Defendant Sue Young ordered the deployment of chemical weapons in violation of the Convention on the Prohibition of the Development, Production, Stockpiling, and Use of Chemical Weapons and on their Destruction of which Asialand was a party to in addition to being party to the Rome Statute of the International Criminal Court and to the United Nations. Sue Young contends that the use of the weapons was a last resort intended to stop the attack posed by the invasion of Punkistan. The tactics of the invading army were such that they would cause incidental injuries and deaths to civilians, damage civilian properties, cause long-term damage to the environment, and would threaten resources that were vital to the survival of the population of Asialand. The Defendant contends that if she had waited to launch a counter-attack, the resources would have fallen into the hands of Punkistan and/or would have risked the potential of being destroyed during the conflict. The Trial Court stipulated that prior to the deployment of the chemical weapons Sue Young did not request the UN-Security Council permission to deploy chemical weapons, citing the inability to repel the invading forces by conventional means, time constraints compounded by the UN Security Council being historically slow to respond, and the threat to essential resources of Asialand.

Finally, the Defendant did not make any effort to warn the population of the impending attack. She asserts that, since she did not have knowledge of the extent of the harm that would result from the deployment of the weapons, she did not anticipate the consequences and believed that the use of chemical weapons to halt the invading army was proportional. As a result of the attack, approximately 2,000 combatants of the army of Punkistan were killed in action, 16,000 Asialand civilians died, and there were 35,000 reported injuries. The estimated total population of Asialand was around four million at the time of the deployment of the chemical weapons. It was also determined that the land was not apt for crop production for a period of four years and that the long-term effects in the region would include a rise in birth defects, widespread disease, crop devastation, and damage to the environment.

Notes

1. The use of chemical weapons by the government, including mustard gas, actually preceded the al-Anfal campaign. The al-Anfal campaign was conducted in three stages; the first in February 1988, the second in early spring and the last offensive in August

1988. Van Brulnessen has categorized the Iraqi government's purposes in the al-Anfal campaign to: "break the Kurdish armed resistance and to enforce a massive resettlement program by frightening the civilian population into leaving their villages. This resettlement program was itself meant to impede future Kurdish guerilla movements." Martin van Brulnessen, "Genocide in Kurdistan?: The Suppression of the Dersim Rebellion in Turkey (1937-38) and the Chemical War Against the Iraqi Kurds (1988)," in *Genocide: Conceptual and Historical Dimension*, ed. George J. Andreopoulos (Philadelphia: University of Pennsylvania Press, 1994), 156. More generally van Brulnessen considers the government's use of chemical weapons to be only one part of a lengthy campaign against Kurdish society in Iraq. For his complete discussion about the chemical attacks, see "Genocide," 154-161. While the trials in Iraq demonstrate the legal consequences of the use of chemical weapons, in other cases involving the use of weapons that indiscriminately target civilians, justice has eluded victims. NATO's aerial bombardment of Yugoslavia and Kosovo 1999 although not involving chemical weaponry, did cause considerable suffering and damage to civilian populations, and included the use of depleted uranium, which some regard as a type of chemical weapon. Similar arguments can be made about the more recent military campaigns conducted in Afghanistan and Iraq. The United States used napalm in World War II's strategic bombing of Germany and Japan, as well as later in the 1960s in Vietnam.

2. William Schabas, *Genocide in International Law: The Crime of Crimes,* 2d ed. (Cambridge, UK: Cambridge University. Press, 2009), 424; see also Gerhard Werle, *Principles of International Criminal Law*, 2d ed. (The Hague: T-M-C-Asser Press, 2009), 115-116.

3. Charter of the United Nations, Art. 2(4) (1945).

4. Common Article 3(1) states: "persons taking no part in the hostilities, including members of armed forces who have laid down their arms and those placed *hors de combat* by sickness, wounds or any other means . . . are, in all circumstances, to be treated humanely, without any distinction founded on race, colour, religion or faith, sex, birth or wealth, or any other similar criteria." See for example, Geneva Convention (III). Geneva, August 12, 1949, www.icrc.org/ihl.nsf/FULL/375?OpenDocument. Also Rome Statute of the International Criminal Court, UN Coc. A/CONF.183/9, Art. 8(c)-(f).

5. For these and other controversies students should consult Antonio Cassese, *International Criminal Law*, 2d ed. (Oxford: Oxford University Press, 2008), 96-97.

6. The former prohibits the use of "asphyxiating, poisonous or other gases, and all analogous liquids, materials or devices," not chemical weapons per se. The latter is a "catch-all provision" which includes weapons that "cause superfluous injury or unnecessary suffering or which are inherently indiscriminate in violation of the international law of armed conflict" but which may only be included by annex to the Statute. Rome Statute, Articles 8(2)(b)(xviii) and (xx). For Werle's discussion on these points, see *Principles*, 457, 459-461.

7. Werle, *Principles*, 463.

8. Protocol for the Prohibition of the Use of Asphyxiating, Poisonous or Other Gases, and of Bacteriological Methods of Warfare. www.icrc.org.

9. Werle, *Principles*, 465.

10. Rome Statute, Art. 8(2)(b).

11. Convention (IV) relative to the Protection of Civilian Persons in Time of War, Geneva, August 12, 1949, http://www.icrc.org/ihl.nsf/FULL/380?OpenDocument (accessed June 30, 2011); Convention (IV) respecting the Laws and Customs of War on Land and its annex: Regulations concerning the Laws and Customs of War on Land, The Hague, October 18, 1907, http://www.icrc.org/ihl.nsf/FULL/195?OpenDocument (ac-

cessed June 30, 2011); see also Protocol Additional to the Geneva Conventions of 12 August 1949, and relating to the Protection of Victims of International Armed Conflicts (Protocol I), http://www.icrc.org/ihl.nsf/FULL/470?OpenDocument (accessed June 30, 2011).

12. Rome Statute, Art. 8(2)(b)(iv) and 8(2)(a)(iii), respectively.

13. As Cassese discusses, these grave breaches targeting "persons or property protected under the provisions of the relevant Geneva Conventions" is one of five different categories of war crimes. The other five are crimes against civilians or combatants that result from prohibited *methods* of warfare; crimes against these same protected groups that arise from prohibited *means* of warfare; crimes against protected persons (i.e., Red Cross officials etc.); crimes involving the fraudulent use of protected emblems and signs, and lastly prohibitions on the use of child soldiers. Cassese, *International Criminal Law*, 88-92.

14. Rome Statute, Art. 30(2)(a) and (b).

15. Rome Statute, Art. 30(3).

16. On this point see Werle, *Principles*, 377-378.

17. Rome Statute, Art. 7(1).

18. The International Criminal Tribunal for Rwanda (ICTR) has defined "widespread" as "'a massive, frequent, large scale action, carried out collectively with considerable seriousness and directed against a multiplicity of victims"; "systematic" as "thoroughly organised and following a regular pattern on the basis of a common policy involving substantial public or private resources." Malcolm N. Shaw, *International Law*, 6th ed. (Cambridge, UK: Cambridge University Press, 2008), 437, citing International Criminal Tribunal for Rwanda, *Prosecutor v. Jean Paul Akayesu*, Case No. ICTR-96-4-T, Judgment, para. 580 (September 2, 1998). For a somewhat different definition of "systematic" see The International Criminal Tribunal for the Former Yugoslavia, *Prosecutor v. Tibomir Blaškić*, Case No. IT-95-14-T, Judgment, paras. 203-204 (March 3, 2000) cited in Shaw, *International Law*, 437. For problems associated with narrow scope of Article 7, see Cassese, *International Criminal Law*, 124-126.

19. Rome Statute, Art. 7(1)(a), (b) and (d); also 7(2)(b) and (d).

20. Rome Statute, Art. 7(1)(k).

21. UN Charter, Art. 51.

22. International Court of Justice, *Military and Paramilitary Activities in and Against Nicaragua (Nicaragua v. United States of America)* 1986 ICJ Reports 14; from Shaw, *International Law*, 1132. Students should become familiar with the *Nicaragua* case and other ICJ cases in which the principle of self-defense is contested. See for example, *Oil Platforms (Islamic Republic of Iran v. the United States of America)*, Judgment 2003 ICJ Reports at 161 and *Armed Activities on the Territory of the Congo (Democratic Republic of the Congo v. Uganda)*, Judgment, 2005 ICJ Reports at 168 all of which can be obtained from the ICJ website: www.icj-cij.org/docket/index.php?p1=3&p2=3.

23. Whereas individual self-defense committed as part of "a defensive operation conducted by forces" is prohibited by Article 31(1)(c) of the ICC Statute. Rome Statute, Art. 31(1)(c); for further discussion on this point, see Werle, *Principles*, 203; also Cassese, *International Criminal Law*, 259-260.

24. It may be useful for instructors at this point to discuss the distinction between necessity and duress. Necessity may be warranted when "threats to life and limb [emanate] from *objective circumstances* [emphasis in original]"; duress when an actor faces "threat or psychological compulsion by one or more persons." Cassese, *International Criminal Law*, 280. Students will discover that Article 31(1)(d) includes *both* together as

a single defense. Article 31(1)(d) reflects and codifies customary international law. *International Criminal Law*, 289.

25. The use of armed force to respond to an imminent threat in self-defense is different from the use of force in anticipation of an attack in that with the latter the attack by the belligerent force is only forcible. Whether the use of force in anticipation is appropriate or not is also a matter of a state's assessment of its options. Miscalculations are especially likely to occur and can have devastating consequences. For further discussion see Shaw, *International Law*, 1137-1140.

26. Werle, *Principles*, 201-208; Cassese, *International Criminal Law*, 281; on self-defense, 259; state self-defense, Shaw, *International Law*, 1131-1143. For further discussion regarding the proportionality requirement see Frederic L. Kirgis, "Some Proportionality Issues Raised by Israel's Use of Armed Force in Lebanon," *ASIL Insights*, 10, no. 20 (2006).

The conditions set forth above are similar in some respects to the requirements for the justification of a military reprisal. Defined as "the unilateral use of military force in an attempt to enforce international law" (see Thomas R. Van Dervort, *International Law and Organization: An Introduction* [London: Sage Publications, 1998], 474) reprisals are used in cases involving serious violations of international law by another state and must not be used as an act of military retaliation. Werle, *Principles*, 225.

27. Rome Statute, Art. 31(1)(d).

28. You also have situations of jury nullification in which a jury completely disregards the offender's violation because they perceive the law violated to be immoral.

29. In this case it would amount to the Respondent making the argument that the use of chemical weapons is justified by the fact that his country was invaded; one bad acts deserves another. As Werle states there are no bases "found in either customary international law or treaty law for taking this as grounds for exclusion." *Principles*, 226-227.

30. Rome Statute, Art. 8(2)(a)(iv).

31. Rome Statute, Art. 31(3).

32. Werle, *Principles*, 225, 421-422, 424.

33. D'Amato contends that the underlying notion to military necessity is the principle of cost effectiveness. In this case destruction of property, harm to a civilian population, may be justified as a means of averting even more deaths should the war continue over the long-term. Anthony D'Amato, *International Law Anthology*, (Cincinnati, OH: Anderson Publishing Company, 1994), 235. On a separate note, in the current case discussed in this section, there is a certain degree of irony associated with the president's choice to destroy property/kill people in order to save property/people.

34. For further discussion on this point, see Werle, *Principles*, 208. The proportionality requirement is also included Article 8(2)(b)(iv) of the Rome Statute. In this instance the damage caused by the attack must not be "clearly excessive in relation to the concrete and direct overall military advantage anticipated." Rome Statute, Art. 8(2)(b)(iv).

35. This again also refers back to the military defense argument. For applicable sources of law students can consult the Geneva Conventions and their Optional Protocols; also Shaw, *International Law*, 1184, 1190.

36. International Criminal Court, *SITUATION IN DARFUR, Sudan, In the Case of The Prosecutor v. Ahmad Muhammad Harun ("AHMADHARUN") and Ali Muhammad Al Abd-Al-Rahman ("A U KUSHAYB")*, ICC No.: ICC-02/05-01/07 (April 27, 2007), 32.

37. International Criminal Tribunal for the Former Yugoslavia (ICTY), *Prosecutor v. Kunarać*, Case No. IT-96-23/1-A, Judgment, para 85 (June 12, 2002).

38. ICTY, *Prosecutor v. Kordić and Čerkez*, Case No. IT-95-14/2-T, Judgment, paras 211-212 (February 26, 2001).

39. This is a requirement for crimes against humanity. See *Prosecutor v. Kunarać,* Appeals Judgment, paras. 85, 90-92.

40. Jefferson D. Reynolds, "Collateral Damage on the 21st Century Battlefield: Enemy Exploitation of the Law of Armed Conflict, and the Struggle for a Moral High Ground," 56 AFLR (2005) 1, http://www.afjag.af.mil/shared/media/document/AFD-081009-011.pdf.

41. Reynolds, "Collateral Damage," 71.

42. On this point, see Gerhard Werle, *Principles of International Criminal Law*, (The Hague: T-M-C Asser Press, 2009), 457.

43. Charter of the United Nations (1945).

44. ICTY, *Prosecutor v. Kordić and Čerkez,* Trial Judgment, para. 449.

45. See Elies van Sliedregt, "Defences in International Criminal Law" (paper presented at the conference Convergence of Criminal Justice Systems). "Building Bridges—Bridging the Gap," *The International Society for the Reform of Criminal Law 17th International Conference*, August 25, 2003, http://www.isrcl.org/Papers/Sliedregt.pdf, 14.

46. Gerhard Werle, *Principles of International Criminal Law*, 1st ed. (Cambridge: Cambridge University Press, 2005), 113, 144.

47. Werle, *Principles*, 1st ed. 144.

48. Protocol for the Prohibition of the Use of Asphyxiating, Poisonous or Other Gases, and of Bacteriological Methods of Warfare (Geneva, 17 June 1925), http://www.icrc.org/ihl.nsf/FULL/280?OpenDocument.

49. Gerhard Werle, *Principles of International Criminal Law*, (The Hague: T-M-C Asser Press, 2009), 461; see especially ff. 830.

50. Convention on the Prohibition of the Development, Production, Stockpiling and Use of Chemical Weapons and on their Destruction (1993).

51. Cathy Scott-Clark and Adrian Levy, "Spectre Orange," *Guardian*, March 29, 2003, http://www.guardian.co.uk/world/2003/mar/29/usa.adrianlevy.

52. Allafrica.com, "Nigeria: Shell to Pay N62.5bn for Oil Spill in Ogoniland," August 4, 2011 http://allafrica.com/stories/201108040007.html (accessed August 5, 2011); also Allafrica.com, "Nigeria: Shell Admits Liability Over Ogoni Oil Spills," August 4, 2011, http://allafrica.com/stories/201108040320.html (accessed August 5, 2011).

53. Dinah Shelton, Decision Regarding Communication 155/96 (Social and Economic Rights Action Center/Center for Economic and Social Rights v. Nigeria), Case No. ACHPR/COMM/A044/1, 96 *Am. J. Int'l L.* 937, 940-941(October, 2002).

54. Fons Coomans, "The Ogoni Case before the African Commission on Human and Peoples' Rights," 52 *Int'l & Comp. L. Q.* 749, 754 (July, 2003).

55. Adam Roberts and Richard Guelff, *Documents on the Laws of War*, 3d. ed. (Oxford: Oxford University Press, 2000), 9.

56. Roberts & Guelff, *Documents on the Laws of War*, p. 9.

57. Article 8(2)(b)(xvii) forbids "employing poison or poisoned weapons," and xviii forbids "Employing asphyxiating, poisonous or other gases, and all analogous liquids, materials or devices."

58. Werle, *Principles*, 461; on this point see also Antonio Cassese, *International Criminal Law*, 2d ed. (Oxford: Oxford University Press, 2008), 95; M. Cottier in *Commentary of the Rome Statute of the International Court*, ed. Otto Triffterer, 2d ed. (Oxford: Hart Publishing, 2008), Art. 8 at marginal no. 180.

59. Cassese, *International Criminal Law*, 54.

60. Gerhard Werle, *Principles*, 143.

61. Rome Statute, Article 39(1).

62. Cassese, *International Criminal Law*, 54.
63. Cassese, *International Criminal Law*, 54.
64. Mohamad Elewa Badar, "The Mental Element in the Rome Statute of the International Criminal Court: A Commentary from a Comparative Criminal Law Perspective," *Criminal Law Forum* 19, Nos. 3-4 (September 2008): 473-518.
65. Roger S. Clark, "The Mental Element in International Criminal Law: the Rome Statute of the International Criminal Court and the Elements of Offences," *Criminal Law Forum*, 12, No. 3 (2001): 305.
66. Cassese, *International Criminal Law*, 55; Werle, *Principles*, 145.
67. A. Eser, "Mental Element—Mistake of Fact and Mistake of Law," in Antonio Cassese, Paola Gaeta, and John R.W.D. Jones, *The Rome Statute of the International Criminal Court: A Commentary*, Vol. 1 (Oxford: Oxford Univ. Press, 2002), 911-20, quoted in Cassese, *International Criminal Law*, 55.
68. Badar, "The Mental Element," 479.
69. Badar, "The Mental Element," 479.
70. Brend v. Wood, 175 L.T.R. 306, 307 (1946); *see also* Harding v. Price, 1 All E.R. 283, 284 (1948), quoted in William A. Schabas, "*Mens Rea* and The International Criminal Tribunal for the Former Yugoslavia," 37 *New Eng. L. Rev.* 1015 (Summer 2003).
71. Schabas, "*Mens Rea*," 1018.
72. Schabas, "*Mens Rea*," 1018.
73. France et al. v. Goering, 22 IMT at 466.
74. William Schabas, *An Introduction to the International Criminal Court*, 3d. ed. (Cambridge & New York: Cambridge University Press), 954.
75. For example see International Criminal Tribunal for the Former Yugoslavia (ICTY), *Prosecutor v Tadić*, Case No. IT-94-1-T, Opinion and Judgment, paras 646-48 (May 7, 1997); as to the necessity of an organized plan see ICTY, *Tadić*, Trial Judgment, paras. 653-655; also ICTY, *Prosecutor v. Kupreškić et al.* Case No. IT-95-16-T, Judgment, paras. 551, 555 (January 14, 2000). Moreover as the Appeals Chamber of the ICTY stated in *Prosecutor v. Kunarać*, Case No. IT-96-23/1-A, Judgment, para 98 (June 12, 2002) a plan or policy is not necessarily a legal requirement of crimes against humanity as per the Statute and international customary law (see ff. 114).
76. Protocol Additional to the Geneva Conventions of 12 August 1949, and Relating to the Protection of Victims of International Armed Conflicts (Protocol I) (with annexes, Final Act of the Diplomatic Conference on the Reaffirmation and Development of International Humanitarian Law Applicable in Armed Conflicts dated 10 June 1977 and resolutions adopted at the fourth session). Adopted at Geneva on 8 June 1977," http://treaties.un.org/doc/Publication/UNTS/Volume%201125/volume-1125-I-17512-English.pdf (Accessed August 5, 2011).
77. Francisco Forrest Martin, Stephen J. Schnably, Richard J. Wilson, Jonathan S. Simon, and Mark V. Tushnet, *International Human Rights & Humanitarian Law: Treaties, Cases, & Analysis* (Cambridge: Cambridge University Press, 2006), 529.
78. Francisco Forrest Martin, "Using International Human Rights Law for Establishing a Unified Use of Force Rule in the Law of Armed Conflict," 64 *Sask. L. Rev.* 347 (2002), extracts published in Martin et al. *International Human Rights*, 529-533.
79. ICTY, *Prosecutor v. Kordić and Čerkez*, Case No. IT-95-14/2-A, Judgment, para. 30 (December 14, 2004).
80. Protocol I, Art. 51.
81. Jean-Marie Henckaerts and Louise Doswald-Beck, *Customary International Humanitarian Law Volume I: Rules* (Cambridge: Cambridge University Press, 2005), 47.

82. Rome Statute, Article 8(2)(b)(iv).

83. Protocol I, Art. 57.

84. Gary D. Solis, *The Law of Armed Conflict: International Humanitarian Law in War* (Cambridge: Cambridge University Press, 2010), 274.

85. Solis, *The Law of Armed Conflict*, 281.

86. Cassese, *International Criminal Law*, 305-306.

87. Roberts and Guelff, *Documents on the Laws of War*, 10.

88. Thomas M. Franck, "On Proportionality of Countermeasures in International Law," 102 *Am. J. Int'l L.* 715, 721 (October 2008).

89. Cassese, *International Criminal Law*, 280.

90. Cassese, *International Criminal Law*, 284.

91. Cassese, *International Criminal Law*, 280-289.

92. See generally, Chapter 4 in Antonio Cassese, et. al., *International Criminal Law*, 3d ed. (Oxford, UK: Oxford University Press, 2013).

93. Cassese, *International Criminal Law*, 38.

94. Cassese, *International Criminal Law*, 38.

95. For historical information regarding the development of the Chemical Weapons Convention, see the web site of the Organisation for the Prohibition of Chemical Weapons, www.opcw.org.

96. Gerhard Werle, *Principles of International Criminal Law*, 2d ed. (The Hague: T-M-C Asser Press, 2009), 491.

97. This is consistent with Art. 2(2)(c) of the U.S. Model Penal Code, which refers to recklessness as occurring when a person "consciously disregards a substantial and unjustifiable risk that the material element exists or will result from his conduct." Similarly, Art. 121-3(3) of the French Penal Code refers to circumstances in which a person "fail[s] to show normal diligence, taking into consideration where appropriate the nature of his role or functions, of his capacities and powers and of the means then available to him." Cited in Cassese, *International Criminal Law*, 41.

98. For historical context see, generally, Cassese, *International Criminal Law*, ch. 5.

99. Cassese, *International Criminal Law*, 89.

100. Claire de Than and Edwin Shorts, *International Criminal Law and Human Rights* (London: Sweet & Maxwell, 2003), 91.

101. De Than and Shorts, 92.

102. Cassese, *International Criminal Law*, 92, citing *Ahlbrecht*, a 1949 Dutch Special Court of Cassation decision concluding that the killing of one person and mistreatment of five others constituted a war crime but not a crime against humanity.

103. Cassese, *International Criminal Law*, 93. Note that a different conclusion can be reached where isolated incidents are linked by a common factor such as individuals serving on the same side in an armed conflict. Cassese, 94.

104. De Than and Shorts, *International Criminal Law*, 92.

105. De Than and Shorts, *International Criminal Law*, 92.

106. Cassese, *International Criminal Law*, 209.

107. Cassese, *International Criminal Law*, 209.

108. Cassese, *International Criminal Law*, 209.

109. Cassese, *International Criminal Law*, 210, 215.

110. Werle, *Principles*, 144.

111. *Prosecutor v. Erdemovic*, ICTY Appeals Chamber no. IT-96-22-A, decided October 7, 1997.

112. Curiously, while not crucial to our consideration of the instant case, the Trial Chamber appeared to base its ruling on the conclusion that Erdemovic had failed to pre-

sent corroborating evidence in support of the defense, even though it had been raised in the context of entering a guilty plea and not in an evidentiary proceeding.

113. 14 QBD 273 (1884).

114. Luis E. Chisea, "Duress, Demanding Heroism, and Proportionality," *Vanderbilt Journal of Transnational Law* 41 (2008): 741-773.

115. On this point we are indebted to the work of Massimo Scaliotti, "Defences before the international criminal court: Substantive grounds for excluding criminal responsibility – part 1," *International Criminal Law Review* 1 (2001): 111-172.

116. *See* Report of the Preparatory Committee on the Establishment of an International Criminal Court, G.A. 51st Session (1996).

117. *See* Report of the Working Group on General Principles of Criminal Law, UN Doc. A/CONF.183/C.1/WGGP/L.4/Add.1, 29 June 1998, 5–6.

118. A. Eser, "Article 31: Grounds for excluding criminal responsibility," in ed. O. Triffterer, *Commentary on the Rome Statute of the International Criminal Court* (Baden-Baden: Nomos Verlagsgesellschaft, 1999), 550–551.

119. U. S. Model Penal Code § 3.02(1)(A).

120. French Criminal Code Art. 122-7.

121. German Penal Code § 34.

122. Eser, 550-551.

123. Scaliotti, "Defences," 156.

124. This is also consistent with the provisions of the penal codes referenced above.

Chapter 6

Authorizing the Use of Torture for Interrogation: Prosecutor versus the Ministers of Defense and Justice

With Aaron Fichtelberg and Robert J. Beck

The fourth case concerns the use of torture by the Government of the Republic of Moresia. The case in question is on appeal in the Moot International Criminal Court. The primary question the Court is asked is to determine is whether or not the Defendants/Appellants—the Ministers of Defense and Justice of the Republic of Moresia—perpetrated torture by legally authorizing what appears to be torture by the definitions of international, not domestic law. By approving certain memoranda concerning torture (see below) are they culpable of authorizing torture? Secondly, did they have command responsibility over those directly responsible for the use of torture prohibited under Article 8 of the ICC Statute, as well as the second indictment for crimes against humanity under Article 7? Finally, the case asks whether or not torture, in a fight against terrorism, can be justified on grounds of necessity.

This case involves a hypothetical situation, based roughly on the actions of the Bush administration with the Justice and Defense Ministers as defendants. The main legal questions stem from two memos they approved, which involve the definition of torture, the standards for command responsibility (e.g., direct orders, knowledge, objective and subjective tests of normative expectations about knowledge), as well as a possible necessity defense (also the core legal question of the chemical weapons case in this book). The Defense Minister has direct responsibility for the conduct of military interrogations in known locations managed by the military. The Justice Minster's memo provides guidance for the entire government, is broader in permissiveness, and is intended for high value detainees in secret locations, though the more loose standards might also migrate to the military. Do these memos authorize torture? If they do not, and torture occurred, is there any command responsibility apart from the drafting of the legal memos that would accrue to the Justice Minister or the Defense Minister?

The charges of crimes against humanity depend on the whether or not the contextual element of a "widespread or systematic attack against a civilian population" can be demonstrated. The Article 8 indictment will be much more closely debated because various legal issues can arise, including command responsibility under Article 28, for the material, mental, and contextual elements violated. The issue then becomes whether or not the Justice Minister would be held responsible for the Office of Legal Counsel memo, which authorized acts more clearly constituting torture (anything short of "organ failure or death"). That latter standard, which was developed independently, was signed and enforced by the Justice Minister, who is both a neutral enforcer of the law, but in practice also a cabinet member and lawyer for the administration. When the memo was leaked, it produced a scandal, which led the OLC to develop a less permissive standard of torture, though that change does not necessarily mean that the first standard was illegal—if a subjective standard for the mental element of crime is accepted by the Court, that is that the Justice Minister only has to prove that he acted in a good faith belief that torture was only constituted by organ failure or death.

A second issue is whether or not the techniques listed in a memo signed by the Defense Minister constitute criminal actions, as they are far less cruel than those in the Justice Minister's memo. However, the techniques from both memos, taken together, certainly could cause severe pain, which indeed constitutes torture. For example, sleep deprivation is authorized, as are stress positions. The problem rests with the fact that nowhere is it indicated that *only* two of these techniques at a time may be used. The issue for the Defense Minister would depend on whether or not he should be held to an objective test—what a reasonable defense minister or person would have or should have done—in listing permissible techniques, without stating how many could be used over any given time period, or simply whether the legal test is subjective (what this defense minister apparently thought at the time he signed his memo).

For both defendants, much will depend on the location of the trial. If the case were to appear before a human rights court, such as through the European Council or the European Union, their treaties, the European Convention of Human Rights and the Charter of Fundamental Rights, respectively, would apply. If the case were tried in a domestic court, then the issue would be the applicability of the Geneva Conventions, which criminalize torture as a grave breach with theoretical universal jurisdiction. However, many countries regard universal jurisdiction as only an option, not a legal obligation. Prosecutors could argue for the applicability of human rights law, regardless of trial location, in order to utilize the clear standard definition of torture found in Article 1 of the Convention against Torture, which is defined as severe pain, mental or physical.

Facts of the Case

Over the past decade the country of Moresia has been fighting a war against the Adeaq La terrorist network; members of which are responsible for a number of attacks on Moresian soil, including a large-scale bombing that occurred in the capital city of Moresia on October 12, 2002. The Government of Moresia—its intelligence and defense communities—were caught completely off-guard by the Adeaq La attacks. Adeaq La is a decentralized terrorist organization with cells in several countries around the world, including Germany, the United Kingdom, and Belgium, not to mention several countries in the Middle East and Southeast Asia. The main hub of Adeaq La is in the country of Gafhanistan which Moresian military forces invaded in late November 2002.

In the weeks and years following the Adeaq La attacks, the Government of Moresia captured and detained thousands of suspects and paramilitary soldiers working for the Nabilat Government in Gafhanistan. Many of those captured were transferred to a Moresian naval base on a territory located approximately ninety miles off the coast of Moresia's southernmost state. Within a month of the October 2002 attacks, Minister of Justice Anthony Croft circulated a top-secret memorandum, written by legal counsel, which addressed the legality of acceptable procedures for interrogators of detainees. Many of the procedures outlined in the November 16, 2002 memorandum were determined by legal counsel at the Ministry of Justice to "fall outside" methods prohibited by the Convention against Torture and Other Inhuman and Degrading Treatment or Punishment (Torture Convention). The stated purpose of the use of these techniques was to obtain valuable information about the workings of the Adeaq La terrorist network in an effort to prevent future attacks against Moresia and other allied countries. Stopping the Adeaq La terrorist network was of paramount importance to Moresia's national security interests. The Government of Moresia considers the war against Adeaq La to be an international conflict.

The procedures addressed by the Minister of Justice in his November 2002 memorandum include the following: (1). head slapping; (2) sleep deprivation; (3) stress positions; (4) loud noises; (5) simulated drowning; (6) extreme temperatures; (7) credible threats to relatives; (8) inadequate diet; (9) restriction of bodily movement; (10) solitary confinement; and (11) hooding. According to Minister Croft none of these methods cause "severe" or "irreparable physical or mental harm" to the detainees. "Severe" in this instance is defined in the memorandum as conduct which leads to death or organ failure. The Minister's memorandum, based on drafting by his Office of Legal Counsel, was intended for the entire government and was supported by additional memoranda written by legal counsel to the Minister of Defense of Moresia, Ronald Mursfeld, which was intended for military detention facilities, none of them secret.

In the years that followed, the techniques included in Appellant Croft's memorandum were utilized by agents of the Government of Moresia in their interrogation of Gafhanistani terrorist suspects detained on Moresia's naval base in Moguatana, as well as in undisclosed locations in countries allied with Moresia in the global war against terror. The Ministers of Defense and Justice were never present in any of these locations when the controversial interrogation techniques were used.

In 2005 both ministers were indicted by the ICC for war crimes and crimes against humanity per Articles 8 and 7 of the ICC Statute, respectively. In October 2007 both were convicted on all charges and sentenced to a period of twenty-five years in a maximum security prison system. Shortly thereafter Ministers Croft and Mursfeld appealed their convictions.

Legal and Other Issues for Discussion

The actions taken by the Government of Moresia occurred in an environment similar to that which existed in the years immediately following the attacks of September 11, 2001 and are reminiscent of the policies followed by the U.S. government in the global "war against terror." The post-9/11 period found the country and its leaders understandably shaken, fearful, and angry. Due to various weaknesses inherent in the international torture regime, "the stage [was] set for impromptu, crisis-based decision-making. Inevitably, a sort of ad hoc balancing [was] substituted in place of formal rules of law leading to excess in the forms of 'judgments based on suspicion and not hard evidence' and the jettisoning of 'checks on unilateral decision-making.'"[1]

Extant policy of the United States on torture was "modified" by the Office of Legal Council in the Bush Administration to permit actions that were highly questionable under international not to mention existing law; actions which include, but are not limited to, "waterboarding," sleep and food deprivation, hooding, sexual abuse, and forcing detainees to remain in painful stress positions for prolonged periods of time.[2] The government's policy—clarified by a series of memoranda—set the bar for torture rather high, initially limiting it to actions causing "severe pain or suffering" of the sort that would cause "death, organ failure, or the permanent impairment of a significant body function."[3] As for mental torture, it was restricted to harm that "results in significant psychological harm of significant duration, e.g., lasting for months or even years."[4]

Ironically checks on the power of the executive branch regarding the use of unsavory methods of interrogation against terror suspects were not necessarily expanded by subsequent congressional action. For example, according to the Military Commissions Act of 2006, statements obtained with the use of torture are generally inadmissible, but in situations in which "the degree of coercion is disputed" they can still be used whether obtained *before* the enactment of the Detainee Treatment Act (2005) or after if it was determined by a military judge that they served the "interests of justice," and/or the "totality of circumstances renders the statement reliable and possessing sufficient probative value."[5]

Scholars have attributed the "room for interpretation" perceived by officials of the Bush Administration to two cases in particular: *Ireland v. the United Kingdom* (1978) and *Public Committee Against Torture in Israel v. State of Israel* (1999) both of which addressed acts considered to be "less than torture."[6] It is advisable for students to become familiar with these cases.

In *Ireland*, the European Court of Human Rights (ECHR) held that the tactics utilized by members of the British Government to interrogate IRA suspects—known as the "five techniques"—did *not* constitute torture in violation of the European Convention for the Protections of Human Rights and Fundamental Freedoms.[7] Students will immediately recognize the similarity between these "five techniques" and those used by agents of the Government of Moresia in this case. They include:

> (a) *wall standing*: forcing the detainees to remain for periods of some hours in a 'stress position' . . . ; (b) *hooding*: putting a black or navy coloured bag over the detainees' heads and, at least initially, keeping it there all the tine except during interrogation; (c) *subjection to noise*: pending their interrogations, holding the detainees in a room where there was a continuous loud and hissing noise; (d) *deprivation of sleep*: pending their interrogations, depriving detainees of sleep; (e) *deprivation of food and drink*: subjecting the detainees to a reduced diet during their stay at the centre and pending interrogations.[8]

Moreover, "claims of beatings [by the applicants] were . . . rejected because they could not be susbstantiated.[9]

Although the Court in *Ireland* made a distinction between torture and acts less than torture, the Israeli Supreme Court avoided defining torture or cruel and inhumane treatment altogether, despite the fact that the case in question concerned interrogation methods that were suspiciously "torture like," and which included the use of the "Shabach" position.[10]

An important aspect of the *Public Committee* case concerns a defense used by the Defendants in the present case, albeit in modified form: the necessity defense. As Lyne discusses in the *Public Committee* case the Justices of the Supreme Court of Israel ruled that torture could *not* be used as state policy, but given certain circumstances (e.g., a "ticking time bomb scenario"), the perpetrators of torture could argue in their defense that torture was necessary to avoid a larger imminent disaster.[11] This addresses the ethnical question of whether or not the prohibition against torture is absolute (as per the Torture Convention and customary international law), or if in fact it is a reasonable option in some situations.

Are "torture warrants," for instance, appropriate in order to save human lives?[12] Yet, As Bennoune states: "intellectual proponents of loosening the bans on torture to confront terror fail to grasp that deconstructing the prohibition of torture in international law inherently destabilizes the notion of terror and why it is wrong."[13] Rather terror and torture are two sides of the same coin in that both are "characterized by the infliction of severe pain and suffering on victims, the intentionality of doing so, and the fact that the action in question is done for a justificatory purpose."[14]

In any event, as scholars such as Rouillard contend, the justification for torture Bush Administration officials derived from these two cases was based on erroneous interpretations of the rulings in question. With *Ireland*, the fact that the ECHR ruled that the "five techniques" were "inhumane and degrading treatment" opened the door to a whole host of tactics, including waterboarding," that were considered by the OLS as suitable for use so long as they did not cross the threshold of "extreme" as set forth by the "torture memoranda."[15] As for *Public Committee* case, the OLS once again misinterpreted the Israeli Supreme Court's decision regarding the legality of the interrogation techniques used by Israeli security forces. As Rouillard discusses, the Supreme Court did not actually determine whether or not these techniques constituted "either torture or cruel and degrading treatment, . . . [rather] it dealt solely and restrictively with question of whether the Government of Israel or the Head of the GSS [General Security Services] had the authority to 'establish directives regarding the use of physical means during the interrogation of [terrorist] suspects . . . beyond the general rules which can be inferred from the very concept of an interrogation itself.'"[16]

This "room for interpretation" is also likely a result of certain deficiencies with the 1984 Torture Convention itself;[17] more specifically the fact that the Convention only requires states to criminalize torture, not cruel, inhuman or degrading treatment or punishment.[18]

Returning to the case of the United States, it is important to recognize the fact that although the Obama Administration, through a series of executive orders, made efforts to bring U.S. policy regarding torture more in line with international humanitarian and human rights law, to date there have been *no* prosecutions of perpetrators of torture by the Government of the United States.[19] As has been suggested, this failure to take appropriate legal action against offenders contributes to the perpetuation of global terrorism and creates a crisis of legitimacy for the United States.[20] The example of the United States demonstrates the difficulties associated with domestic prosecutions for torture. Prosecutors in the case against Ministers Croft and Mursfeld are aiming to correct this imbalance through their prosecution in an international venue of two high-level politicians for a government's use of torture as a counter-terrorism measure.[21]

The International Torture Regime

Under the international torture regime,[22] torture is a non-derogable prohibition, grounded in customary law; its commission now considered a violation of *jus cogens* norms.[23] The protections against torture extend not only to noncombatants and combatants, but also to "illegal combatants, such as spies and *saboteurs* [emphasis in original]" (under humanitarian law), as well as to individuals during peacetime, including detainees more generally, under international human rights law.[24]

Because this case pertains to the use of torture in a very specific set of circumstances, it will be useful for instructors to explain the distinction between torture as part of a broader category of international criminal offenses, and torture as a separate offence (a "discrete crime").[25] The latter pertains to the use of torture by state officials or others (with the tacit or express approval of state officials), which is *not* linked to war or committed within the context of a crime against humanity.

As Cassese discusses prohibitions against torture as a "discrete" offense under international criminal law are grounded in international human rights law;[26] notably Article 7 of the International Covenant on Civil and Political Rights or ICCPR,[27] Article 5 of the Universal Declaration of Human Rights (UDHR),[28] and of course the 1984 Torture Convention, among others.[29] Article 1 of the Torture Convention defines torture as:

> any act by which severe pain or suffering, whether physical or mental, is intentionally inflicted on a person for such purposes as obtaining from or a third person information or a confession, punishing him for an act he or a third person has committed or is suspected of having committed, or intimidating or coercing him or a third person, or for any reason based on discrimination of any kind, when such pain or suffering is inflicted by or at the instigation of or with the consent or acquiescence of a public official or other person acting in an official capacity.[30]

When it comes to state responsibility the Torture Convention grants little room for exception or justification. Article 2 states that it makes no difference whether or not the country is at war, encountering severe political instability, or "public emergency," torture is prohibited and inexcusable.[31] Unfortunately the Torture Convention leaves it up to member states to enforce these prohibitions, including the prosecution of offenders. As Harper, Rouillard, and others discuss, because the definition of torture provided by the Torture Convention is vaguely worded, "the parameters of torture and ill treatment remain open to interpretation."[32] As the example of the United States demonstrates, in practice this means that states will define and re-define torture (and its exceptions) as befits their interests.[33] The Torture Convention is similar in this way to the Genocide Convention and is another excellent example of a treaty whose limitations reflect the tensions between national and international prerogatives. This is an excellent place for instructors to broaden the discussion to arguments about state sovereignty, national security, and international law. Do state interests trump international law? Is international law merely the pursuit and protection of lofty moral objectives that have little basis in the every-day decisions states are forced to make in the pursuit and protection of national interests; especially national security? As Welsh states: "ethicality is the most difficult rule to define in the context of terrorism because there is an inherent tension between individual standards of morality, the laws of nations, and international laws and customs. Crisis exacerbates these tensions, as moral and legal standards often appear to be at odds with effectiveness and necessity."[34] Does a rational-choice, realpolitik argument hold water when it comes to the use of torture as a means to combat global terrorism or does it merely weaken the international torture regime?

Moreover, as Knoops asks, is it permissible to use methods such as torture that violate *jus cogens* norms to protect society from other crimes that violate such norms (e.g., war crimes, crimes against humanity, and so forth)?[35] What implications does this type of situation have for the ICC? Knoop's conclusion is worth quoting at some length:

> This view, . . . carries the risk of opening the door to arbitrary application of interrogation methods which are deemed to be justified by allegedly exceptional circumstances, amounting to a form of self-defense on the part of the State. The nuanced approach of the Israeli Supreme Court, itself, in strictly applying the rule of law within the framework of existing criminal law concepts, is to be preferred. It is not unlikely that the ICC, once confronted with a case involving a military commander charged with torture in relation to interrogation methods, will resort to the opinion of the Israeli Supreme Court. The ICC's primary responsibility is the upholding of the rule of law, even in the context of trying circumstances.[36]

As a *jus cogens* violation torture has emerged as an offense to which universal jurisdiction applies,[37] although many states see torture as a discrete offense more suitable for domestic jurisdiction. In any event, Cassese states that it shares with torture as a war crime and as a crime against humanity the fact that its purpose is not limited to obtaining admissions of guilt or extracting confessions from suspects. More broadly, torture can be used for a variety of purposes including to "punish, intimidate, or humiliate a person," and/or to coerce certain behavior from its subjects.[38]

The case in this section, however, concerns the use of torture in violation of international humanitarian law, which of course includes the four Geneva Conventions (specifically Common Article 3) and their Additional Protocols.[39] Similar to the example of the United States, the use of torture by representatives of the Government of Moresia is being utilized against terrorist suspects captured abroad in Gafhanistan; specifically those with suspected links to the Adeaq La terrorist network or who are suspected of involvement in actual terrorist and/or military offenses against Moresian forces.

Torture as a war crime is prohibited under Articles 8(2)(a)(ii) and 8(2)(c)(i) of the ICC Statute as pertains to interstate and intrastate conflicts, respectively. As indicated above the case in this section concerns an interstate conflict; an international war on terror. Similar to the third case in this book, all parties are in agreement as to the contextual element of the war crime. In other words, all parties recognize that all of the acts in question were perpetrated during an interstate armed conflict. Unlike the previous cases all parties are also in agreement with respect to the material elements. In other words everyone acknowledges a war existed and that torture was in fact committed by agents of the Government of Moresia; the question is, are the Appellants liable for the actions of others?

Appellants have also been convicted by the Trial Chamber of the ICC for violation of Article 7(1)(f) of the ICC Statute. Interestingly, compared to the definition of torture as a war crime and as a separate offense under international law more generally, torture as a crime against humanity, defined by Article 7(2)(e), does *not* necessitate a cause.[40] Despite the looser definition of torture provided by the Statute, in most cases, the ICC Prosecutor would face an up hill battle in terms of demonstrating that the use of torture was part of a widespread and/or systematic attack on a civilian population.

In this case students can discuss and debate whether or not the use of torture as a means to gather information, to coerce etc. was or can be part of a systematic or widespread attack on a civilian population. Is it a matter of the number of incidences of torture? In other words how much torture is necessary to constitute a widespread or systematic attack? What if the use of torture was sporadic? And of course students will remember from the previous cases that the contextual and mental elements are closely intertwined with crimes against humanity. The question thus becomes: did the Defendants act with the knowledge that the use of torture would contribute to the furtherance of an attack against a civilian population?[41] Who were the "real" targets of the torture?

Command or Superior Responsibility

The Ministers of Defense and Justice are appealing their convictions on the grounds that neither had command responsibility over those directly responsible for the crimes in question. The case in this section provides students with an excellent example of the application of a general principle of international law that has not as yet come up: command or superior responsibility. Outlined in Article 28 of the ICC Statute command responsibility incorporates liability for both military commanders and "other superiors" for crimes committed by subordinates within their "effective [command]/responsibility and control," having occurred with their "knowledge" and absent any attempts on their part to prevent or repress these crimes.[42] The "knowledge" requirement under Article 28 differs between military commanders and non-military civilian superiors. As to the former it refers to what the "commander or person [acting as de-facto military commander] knew or, . . . should have known"; with civilian superiors "knowledge" means "the superior either knew, or consciously disregarded information" about the crimes committed or about to be committed.[43] Superiors can thus be liable for war crimes, crimes against humanity, and genocide under this doctrine.

The concept of command or superior responsibility is grounded in international customary law including military manuals, the decisions of the international *ad hoc* tribunals and Articles 86 and 87 of the First Additional Protocol to the Geneva Conventions.[44] Historically the issue of command responsibility has been a sticky issue with respect to civilian leaders. The Nuremberg and Tokyo Tribunals were at odds somewhat in their interpretations of the degree of responsibility civilian leaders held over decision-makers on the battlefield.[45] This was an issue of course with which the judges of the International Criminal Tribunal for the Former Yugoslavia and the International Criminal Tribunal for Rwanda had to contend, deciding in the end that civilian command was a matter of the commander's degree of "effective" control over his/her subordinates.

In any event questions over liability remain. Instructors can use as examples of cases heard by the ICTY, the ICTR, the Nuremberg Tribunal and so forth that raise a host of different questions about responsibility and knowledge.[46] Should military and civilian leaders be liable for actions committed by subordinates thousands of miles away? Should their liability under this scenario be equal to that of their subordinates, whether or not they shared the intent of the subordinates or made a "positive" contribution to the commission of the offense? Should it be less? Should command responsibility be treated as a separate offense (e.g., dereliction of duty)?[47] These questions are important as they address the issue of whether holding a superior vicariously liable for the offenses of his/her subordinate is or is not a violation of the principle of individual criminal liability.

Further questions worth asking include the following: Does command responsibility assume a degree of knowledge that leaders cannot possibly have, or is the "should have known" concept reasonable under these circumstances? Why should civilian leaders be included at all? Moreover, with their inclusion, as per Article 28(b)(i) of the ICC Statute, how does the prosecution demonstrate a "conscious disregard" on the part of a civilian leader? Is this a stricter or looser standard for liability? These are the types of questions with which student lawyers will have to grapple when conducting their own moot courts.

To demonstrate superior responsibility Werle outlines three elements the prosecution must demonstrate. First a superior-subordinate relationship must be present. What does this mean exactly? This issue addresses the concept of "control." For superiors control can be *de jure*, as well as *de facto*. Moreover, control must be "effective." If a superior lacks control of his subordinates independently of the circumstances then a true superior-subordinate relationship does *not* exist.[48] The second element is the knowledge requirement. The prosecution has to demonstrate that the superior knew or should have known that acts of torture were about to be or had in fact been committed by subordinates. Unlike many of the other crimes discussed in this text, the mental element at issue is not *dolus directus* (unless the superior actually took part in the offense), but negligence.

The concept of negligence was introduced in Chapter 3 of this book. Expanding on the initial discussion, a distinction can be made between two types of negligence: "ordinary/simple" and "gross." The former refers to an accused's knowing disregard of the risks associated with his/her violation of an extant standard of care. In the latter form, the accused not only knowingly violates an existing standard of care to which he/she must adhere, but believes the risks associated with this violation will not occur; additionally, he/she engages in "conduct that is blatantly at odds with the prescribed standards."[49] Gross or culpable negligence includes the knowledge requirement ("conscious disregard") plus the superior's failure to take the "necessary and reasonable measures" to prevent and/or punish the conduct in question. The latter refers to a third element of superior responsibility which, as Werle discusses, has to do with a failure on the part of superiors to prevent the commission of a crime by their subordinates and/or punish those subordinates who committed the offense as required under international law.[50]

Instructors should make a distinction for students between command responsibility and joint criminal enterprise (JCE) both of which have been presented as a mode of liability by the international tribunals. JCE extends to actions perpetrated with the intent of furthering a larger criminal enterprise, such as war or crimes against humanity. Everyone is equally liable for the same offense because everyone shares the same intent.[51] As Cassese states, in cases of command responsibility it may be the case that superiors act in pursuance of a larger goal, however, for liability to attach, the prosecution need only demonstrate culpable negligence on the part of the superior.[52] In the current case law of the two *ad hoc* tribunals, the superior is liable for his breach of duty separately from the crimes committed by others.[53]

The knowledge requirement of commanders can vary from "conscious" disregard, to simple ignorance ("should have known").[54] As per the ICC Statute, what is important is that the superior did not act on this knowledge and "take all necessary and reasonable measures within his or her power to prevent or repress . . . commission [of these acts]."[55] Students must take note of the fact that the ICC Statute differs from the statutes of the two *ad hoc* tribunals, in addition to the Special Court for Sierra Leone, in that command responsibility in the ICC makes the superior criminally liable as a participant for the acts of his/her subordinates—albeit liable to a lesser extent.[56] By way of contrast the ICTY now utilizes command responsibility as an aggravating factor at sentencing.[57]

Students will no doubt have questions as to the definitions of "necessary" and "reasonable." Does this depend on the circumstances of the case? As Werle discusses international humanitarian law is clear on what each means: "Necessary measures have been defined as measures appropriate to discharging the superior's obligations, showing that he or she genuinely tried to prevent or to punish. Reasonable measures . . . are those reasonably falling within the superior's substantive powers"; in other words, those powers which would have stopped the crime or punished the offenders (e.g., his capacity).[58]

Due to the difficulties surrounding the demonstration of command responsibility as a mode of liability over the years both *ad hoc* tribunals have come to rely on a very narrow interpretation of the doctrine. Bonafé attributes the preference of the *ad hoc* tribunals for direct responsibility to the judges' preference for clear displays of individual criminal liability in addition to and over the otherwise murky causal nexus between superiors and subordinates associated traditional command responsibility.[59] In very few cases have individuals in fact been convicted by these tribunals strictly on the basis of command responsibility.[60]

LEGAL BRIEF OF THE DEFENDANTS/APPLICANTS

THE QUESTION

The Court is asked to determine whether the Appellants, Ministers of Defense and Justice for the Republic of Moresia, Ronald Mursfeld and Anthony Croft, respectively, exercised command responsibility over those directly responsible for the use of internationally impermissible methods of interrogation against some of the Gafhanistani nationals interned at Moguatana naval base. The Court is therefore asked to assess the legality of the Appellants' convictions for torture as a war crime and a crime against humanity.

ISSUES

The following issues will be addressed in this brief: (I) the Prosecution's failure to demonstrate that both Appellants exercised effective command responsibility over those who perpetrated torture as a war crime at the Moguatana naval base; (II) the Prosecution's failure to demonstrate the contextual element of torture as a crime against humanity in this case; and (III) if the Court should find that Appellants Mursfeld and Croft in fact exercised command responsibility over those directly responsible for the use of unlawful interrogation tactics at the Moguatana naval base, Appellants further contend that these tactics were necessary in order to prevent larger humanitarian catastrophes in Moresia, as well as the rest of the world, catastrophes orchestrated and carried out by the Adeaq La terrorist network and its affiliates.

SUMMARY OF ARGUMENTS FOR APPELLANTS MURSFELD AND CROFT

Appellants Mursfeld and Croft acknowledge that the country of Moresia is involved in an inter-state war with the country of Gafhanistan, and that some torture tactics were utilized by military personnel against Gafhanistani soldiers held captive at the Moguatana naval base. Neither Appellant ordered these tactics be used, however, nor had any knowledge of their actual use. Both are civilian leaders in the political hierarchy of the Government of Moresia. The geographical separation of Appellants Mursfeld and Croft from the Moguatana naval base (the government offices of the Appellants are over 1,000 miles distant from Moguatana) prevented the Appellants from having the requisite knowledge and ability to exercise effective command control over the perpetrators of these crimes. Consequently, neither civilian leader could take the necessary and reasonable measures to prevent these war crimes from taking place. Furthermore, the Prosecution's contention that Appellants Mursfeld and Croft are responsible for torture as a crime against humanity per Article 7(1)(f) is completely without merit: the Prosecution failed to demonstrate at the trial stage the existence of the contextual element of the crime of torture as a crime against humanity in this case. Lastly, if the Court should find that Appellants Mursfeld and Croft are responsible for torture as a war crime, Appellants Mursfeld and Croft contend that the use of torture tactics against Gafhanistani captives at the Moguatana naval base was necessary and legally justified in order to prevent imminent terrorist attacks conducted by the Adeaq La terrorist network and its affiliates against the country of Moresia and its allies.

THE PROSECUTION'S CASE AGAINST APPELLANTS MURSFELD AND CROFT

The Prosecution bases its entire case against the Appellants on two claims. First, the Prosecution submits that the use of torture by agents of a government constitutes a violation of *jus cogens* law on par with other international crimes, including genocide. The Prosecution goes to great lengths to remind this Court of the horrific nature of torture and international efforts to prohibit its use as a crime under *any* and *all* circumstances.

Secondly, the Prosecution contends that both Appellants exercised command responsibility over the alleged acts per Article 28 of the ICC Statute. Specifically, they argue that both Appellants had effective control over those using torture, had knowledge that torture tactics were being used, and nevertheless failed to undertake necessary and reasonable measures to prevent and to punish members of the Moresian military for their use of torture as a means of interrogation.

The Prosecution contends that it met the contextual, material, and mental criteria for each of the crimes with which Appellants Mursfeld and Croft were charged per Articles 7 and 8 of the ICC Statute.

Appellants Mursfeld and Croft were charged with and convicted by the Trial Chamber of this Court of the use of torture as a grave breach of the four Geneva Conventions of 1949 per Article 8(2)(a)(ii) of the ICC Statute.

The Prosecution bases this charge on the fact that torture tactics were used by members of the Moresian military against Gafhanistani prisoners of war interned at the Moguatana naval base. Tactics allegedly ranged from sleep deprivation to solitary confinement. Moreover, the Prosecution contends that, by virtue of their positions within the hierarchy of the Government of Moresia, Appellants Mursfeld and Croft exercised command responsibility over those directly responsible for the use of torture at Moguatana.

On the one hand, the Prosecution contends that each of the Appellants "should have known" that torture tactics were used, regardless of their physical remoteness and their lack of direct knowledge. On the other hand, the Prosecution also bases its war crimes charge against Appellants on a November 16, 2002 memorandum written by Appellant Croft to civilian leaders in the executive branch of the Government of Moresia, which included Appellant Mursfeld. This memorandum, the Prosecution contends, constitutes direct evidence of the command responsibility exercised by Appellants Croft and Mursfeld.

Appellants Mursfeld and Croft were charged with and convicted of torture as a crime against humanity pursuant to Article 7(1)(f).

The Prosecution bases this charge on the claim that the use of torture by members of the Moresian military satisfied the contextual criterion of a "widespread or systematic attack" against the civilian population of Gafhanistan because many of those interned and interrogated by agents of the Government of Moresia were in fact Gafhanistan citizens "indiscriminately rounded up" by the Moresian military. The use of torture, the Prosecution contends, served no other purpose than to maliciously intimidate the population of Gafhanistan into cooperating with the Government of Moresia.

The Prosecution contends that Appellants Mursfeld and Croft exercised effective command responsibility over those responsible for the use of torture as a crime against humanity perpetrated against these Gafhanistanis civilians. The Prosecution bases this argument on the same evidence described above.

INAPPLICABILITY OF DOCTRINE OF SUPERIOR RESPONSIBILITY TO TORTURE AS A WAR CRIME IN THIS CASE

Contextual and Material Elements of Torture as a War Crime.

Appellants Croft and Mursfeld do not dispute that some unlawful interrogation tactics, which might constitute torture, were used against Gafhanistani prisoners of war interned at Moguatana naval base. However, they might be construed, the tactics were used to gather intelligence information about the Adeaq La terrorist network: its strategies, inner-workings, and future attacks. Appellants submit, however, that those responsible for these tactics were rogue members of the military who were acting outside the scope of domestic and international laws prohibiting the use of torture as an interrogation method. These rogue military staff members were not acting under commands from civilian or military authorities at the time these acts were committed. Accordingly, the civilian leadership bear no liability for the acts of the subordinates.

Liability of Appellant Minister of Justice Anthony Croft

Appellant Minister of Justice Anthony Croft's Degree of "Control"

The Appellant Minister of Justice Anthony Croft submits that the degree of "control" he exercised over subordinate interrogators at the Moguatana naval base does not rise to the level of "command responsibility" as understood by international criminal law. Under Article 28(b) of the Statute of the ICC, non-military superiors are responsible for the acts of their subordinates if they are "committed by subordinates under his or her effective authority and control." Furthermore as outlined in Article 28(b)(ii), the crimes in question "were within the effective responsibility and control of the superior." There is no reason to ascribe the required effective authority or control to the Appellant due to the civilian nature of the Appellant's position in the Moresian government, as well as his geographic distance from the location of the acts of torture. Nor is there reason to believe that the alleged crimes in question were under Appellant Croft's authority or control. As was noted in the Trial Judgment of the International Criminal Tribunal for the Former Yugoslavia (ICTY) in *Celebici* [*Delalic*]: "great care must be taken lest an injustice be committed in holding individuals responsible for the acts of others in situations where the link of control is absent or too remote."[61]

Čelebići held that for non-military commanders "effective control" is crucial; specifically "superior responsibility extends to civilian superiors only to the extent they exercise a degree of control over their subordinates which is similar to that of military commanders."[62] Appellant Croft lacked this degree of effective control. Appellant Croft is a civilian leader of the Moresian government, with no legal position within the military chain of command. Accordingly Croft lacked any clear avenue by which to discipline soldiers who had violated Moresian policy. Additionally, Appellant Croft had no control over the decision-making of military leaders. Moreover, the geographic distance separating Appellant Croft from the scene of the alleged crimes prevented him from exercising effective control over the actions of the interrogators. In short, Appellant Croft was not a commander or superior to those who perpetrated the alleged acts of torture and therefore is not liable for their actions.

Appellant Minister of Justice Anthony Croft's "Knowledge" of the Use of Torture

Along with the requirement of effective control, Article 28(b)(i) of the ICC Statute requires that the "superior either knew, or consciously disregarded information which clearly indicated, that the subordinates were committing or about to commit" any of the crimes subject to ICC jurisdiction. Appellant Croft possessed neither direct nor indirect knowledge that torture tactics were being used by members of the military at Moguatana naval base, a location many miles away from the capital of Moresia. His position in the political-military hierarchy of the Government of Moresia, as well as the geographic distance between Croft and Moguatana naval base prevented him from knowing that torture tactics were being used by the military. There is no evidence that Appellant Croft consciously disregarded information regarding the use of torture in interrogations at Moguatana naval base.

Appellant Minister of Justice Anthony Croft's Use of "Necessary and Reasonable Measures"

Article 28(b)(iii) of the ICC Statute requires the civilian superior to "take all necessary and reasonable measures within his or her power to prevent or repress [the] commission [of international crimes] or to submit the matter to the competent authorities for investigation and prosecution." Both ICTY and the International Criminal Tribunal for Rwanda (ICTR) jurisprudence have clearly established a different, arguably *lower*, expectation that civilians will be capable of exerting discipline in this regard than with military officials. The Trial Chamber of the ICTY noted in its 1999 *Aleksovski* opinion, for example that, "It cannot be expected that a civilian authority will have disciplinary power over his subordinate equivalent to that of the military authorities in an analogous command position."[63] Even if Appellant Croft has *prima facie* command responsibility for acts of torture committed at Moguatana naval base, he nonetheless is not liable for these acts because he took all necessary and reasonable measures to prevent the commission of torture.

As the celebrated international legal publicist, Gerhard Werle, observed in his seminal 2009 Cambridge University Press monograph, *Principles of International Criminal Law*:

> [With regard to Article 28(b)(iii) . . .] It is not possible to generalize as to what measures are reasonable. Most important is the extent of control and influence that the superior has at his or her disposal in dealing with subordinates . . . This, in turn, determines the extent to which the superior is able to prevent or punish violations of the law by subordinates.[64]

To demonstrate this point, Werle cites the ICTY's 1999 *Aleksovski* Trial Chamber decision, the 2004 *Blaškić* Appeals Chamber decision, and the decision of the ICTY Appeals Chamber of 2007 in *Blagojević and Jokić*. In the latter case, the Appeals Chamber, referring to the *Čelebići* Appeals judgment, held that "'possession of *de jure* power in itself may not suffice for the finding of command responsibility if it does not manifest in effective control.'"[65]

Moreover, the ICTY Trial Chamber in *Boškoski and Tarčulovski* held that,

> civilian superiors, who may lack the disciplinary or sanctioning powers of military commanders, may discharge their obligation to punish by reporting to the competent authorities whenever a crime has been committed if these reports are likely to trigger an investigation or initiate disciplinary or criminal proceedings.[66]

As chief legal officer of the Government of Moresia, Appellant Croft does not deny that he wrote and circulated a memorandum on November 16, 2002 assessing the legality of interrogation tactics. Nor does Appellant Croft deny that his memorandum could be used by military officials in their interrogation of Gafhanistani terrorist suspects. A copy of the memorandum was given to the Appellant Minister of Defense Ronald Mursfeld. Nevertheless, Appellant Croft in no way communicated to Appellant Mursfeld, or to any other official in the executive branch of the Government of Moresia, that these tactics were to be used by members of the military against suspects detained at Moguatana naval base. He simply performed his duty as a legal advisor to the Government of Moresia, providing his best legal advice on the lawfulness of certain interrogation tactics.

Appellant Croft possessed no knowledge regarding the *actual* commission of internationally prohibited acts during the interrogations at Moguatana naval base. As chief legal officer of Moresia, had he been made aware of allegations of torture, he would have immediately instituted an investigation and prosecuted anybody suspected of unlawful interrogation techniques. As no information was provided on such charges, Appellant Croft was not put on "'notice of offences committed by subordinates.'"[67] Hence, no investigation to halt these crimes (a "reasonable" and "necessary" measure, given the circumstances) was undertaken.

Liability of Appellant Defense Minister Ronald Mursfeld

Appellant Minister of Defense Ronald Mursfeld's Degree of "Control"

As a civilian leader of the Ministry of Defense of the Government of Moresia, Appellant Mursfeld lacked effective control over his military colleagues and subordinates. To a large extent, Mursfeld's lack of effective control reflected his very significant geographic distance from the location where the alleged crimes of torture occurred. Though some might seek to characterize Appellant Murfeld's degree of influence over those responsible for these alleged crimes as "substantial," his degree of influence was certainly not "controlling," as the Prosecution suggests. Appellant Mursfeld was not, and never has been, the military commander of Moresian forces.

Appellant Mursfeld categorically rejects the notion that his influence over military interrogators at the Moguatana naval base was, in fact, "substantial." However, even if he were to concede that his influence had been "substantial," though, the ICTY has consistently denied in its rulings that "substantial influence" by civilian superiors is sufficient to impute criminal liability. In *Kordić and Čerkez*, for example, the Trial Chamber held that,

> Evidence that an accused [a civilian authority] is perceived as having a high public profile, manifested through public appearances and statements, and thus as exercising some authority, may be relevant to the overall assessment of his actual authority although not sufficient in itself to establish it, without evidence of the accused's overall behavior towards subordinates and his duties.[68]

More than mere perception or belief of authority is required to demonstrate genuine "authority," and therefore, potential criminality. The Trial Chamber in *Kordić and Čerkez* went on to say:

> While in the case of military commanders, the evidence of external observers such as international monitoring or humanitarian personnel may be relied upon [to determine authority], in the case of civilian leaders evidence of perceived authority may not be sufficient, as it may be indicative of mere powers of influence in the absence of a subordinates structure.[69]

Appellant Mursfeld reiterates that his duties *do not* include command and control of Moresian military forces.

Appellant Minister of Defense Ronald Mursfeld's "Knowledge" of the Use of Torture

As has already been noted, Appellant Mursfeld was not present and was nowhere near the Moguatana naval base when the alleged offenses occurred. On this point the Trial Chamber of the ICTY held in *Naletilić and Martinović*: "Considering geographic and temporal circumstances . . . the more physically distant the superior was from the commission of the crimes, the more additional *indicia* are necessary to prove that he knew of the crimes."[70]

It is worth noting that post-cold war international criminal tribunals have almost never ruled on a case where a superior was a senior civilian, physically removed from the scene of alleged crimes, and did not directly solicit torture. Most ICTY jurisprudence, for example, has addressed prison "camp commanders," individuals much closer in terms of geographical location and by virtue of their position in the chain-of-command, to the alleged criminal acts. The present case therefore represents a novel interpretation of customary law regarding the concept of high-level civilian "superiority."

It must be emphasized that nothing in the factual record supports the Prosecution's contention that the Appellant Mursfeld "consciously disregarded information" about the acts of torture at Moguatana naval base, the standard to which he should be held as civilian superior.

Appellant Minister of Defense Ronald Mursfeld's Use of "Necessary and Reasonable Measures"

As we have already demonstrated, the extent of the Moresian Minister of Defense's control and influence was significantly limited by his civilian status and his physical remoteness from the interrogation site. His omission in and of itself is insufficient to establish *civilian* "superior responsibility." At most, it might perhaps constitute "accessory liability after the fact," a form of liability that falls far beyond this Court's proper jurisdiction.

The Memorandum Does Not Establish Command Responsibility for the Appellants

Further, the memoranda for which the Appellants accept authorship are insufficient for attaching liability to the Appellants. The first memorandum (written on November 16, 2002) was written by Minister of Justice Croft and set out various interrogation techniques that he believed did not violate the Torture Convention. This legal opinion was meant for guidance only and did not require, much less "command" that any particular actor use the tactics outlined in the text of the memorandum in any case. Thus the Appellant cannot be linked to the criminal actions committed at Moguatana naval base. As the Minister of Justice does not have effective responsibility or control over those individuals who committed torture at Moguatana naval base, the memorandum he authored is insufficient to establish a chain of liability between the Appellant and the acts of torture in question. If his legal analysis were inadequate, the proper forum for adjudicating this matter would be in the Moresian Bar Association, not the International Criminal Court.

While Appellant Mursfeld signed a similar memorandum authorizing the use of harsh interrogation tactics against prisoners one month after the aforementioned Croft memorandum, this second memorandum needs to be placed within the context of the international laws of command responsibility more generally. According to the International Criminal Court's criteria, a commander is only responsible for acts that he "knew or, owing to the circumstances at the time, should have known" were occurring under her command. As the ICTY in the *Čelebići*[71] case established, liability can only be established if commanders "had actual knowledge, established through direct or circumstantial evidence, that his subordinates were committing or about to commit crimes," or "he had in his possession information of a nature, which at the least, would put him on notice of the risk of such offences by indicating the need for additional investigation in order to ascertain whether such crimes were committed or were about to be committed by his subordinates." Further, the Chamber in this case declared that, "in the absence of direct evidence of the superior's knowledge of the offences committed by his subordinates, such knowledge cannot be presumed, but must be established by way of circumstantial evidence." As no evidence of such knowledge has been proven, the existence of a memo authorizing such behavior is insufficient to establish the required knowledge for establishing command responsibility.

FAILURE OF PROSECUTION TO DEMONSTRATE THE CONTEXTUAL ELEMENT OF TORTURE AS A CRIME AGAINST HUMANITY IN THIS CASE

At trial, the Appellants were convicted of torture as a crime against humanity; a violation of Article 7(1)(f). Appellants Mursfeld and Croft argue that the Prosecution did not meet the contextual element of torture as a crime against humanity, and therefore, that their conviction ought to be overturned.

As international courts have repeatedly ruled, to demonstrate the perpetration of crimes against humanity the burden is on the Prosecution to demonstrate that the offenses occurred within the context of a "widespread or systematic attack directed against any civilian population." Absent this, the crime in question—in this case, torture—is not in fact a crime against humanity.

The crucial element in this case concerns the population in question: the "victims" of the attack, as it were. The ICTY Appeals Chamber in *Kunarac et al.* held that a civilian population must be "the primary rather than an incidental target of the attack.[72] Moreover, the Court ruled that "the assessment of what constitutes a 'widespread' or 'systematic' attack is essentially a relative exercise in that it depends on the civilian population which, allegedly, was being attacked."[73] Moreover, as the Trial Chamber in *Kunarac et al.* ruled: "customary international law obliges parties to the conflict to distinguish at all times between the civilian population and combatants, and obliges them not to attack a military objective if the attack is likely to cause civilian casualties or damage which would be excessive in relation to the military advantage anticipated."[74]

Appellants contend that, as a point of fact, the efforts by the Moresian military to capture and to detain Gafhanistanis were strategically conducted to *avoid* targeting the civilian population of Gafhanistan. Those presently in custody of the Government of Moresia and who are interned at Moguatana naval base, are *not* Gafhanistani civilians unfairly targeted. Rather, those interned are persons suspected of possessing a connection to the Adeaq La terrorist network and/or who are responsible for attacks against Moresian military personnel. They have been detained as prisoners of war and therefore cannot be considered the victims of a crime against humanity.

Moreover, Appellant Croft reiterates that his memorandum of November 2002 addressed the legality of the use of various interrogation tactics against *Gafhanistani prisoners of war* exclusively. The Prosecution has failed to demonstrate that this memorandum in any way constitutes evidence of the Appellant's intention to perpetrate a *widespread or systematic* attack against the *civilian* population of Gafhanistan.

Because there was no widespread or systematic attack against the civilian population of Gafhanistan, no crimes against humanity can be considered to have been perpetrated by the military of Moresia acting as agent of the Government of Moresia. Consequently, the material and mental elements of the crimes against humanity charge are therefore moot.

TORTURE AS A NECESSARY STRATEGY IN THE CURRENT WAR ON TERROR

Appellants Mursfeld and Croft acknowledge that the use of torture is illegal under international law, as well as the laws of the Republic of Moresia. Contrary to the Prosecution's argument, neither Appellant ordered nor condoned these practices. The use of torture by members of the Moresian military was *not* official government policy and was not carried out at the command of the Appellants or with their knowledge or assent. Rather, its use was a result of the misbehavior of a few rogue officers who acted independently, thousands of miles away from the location of the defendants at the time. These soldiers were acting outside the scope of permissible interrogation techniques laid out in Moresian civilian and military law.

However, even if the Court finds that the Appellants bear command responsibility for the acts of torture committed at Moguatana naval base, and that these acts met the legal requirements of a crime against humanity, we further contend that the defense of necessity ought to be invoked and the conviction overturned. According to Article 31 of the ICC Statute, "At trial, the Court may consider a ground for excluding criminal responsibility other than those referred to in paragraph 1 where such a ground is derived from applicable law as set forth in article 21." We maintain that a defense of necessity meets the requirements set out in Article 31(c), namely, that of the "general principles of law derived by the Court from national laws of legal systems of the world."

The requirements for determining the existence of a general principle of law in international law are established in numerous cases. In the *Erdemovic* ruling, for example, in determining the precise nature of the defense of duress, the Appellate Chamber of the ICTY turned to "a survey of those jurisdictions whose jurisprudence is, as a practical matter, accessible to us in an effort to discern a general trend, policy or principle underlying the concrete rules of that jurisdiction."[75] Using this as a guideline it is clear that in both common law and civil law traditions, the defense of necessity has been recognized in both statute and in practice. Under the various state laws of the United States, "The defense of necessity is available when a person is faced with a choice of two evils and must then decide whether to commit a crime or an alternative act that constitutes a greater evil."[76] Similarly, under English law, there has long been a recognized defense of necessity.[77] In civil law systems, a similar principle exists. Under Article 122-7 the French Code Penal, for example, "N'est pas pénalement responsable la personne qui, face à un danger actuel ou imminent qui menace elle-même, autrui ou un bien, accomplit un acte nécessaire à la sauvegarde de la personne ou du bien, sauf s'il y a disproportion entre les moyens employés et la gravité de la menace." ("A person is not criminally liable if confronted with a present or imminent danger to himself, another person or property, he performs an act necessary to ensure the safety of the person or property, except where the means used are disproportionate to the seriousness of the threat.") The defense of necessity is clearly established as a general principle of criminal law and therefore ought to be considered by the Court in relation to the Appellants.

In this case, the actions taken against the prisoners held at Moguatana naval base meet the legal standard of necessity. This Court must balance the life-saving information obtained from the use of these interrogation techniques *against* the likely consequences of additional attacks perpetrated by the Adeaq La terrorist network in Moresia and elsewhere around the world. This is the position taken by the Israeli Supreme Court in the *Public Committee* case.[78] Specifically that Court held that (a) the use of torture was illegal as a matter of state policy; but that (b) in certain circumstances those accused of torture could argue in their defense that torture was necessary to avoid a larger imminent disaster.

Several well-known scholars, including eminent American jurist Alan Dershowitz, have repeatedly argued in defense of the limited use of torture in scenarios in which the threat of harm to a country's population is severe and imminent; a "ticking time bomb scenario," in other words.[79] In these situations, torture stands as the "lesser of two evils" compared to other *jus cogens* violations of arguably larger scope and scale.

Legal scholars contend that the use of torture—as a violation of international humanitarian law (IHL)—could be justified on the grounds that it "would do *less* [emphasis in original] damage to the values IHL seeks to protect than would any licit alternative."[80] Appellants submit that this humanitarian approach raises a question that the Prosecution and the Trial Chamber of this Court neglected to address: specifically "if torture can, however narrowly, be justified for the obtainment of otherwise unavailable information that would save the lives of innocent people, why would it be *un*justified, if it leads to the same result—the saving of innocent people—by different means?"[81] The justification of humanitarian necessity can be derived from domestic systems and aspects from international humanitarian law itself, which permits harm to some if it is proportional to the legitimate outcome sought, and which "states as its own goal maximizing humanitarian protections from harms of inevitable wars."[82] Although not the same as the military necessity defense, a humanitarian necessity defense "would center only on humanitarian needs."[83]

Appellants are making an identical argument in this case. Both contend that the larger imminent humanitarian threat posed by future attacks perpetrated by the Adeaq La terrorist network on Moresia and elsewhere throughout the world justified the limited use of torture in this instance. Appellants remind this Court that the immediate beneficiaries of the use of torture were not merely Moresian citizens, but citizens in countries throughout the world. Though they were not formally advocating torture *per se*, Appellants Mursfeld and Croft were nevertheless rightly focused on the future victims of the Adeaq La terrorist network. Given the nature of the Adeaq La terrorist network—its ability easily to infiltrate other countries, its hatred for Moresia and its allies—a reinterpretation of existing international humanitarian law regarding the use of torture is required. The threat posed by the Adeaq La network was clear and its willingness and ability to kill thousands of innocent civilians has been established, making extreme actions like the acts of torture that occurred at Moguatana naval base a justifiable necessity.

CONCLUSION

Appellants reiterate that the use of torture is not an accepted policy of the Republic of Moresia and is illegal under the international torture regime, including the Convention against Torture and Other Inhuman and Degrading Treatment or Punishment to which Moresia is a signatory.

Appellants do not dispute that torture techniques were used by rogue members of the Moresian military at the Moguatana naval base against Gafhanistani prisoners of war. Appellants Mursfeld and Croft, however, lacked requisite *control* over these interrogators to be held criminally responsible by the International Criminal Court. Both Appellants lacked the requisite *knowledge* to be held criminally responsible. Lastly neither can be held criminally responsible by this Court for failure to undertake *reasonable measures* to prevent the use of torture.

Appellants strenuously contest the Prosecution's contention that both are responsible for the perpetration of torture as a crime against humanity. Torture was used by rogue members of the military against Gafhanistani prisoners of war only. No widespread or systematic attack was launched against the civilian population of Gafhanistan. The Prosecution has failed to demonstrate that the Government of Moresia was, in fact, directly targeting Gafhanistani civilians.

Finally, should this Court find either or both Appellants responsible for the use of torture as a war crime, Appellants Mursfeld and Croft contend that its use was necessary in order to prevent a larger humanitarian disaster that would have affected not only Moresian citizens, but innocent citizens throughout the world. Appellants remind this Court of the words of the Israeli Supreme Court in the *Public Commission* case: "Just as the existence of the 'necessity defense' does not bestow authority [to use torture], the lack of authority does not negate the applicability of the necessity defense or other defenses from criminal laibility."[84]

LEGAL BRIEF OF THE RESPONDENT

THE QUESTION

The Appeals Chamber of this Court is being asked to assess the legality of the Appellants' convictions for war crimes and crimes against humanity. The key legal issue before the Appeals Chamber of this Court is whether or not Appellants exercised effective control over those responsible for the utilization of torture against suspects interned at the Moguatana naval base. The Court is also asked to consider whether or not the humanitarian necessity defense, on which Appellants rely, is warranted in this case.

ISSUES

The following issues will be addressed in this brief: (I) torture as a violation of *jus cogens* norms and its prohibition under international law; (II) the legality of the Appellants' conviction for crimes against humanity and war crimes on the basis of the command responsibility doctrine; and (III) the merit of Appellants' "humanitarian necessity" defense.

SUMMARY OF ARGUMENTS

The use of terrorism is an inhumane practice that has been banned domestically and internationally. Torture is prohibited regardless of the existence of a state of public emergency, war, or any other similar circumstance. Appellants Mursfeld and Croft, by virtue of their positions in the political-military hierarchy of the Government of Moresia, exercised effective command responsibility over those responsible for the use of torture against Gafhanistani civilians and prisoners of war detained at the Moguatana naval base. This authority is demonstrated by the November 16, 2002 memorandum written by Appellant Croft, a copy of which was presented to Appellant Minister of Defense Ronald Mursfeld and other top officials of the Moresian government. This memorandum was intended to direct the activities of interrogators at the Moguatana naval base. The use of torture at Moguatana commenced shortly thereafter. The fact that torture was used as an interrogation method against Gafhanistani prisoners of war makes its use a war crime; that it was used as part of a widespread *and* systematic campaign against the Gafhanistani *civilian* population makes its use a crime against humanity. The notion that its use can be justified as a pre-emptive method of self-defense, a "lesser-of-two-evils" means of preventing future humanitarian disasters, is completely without any basis in international humanitarian law.

Torture is a *jus cogens* violation and *cannot* be used by any government regardless of the rationale. Torture violates the fundamental human rights of those against whom it is used and is an affront to all humankind. Moreover, it creates a culture of impunity that only increases the likelihood for future *jus cogens* violations. The Appellants' argument that torture can be a valid method of interrogation based on "humanitarian necessity" is completely without merit and has no basis in international law.

THE USE OF TORTURE AS NON-DEROGABLE UNDER INTERNATIONAL LAW

Torture has long been prohibited by international humanitarian law, including the four Geneva Conventions of 1949. Article 17 of the Third Geneva Convention bans the use of torture on prisoners of war,[85] Article 32 of the Fourth Geneva Convention bans the use of torture against non-combatants and other protected persons;[86] Common Article 3(a) to all four Conventions applies the ban on the use of torture to internal conflicts.[87]

Owing to its gravity and its actual and potential use as a method of interrogation and individual degradation by government officials and their agents, torture as a crime *per se* is banned worldwide. "Torture" is defined by Article 1 of the 1984 United Nations Convention against Torture and Other Inhuman and Degrading Treatment or Punishment (Torture Convention) as:

> any act by which severe pain or suffering, whether physical or mental, is intentionally inflicted on a person for such purposes as obtaining from or a third person information or a confession, punishing him for an act he or a third person has committed or is suspected of having committed, or intimidating or coercing him or a third person, or for any reason based on discrimination of any kind, when such pain or suffering is inflicted by or at the instigation of or with the consent or acquiescence of a public official or other person acting in an official capacity.[88]

Moreover, Article 2 of the Torture Convention states that the right to be protected against torture is a non-derogable right: "No exceptional circumstances *whatsoever* [emphasis added], whether a state of war or a threat of war, internal political instability or any other public emergency may be invoked as a justification of torture."

Similarly the International Covenant on Civil and Political Rights (ICCPR), the European Convention for the Protections of Human Rights and Fundamental Freedoms (European Convention), and the American Convention on Human Rights (American Convention), among others, outline the protections against torture as non-derogable.[89]

Decisions by national and regional courts demonstrate the absolute ban on the use of torture by domestic security officials against detainees. In Chile, for example, numerous officials associated with the Pinochet regime, including the former president himself, have been prosecuted for the use of torture. Moreover, in cases such as *Mikheyev v. Russia,*[90] *Aksoy v. Turkey,*[91] *Aydin v. Turkey,*[92] *Selmouni v. France,*[93] and more recently *Carabulea v. Romania,*[94] for example the European Court of Human Rights (ECHR) held that interrogation tactics such as beatings, rape, and electric shocks, used against detainees by security officials to extract information, confessions of guilt etc. constituted torture in violation of Article 3 of the European Convention. These tactics also include threats of harm ("psychological torture") as addressed by the ECHR more recently in *Gäfgen v. Germany*.[95] In *Gäfgen* the ECHR reiterated that the

> prohibition on ill-treatment of a person applies irrespective of the conduct of the victim or the motivation of the authorities . . . No derogation is allowed . . . The philosophical basis underpinning the absolute nature of the right under Article 3 does not allow for any exceptions or justifying factors or balancing of interests.[96]

In *Selmouni*, the ECHR described the Convention as

> a 'living instrument which must be interpreted in the light of present-day conditions' . . . [such that] the Court considers that certain acts . . . classified in the past as 'inhuman and degrading treatment' as opposed to 'torture' could be classified differently in the future. [The Court] . . . takes the view that the increasingly high standard being required in the area of the protection of human rights and fundamental liberties correspondingly and inevitably requires greater firmness in assessing breaches of the fundamental values of democratic societies.[97]

The ECHR, and international courts have expanded the offenses that constitute torture; this crucial in a period in which highly questionable interrogational methods used by security forces in the name of the "war on terror" have been classified by some countries as "less than" torture.[98]

The case before this Court differs from those tried by the ECHR to the extent that it concerns the prohibition of torture as a war crime, and a crime against humanity. Building on the decisions of the two *ad hoc* Tribunals in *Furundzija*,[99] *Akayesu*,[100] and *Mucić et al.*[101] the International Criminal Tribunal for the Former Yugoslavia (ICTY) Trial Chamber in *Kunarac et. al.* acknowledged that the prohibition against torture has roots both in international humanitarian and human rights law; the former differing from the latter in that "international humanitarian law does not depend on the participation of the state and, conversely, its participation in the commission is no defense to the perpetrator."[102] In keeping with the definitions of torture outlined above in the Torture Convention, the ICTY defined "torture" in *Kunarac* as

> (i) The infliction, by act or omission, of severe pain or suffering, whether physical or mental. (ii) The act or omission must be intentional. (iii) The act or omission must aim at obtaining information or a confession, or at punishing, intimidating or coercing the victim or a third person, or at discriminating, on any ground, against the victim or a third person.[103]

Appellants in this case are appealing their convictions by the Trial Chamber of this Court on the grounds that neither holds command responsibility for the acts of torture committed in Moguatana by "rogue" agents of the Moresian military per Article 28 of the Rome Statute. The Prosecution has argued to this

Court that neither civilian status, geographic separation from the crime scene, their self-contained locations in the civilian-military institutional hierarchy of the Government of Moresia, nor any other excuses Appellants provide to "distance" themselves from the offenses negate liability for either Appellant. Both had a duty to prevent and punish the acts in question and failed to do so.

CONTEXTUAL, MENTAL, AND MATERIAL ELEMENTS OF WAR CRIMES AND CRIMES AGAINST HUMANITY

Crimes against Humanity

Appellants were charged and convicted for the use of torture as a crime against humanity per Article 7(1)(f) of the Rome Statute.

Contextual Element

As this Court and other international courts including the Special Court for Sierra Leone, the Extraordinary Chambers of the Courts of Cambodia, and the two *ad hoc* criminal tribunals—the ICTY, ICTR—have ruled, what is required in order to demonstrate that an offense (in this case torture) is a crime against humanity, it must be shown, as the contextual element required under Article 7 of the ICC Statute, that the crime was part of "a widespread or systematic attack against any a civilian population."[104] The five-point test laid out by the Appeals Chamber of the ICTY in *Kunarac et. al.* is particularly useful as a guide in this case.

Reaffirming the conclusions of the Trial Court on this point, the Appeals Chamber in *Kunarac* et. al. ruled:

> In order to amount to a crime against humanity, the acts of an accused must be part of a widespread or systematic attack 'directed against any civilian population.' This phrase has been interpreted . . . , as encompassing five elements: (i) There must be an attack. (ii) The acts of the perpetrator must be part of that attack. (iii) The attack must be directed against any civilian population. (iv) The attack must be widespread or systematic. (v). The perpetrator involved must know that his acts constitute part of a pattern of widespread or systematic crimes directed against a civilian population and know that his acts fit into such a pattern.[105]

Moreover, the Court ruled that the target, "any civilian population," does not necessitate that the victims of the attack be associated with any particular side of the conflict.[106]

Moreover, as the Trial Chamber of the ICTY affirmed in *Gotovina et. al.* an attack "does not have to be directed against the civilian population of the entire area relevant to the indictment."[107] What the Prosecution will demonstrate is that "enough individuals were targeted in the course of the attack, or that they were targeted in such a way as to satisfy the Trial Chamber that the attack was in fact directed against a civilian 'population,' rather than against a limited and randomly selected number of individuals."[108]

As the Prosecution demonstrated to the Trial Chamber of this Court through the use of extensive witness testimony, many of those interned at the Moguatana naval base were Gafhanistani civilians who were deliberately "rounded up" by Moresian military forces during the initial phases of military operations in Gafhanistan. That they might have occasionally helped or were suspected of helping the combatants does not mean that they were not actually civilians. They were illegally interned alongside Gafhanistani prisoners of war suspected of having direct links to, and therefore broader knowledge of, the identity of the actual perpetrators of the October 2002 Adeaq La terrorist attacks.

International courts have been clear on the fact that the presence of non-civilians among a mostly civilian population *does not* deprive the civilian population of their civilian status.[109] When there is doubt as to the civilian status of a population, a military is to assume the population in question *is civilian*.[110] These points of customary international law were routinely ignored by the Moresian military who captured women, children, and the elderly in their round up of civilian suspects; particular persons who were extremely *unlikely* to have had any substantive connection to, or knowledge of, the Adeaq La terrorist network, not to mention its inner-workings. In any event the Prosecution successfully demonstrated to the Trial Chamber that these civilian persons were subjected to cruel and degrading treatment that meets the definition of torture under this Court's Statute, as well as under customary international law.

Material Element

Article 7(2)(e) further defined "torture" as "intentional infliction of severe pain or suffering, whether physical or mental." Unlike torture as a war crime, or for that matter a discrete offense, torture as a crime against humanity requires no specific purpose for its use.[111]

As demonstrated by the Prosecution in the trial-stage of the proceedings, the November 16, 2002 memoranda issued by the Appellant Minister of Justice Anthony Croft listed a number of possible interrogation tactics to be used by military interrogators against Gafhanistani prisoners of war interned at the Moguatana naval base. These methods (mentioned above), which included sleep deprivation, simulated drowning, and hooding, were judged by Appellant Croft, acting in his capacity as chief legal officer of the Republic of Moresia, as legally acceptable because they were acts that, although cruel and inhuman, did *not* constitute torture. A copy of this memorandum was presented to Appellant Minister of Defense Ronald Mursfeld on November 16, 2002.

The Prosecution clearly demonstrated to the Trial Chamber of this Court that a number of these tactics were used against persons held in the Moguatana naval base a short time after the November 2002 Croft memo was issued. Medical records of the victims, witness testimony, and photographic evidence introduced to the Trial Chamber substantiated these accusations.

What is at issue here is the identity of those interned at Moguatana naval base. Appellants Mursfeld and Croft readily acknowledge that some of the torture tactics outlined in the November 16, 2002 memorandum were used by some members of the military against Gafhanistani suspects interned at Moguatana naval base. However, these suspects, they contend, were prisoners of war. They neglect to acknowledge the fact that Gafhanistani civilians having *no* proven connection to the conflict or the Adeaq La terrorist network were also detained for questioning at Moguatana and subjected to similar illegal methods of interrogation.

Article 7(2)(e) of the ICC Statute does not require the Prosecution to demonstrate the purpose of the torture used by the Moresian military against Gafhanistani civilians in this case. However, the Prosecution nevertheless successfully demonstrated to the Trial Chamber of this Court, through the use of statements from civilian torture victims detained and then released from Moguatana and deported back to Gafhanistan, that the Moresian military's use of torture tactics against these persons was for the purposes of terrorizing and degrading members of the Gafhanistani population in order to strike fear among the Gafhanistani citizenry as a whole.

Mental Elements

As the November 16, 2002 memorandum demonstrates the Appellants had knowledge that torture tactics would be used against Gafhanistanis captured and interned at Moguatana naval base and because both Appellants are disputing the Prosecution's application of Article 28 of the ICC Statute to this case, the Prosecution will address superior/command responsibility as it pertains to both crimes in a separate section of this brief (see below).

War Crimes

Appellants Ronald Mursfeld and Anthony Croft were charged and convicted of torture as a grave breach of the Geneva Conventions of August 12, 1949 pursuant to Article 8(2)(a)(ii) of the ICC Statute.

Contextual Elements

The contextual element of torture as a war crime has been met by the Prosecution. Appellants Mursfeld and Croft acknowledge the presence of an armed conflict of international character fought between the Government of Gafhanistan and the Government of the Republic of Moresia pursuant to Article 8 of the ICC Statute.

Material Elements

Appellants Mursfeld and Croft readily acknowledge that a number of the torture tactics outlined in the November 16, 2002 memorandum written by Appellant Croft and presented to Appellant Mursfeld were used by some members of the military against Gafhanistani prisoners of war interned at Moguatana naval base. These members, they contend, were "rogue" members of the Moresian military.

Mental Elements

What the Appellants dispute in this case is the applicability of Article 28 of the ICC Statute to this case. As the Prosecution demonstrates below both Appellants had requisite knowledge and effective control over those responsible for the use of torture in this case and both are liable for their failure to take adequate measures to prevent and punish the misbehavior of these "rogue" agents of the military.

LIABILITY OF APPELLANTS UNDER ARTICLE 28 OF THE ROME STATUTE

The Prosecution is applying Article 28 of the ICC Statute to this case as a mode of liability for the offenses perpetrated by Moresian military interrogators at the Moguatana naval base. To demonstrate that Appellants Mursfeld and Croft are liable for these offenses the Prosecution must show that (a) both had knowledge of the commission or likely commission of these acts and (b) that both exercised effective control over those responsible for the actual perpetration of the crimes in question.

Liability of Appellant Minister of Justice Anthony Croft

Addressing the liability of the Minister of Justice Anthony Croft first, Article 28(b) states that a civilian superior "shall be criminally responsible for crimes within the jurisdiction of the Court committed by subordinates under his or her effective authority and control, as a result of his or her failure to exercise control properly over such subordinates." As the Republic of Moresia's chief legal officer, the Minister of Justice had issued particular instructions to officials in the executive branch of the Government of Moresia regarding the use of torture within a context where it was foreseeable that torture would be the result.

As with other *jus cogens* violations the material and mental elements of torture as a war crime are closely linked. The Appellant contends that his position in the political-military hierarchy of the Moresian government, in addition to his geographical distance from the location at which acts of torture were being committed, is demonstration of (a) his lack of effective control and (b) his lack of knowledge. With respect to the both, the Trial Chamber of the ICTY in *Blaškić* held:

> if a commander has exercised due diligence in the fulfillment of his duties yet lacks knowledge that crimes are about to be committed, such lack of knowledge cannot be held against him. However, taking into account his [*Blaškić's*] particular position of command [in the Croatian Army] and the circumstances prevailing at the time, such ignorance cannot be a defence where

absence of knowledge is the result of negligence in the discharge of his duties.[112]

Applicant Croft is raising the issue of whether or not his *civilian* position in the chain-of-command in the Government of Moresia obviates his responsibility as a superior for the commission of these crimes; specifically his failure to prevent and punish. As this Court knows, one's civilian status does not negate ones' responsibilities under international criminal and humanitarian law per Article 28(b) of the ICC Statute. This is an argument that applies equally to Appellant Mursfeld as discussed below.

Case law is clear on the fact that the doctrine of command responsibility extends to civilian authorities as well as military. The *ad hoc* Tribunals established in Nuremberg and Tokyo resulted in the conviction of a number of high-ranking civilian authorities for war crimes: one of the most prominent, Koki Hirota, the Prime Minister and Foreign Minister of Japan for the "Rape of Nanking." A crucial point made by the United States Supreme Court is that: "The true test, which is found in varying degrees in the criminal law of most nations, is not the existence of the order, but whether moral choice was in fact possible." [113]

More recently the ICTR and the ICTY have addressed the liability of civilian leaders for their failure to fulfill their duties as superiors. In *Kordić and Čerkez*, for example, the Trial Chamber of the ICTY held that:

> At the top of the chain, political leaders may define the policy objectives. These objectives will then be translated into specific military plans by the strategic command in conjunction with senior government officials. At the next level the plan would be passed on to senior military officers in charge of operational zones. The last level in the chain of command would be that of the tactical commanders which exercise direct command over the troops.[114]

We disagree with the Appellants' contention that neither can be held vicariously liable for the crimes in question "insofar as vicarious liability may suggest a form of *strict* imputed liability."[115] Per the Statute of the ICC, commanders are responsible for the acts of their subordinates. Failure to prevent and punish is a subsidiary crime of participation similar to aiding and abetting. Appellants are therefore responsible for the crimes committed by actors under their effective control as a consequence of their knowledge of these crimes and their dereliction of duty to prevent and punish same.

Regarding the issue of effective control, in this case the ruling of the Trial Chamber in *Kambanda* is particularly instructive. In holding the former Prime Minister of Rwanda, Jean Kambanda, liable for crimes against humanity and genocide the ICTR held that as "Prime Minister of the Interim Government of Rwanda . . . he also exercised de jure and *de facto* authority over senior civil servants and senior officers in the military."[116] Moreover, the ICTR has found that effective superior authority extends to a variety of positions in a state including businessmen and those in the media as demonstrated in *Musema* and in *Nahimana et al.* respectively.[117]

In the *Čelebići* Appeals judgment the ICTY, affirming the Trial Court's ruling on this issue, held that "Although the degree of control wielded by a *de jure* or *de facto* superior may take different forms, a *de facto* superior must be found to wield substantially similar powers of control over subordinates to be held criminally responsible for their acts."[118] The Prosecution agrees with Appellants on this point of law. In this same decision "effective control" was defined by the ICTY as the superior's ability to "prevent them [his subordinates] from committing crimes or punish them after they committed the crimes."[119]

Under the ICC Statute effective control for civilian leaders requires knowledge or a "conscious [disregard] of information" that one's subordinates had committed or are about to commit a crime within the jurisdiction of the Court.[120] The *ad hoc* tribunals have held that the information held by superiors need only be general information.[121] Appellant Croft surely exceeded this standard as he is the chief legal officer of the Republic of Moresia and the author of the now-infamous November 2002 "torture memo."

The position of Appellant Croft in the "political-military hierarchy" of the government makes his "absence of knowledge" defense ludicrous. Appellant's memorandum, based on an erroneous interpretation of domestic[122] and international laws prohibiting torture no less, was written shortly after the October 2002 attacks. The Republic of Moresia went to war against Adeaq La and the Nabilat Government in Gafhanistan shortly thereafter. It was during this period that Moresian military forces captured and detained countless Gafhanistani suspects—soldiers and civilians—and implemented the extralegal interrogation tactics mentioned in the November 2002 Croft memorandum at the Moguatana naval base.

Respondent acknowledges Appellants' contention that *ad hoc* Tribunals such as the ICTY have consistently held that the influence superiors have over their subordinates must be controlling, not merely substantial. The extralegal treatment of terrorist suspects in the current global environment, however, requires an expanded interpretation of the command/superior responsibility doctrine. The case before this Court involves a key non-military official of the Moresian government whose erroneous interpretation of the law served to point the military arm of the state toward practices that, while perhaps anticipated to yield valuable intelligence information, clearly violate Moresia's international legal obligations under the Rome Treaty, the Torture Convention, not to mention its own domestic laws. Appellant Croft's position in the chain-of command of the Moresian government does not detract from his power to command the law toward what were predictably unlawful ends. Appellant Croft, as well as Mursfeld, should therefore be barred from resorting to a narrow interpretation of command responsibility that requires a more direct superior-subordinate relationship and a clear command and control hierarchy through which to trace criminal responsibility. Clearly, the judgment at trial suggests that it is not that simple.

Article 28 implies a superior-subordinate relationship such that omissions of the former lead to illegal acts by the latter. Due to his superior authority in legal matters via the discharge of opinion upon questions of law when required by the Moresian President, Appellant Croft had a command responsibility to dispense advice that upholds the Republic of Moresia's legal obligations. Given the circumstances of the day and his position of authority, the Prosecution contended that Applicant Croft knew that use of torture tactics by members of the military would be the likely result of his November 2002 memorandum; particularly given that his "torture memo" was circulated among higher-ups in the executive branch of the government, including fellow-Applicant Minister of Defense of Moresia Ronald Mursfeld. Again, the fact Minister of Justice Croft was not strictly in the military chain-of-command and was geographically distant from the crime scene does not detract from his role in *commanding*, via legal interpretation, and *controlling*, via his power to enable unlawful conduct through the office of Appellant Minister of Defense Ronald Mursfeld.

From this it follows that, by his actions, Applicant Croft obviously failed to "take all necessary and reasonable measures within his . . . power to prevent or repress" the crime in question or for that matter "submit the matter to the competent authorities for investigation and prosecution" as required under the ICC Statute. As the ICTY held in *Boškoski and Tarčulovski,* control and "necessary and reasonable measures" are "interrelated, as the degree of effective control over subordinates can be evidence for the necessary and reasonable measures within the competence of a superior."[123]

"Necessary" acts have been defined by international courts as "those required to discharge the obligation to prevent or punish, in the circumstances prevailing at the time"; "reasonable" as those measures "which the commander was in a position to take in the circumstances prevailing at the time."[124] As international legal scholar Gerhard Werle discusses, to determine "reasonable" the *ad hoc* Tribunals have relied on "the extent of control and influence that the superior has at his or her disposal in dealing with subordinates."[125]

The use of torture by agents of the military could not have happened had Appellant Croft indicated to Appellant Mursfeld that the use of torture tactics prohibited by Moresian and international human rights and humanitarian law were extralegal. The evidence demonstrates that Applicant Croft knew that his "liberal" interpretation of international law, occurring within such an emotionally charged post-October 2002 atmosphere, would travel through the office of the Minister of Defense down to his subordinates in the form of authorized torture. Moreover, Appellant Croft, as chief legal officer of the Government of Moresia had "the possession of material abilities to prevent subordinates offences or punish subordinate offenders"[126] which he completely and consciously disregarded. As the Trial Chamber stated in *Gotovina et. al.*, "A deliberate failure to conduct or conclude such an inquiry, despite having the means to do so, satisfies this standard."[127]

Liability of Appellant Minister of Defense Ronald Mursfeld

Appellant, Minister of Defense Ronald Mursfeld, exercised command authority over his subordinates; whether his command was *de jure* or *de facto,* is of no significance in light of the serious violations of international humanitarian law which occurred under his watch. Appellant Mursfeld, like Appellant Croft, may have been geographically distanced from the place in which the atrocities occurred. Appellant Mursfeld must have known or should have known that personnel under his command would engage in methods of interrogation that amounted to torture. As is obvious from the reports of maltreatment of detainees at Moguatana naval base, that have now become widely known to the public, it is apparent that Appellant Mursfeld failed to take reasonable and necessary measures that were within his power to prevent and punish subordinates for these offences.

It is important to reiterate that the superior-subordinate relationship required by Article 28 of the ICC Statute may be direct *or* indirect, including command of informal structures. On this point the Appeals Chamber of the ICTY acknowledging the decision of the Trial Chamber in "*Čelebići*" (*Delalič*) case stated: "the superior-subordinate relationship is based on the notion of control within a hierarchy and that this control can be exercised in a *direct or indirect manner* [italics added], with the result that the superior-subordinate relationship itself may be both direct and indirect."[128] The Court also pointed out that this relationship *must be* one in which the superior exercises effective control.[129]

Moresia followed a model whereby a civilian minister commanded and controlled the military branch of the state and thereby the military personnel in the detention center. Appellant Mursfeld, as Defense Minister of the Government of Moresia, held formal power via a *de jure* position as military commander. Nonetheless, we noted earlier that the superior-subordinate relationship could be *de facto* or *de jure.* The Trial Chamber of the ICTY held that: "a relationship cannot be determined by reference to formal status alone. Accordingly, formal designation as a commander is not necessary for establishing command responsibility, as such responsibility may be recognised by virtue of a person's *de facto,* as well as *de jure*, position as a commander."[130]

By virtue of his command position, Applicant Mursfeld must have known, or at the very least should have known that, in the highly charged atmosphere of an interrogation center holding terrorist suspects and/or their sympathizers, the interrogation methods recommended by Applicant Croft as chief legal officer of Moresia (already falling outside the prevailing view of legality), would be utilized and taken to excess. That this point can be inferred from information on record is drawn from the ICTY determination that:

> Actual knowledge, which may be defined as the awareness that the relevant crimes were committed or were about to be committed, may be established through direct or circumstantial evidence. Circumstantial evidence will allow for an inference that the superior 'must have known' of subordinates' criminal acts.[131]

By his pursuit of interrogation methods ultimately approved by the Applicant Minister of Justice, Minister of Defense Mursfeld knew or should have known about these crimes.

Respondents acknowledge that geographical distance, under different circumstances, may make it difficult for a commanding officer to know of the crimes committed under his watch. A similar challenge was addressed by the Trial Chamber of the ICTY in *Naletilić and Martinović* which held: "Considering geographical and temporal circumstances . . . the more physically distant the superior was from the commission of the crimes, the more additional indicia are necessary to prove that he knew of the crimes."[132] Yet Respondents find that the circumstances of the case point in a different direction. Applicant Mursfeld had every reason to know, as the use of the interrogation methods in question was both *investigated* and *approved* by Appellant Croft. Respondents contend that Applicant Mursfeld's reason to know *more than* surpasses the legal standard as emphasized by the ICTY in *Čelebići*:

> A showing that a superior had some general information in his possession, which would put him on notice of possible unlawful acts by his subordinates would be sufficient to prove that he 'had reason to know' . . . the relevant information only needs to have been provided or available to the superior.[133]

Applicant possessed information that the use of torture against detainees was not only likely but imminent; information he consciously disregarded.

Applicant Mursfeld failed to take the necessary and reasonable measures to prevent or punish the use of torture. Mursfeld had an obligation under international and Moresian military law to prevent crimes which, as stated above, were predictable after the circulation of the Croft "torture memo" as well as in the charged atmosphere of the interrogation center, and punish the perpetrators thereof. As the ICTY Trial Chamber held in *Kordić and Čerkez*:

> The duty to prevent should be understood as resting on a superior at any stage before the commission of a subordinate crime if he acquires knowledge that such a crime is being prepared or planned, or when he has reasonable grounds to suspect subordinate crimes . . . The duty to punish naturally arises after a crime has been committed.[134]

The same Court further argued that: "This duty includes at least an obligation to investigate the crimes to establish the facts and to report them to the competent authorities, if the superior does not have the power to sanction himself."[135] This duty has been interpreted by the Appeals Court of the ICTY in *Boškoski and Tarčulovski* to constitute "a *type of measure* that satisfied the legal standard which was correctly identified [by the Trial Chamber] as the "necessary and reasonable measures."[136] Pursuant to Moresian law, Appellant Mursfeld's ability to sanction more than exceeded the standard set by the ICTY. That the Applicant neither prevented nor punished reflects his intention to pursue what he wanted the law to be rather than what it really is. Respondents contend that all elements of command responsibility under Article 28 of the Rome Statute are satisfied as described above.

INAPPLICABILITY OF THE "NECESSITY" DEFENSE

Lastly Appellants are asserting a necessity defense per Article 31(3) of the ICC Statute. In this respect they assert that the use of torture, a violation of international law, was necessary given the presence of exigent circumstances beyond their control; specifically the uncertainty of the intentions of the leadership of the Adeaq La terrorist network and the fear that another attack or attacks against Moresia were imminent.

Respondents submit that that the use of torture under these circumstances does not negate its illegality. As an international crime—a war crime or a crime against humanity—its use is strictly forbidden. This was reaffirmed in *Furundžija* wherein the Trial Court stated:

> Clearly, the *jus cogens* nature of the prohibition against torture articulates the notion that the prohibition has now become one of the most fundamental standards of the international community. Furthermore, this prohibition is designed to produce a deterrent effect, in that it signals to all members of the international community and the individuals over whom they wield authority that the prohibition of torture is an *absolute* [emphasis added] value from which nobody must deviate.[137]

Moreover, in this same decision the Trial Court held that the prohibition against torture, "At the inter-state level . . . serves to internationally de-legitimise any legislative, administrative or judicial act authorizing torture."[138]

Nevertheless some scholars have opined that torture is warranted, under some circumstances, to head off a larger disaster.[139] Some suggest that a humanitarian necessity is suitable as a defense in situations in which torture prevents future *jus cogens* violations such as crimes against humanity; this despite the fact that torture itself is a *jus cogens* violation.[140]

Appellants base a great deal of their argument for the "humanitarian necessity defense" on the work of one scholar, Gabriella Blum. It is worth noting that in the Blum article the Appellants cite, the author herself contends that the use of a humanitarian necessity defense would only be consistent with international humanitarian law if it were applied to instances in which torture was used in an attempt to avoid future "significant" harm to *enemy* combatants and civilians.[141] The Appellants are gravely misinterpreting and therefore misapplying Blum's humanitarian defense argument.

Moreover, it is worth noting that the Israeli High Court is the *only* court to entertain any sort of *ex post facto* necessity defense for the use of torture. Respondent contends that this Court should not wish or attempt to embark on a pathway in which torture becomes a justifiable practice. The use of torture degrades its international prohibitions, as well as the international human rights regime as a whole. International courts have *consistently* held that torture as a war crime and crime against humanity is *absolutely* prohibited under international law. The "humanitarian necessity" defense offered by Appellants has no basis in customary international law and is therefore without merit.

CONCLUSION

Prosecution/Respondents contend that the fight against terrorism and, in particular, the treatment of terrorist suspects in the post-October 2002 era calls for a more expansive view of the command and control doctrine. In the context of blurred lines of civilian-military authority and the tendency of legal advice to fulfill the dubious expectations of those who request it, a country's chief legal officer has the ability to exercise effective command responsibility over those who are directly responsible for criminal acts; in this case, the use of interrogation practices that amount to torture. The absence of a more direct command relationship does not signify an absence of command responsibility. Appellants were convicted for torture as a war crime and a crime against humanity on the basis of this relationship by the Trial Chamber. Respondents request this Court to uphold the Appellants' convictions and deny their supplementary justification for the use of torture on the grounds of humanitarian necessity.

In *Kunarac et. al.*, the Appeals Court's opinion regarding crimes against humanity reflects well the *opinio juris* regarding the use of torture:

> when establishing that there was an attack upon a particular civilian population, it is not relevant that the other side also committed atrocities against its opponent's population. The existence of an attack from one side against the side's civilian population would neither justify the attack by that other side against the civilian population of its opponents nor displace the conclusion that the either side's forces were in fact targeting a civilian population as such. Either . . . would be equally illegitimate and crimes committed as part of this attack could, all other conditions being met, amount to crimes against humanity.[142]

The gravity of the October 2002 terrorist attacks perpetrated by members of the Adeaq La terrorist network does not eliminate the responsibility of the Government of Moresia to adhere to prohibitions against the use of torture under international criminal and humanitarian law.

JUDGMENT

The case before the International Criminal Court is *Prosecutor vs. Mursfeld and Croft*. The case concerns the alleged torture on Gafhanistani detainees that were being held at Moguatana Naval Base following the attack by Adeaq La terrorists on Moresian soil. The Appellants are being charged with the following: Article 7; Crimes against Humanity, Section 1 subsection f (Torture); and Article 8; War Crimes; Section 2 subsection ii (Torture or inhumane treatment, including biological experiments). In this case, we have two defendants and similar, but distinct legal issues raised. Torture was in fact committed by agents of the Government of Moresia.

The question is whether or not two senior government ministers authorized this torture, or that torture was the reasonably likely consequence of their memos authorizing these practices and whether, upon learning that torture was being perpetrated, they perpetrated crimes of omission for failing to investigate and have the torture prosecuted. To answer these questions, this Court will rely not only on the ICC statute, but also all sources of international criminal law, including human rights law, especially the Convention against Torture and Other Cruel, Inhuman and Degrading Treatment and Punishment, as well as the customary international law confirmed in the decisions of the International Criminal Tribunals for the former Yugoslavia and Rwanda.

The case will revolve around the ICC Statute's Article 28 (command responsibility), Article 30 (mental element), and Article 31 (applicable grounds for exclusion). The defense bases its argument on suggestive intent, that the legal memo(s) did not authorize torture but rather offered advanced methods of interrogation, since previous methods had not worked. The memo clearly outlined what should and can be done, and the two appellants handed down orders which a *reasonable* individual would have obeyed, along with the established rules for interrogations, including Army Field Manual, which explicitly states the specific rules. The defense argues that neither Croft nor Mursfeld can be held liable for the actions of those who disobeyed the rules in the Army Field Manual.

Second, the contextual elements for crimes against humanity and war crimes are not met, according to the defense. Neither Appellant authorized or called for the implementation of a widespread or systematic attack against civilians, the criterion for crimes against humanity. Nor were the alleged tortures occurring war crimes. The detainees may have had fewer rights, because they were suspected terrorists and therefore were unlawful enemy combatants, according to the Appellants, representing only a small portion of the population which were subjected to the advanced interrogation techniques authorized in the two memos of the Appellants. The authorized techniques were limited to mental and physical pain and distress. This was not enough to be labeled severe, and therefore failed to constitute torture.

On the other hand, the Prosecution argues that each Minister should be held responsible for torture. First, were the contextual elements of torture as a war crime and crimes against humanity met? As for crimes against humanity, the Prosecution argues that a widespread or systematic attack is a quantitative measure and cites case law to reinforce that it is the number of victims that were attacked that defines the widespread nature of the attack.[143] *Blaškić* defines widespread by the scale of the attack and the number of victims, and there were thousands of detainees. The *Blaškić* case also defines "systematic" as the organized nature of conduct concerned by planning or organization, and in this case the detainees were systematically arrested. There was an aggressive campaign of apprehension according to reports with little evidence with regard to combat status. Given that thousands of individuals were arrested, detained, and subjected to torture, the Prosecution argues that civilians were attacked in large numbers was therefore widespread. With regards to any systematic nature of the attacks, the Prosecution argues in accordance with previous case law "the organized nature of the conduct concerned which will very often be evidenced by planning or organization of the accused."[144] The Prosecution argues that the attacks were systematic, given that the detainees were arrested from an aggressive plan of apprehension. In regards to the nature of the attack, the Prosecution argues that an attack would include, but is not limited to acts of violence such as torture.[145] Given the fog of war and the context of the hostile nature of war, intelligence could be misinformed and thus innocent civilians can be arrested and detained. Acts of torture can predictably result from interrogations where the detainees, who were mistakenly apprehended, had no actionable intelligence to offer. While no torture is legally justified, it is a sad irony that those without any useful information may receive even worse treatment, including torture and cruelty.

However, the contextual element for crimes against humanity would have applied to some of the suspected terrorists who were subsequently detained and allegedly tortured only if the attacks were not proportionate and necessary during attacks where civilians were killed. Moreover, courts have held that for the contextual and material elements for both Article 7 and 8 of the ICC Statute, "There must be some kind of preconceived plan or policy."[146] It is clear that the government of Moresia intended to arrest "with all means necessary," and where impossible, to shoot to kill, as if the suspected terrorist had no right to arrest and due process. The Appellants contend that the attacks are not systematic and also were not directed at a civilian population, but at suspected Adeaq La terrorists. That "some civilians would be caught up in the arrests,"[147] is inevitable but not intended as such. In the absence of evidence that the civilian collateral damage suffered in pursuit of disproportional and unnecessary attacks on terrorists, the contextual element for crimes against humanity is missing, while it is met for war crimes.

The Appellants' position on the contextual element for war crimes, that armed conflict characterized some of the arrests, but not the majority, does not mean that some war crimes could have occurred because of their memos. For crimes against humanity, if the contextual element requires either widespread or systematic attacks on civilians as if they were a quantitative measure,[148] then the issue would depend on whether arrests were part of attacks on civilian populations. Arrests directed at suspected Adeaq La terrorists could only be called "attacks" in this legal view, if civilians were also attacked as part of these arrests. Again, it is clear that some of these arrests involved attacks on homes where innocent civilians, such as family members, also were involved in the combat.

The Court agrees with the Defense since the attacks were directed at suspected terrorists and given that the terrorists failed to distinguish themselves from the civilian population, the consequence that some civilians within the arrested population were caught was an unintended consequence.

Turning to the material element of crime, the Court is seized of the question of whether or not they are responsible for the war crimes, here torture, because they had command responsibility over the detainees. In 2002, the Justice Minister authorized a legal memo for the whole government that defined criminal torture as that which results in organ failure or death, while the Defense Minister authorized more rigorous standards restricting torture intended for the Moguatana Bay detention center and other military sites, where systematic torture certainly occurred. There is little doubt that the Justice Minister authorized criminal standards of conduct. Is that necessarily a violation of international criminal law as a form of confidential legal advice—if that was its purpose?

Confidential legal advice, however, is not what the Justice Minister offers, even if he has legal office providing standards for the government. As the chief legal officer of his country, the Justice Minister signed a document that constituted an order for the whole government, especially intended for intelligence agencies charged with high value detainees, not confidential advice to one client. Therefore, there can be little doubt that a definition of torture that eliminates most torture covered by customary international law authorizes torture. Article 1 of the Convention against Torture establishes this standard as "severe pain, mental or physical." His memo subverted the law-abiding standards of the Army Field Manual. It is also possible that the torture occurring under the possible command responsibility of the Defense Minister reflected the much looser standards defining torture in the Justice Minister's legal memo. Whether permitting torture is the same as ordering or having command responsibility for banned torture is the remaining legal question in the case of the Justice Minister.

The Defense Minister, as a superior within the defense department is closer to the chain of command, and thus has more direct responsibility. However, his memo was closer to the Article 1 definition from the Torture Convention than that provided by the Justice Minister. The approximate dozen techniques approved are individually not necessarily tortuous, but the memo was arguably reckless in specifying any rules about combining the techniques or in specifying limits to individual techniques. For example, stress positions and sleep deprivation, which could be torturous, both individually and in combination, are approved. The criminal law is meant to apply to legal memoranda, especially those promulgated by commanders in the line of responsibility, as legal advice cannot include the authorization of crimes. The techniques listed in the Defense Minister's legal memo makes his case almost as dangerous as that of the Justice Minister's surreal redefinition of torture. Indeed, the amount of time and thus the total suffering under the Defense Minister's criteria would or could be vastly greater than from a quick, but lethal form of torture that might result from the Justice Minister's legal advice.

The mental element of crime is whether torture was intended in the memos, or the lower and more controversial standard of recklessness or negligence. With the benefit of hindsight and even beforehand, it is clear that by an objective standard, a reasonable justice minister would know that he was authorizing torture. (We will turn to the Defense Minister's intent and knowledge below.) The normal mental element criteria are objective: what a reasonable government minister would have foreseen as the likely consequence in the normal course of events. If the Court were to assume neither Appellant intended torture and did not have knowledge, there is some international jurisprudence in international criminal law that says that occasionally one can argue for a lower standard because of the stakes, that it would be reckless or criminally negligent not to have foreseen what is reasonably foreseeable, then these memos would effectively have authorized torture, or make torture inevitable.

The mental element turns on whether one assumes that the Appellants did not have intent and knowledge of torture. All these memos are saying technically what is allowed. If one knows that torture is going to be used, does it have the same effect of saying, "Do this"? We say, "You can use any of these techniques, but don't torture." Is it possible to conclude that one ordered torture even though they have only written a memo that says what is allowed? Politically, we know that that such a memo can have the effect of an order because it is easily foreseeable that someone would know that the lowest common denominator would be practiced. It is also possible that the mental element could be based on a subjective test, what the Appellants actually thought, where their apparent belief that they were not authorizing torture would absolve them of what a reasonable minister would have thought. Both have consistently claimed that near-death is not torture. It would be difficult to show beyond a reasonable doubt that they did not secretly believe they were authorizing torture, given the legal advice that they received. In the absence of proof of prevarication, the Court must decide whether a subjective test for a *jus cogens* prohibition could be warranted. Clearly, this cannot be the case, as an absolute a crime of torture cannot be subjectively accepted as a matter of law. However, could an objective mental standard of recklessness or negligence constitute the standard? Again, the same logic applies: an absolute prohibition under law cannot excuse senior officials for their irresponsible behavior, given the manifestly required vigilance in international criminal law. The ICC statute does not offer any clear standard on these lower mental elements of crime. If they were to be applied, it would be over matters that did not constitute state policy, and rather those in combat who might be involved in ambiguous circumstances, not the clear-cut authorizations at stake here.

Since the mental and contextual elemental elements for war crimes have been met, what about the material element? Do the memos reveal command responsibility of superior officers for legal advice, since these memos, by themselves, do not represent direct orders. A first question is whether or not authorizing behavior can be criminal, if there were an expectation, based on either a subjective and/or objective test of intent, that they would be tantamount to facilitating torture? This is similar to the typical question of whether superiors are responsible for the behaviors of their inferiors. One could argue that legal advice is the same as giving explicit orders if the Appellant (subjectively or objectively) would have reasonably expected that legal advice to be followed in the ordinary course of events. There might be some tiny doubt about either the subjective intent or a reasonable expectation that these legal rules would be followed. The Court finds that there is neither a reasonable doubt nor any evidence that the subjective intent was that these legal memos were not intended to result in the activities outlined.

Even though the acts that took place at Moguatana Naval Base occurred after the memoranda from Mursfeld and Croft were received, the Appellants cannot necessarily be held accountable for command responsibility over the Moresian military. Their distance from the naval base left them unable to exercise direct authority. Individuals should not be held responsible where control is absent or too remote. *Prosecutor v. Aleksovski* explains that "it cannot be expected that a civilian authority will have disciplinary power over his subordinate equivalent to that of the military authorities in an analogous command position."

While the Justice Minister had no direct command responsibility, the evidence shows that the legal memos were actually intended for intelligence agency interrogations, which had been unprecedented until that time. There is little doubt that the Justice Minister would have had some knowledge of these intelligence agency activities, even if he had no supervision of their interrogations—and that this memo might have also migrated to the Defense Ministry interrogations, which may explain why many of the techniques authorized were mixed together in a way that undoubtedly constituted torture. The Justice Minister, in approving the legal memorandum drafted by the Office of Legal Counsel does give legal opinions about active policy. With an objective test, one can ask if it is reasonable not to expect this to result, as a conspiracy or direct criminal enterprise, as opposed to merely giving advice. The Justice Minister argues that he does not meet the criteria of command responsibility under international criminal law. The Justice Minister is not in the hierarchy of either intelligence agency or defense ministry decision making (as opposed to the Defense Minister).

One defense would be necessity, but we can dispense with this because the Torture Convention states unequivocally that torture is never legal. Nor has either Appellant provided any compelling evidence for this position. The memo of the Defense Minister outlined methods and made recommendations of advanced counter resistance techniques, which included: stress positions (standing for four hours, sitting, etc.); the use of false documentation and false reports to induce a reaction; an isolation period of thirty days with the potential for extended isolation upon request; interrogation of the detainee outside of a standard interrogation booth; depravation of light and auditory stimuli; hooding during both transportation and interrogation; the use of twenty hour long interrogations; removal of comfort items including religious items; removal of clothing and forced grooming; and the use of phobias (i.e., dogs) to induce stress.

Ultimately, only one item from the most aggressive techniques listed, the use of mild non-injurious contact such as poking, grabbing, and light pushing, was approved by the Defense Minister. However, the methods were used (illegally) consecutively, in combination, and for longer periods of time than outlined in the Defense Minister's memo. The mental element for intent is fulfilled here as the memo included both vague language for the methods used, as well as omissions of further guidelines as to the use of constructive methods and in combination of different methods. The memo indicated that a certain amount of individual discretion on the part of the commanding officer/armed forces was authorized. However, in the climate of the conflict individual discretion, not clear rules, were used to determine how far an interrogation will go and what tactics will be used.

The two Appellants were kept up to date on the interrogations and both failed to apply any repressive measures or negative consequences, allowing the techniques to continue. By failing to employ repressive consequences after the fact, both are criminally responsible under Article 28 A(1) and 28 B(3) of Rome Statute. In the ICTY case of *Kvakra,* the Court ruled that torture *per se* could occur through negligence and gross recklessness (see also *Blaškić* and *Stakić*). In these cases recklessness was more than enough to establish liability for crimes in terms of intent. Criminal responsibility must take into consideration both international and customary law. *Blaškić* defines "widespread" by the scale of the attack and the number of victims, and there were thousands of detainees. *Blaškić* also defines "systematic" as the organized nature of conduct concerned by planning or organization, and in this case the detainees were systematically arrested and there was an aggressive campaign of apprehension according to reports with little evidence to regard for combat status.

If an objective legal test of intent constitutes the mental element of an alleged crime, then the Defense Minister would be criminally liable as well. Acts of omission are criminally liable if the law calls for a reasonable standard of behavior, which in this context would be to specify not only approved techniques, but also with clarity and specificity. Here, the Defense Minister omitted critically defining details, not only on the limits of each technique and how they could be combined, but also in failing to provide a definition of torture. One might infer that the definition of torture migrated from the Justice Minister's legal memo, which was intended for the entire government. However, the Defense Minister's memo did not include the definition of torture. If he intended to use the existing definition found in the Army Field Manual for interrogation, that torture was any severe mental and physical pain, then that subjective evidence would exonerate him since many apparently felt his list of individual methods were individually not going to cause severe pain. If the legal test of the mental element was meant to be subjective, the Court finds that the burden of proof has not been met, if that were the apt legal criterion, since the issue is the apparent authorization of an entire list of techniques.

Should the law apply the orthodox legal standard of an objective test of reasonableness for situations where the defendant is in the direct chain of command, but is only issuing legal advice that does not automatically constitute direct orders and where he *might* not have direct knowledge of whether or not interrogation techniques are criminally coercive (even if it would be reasonable for him to know as part of his job, what those techniques were in practice)? The Prosecution notes that both memos omit guidelines for consecutive and combined administration, which amounts to torture. Vague language such as "at this time" and "multiple interrogation techniques" is used. There was also a failure to prevent torture or employ repressive acts once it became known torture was taking place in Moresian territory. The Appellants argue that a subjective test should be used when determining intent and cites case law, particularly *Celebici*, which states "An assessment of the mental element . . . should be conducted in the specific circumstances of each case, taking into account the specific situation of the superior concerned at the time in question."[149]

The Court does not find direct intent, citing the ICTY *Blaškić* case for the responsibility of "a person who orders an act or omission with the awareness of the substantial likelihood that a crime will be committed"[150] and *Kayishema*, which held: "The act(s) or omission(s) may be done with intention, recklessness, or gross negligence."[151] The defense argues that there is no clear intention present in the Defense Minister's memo, which only goes as far as to outline interrogation methods which were deemed legal (categories I, II, and the fourth technique in Category III)[152] and did not authorize the more severe techniques or the consecutive and combined use of techniques. The defense uses a subjective test by citing the ICTY Appeal judgment in the *Celebici* case, which places more emphasis on actual knowledge rather than negligence as a standard.[153] The Justice and Defense Ministers argue that they were outside the chain of command responsibility because of their status as civilian leaders outside the military hierarchy and distance from acts, which amounts to a lack of military authority as cited in ICTY *Aleksovski*.[154]

The answer would imply that some objectivity is required under the Nuremberg doctrine, which has been incorporated into the ICC statute that a manifestly unjust order cannot be obeyed. However, that is a responsibility of inferiors to superior orders. There is at least some reasonable doubt that the Justice Minister would be held to a standard of knowing that anything less than death is not an acceptable definition of torture. Does omitting the obvious constitute commanding torture to take place? Clearly not, since the Appellant cannot be shown to have thought that torture should or was defined by death. The Court does find that the mental element cannot be reduced to only the subjective intent of the Appellant; otherwise torture could not be prohibited in practice. However, by the objective standard, there is no proof beyond a reasonable doubt that the Defense Minister's acts of omission were unreasonable, given the conflicting definitions of torture from the Justice Ministry and the Army Field Manual. So, the Justice Minister had intent, but no command responsibility and the Defense Minister had no objective intent to torture, only negligence and recklessness in his command responsibility. Given the importance of the torture prohibition, the

Court finds the lower standards for the mental element would apply to the Defense Minister's possible criminal conduct.

However, the Justice Minister, as the country's chief legal officer, did have command responsibility over law enforcement, including for torture. The Torture Convention's requirement of investigating and, where appropriate, prosecuting torture constitutes a customary international law requirement. The same standard would apply to a defense minister whose inferior agents were credibly committing acts that could reasonably be called torture. The Defense Minister's alleged criminal liability, therefore, does not appear to be based on different evidence, not the legal memos themselves, but subsequent conduct, the supervision of his inferiors using interrogation techniques. By an objective test, should the Defense Minister have known that torture was being used at interrogation facilities under his direct command, and if yes, did he reasonably respond to these reports? There is little doubt that he did know that torture was occurring at the detention center in question. Therefore, the Defense Minister, while not liable for his omission in his legal memo, is liable for failing to respond in a timely fashion to reports that torture and abuse were occurring under his command. However, would these acts have been constituted as the acts of isolated individuals or the result of government policy generally? In the former case, the Defense Minister would not be liable unless he obstructed justice. However, it is clear that both Appellants would be responsible for implementing or failing to correct policies clearly at odds with the objective standard of prohibition required under the standards of the Nuremberg Principles. The burden of proof is on the Prosecution, but it has shown that the Justice and Defense Ministers took no investigative and corrective action to these credible reports of torture that they certainly would have received, often in real time. Therefore, the Court would find the Justice and Defense Ministers guilty for failing to respond to the reports of systematic torture conducted under their authority, under the principle of absolute prohibition required under international criminal law.

It is imperative to emphasize that neither human rights law, nor criminal law authorizes arbitrary arrests. Suspicions of terrorism must be reasonable and not subjective. While this case does not consider the arbitrariness of detention, both legal memos omitted details providing for release of those whom interrogation reveals there is neither reasonable suspicion of terrorism or probable cause of commission of a crime. It is essential to establish that both Appellants have an obligation to prevent acts of omission with respect to torture and must monitor the acts that are the likely consequences of their actions in the ordinary course of events. Both ministers are guilty of arbitrary detention, which the Human Rights Committee has made clear is a major facilitating condition of torture. The torture that occurred at resulted from the sweeps of neighborhoods that resulted in arbitrary arrests and subsequent torture of the innocent to obtain information that they actually lacked. For those detained in secret sites, mostly real terrorists as far as we know, both Ministers were also responsible for not following customary international law prohibiting secret detention, as mandated by the additional commentary by both the Human Rights and Torture treaty Committees (see the *habeas corpus* case in this book for additional details).

The European Court of Human Rights in the *El-Masri* case noted that an unjustifiably broad interpretation of state secret privilege had been asserted by the United States Government in proceedings before United States courts in that case, and that the same approach had led the authorities of the former Yugoslav Republic of Macedonia to hide the truth.[155] In the context of the secret detention, rendition, and torture program of the Bush-era CIA, the Court rightly concluded that the concept of state secrets "has often been invoked to obstruct the search for the truth."[156]

As a State Party to the Torture Convention, the Government of Moresia, led by both Appellants, is responsible to monitor, evaluate, and report on victims of torture or ill-treatment. Both Appellants are obliged by international law to know, as a result of their legal memos: (1) The number of victims of torture or ill-treatment; (2) measures taken to assist victims in the direct aftermath of torture; (3) The rehabilitation facilities available to victims of torture or ill-treatment and the accessibility thereof, as well as the budget allocation for rehabilitation programs and the number of victims who have received rehabilitative services appropriate to their needs; (4) The complaint mechanisms available for victims of torture or ill-treatment, including how such mechanisms are made known and accessible to all victims; (5) The measures taken by states parties to ensure that all allegations of torture and ill-treatment are effectively investigated; (6) The available avenues for a victim of torture or ill-treatment to obtain redress, including all criminal, civil, administrative and non-judicial procedures. These human rights obligations are legal and mandatory, though they are not yet clearly crimes under international criminal law. However, the Court is empowered to offer remedies for torture, and hereby orders the current officials in Moresia to desist from arbitrary and secret detention.

The International Criminal Court is empowered to order remedies that emerge from individual criminal cases, as empowered by the ICC Statute, and hereby orders the Appellants to make sure that their respective agencies compile this information and report to the Court on compliance at regular intervals. Both the Defense and Justice Ministers are liable, the former for command responsibility and the latter for failing to investigate and prosecute. However, the criminal liability of both might be overturned by a claim of necessity or that the detainees were unlawful combatants not entitled to the protections of the Geneva Conventions. The latter claim can be immediately discarded because torture violates the human dignity to which all human beings are entitled, both as human beings and under the Geneva Conventions, which mandates humane treatment of all. Clearly, human rights law calls for absolute prohibitions on torture, as the Torture Convention explicitly prohibits torture's use in all circumstances. However, human rights law is not automatically incorporated into international criminal law, which also explicitly authorizes a necessity defense. Both Defendants maintain that they felt that they had to use coercive measures necessary to protect the security of their country. By a subjective test, assuming they were and are sincere in this stated belief, both Appellants are not guilty. Does the necessity defense require reasonable intent, not just subjective belief?

Even if it were true that both Appellants authorized policies that constitute violations of criminal definitions of torture, which was only proven in the Justice Minister's case, and even if it were true that both knew torture was going on, which would implicate both the Justice and Defense Ministers, the necessity defense doctrine holds that that sometimes there are situations where one must commit a crime for the greater good. By an objective test, this would not be with benefit of hindsight, but rather the test of what a reasonable official would and should have believed at the time. The Appellants argue that, in the wake of the attack, one had to be risk averse, considering the apocalyptic threats perceived by many or most people as a distinct possibility. However, these do not mean that necessity can be defined subjectively to whatever is intended, Paranoids can intend things which are subjectively genuine, but they are not absolved of guilt because of mental illness, unless that reaches the standard of insanity. No one has argued that either Appellant was or is insane.

This defense of necessity must be the very rare exception. In conformity with most criminal laws, intent must be at least partly objective. That would mean that any criminal measures authorized must be reasonably chosen because of the absence of alternatives. While there can be little doubt that a relationship form of interrogation is more accurate than one based on criminal coercion, the former method is time consuming and conceivably too slow under the conditions of the environment. However, this Court cannot possibly take the position that it was reasonable to torture anyone to get information in the fastest way possible, if only because there is no evidence that, on average, the information obtained is reliable. By the standards of the time, a reasonable Justice and Defense Minister would or should have known that coercive interrogation is only fast, but not accurate and actually likely to produce reckless consequences. There are almost no documented cases of a "ticking time bomb scenario," but there are many documented cases of false information obtained under torture that produced disastrous consequences, such as the torture of al-Libi by the Egyptian Interior Minister, which led to the false information about Saddam Hussein used to justify the illegal invasion of Iraq. One criminal act led to another illegal one. Therefore, the torture was not necessary and cannot be used as a defense in these two criminal cases because objectively, the Ministers should have obtained professional advice from their criminal justice investigative agency, which was the most experienced on the value of interrogation techniques needed for intelligence.

Of the two Appellants, it can be said that the Justice Minister's crime, approving in his memo unequivocal torture for the entire government of Moresia, was more reckless and unjust. He is sentenced to twenty-five years in prison, which also reflects his acts of omission to investigate and prosecute as the country's chief legal officer, even though he was not in command of any interrogators. The Defense Minister's acts of negligence and recklessness, in addition to his similar acts of omission, also cannot be tolerated is sentenced to twenty years in prison.

APPENDIX A: Examples of Judges' Questions and Lawyers' Answers from Student Moot Courts

Q: Are you arguing that these suspected members of the terrorist network were lawful combatants?
A: They were suspected members of the Adeaq La terrorist network. They were unlawful combatants, but still protected under the Geneva Conventions.
Q: If they had been established terrorists, would coverage apply to them? How are suspected terrorists, who are unlawful combatants, covered?
A: International Humanitarian Law requires that everyone be treated humanely, including those not eligible for prisoner of war status.
Q: I have questions regarding the intent which you say can be inferred from the actual memo. The first is that the language is vague and facts have been omitted concerning certain policies and standards that could have been in place to ensure that these crimes were not committed. How can you be sure that the memo demonstrates the intent of the defendants to carry out these acts of torture?
A: By using the objective test I am assuming that a reasonable person, given the context of the hostilities at the time, the political climate, would have taken the omissions to indicate that there was personal discretion on the part of commanding officers on the ground and those carrying out the interrogations as to what tactics were appropriate for use.
Q: Also as you state that the memo does indicate that there was individual discretion on the part of the armed forces. My question is does that separation alleviate the responsibility of the two appellants. Can they be held responsible for the actions of the armed forces?
A: The separation does not alleviate their responsibility. The appellants are responsible for the behavior of those under their command.
(space indicates a new topic)

Q: If the judge does not accept direct intent you're going to have to prove recklessness. You'll need to explain the recklessness standard, which case law applies. Also you didn't mention whether negligence applied. I wondered if you're not going to make a case for negligence for the mental element?
A: I wasn't planning on it. I feel that recklessness will be sufficient.
Q: Okay and assuming the definition of recklessness is clear enough from the case that you cited, I would also appreciate if you can determine why the recklessness standard should apply to this particular situation, which is not a traditional armed attack but involves the widespread and systematic detention of detainees?

A: My answer to that is the detainees are suspected terrorists rather than established ones. Moresia is fighting a terrorist cell rather than established combatants or terrorists.
Q: So you're saying that the fact that they were suspected terrorists is equivalent to saying that it was an attack on civilians?
A: Yes.

Q: The first question has to do with intent. You claim that there was no intent for torture spelled out in the memo which details advanced interrogation techniques to be used against the detainees. However, Moresia is a signatory to the UN Torture Convention which defines torture in Article 1 as "any act by which severe pain or suffering, whether physical or mental, is intentionally inflicted on a person for such purposes as obtaining from or a third person information or a confession, punishing him for an act he or a third person has committed or is suspected of having committed, or intimidating or coercing him or a third person, or for any reason based on discrimination of any kind, when such pain or suffering is inflicted by or at the instigation of or with the consent or acquiescence of a public official or other person acting in an official capacity." The categories referred to in the memo, some of them refer to isolation, hooding, and a variety of other methods that could cause mental and physical pain or suffering. In light of this, how can you justify the use of the techniques you label as "advanced interrogation techniques? Do they not constitute torture?
A: Although these methods may have caused physical and mental pain, the defense does not believe they meet the definition of "severe." The intent of the memo is that these are to be individual acts which individually do not constitute severe physical or mental pain.
Q: But they did intend for the advanced interrogation methods to be used?
A: Correct.
Q: There were no guidelines as to how they should be used?
A: Yes there are. The defendants were relying on the field manual for interrogation, the Uniform Code of Military Justice, the military hierarchy, and discretion to govern the use of the approved interrogation techniques.

Q: My next questions have to do with the crimes against humanity charges. A systematic attack cannot be random. According to the Prosecution, which cited to *Akayesu*, there must be a plan or policy although that policy does not have to be absolutely defined. Given that those with suspected ties to the Adeaq La network were detained and removed to an area that was controlled by the Moresian government, indicates that this was not random. They were then subjected to advanced interrogation methods, approved by Moresian military and political leaders, which were carried out by armed forces following a strict chain-of-command in adherence to the, as you say, Uniform Code of Military Justice and other official guidelines. How can you say that that was not a systematic plan?

A: The detention and arrest of the individuals was planned. However, the use of torture on them is not a plan. Advanced interrogation was the plan.
Q: Advanced interrogation was the plan?
A: That is correct.
Q: Advanced interrogation which can be considered torture.
A: But the plan, the intent of the plan, was not for them to be subjected to torture at the time of their detention.
Q: But was the process of detaining and questioning systematic?
A: The process of collecting them was but that is not the basis of the charges against them. Rather the charge against them has to do with the act of torture.

Q: My next question has to do with it being widespread. Thousands of individuals were gathered and detained by Moresian forces. How can you claim that that was not widespread?
A: Given that the victims of the collection were from one category . . .
Q: So the number of victims doesn't play a part?
A: We see this case as pertaining to one victim who was a suspected terrorist. One victim, not thousands were gathered.
Q: So the act was isolated?
A: Correct

Q: You claim that they are unlawful combatants and that civilians may have been detained as well as members of the Adeaq La network and that's because members of Adeaq La do not wear recognizable symbols that distinguish them from the civilian population. But you do agree that innocent civilians were detained?
A: That's a possibility. Given that the Adeaq La members did not separate themselves from the population it is very possible that civilians were detained.

Q: You talk about the Čelebići judgment and I do agree that specific circumstances must be taken into account with relation to command responsibility. That was your subjective test. For your objective test you claim that any reasonable person would not read the memo and think it was allowing for torture. However, it was read and could be construed as permitting torture and that people did step outside of the line. Does that make sense?
A: Yes. I understand what you're saying.
Q: The acts were committed.
A: The intent of the memo was not to have them committed outside of the original authorization of the categories. Therefore because the authorization specifically states that you're not allowed to do acts that are clearly defined as torture under the Torture Convention a reasonable person would not see the intent of the memo to be condoning torture.

Q: First of all the ICC Statute says you must also prevent torture. So regardless of what was intended by the memo or what was in the minds of the defendants it seems to me that if torture was going on and it was reported the defendants had a duty to stop it. There is command responsibility, which you have not addressed, for halting the torture once it started.

A: I believe that the command responsibility was going to be addressed in the rebuttal part, but I can address it now.

Q: I'm addressing it because in an inquisitorial system the judge asks legal questions.

A: That's fine. I can answer that. Given their positions as civilians within the military hierarchy they have presumed authority over individuals in the military and not direct command authority.

Q: The ICC Statute says very clearly that that's irrelevant. The Statute says that if they are commanding that they have responsibility. The fact that they wrote the memo suggests that they have command responsibility does it not? Otherwise if they have no command responsibility, why write the memo in the first place?

A: Yes it does demonstrate command responsibility.

Q: So will you concede that there is a duty of care to make sure that torture is not being inflicted on detainees?

A: Yes.

Q: And did they exercise that duty of care after they learned that torture had taken place?

A: After, no.

Q: So you're saying they're guilty?

A: That they didn't take action after the fact.

Q: You should argue that it's still not a violation of the Statute.

A: I don't see how it wouldn't be.

Q: Well, it's your job to argue for your clients. Well, we'll let your partner deal with that particular question.

Q: Now did I hear you say that the Geneva Conventions don't apply?

A: Given that they were unlawful combatants.

Q: Okay. Well, the fact is the Geneva Conventions say that unlawful combatants must be treated humanely. They also say that you need a battlefield tribunal to determine the detainees' status as unlawful or lawful. You admit there were no battlefield tribunals, right?

A: Correct.

Q: So would you say that the treatment that has been reported is consistent with being treated humanely?

A: No not the treatment that was reported. They were not treated according to the guidelines of the memorandum.

Q: Okay so with respect to the absence of battlefield tribunals and the fact that they were not treated humanely in fact would suggest that these two indi-

viduals, if command responsibility is shown, are in violation of the Geneva Conventions and therefore guilty of war crimes?
A: If command responsibility is shown then yes.
Q: And they did write the memos because they did have command responsibility?
A: Correct.

Q: You also said that these acts were isolated?
A: Correct.
Q: Well, they fit a pattern did they not? They all involve techniques that the Prosecution states amount to torture. How can they be regarded as isolated acts if all detainees are getting the same kinds of harsh treatment?
A: Because it was only isolated to a certain set of individuals and not a section of the population.
Q: Right, but the attack was on them because they were denied due process. If they were given a battlefield tribunal then that would not be an attack. These people were arrested at the point of arms, and the majority was innocent of any crime whatsoever. So in the absence of battlefield tribunals this was an attack was it not?
A: Given the nature of the organization that was . . .
Q: But these people had nothing to do with the organization.
A: But the military couldn't distinguish if they did or not at the time.
Q: Must there not be probable cause for a lawful arrest?
A: Given that they were suspected terrorists . . .
Q: But you can't arrest anyone just on suspicion . . .
A: They were detained . . .
Q: There must be probable cause.
A: They were detained . . .
Q: They were detained incommunicado which is worse than arrest where it's not incommunicado.
A: The intent of it was to detain the individuals who were suspected of having ties with the terrorist organization.
Q: We have the word of the government which is at odds with the facts. The truth was that the majority were innocent. They had no ties to the terrorist network.
A: After they determined that . . .
Q: In any event they were denied due process.
A: Correct.
Q: The Geneva Convention says that if there is doubt a tribunal is required. Should the government have known that there was doubt, that many of them were not unlawful combatants?
A: I would say that it's probable that great care was taking in separating the suspected terrorists from civilians and that the individuals who were detained . . .
Q: It's not probable. In fact it's quite the opposite.

A: I would say that it was probable given that Moresia is a signatory to the Torture Convention. They would take all measures possible to only detain those individuals who were suspected . . .
Q: Many countries that have ratified the Torture Convention have violated it, so the fact that Moresia ratified the Torture Convention is irrelevant is it not?
A: Yes I guess.
Q: All right let's turn to intent. You said that there is no intent to use torture in the memo. The issue is not the memo but what the defendants' intent was is it not?
A: But the vessel of this intent was the memo.
Q: It's not the only evidence before the Court. The very fact that they didn't do anything to halt the torture once it was reported casts doubt on whether the memo was a serious set of orders. They did nothing to say "hey we only meant one item." A reasonable person could say that the combination amounted to torture.
A: I would think that a reasonable person would look at all of the different mechanisms involved . . .
Q: This memo exceeded all of the other mechanisms. The army field manual doesn't authorize all of these techniques.
A: No but it has the guidelines for how interrogations are to proceed and doesn't . . .
Q: This memo was in violation of the army field manual so the manual was not a controlling institution.
A: But it does govern how interrogations are to be conducted.
Q: So you're conceding that this violated the army field manual?
A: I think that it superseded it but at the same time . . .
Q: How did it supersede it if it contradicts it.
A: I think the memo updates the army field manual in a way that it . . .
Q: It makes it irrelevant?
A: I don't think it would make the entire manual irrelevant.
Q: How would someone know which part of it is irrelevant?
A: The procedures would be relevant because they . . .
Q: But they're contradicted by the memo.
A: The memo only contradicts the acts that can be done because of the resistance that the individuals were facing.
Q: They were resisting because they were innocent. They didn't know anything.
A: But I think at the same time they could have resisted because of the nature of the resistance . . .
Q: So we persecute the innocent to get at the guilty?
A: I think sometimes when you're looking for the guilty sometimes innocents . . .
Q: I hope it's not your family.
A: I hope not too but sometimes that happens within legal systems. Sometimes innocent individuals are convicted of being guilty of a crime.

Q: Okay you cited the Čelebići case as the basis for the subjective test. And you quoted that the mental element and the specific circumstances of each case should be taken under consideration. What does that have to do with the subjective test which has to do with the mindsets of the defendants?
A: The circumstances surrounding the case affect the individual's mindset at the time. The context needs to be taken into consideration.
Q: Why shouldn't a judge interpret that the circumstances of the case, that the mindset of the defendants, condoned torture, especially given the fact that they went ahead and used torture anyway as if the memo was irrelevant? If the defendants only intended to use one or two of the techniques outlined in the memo, the subjective element could be used against you.
A: That's why if the subjective is not found we offer an objective test to counter that.
Q: Normally the subjective test is used because the objective test would say that any reasonable person would find that memos such as these lead to torture. There's nothing that says "only use one technique."
A: Again referencing back to the other institutions that are in place they would follow those guidelines and the discretion of military commanders. If the interrogations were not working they could step it up within the guidelines of the memo.
Q: Why did the defendants not state that only one of these techniques should be used? If the intent really was not to use torture why not say "you can only use one of these methods?"
A: That would have limited the information they were gathering. They didn't want to limit the interrogation methods too much to the point they were ineffective.
Q: Why not place some limits short of torture. Why not say "you can use two or three of these techniques but not all of them?"
A: I believe it was because they were separated by a distance as well as the fact that they were civilians. They didn't understand exactly what was happening. They couldn't make a judgment as to what the limits were as to the techniques used.
Q: Wouldn't it be reasonable to assume that those who were resisting were resisting because they didn't know anything?
A: Or that they have been trained to resist. It could go either way.
Q: But the possibility also exists that a lot of them don't know anything. A reasonable person might say that you're torturing someone.
A: But a reasonable person could also say that they're resisting torture because of their ideology and convictions. A reasonable person could say that these interrogation methods are needed.
Q: Except that most people will talk if they're tortured. They'll say whatever you want to get you to stop.
A: I believe that there is a threshold for every individual.
Q: Well, how about you? What's your threshold?

A: Given that I was in the military and we did go through training for that . . .

Q: Could you go through all of the techniques and not talk?

A: Probably not, however, they could have had training or their ideology could have motivated them. Again the threshold for each individual is different.

Q: So American ideology is not that strong?

A: They could have had stronger conviction given that it was engrained inside of their religion. Their religion is a part of their culture. In order to get to that threshold you need advanced interrogation techniques.

Q: Is it reasonable to use techniques if people are only saying what you want to hear?

A: I think you're going to get some who say what you want to hear, but you're also going to get others who will provide you with valuable information. Again is it reasonable to subject innocent individuals to these methods for the sake of getting one or two who provide information you can use? Given the threat of imminent danger to Moresia it was reasonable to subject all individuals to these techniques.

APPENDIX B: Alterable Facts that Students and Faculty Could Adopt to Change the Legal Arguments

In order to generate different legal arguments and papers from those in this chapter, students and faculty should consider factual changes from those suggested below:

1. Over the past decade the country of Moresia has or has not been fighting a war against the Adeaq La terrorist network; members of which are or are not responsible for a number of attacks on Moresian soil, including a large-scale bombing that occurred in the capital city of Moresia on October 12, 2002.
2. During the its military campaign in Gafhanistan, the Moresian military captured and detained thousands of innocent or guilty suspects for terrorism and/or paramilitary soldiers working for the Nabilat Government in Gafhanistan, which was overthrown on December 31, 2002.
3. Most Gafhanistani suspects detained by the Moresian military were transferred to the Moguatana naval base located approximately ninety miles off the coast of Moresia's southernmost state, but under Moresian jurisdiction. The large majority was or was not innocent of any crime, despite Moresian suspicions.
4. At the Moguatana naval base a number of Gafhanistanis were or were not subjected to torture by members of the Moresian military and/or intelligence agencies as a means to attempt to gain information regarding the Adeaq La terrorist network.

5. Anthony Croft is Minister of Justice of the Government of Moresia and the chief legal officer of the Republic of Moresia. Croft is the author of the November 16, 2002 memorandum regarding the legality of the use of torture interrogation tactics under international law, where his definitions of torture were or were not consistent with Article One of the Convention against Torture.
6. Ronald Mursfeld is Minister of Defense of the Government of Moresia and is or not responsible for interrogation tactics used in the Moresian military, as well as its intelligence agencies.
7. The Republic of Moresia has or has not ratified the United Nations Convention against Torture and Other Inhuman and Degrading Treatment or Punishment (1984).
8. The Minister of Justice in signing the OLC memorandum and the Defense Minister in his December 2002 memorandum, did or did not ever order anyone to commit torture, only authorized techniques, which were or were not tantamount to torture or cruel, inhuman or degrading treatment or punishment.
9. The Minister of Justice was or was not geographically separated from the crimes committed and his actual or lack of effective knowledge that torture was being used there. The Minister of Defense was or was not geographically separated from the crimes committed and had or lacked sufficient knowledge and control over the use of extralegal interrogation tactics by military personnel at Moguatana naval base.

Students and faculty could consider this analogous scenario that raises similar issues:

An African country is faced with a separatist insurgency. A number of senior rebel officers are captured and interrogated. The regime has doctors present to keep people from suffering or dying, but still trying to give them enough pain to break and provide really good information that can help suppress the illegal, if justified rebellion. The government claims that critical strategic information was obtained by these interrogations. The rebels regard the interrogation techniques as terror motivated by vengeance and intimidation. This is what rebels can expect if captured; so they should desist. The issue of whether or not the regime is truthful about interrogation is unclear or the actual techniques used.

The enhanced interrogation techniques used on the victims appear to have traumatized them. However, psychologically they began a long-term healing process from the humiliation and degradation they experienced. The rebellion was suppressed and no one in the regime was prosecuted for torture. So, the International Criminal Court indicted the head of the African state. He, in turn, refused to accept the Court's legitimacy, claiming that this is a biased "African Criminal Court," which has not indicted anyone from any other continent. This

Court, he claimed, is financed by the West to maintain an illegal postcolonial domination of the third world and is racist by only selecting Africa. This Court did not even indict anyone responsible for much worse torture, such as Sri Lanka, where the alleged crimes had occurred after the Court had jurisdiction, Moreover, there no Americans or British indicted for instances of torture perpetrated at the Abu Ghraib or Bagram Air Base.

Notes

1. David Welsh, "Procedural Justice Post-9/11: The Effects of Procedurally Unfair Treatment of Detainees on Perceptions of Global Legitimacy," 9 *Univ, N. H. L. Rev.* 266 (2010-2011). He is partially quoting Jules Lobel, "The Preventative Paradigm and the Perils of Ad Hoc Balancing," 91 *Minn. L. Rev.* 1407, 1413 (2007).

2. Therese Lyne, "Lessons on Lesser Evils: Israel and the Prohibition against Torture," 14 *ISLR* 207, 213-215 (2006); also Fran Quigley, "Torture, Impunity, and the Need for Independent Prosecutorial Oversight of the Executive Branch," 20 *Cornell J. L. & Pub. Pol'y.* 271, 274 (2010-2011). The use of torture is technically prohibited by Title 18 of the U.S. Code, §§2340-2340A which implements the UN Convention against Torture (CAT).

3. This was spelled out clearly in the memo written by Assistant Attorney General Jay Bybee in August 2002. See Memorandum from the U.S. Department of Justice, Office of the Assistant Attorney General, to Alberto R. Gonzales, Counsel to the President, Re: Standards of Conduct for Interrogation Under 18 U.S.C. §§2340-2340A (August 1, 2002), http://www.justice.gov/olc/docs/memo-gonzales-aug2002.pdf (accessed July 7, 2011), 1; see also Memorandum from John C. Yoo, Deputy Assistant Attorney General, Office of the Legal Counsel, to William J. Haynes II, General Counsel of the Department of Defense. Re: Military Interrogation of Alien Unlawful Combatants Held Outside the United States (March 14, 2003), http://www.justice.gov/olc/docs/memo-combatantsout sideunitedstates.pdf (accessed July 9, 2011). For a fuller discussion regarding the memoranda in question see David Cole ed., *The Torture Memos: Rationalizing the Unthinkable*, (New York: New Press, 2009) cited in Quigley, "Torture," 276. Access to the memoranda can be attained through the U.S. Department of Justice website at www .justice.gov/olc.

4. See Bybee Memorandum, August 1, 2002, 1. Although a subsequent 2004 memo by Acting Assistant Attorney General Daniel Levin softened the administration's approach to torture somewhat, it maintains similar conclusions regarding the treatment of detainees reached in the original Bybee memo. Memorandum from the U.S. Department of Justice, Office of Legal Counsel, Office of the Assistant Attorney General, for James B. Comey, Deputy Attorney General, Re: Legal Standards Applicable under 18 U.S.C. §§2340-2340A (December 30, 2004), http://www.justice.gov/olc/18usc23402340a2.htm (accessed July 7, 2011). Moreover, as Harper states: "the new interpretation of the torture definition [as set forth in the Levin memo] did not provide new practices; it merely shielded the United States with ambiguous phrasing." Julianne Harper, "Defining Torture: Bridging the Gap between Rhetoric and Reality," 49 *Santa Clara L. Rev.* 893, 918 (2009).

5. United States Government, Military Commissions Act 2006 (MCA), Pub. Law No. 109-366, 109th Congress, Sections, 948r (b) through (d), (October 17, 2006). Section

948r(d)(3) adds an additional requirement: "that the interrogation methods used to obtain the statement do not amount to cruel, inhuman, or degrading treatment prohibited by section 1003 of the Detainee Treatment Act." According to the Detainee Treatment Act of 2005 "cruel, inhuman or degrading treatment or punishment" was limited to that which violates Amendments 5, 8 and 14 of the US. Constitution. United States Government, Detainee Treatment Act of 2005 (DTA), Pub. Law No. 109-148, 108th Congress (December 30, 2005), Section 1003(d), This is identical to the definition included in the Senate's reservations to the Torture Convention which as Lyne discusses, created problems for foreign detainees held outside of the U.S. as the provision was liberally interpreted by Attorney General Alberto Gonzales to mean that "US officials interrogating and detaining non-US citizens abroad would be free to engage in cruel and inhumane treatment short of torture without violating the Convention." "Lessons," 224. For an argument in *defense* of John Yoo's position that U.S. interrogation tactics of alien enemies detained outside of the U.S. do not violate the 5th and 8th Amendments, see Carrie L. Flores, "Unfounded Allegations that John Yoo Violated his Ethnical Obligations as a Lawyer: A Critical Analysis of the Torture Memo," 25 *BYU J. Pub. L.* 14-18 (2011). The Military Commission Act essentially "pledged immunity for post-9/11 interrogators"; see also Quigley, "Torture," 286.

The U.S. Government is also responsible for the return of terrorist suspects to countries in which they were subsequently subjected to torture in clear violation of Article 3 of the Torture Convention (a practice otherwise known as "irregular rendition"). The result has been "the manipulation of the international law system, as well as the circumnavigation of domestic law prohibitions against torture." Andrew A. Moher, "The Lesser of Two Evils?: An Argument for Judicially Sanctioned Torture a post-9/11 World," 26 *T. Jefferson L. Rev.* 469, 481 (2003-2004). For his full discussion about rendition, see "Lesser of Two Evils," 479-481. Interestingly section 7(a) of the MCA states that "no court, justice, or judge shall have jurisdiction to hear or consider any other action against the United States or its agents relating to any aspect of the detention, transfer, [etc.] . . . of an alien who is or was detained by the United States and has been determined by the United States to have been properly detained as an enemy combatant, or is awaiting such determination."

6. Israeli High Court of Justice, *Public Committee Against Torture in Israel v. State of Israel*, HCJ 5100/94 (September 6, 1999). European Court of Human Rights, *Ireland v. United Kingdom*, 25 Eur. Ct. H.R. (ser. A) 5310/71 (January 18, 1978) For a fuller discussion on the impact these cases had on the Bush Administration see Lyne, "Lessons," 220, 225-232.; and especially Louise-Philippe Rouillard, "Misinterpreting the Prohibition of Torture Under International Law," 21 *Am. Univ. Int'l L. Rev.* 9, 23-30 (2005-2006).

7. Rouillard, "Misinterpreting," 24; see also Council of Europe, European Convention for the Protections of Human Rights and Fundamental Freedoms, Arts. 3, 15, Rome, April 11, 1950, http://conventions.coe.int/Treaty/en/Treaties/Html/005.htm (accessed August 25, 2011).

8. Rouillard, "Misinterpreting," 24, citing *Ireland*, 25 Eur. Ct. H.R. (ser. A) at 41.

9. Rouillard, "Misinterpreting," 24-25.

10. In brief, persons placed in a Shabach position are subjected to loud music while sitting in a chair tilted face-forward with his hands tied to the back to the chair. Rouillard, "Misinterpreting," 28 quoting *Public Committee*, Judgment, paras. 10-13; see also Geert-Jan Alexander Knoops, "International Criminal Liability for Interrogation Methods by Military Personnel under Customary International Law and the ICC Statute," *International Criminal Law Review*, 4 (2004): 216.

11. Lyne, "Lessons," 230-231. She also contends that this *post facto* necessity defense indirectly became a justification for a continued use of torture in Israel. "Lessons," 231.

12. According to legal scholar Alan Dershowitz in "ticking time bomb" scenarios, torture would be permissible if conducted in an open and transparent manner pursuant to a warrant. Lyne, "Lessons," 232-234. For a very similar argument, including discussion of Dershowitz' argument, see Moher, "Lesser of Two Evils," 482-489.

13. Karima Bennoune, "Terror/Torture Redux," 19 *Tul. J. Int'l & Comp. L.* 173, 181 (2010). As Welsh discusses ticking time bomb scenarios are fairly unrealistic to begin with, but regardless the long-term costs associated with using torture as a means to gain information are ignored in favor of short-term advantages. "Procedural Justice," 293-294.

14. Bennoune, "Terror/Torture Redux," 180.

15. As Rouillard states part of the OLS' "misreading" of the *Ireland* decision can be associated with, among other things, the fact that at the time the ruling was handed down, the Torture Convention had not entered into force. Based on this and a number of other facts, the OLS' reading of the *Israeli* decision was selective indeed, For his full discussion Rouillard, "Misinterpreting," see 25-28.

16. Rouillard, 29, citing in part *Public Committee* Judgment, para. 30.

17. Convention against Torture and Other Inhuman and Degrading Treatment or Punishment, UN Doc. A/39/51 (1984). Art. 4.

18. Harper, "Defining," 903.

19. Jordan J. Paust, "Ending the U.S. Program of Torture and Impunity: President Obama's First Steps and the Path Forward," 19 *Tul. J. Int'l & Comp. L.* 151, 153-154 (2010); also Bennoune, "Terror/Torture Redux," 178-179, Quigley, "Torture," 284-289. For more regarding the changes made by Obama see Harper, "Definitions," 918-919. Others have called for truth commissions and the creation of greater independent oversight of the executive branch. For the former see Kim. D. Chanbonpin, "'We Don't Want Dollars, Just Change': Narrative Counter-Terrorism Strategy, an Inclusive Model for Social Healing, and the Truth About Torture Commission," 6 *NW. J. Pub. L. & Soc. Pol'y.* 1 (2011); with regard to the latter see, Quigley, "Torture," 293-311.

20. Paust, "Ending the U.S. Program"; Quigley, "Torture," Welsh, "Procedural Justice," and Bennoune, "Terror/Torture." As Harper discusses the absence of prosecution of perpetrators of torture is not a problem that is limited to the United States but extends to a number of countries. "Definitions," 913.

21. Interestingly foreign investigation and/or prosecution of U.S. officials for the use of torture has been tried in a few instances. One of these is a 2009 trial in Italy of twenty-three Americans for the kidnap and transport of a Muslim cleric to Egypt where he was tortured. Most of those on trial were CIA operatives; all were tried in *absentia*. For further discussion see Quigley, "Torture," 309-310.

22. The international torture regime is what Donnelly refers to as a "single issue regime." Compliance with the 1984 Convention against Torture (see above) is overseen by a Committee against Torture. Established under Part II of the Convention its responsibilities include reviewing reports from parties to the Convention and receiving and investigate complaints from states. The Committee works closely with the UN Special Rapporteur on Torture who also investigates cases of torture. Jack Donnelly, *Universal Human Rights: Theory and Practice,* 2d. ed. (Cornell University Press, 2003), 149-151; also Malcolm N. Shaw, *International Law*, 6th ed. (Cambridge, UK: Cambridge University Press, 2008), 327-330.

23. Shaw, *International Law*, 326.

24. The latter are protected by the Fourth Geneva Convention. See Rouillard, "Misinterpreting," 13.

25. Antonio Cassese, *International Criminal Law*, 2d. ed. (Oxford: Oxford University Press, 2008).

26. It will be useful for instructors to make the distinction between international criminal law and international human rights law for students. As Cassese states, international human rights law protects the fundamental rights (political, civil) of individuals and is a foundation for international criminal law, particularly in the area of due process guarantees for the accused. Cassese, *International Criminal Law*, 6.

27. International Covenant on Civil and Political Rights, UN Doc. A/6316 (1966).

28. Universal Declaration of Human Rights, A/Res. 217k, UN Decl. A/810 (1948). Although not a treaty, the UNDHR has acquired the status of customary international law.

29. For a much fuller list of conventions and resolutions prohibiting torture including regional conventions, see Rouillard, "Misinterpreting," 15-17.

30. Torture Convention, Art. 1.

31. Torture Convention, Art. 2.

32. Specifically he is referring to the elimination of the reference to torture as an "aggravated and deliberate form of ill treatment" that was included in the UN Declaration on the Protection of All Persons from Being Subjected to Torture and other Cruel, Inhuman or Degrading Treatment or Punishment, UN Doc. A/10034 (1975). Rouillard, "Misinterpreting," 20. As Harper discusses one of the largest challenges associated with the vague definition of torture provided by the Torture Convention is "severe pain or suffering." This is where torture and less than torture come into play. "Defining," 898, 900-903; see also the tortured (pardon the pun) attempts to define "severe" in the December 2004 Levin memorandum.

33. This is an example of what Donnelly refers to as a "promotional regime," which is to say one in which international standards are in place, compliance is encouraged through monitoring processes, but enforcement of these standards is left up to individual states. Donnelly, *Human Rights*, 127-129. Promotional regimes are weaker compared to those with binding authority. The structural deficiencies of the Torture Convention demonstrate this weakness, particularly Articles 20 through 22 and Article 28. Moreover, as Shaw discusses the Committee is plagued with the problem of "overdue reports" from member states. *International Law*, 328. For an excellent discussion about the definitional problem, specifically when it comes to defining "severity," see Harper, "Definitions," 910-918.

34. Welsh, "Procedural Justice," 287.

35. Geert-Jan Alexander Knoops, "International Criminal Liability for Interrogation Methods by Military Personnel under Customary International Law and the ICC Statute," 4 *Int'l Crim. L. Rev.* 211, 211-229 (2004).

36. Knoops, "International Criminal Liability," 218.

37. Cassese, *International Criminal Law*, 151.

38. Cassese, *International Criminal Law*, 150-151.

39. Convention (I) for the Amelioration of the Condition of the Wounded and Sick in Armed Forces in the Field (1949), http://www.icrc.org/ihl.nsf/FULL/365?OpenDocument; Convention (II) for the Amelioration of the Condition of Wounded, Sick and Shipwrecked Members of Armed Forces at Sea, Geneva (1949), http://www.icrc.org/ihl.nsf/FULL/370?OpenDocument; Convention (III) relative to the Treatment of Prisoners of War (1949), http://www.icrc.org/ihl.nsf/FULL/375?OpenDocument; Convention (IV) relative to the Protection of Civilian Persons in Time of War, Geneva (1949); Proto-

col Additional to the Geneva Conventions of 12 August 1949, and relating to the Protection of Victims of International Armed Conflicts (Protocol I) (1977), Art. 75(2), http://www.icrc.org/ihl.nsf/FULL/365?OpenDocument; and Protocol Additional to the Geneva Conventions of 12 August 1949, and relating to the Protection of Victims of Non-International Armed Conflicts (Protocol II) (1977), Art. 4(2), http://www.icrc.org/ihl.nsf/FULL/475?OpenDocument.

40. See also Cassese, *International Criminal Law*, 151.

41. For further comment on knowledge with regard to crimes against humanity see Werle, *Principles*, 162-163.

42. Rome Statute, UN Coc. A/CONF.183/9, Art. 28(a) through (b).

43. Rome Statute, Art. 28(a) and 28(b)(i).

44. Protocol I, Art. 86, 87.

45. See for example the ruling of the International Military Tribunal (Nuremberg Tribunal) in the *High Command Case* versus that of the IMFTE (Tokyo Tribunal) in *Yashimata* (at *United States v. Wilhelm von Leeb et al.*, U.S. Military Tribunal at Nuremberg, judgment of October 28, 1948 in *Trials of War Criminals before the Nuremberg Military Tribunals under Control Council Law No. 10*, Vol. XI, 462, 513-514 and *United States v. Tomoyuki Yashimata*, U.S. Military Commission Manila, judgment of February 4, 1946 in United Nations War Crimes Commission, *Law Reports of Trials of War Criminals*, Vol. IV, 35.

46. See the examples of case law in Werle, *Principles*, 187-197. For an excellent historical overview of the evolution of the doctrine, see Cassese, International Criminal Law, 236-242; also Otto Triffterer, "Causality, a Separate Element of the Doctrine of Superior Responsibility as Expressed in Article 28 of the Rome Statute," 15 *Leiden J. Int'l L.* 179-185 (2002).

47. With respect to issues associated with the command responsibility as a mode of liability or a dereliction of duty see Chantal Meloni, "Command Responsibility: Mode of Liability for the Crimes of Subordinates or Separate Offence of the Superior?" 5 *J. Int'l Crim. Just.* 619 (2007): 619-637.

48. Werle, *Principles*, 190.

49. Cassese, *International Criminal Law*, 70. Culpable or gross negligence is clearly applicable to command responsibility; in other words as Cassese states in these instances "the military or civilian commanders' conduct glaringly falls short of the standard set by the reasonably prudent and competent commander test." *International Criminal Law*, 251. Here mere recklessness doesn't not suffice.

50. When it comes to the use of repressive measures against a subordinate believed to be responsible for a war crime it's not an either/or situation. Punishment of the subordinate after the fact does not relieve the commander of his/her failure to prevent the subordinate's crime in the first place. Werle, *Principles*, 194. Werle also discusses a fourth element that must be demonstrated by the prosecution: failure of a superior to take proper control over his/her subordinates. This fourth aspect is linked with the failure to punish/report and prevent and somewhat difficult to establish independently of the two offenses (*Principles*, 196-197). In any event Cassese states that "failure to properly supervise" is a lesser standard of negligence in that the superior may not have knowledge of the crimes of his underlings, but as their superior he had a duty to monitor their actions. *International Criminal Law*, 245.

51. For a fuller explanation of JCE see Werle, *Principles*, 172-176. For the ways in which JCE could be associated with superior responsibility see Knoops "International Criminal Liability," 221-223.

52. Cassese, *International Criminal Law*, 244.

53. Cassese, *International Criminal Law*, 244-245; 250; for his full discussion of intent and superior responsibility see 249-252. For a good demonstration of the notion of separate liability for commanders see ICTY, *Prosecutor v. Halilović*, Case No. IT-01-48-T, Judgment, para. 54-100 (November 16, 2005).

54. Cassese, *International Criminal Law*, 250-251.

55. Rome Statute, Art. 28(a)(ii).

56. Werle, *Principles*, 189.

57. On this point see Beatrice I. Bonafé, "Finding a Proper Role for Command Responsibility," 5 *J. Int'l Crim. Just.* 599, 613 at ff. 57 (2007).

58. Werle, *Principles*, 195-196.

59. The ICTY originally opted to convict defendants under both direct *and* command responsibility for the same acts. This was changed by *Krnojelac* at which the Trial Chamber held "that it was inappropriate to convict under both heads of responsibility for the same count based on the same acts . . . The Trial Chamber has the discretion to choose which is the most appropriate head of responsibility." The ICTY Appeals Court "settled the matter" in *Blaskić* wherein it held that in cases in which direct and superior responsibility forms of liability are present for the same count, the Trial Chamber should convict for direct liability. Command responsibility, not forgotten, should be considered an aggravating factor at sentencing. Bonafé, "Proper Role," at 613, ffs. 45 and 47 respectively; see also 612.

60. As Bonafé discusses, the only persons convicted for "pure" command responsibility have been military leaders. For her full discussion see "Proper Role," 616-617.

61. International Criminal Tribunal for the Former Yugoslavia (ICTY), *Prosecutor v. Mucić et al.* ("Čelebići"), Case No. IT-96-21-T, Judgment, para. 377 (November 16, 1998).

62. ICTY, *Čelebići*, Trial Judgment, para 378.

63. ICTY, *Prosecutor v. Aleksovski*, Case No. IT-95-14/1-T, Judgment, para. 78 (June 25, 1999).

64. Gerhard Werle, *Principles of International Criminal Law*, 2d edition (The Hague: T-M-C-Asser Press, 2009), 196.

65. ICTY, *Prosecutor v. Blagojević and Jokić*, Case No, IT-02-60-A, Judgment, para. 302 (May 9, 2007). See also ICTY, *Prosecutor v. Mucić et al.* ("*Čelebići*" [*Mucić*]), Case No. IT-96-21-A, Judgment, para. 197 (February 20, 2001).

66. ICTY, *Prosecutor v. Boškoski and Tarčulovski*, Case No. IT-04-82-T, Judgment para. 418, (July 10, 2008); see also ICTY, *Aleksovski*, Trial Judgment para. 78 and ICTY, *Prosecutor v. Brđanin*, Case No. IT-99-36-T, Judgment, para. 281 (September 1, 2004).

67. ICTY, Prosecutor v. *Blaškić*, Case No. IT-95-14-A, Judgment, para. 62 (July 29, 2004) citing to *Čelebići* Appellate Judgment, para. 241; also International Criminal Tribunal for Rwanda, *Prosecutor v. Bagilishema*, Case No. ICTR-95-1A-A, Judgment (Reasons for July 3, 2002 decision), para. 42 (December 13, 2002). and ICTY, *Prosecutor v. Krnojelac*, Case No IT-97-25-A, Judgment, para. 151 (September 17, 2003).

68. ICTY, *Prosecutor v. Kordić and Čerkez*, Case No. IT-95-14/2-T, Judgment, para. 424 (February 26, 2001).

69. ICTY, *Prosecutor v. Kordić and Čerkez*, Case No. IT-95-14/2-T, para. 424.

70. ICTY, *Prosecutor v. Naletilic and Martinovic*, Case No. IT-98-34-T, Judgment, para. 72 (March 31, 2003).

71. ICTY, *Čelebići*, Trial Judgment, para 383.

72. ICTY, *Prosecutor v. Kunarac et al.*, Case No. IT-96-23, IT-96-23/1-A, Judgment, para. 92 (June 12, 2002).

73. ICTY, *Kunarac et al.*, Appeals Judgment, para. 95; reinforcing the judgment of the Trial Chamber, *Prosecution v. Kunarac et al.*, Case Nos. IT-96-23-T, IT-96-23/1-T, Judgment, para. 430 (February 22, 2001).

74. ICTY, *Kunarac et al.*, Trial Judgment, para. 426.

75. ICTY, Prosecutor v. Drazen Erdemovic, IT-96-22, Joint Separate Opinion of Judge McDonald and Judge Vorah, 7 October 1997, para. 57.

76. Dressler, Joshua, *Cases and Materials on Criminal Law*, 585.

77. *Regina v. Dudley and Stevens*, Queen's Bench Division, 1885 W.B.D. 273.

78. Israeli High Court of Justice, *Public Committee Against Torture in Israel v. State of Israel*, HCJ 5100/94 (September 6, 1999).

79. Alan Dershowitz, *Why Terrorism Works: Understanding the Threat, Responding to the Challenge* (New Haven: Yale University Press, 2002); see also "Democrats and Waterboarding," Wall Street Journal (November 7, 2001), http://www.opnionjournal .com/editorial/feature.htm?id=110010832; Stanford Levinson (ed.), *Torture: A Collection* (New York; Oxford: Oxford University Press, 2004).

80. Gabriella Blum, "The Laws of War and the 'Lesser Evil,'" 35 *Yale J. Int'l L.* 1, 14 (2010).

81. Blum, "The Laws of War," 22.

82. Blum, "The Laws of War," 35-36.

83. Blum, "The Laws of War," 51.

84. HCJ, *Public Committee*, para. 38.

85. Convention (III) relative to the Treatment of Prisoners of War (1949), Art. 17, http://www.icrc.org/ihl.nsf/FULL/375?OpenDocument.

86. Convention (IV) relative to the Protection of Civilian Persons in Time of War (1949), Art. 32, http://www.icrc.org/ihl.nsf/FULL/380?OpenDocument.

87. Use of torture is also banned in Articles 75 and 32 of Additional Protocol I and Additional Protocol II, respectively. See Protocol Additional to the Geneva Conventions of 12 August 1949, and relating to the Protection of Victims of International Armed Conflicts (Protocol I) (1977), Art. 75, http://www.icrc.org/ihl.nsf/FULL/470?OpenDocument; and Protocol Additional to the Geneva Conventions of 12 August 1949, and relating to the Protection of Victims of Non-International Armed Conflicts (Protocol II) (1977), Art. 32, http://www.icrc.org/ihl.nsf/FULL/475?OpenDocument.

88. Convention against Torture and Other Inhuman and Degrading Treatment or Punishment (1984), UN Doc. A/39/51, Art. 1.

89. International Covenant on Civil and Political Rights (1966), UN Doc. A/6316, Arts. 4, 7, http://www2.ohchr.org/english/law/ccpr.htm. Council of Europe, European Convention for the Protections of Human Rights and Fundamental Freedoms (1950), Arts. 3, 15, http://conventions.coe.int/Treaty/en/Treaties/Html/005.htm; Organization of American States, American Convention on Human Rights, "Pact of San Jose" (1969), Arts. 5, 27(2), http://www.unhcr.org/refworld/docid/3ae6b36510.html.

90. European Court of Human Rights (ECHR), *Case of Mikheyev v. Russia*, Application no. 77617/01, Judgment, paras. 135-136 (January 26, 2006).

91. ECHR, *Case of Aksoy v. Turkey*, Application no. 21987/03, Judgment, para. 62-64 (December 18, 1996).

92. ECHR, *Case of Aydin v. Turkey*, Application no. 57/1996/676/866, Judgment, paras. 80-86 (September 25, 1997).

93. ECHR, *Case of Selmouni v. France*, Application no. 25803/94, Judgment, paras. 96-105 (July 28, 1999).

94. ECHR, *Case of Carabulea v. Romania*, Application no. 45661/99, Judgment, para. 144-150 (July 13, 2010).

95. ECHR, *Case of Gäfgen v. Germany*, [GC] Application no. 22978/05, Judgment, para. 108 (June 1, 2010). However, it is important to note that the Court found that, due to the lack of cruelty associated with the threats made to the applicant they constituted "inhuman treatment" that did not reach the level of torture. (para. 108). For threats of torture held as constituting acts of torture see Inter-American Court of Human Rights, *Case of Maritza Urrutia v. Guatemala*, Judgment, paras. 85, 92-98 (November 27, 2003).

96. ECHR, *Gäfgen* [GC], paras. 107-108.

97. ECHR, *Selmouni*, para.101.

98. For example see the memo written by Assistant U.S. Attorney General Jay Bybee in August 2002. "Torture" in this instance was limited to actions causing "severe pain or suffering" of the sort that would cause "death, organ failure, or the permanent impairment of a significant body function." Memorandum from the U.S. Department of Justice, Office of the Assistant Attorney General, to Alberto R. Gonzales, Counsel to the President, Re: Standards of Conduct for Interrogation Under 18 U.S.C. §§2340-2340A (August 1, 2002), http://www.justice.gov/olc/docs/memo-gonzales-aug2002.pdf (accessed July 7, 2011), 1.

99. International Criminal Tribunal for the Former Yugoslavia (ICTY), *Prosecutor v. Furundžija*, Case No. IT-95-17/1-T, Judgment, para 159, 162 (December 10, 1998).

100. International Criminal Tribunal for Rwanda (ICTR), *Prosecutor v. Akayesu*, Case No, ICTR-96-4-T, para. 593 (September 28, 1998).

101. ICTY, *Prosecutor v. Mucić et al.* ("Čelebići"), Case No. IT-96-21-T, Judgment, paras. 459; 470-472 (November 16, 1998).

102. ICTY, *Prosecution v. Kunarac et al.*, Case Nos. IT-96-23-T, IT-96-23/1-T, Judgment paras 470(i), (February 22, 2001).

103. ICTY, *Kunarac et al.*, Trial Judgment, para. 497.

104. Special Court for Sierra Leone (SCSL), *Prosecutor v Fofana and Kondewa*, Case No SCSL-04-14-T, Judgment paras. 110-119 (August 2, 2007); with some alterations see also Extraordinary Chambers of the Courts of Cambodia, *Prosecutor v Kaing Guek Eav ("Duch")*, Case No. 001/18-07-2007/ECCC/TC, Judgment, paras. 297-312 (July 29, 2010).

105. ICTY, *Prosecutor v. Kunarac et al.*, Case No. IT-96-23/1-A, Judgment, para 85 (June 12, 2002); see also *Kunarac et al.*, Trial Judgment, para. 410.

106. ICTY, *Kunarac et al.*, Appeals Judgment, para 88.

107. ICTY, *Prosecutor v. Gotovina et al.*, Case No. IT-06-90-T, Judgment, para. 1704 (April 15, 2011).

108. ICTY, *Prosecutor v. Gotovina et al.*, Trial Judgment, para. 1704.

109. See for example, ICTR, *Prosecutor v. Musema*, Case No ICTR-96-13-T, Judgment, para. 207, (January 27, 2000); also ICTY, Prosecutor v. *Blaškić*, Case No. IT-95-14-T, Judgment, para 214 (March 3, 2000).

110. ICTY, *Kunarac et al.*, Trial Judgment, para 426.

111. Antonio Cassese, *International Criminal Law*, 2d. ed. (Oxford: Oxford University Press, 2008), 151. William A. Schabas, *An Introduction to the International Criminal Court*, 3d ed. (Cambridge: New York: Cambridge University Press, 2007), 111. This is reflected in the rulings of the *ad hoc* tribunals, see for instance ICTY, *Kunarac et al.*, Trial Judgment, para. 486.

112. ICTY, *Blaškić*, Trial Judgment, para 332.

113. United States Supreme Court, *Koki Hirota v. General of the Army MacArthur*, 338 U.S. 197 (1948).

114. ICTY, *Prosecutor v. Kordić and Čerkez*, Case No. IT-95-14/2-T, Judgment, para. 419 (February 26, 2001).

115. ICTY, *Prosecutor v. Mucić et al.*("Čelebići" [*Delalić*]), Case No. IT-96-21-A, Judgment, para. 239 (February 20, 2001).

116. ICTR, *Prosecutor v. Kambanda*, Case No. ICTR-97-23-T, Judgment, para 39(A)(ii) (September 4, 1998).

117. See also ICTR, *Prosecutor v. Musema*, Case No. ICTR-96-13-T Judgment, paras. 880, 882 (January 27, 2000); also ICTR, *Nahimana et al.*, Case No. ICTR-96-52-A, Judgment, para. 605-608 (November 28, 2007).

118. ICTY, "Čelebići" *(Mucić)*, Appeals Judgment, para. 197.

119. ICTY, "Čelebići" (*Mucić*), Appellate Judgment, para. 198. See also ICTR, Prosecutor v *Kajelijeli,* Case No. ICTR-98-44A-A, Judgment, paras. 85-87 (May 23, 2005) and ICTR, *Prosecutor v, Bagilishema*, Case No. ICTR-95-1A-A, Judgment (Reasons for), paras. 50-55 (December 13, 2002).

120. This is consistent with the ICTY appeals ruling in "Čelebići" (*Delalić*), para. 232-239.

121. ICTY, "Čelebići" (*Delalić*), Appeals Judgment, para. 238.

122. The Government of Moresia ratified the UN Torture Convention and has incorporated the Convention via national legislation.

123. ICTY, *Prosecutor v. Boškoski and Tarčulovski*, Case No. IT-04-82-A, Judgment, para. 231, (May 19, 2010). Here the Court cited to *Prosecutor v. Blaškić,* Case No. IT-95-14-A, Judgment, para. 72, (July 29, 2004).

124. ICTY, *Blaškić*, Trial Judgment, para 333.

125. Gerhard Werle, *Principles of International Criminal Law*, 2d ed. (The Hague: T-M-C-Asser Press, 2009), 196.

126. ICTY, "*Čelebići,*" Appeals Judgment, paras. 266.

127. ICTY, *Prosecutor v. Gotovina et al.*, Trial Judgment, para. 1964.

128. ICTY, "*Čelebići*" (*Delalić*), Appeals Judgment, para. 251.

129. ICTY, "*Čelebići*" (*Delalić*), Appeals Judgment, para. 252; ICTY, *Prosecutor v. Hadžihasanovič and Kabura*, Case No. IT-01-47-T, Judgment, para. 77-89 (March 16, 2006); *Prosecutor v. Blaškić*, Case No. IT-95-14-A, Judgment, para. 72 (July 29, 2004).

130. ICTY, *Kunarac et al.*, Trial Judgment, 396; also ICTY, ICTY, "*Čelebići,*" Trial Judgment, paras. 354, 370.

131. ICTY, *Kordić and Čerkez*, Trial Judgment, para. 427; ICTY, *Blaškić* Trial Judgment, para. 307; ICTY, "*Čelebići,*" Trial Judgment, para. 386.

132. ICTY, *Prosecutor v. Naletilić and Martinović*. Case No. IT-98-34-T, Judgment, para. 72 (March 31, 2003).

133. ICTY, "*Čelebići*"(*Delalić*), Appeals Judgment, paras 238-239.

134. ICTY, *Kordić and Čerkez*, Trial Judgment, paras. 445.

135. ICTY, *Kordić and Čerkez*, Trial Judgment, para. 446.

136. ICTY, *Boškoski and Tarčulovski*, Appeals Judgment, para. 232.

137. ICTY, *Furundžija*, Trial Judgment, para. 154.

138. ICTY, *Furundžija*, Trial Judgment, para. 155.

139. See for example Gabriella Blum, "The Laws of War and the 'Lesser Evil,'" 35 *Yale J. Int'l L.* 1 (2010); Alan Dershowitz, "Is it Necessary to Apply 'Physical Pressure to Terrorists—and Lie about It,? 23 *Isr. L. Rev.* 192 (1989) and *Why Terrorism Works: Understanding the Threat, Responding to the Challenge* (New Haven: Yale University Press, 2002).

140. Geert-Jan Alexander Knoops, "International Criminal Liability for Interrogation Methods by Military Personnel under Customary International Law and the ICC Statute," 4 *Int'l Crim. L. Rev.* 211 (2004).

141. Blum, "The Laws of War," 58-67.

142. ICTY, *Kunarac et. al.*, Appeals Judgment, para. 87.

143. *Prosecutor v. Blaskic*, ICTY (Appeals Chamber), judgment of 29 July 2004.

144. *Prosecutor v. Blaskic*, ICTY (Appeals Chamber), judgment of 29 July 2004.

145. *Prosecutor v. Kunarac*, ICTY (Appeals Chamber), judgment; "in the context of a crime against humanity, "attack" is not limited to the conduct of hostilities."

146. *Prosecutor v. Akayesu*, ICTR (Appeals Chamber) and Prosecutor v. Kayishema and Ruzindana, ICTR (Appeals Chamber).

147. ICRC Rule 106; "Combatants must distinguish themselves from the civilian population while they are engaged in an attack or in a military operation preparatory to an attack. If they fail to do so, they do not have the right to prisoner-of-war status."

148. *Prosecutor v. Blaskic*, ICTY (Appeals Chamber), judgment of 29 July 2004.

149. *Prosecutor v. Celebici*, ICTY (Appeals Chamber).

150. ICTY, *Prosecutor v. Blaskic*, Appeals Chamber, July 29 2004 Para. 42.

151. The *Prosecutor v. Clément Kayishema and Obed Ruzindana (Trial Judgment)*, ICTR-95-1-T, International Criminal Tribunal for Rwanda (ICTR), 21 May 1999 Para 146.

152. November 27, 2002 Action memo, p.1, approved one week later.

153. ICTY, Appeal judgment in the Celebici case, case no. IT-96-21, Para. 239.

154. ICTY, *Prosecutor v. Aleksovski*, Case no. IT-95-14/1-T, Judgment, para. 78.

155. *El-Masri*, footnote 26, paras. 191 to 193.

156. *El-Masri*, footnote 26, paras. 191 to 193.

Chapter 7

Suspending Habeas Corpus during the War against Terrorism: Middle Eastern Country versus Western Country

This final case involves civil liability, not criminal, in evaluating competing claims regarding the legality of the detention of alleged terrorists. Liability must be evaluated independently, and not by an executive or military official based on competing interpretations of obligations from international humanitarian law, as well as human rights law. As a civil right, *habeas corpus* is perhaps the oldest, dating back to about 1215 with the *Magna Carta*. Specifically, the International Court of Justice (ICJ) is the setting for a case judging the legality of a Western country allegedly arbitrary detention of those it claims to regard as terrorist suspects without meeting the standards of *habeas corpus* or *amparo*. These are the terms (in common law and in Spanish-speaking, civil law systems respectively) for the independent, third party review, usually by a judge, of the legality of detention. This right is normally required of *both* human rights and humanitarian law for those accused of a crime.

The Middle Eastern country in this case denies that non-state actors have belligerent status against whom war can be declared and that if they were unlawful combatants, they should be tried for those war crimes, as part of the normal due process protections of international humanitarian law (IHL, or war law) based on the standards of civilized legal systems. However, the Western Country asserts that criminal or human rights law is not even at issue, since the detainees were captured as combatants during its war against terrorism and therefore can be detained until the end of that armed conflict. The Respondent Western Country has restricted civil liberties on the grounds that suspected terrorists are not entitled to the same rights as ordinary criminals because of the exigencies of fighting terrorism, which constitutes armed conflict governed by IHL, with additional restrictions warranted because IHL only provides rights to those who qualify for prisoner of war status. Not only are actions taken by the government in question strikingly similar to those by the United States and other Western governments over the past decade, the legal doctrine invoked by Respondent claims that human rights law is irrelevant and that only IHL applies and can be reinterpreted in counter-terrorism to restrict some civil liberties like *habeas corpus* because "national security" and "national defense" trump these legal protections. The scenario presented in these legal briefs, therefore, raises not only the specific issue about the legality of detention, but also the requirements for rights to be suspended. It is noteworthy in the case of the United States, many independent studies have concluded that the large majority of those detained at Guantánamo Naval Base are and were not guilty of any crime. President Barrack Obama's own task force cleared all but some sixty detainees, out of the 850 that were imprisoned there, on the grounds that they were not dangerous to the United States. At the time of writing, some five years after the case portrayed in these facts, about 150 detainees are still there, and are provided some measure of independent review, though the decisions of the DC Circuit courts rarely grant the release of remaining detainees.

In the case in this chapter the Western Country claims the need to be cautious and to detain suspected terrorists on suspicions that are normally not permitted in ordinary criminal law, but which are permitted in IHL. If not permitted to arrest all genuinely suspicious people in order to find out who were or are the real terrorists, the Western Country would miss capturing and interrogating the real terrorists, who are capable of gaming any system requiring *habeas corpus*; who could then continue on with their plans to commit mass murder. Ordinary soldiers cannot be interrogated, but unlawful combatants, including real terrorists, can be interrogated under IHL on the grounds that they do not qualify for the rights of prisoners of war. Furthermore, *habeas corpus* can be suspended under the U.S. Constitution during rebellions.

The plaintiff, a Middle Eastern country, argues that human rights law is very rigorous and does not permit easy and simple derogation of *habeas corpus* on demand. It will cite various legal sources, such as General Comment no. 29 of the Human Rights Committee which establishes strict standards for any derogation, including for due process rights. Draft General Comment 35, on Article 9 of the International Covenant on Civil and Political Rights (ICCPR) specifically states, "[t]he important guarantees laid down in paragraph 4, i.e., the right to review by a court of the legality of detention, applies to all persons deprived of liberty." Paragraph 13 of General Comment no. 2 of the Committee against Torture also underscores the right to *habeas corpus*:

> Certain basic guarantees apply to all persons deprived of their liberty. Some of these are specified in the Convention, and the Committee consistently calls upon States parties to use them. The Committee's recommendations concerning effective measures aim to clarify the current baseline and are not exhaustive. Such guarantees include, inter alia, maintaining an official register of detainees, the right of detainees to be informed of their rights, the right promptly to receive independent legal assistance . . . to defend their rights, and to challenge the legality of their detention or treatment.

According to this perspective, the right to an independent review is not at all derogable, even if other issues of due process are derogable. Even if human rights law is regarded as irrelevant, the Third Geneva Convention of 1949, which applies to armed conflict, mandates battlefield tribunals, when any doubt about the legality of a combatant's status as a prisoner of war exists.

The judge, in turn, could examine any claim to a right to derogation of *habeas corpus* under legal standards such as "strict scrutiny," which developed in U.S. jurisprudence on the Fourteenth Amendment's Equal Protection clause. Here if there is a fundamental state interest, such as national security, the least intrusive standard must be used. IHL may also be a source of judicial review of the methods used, where the means of detention must be proportionate to a legitimate military objective and discriminate between arbitrary sweeps of villages and neighborhoods. There must also be a reasonable basis for suspicion, grounded not in whim or rumor, but in evidence.

Is suspension of *habeas corpus* the most efficient way of stopping terrorism? Even with strict scrutiny of any suspension of the right from arbitrary detention, there needs to discussion about efficiency, such as: how many people are being rounded up, what evidence exists and is required to form the basis of suspicion of terrorism, how independent is anyone conducting a review of the initial evidence, whether human rights law or IHL is the *lex specialis* to apply in such situations, and under what conditions notification of derogation is required. The Western Country says it can round up anyone who appears dangerous after a prior terrorist attack to decrease the probability of additional terrorist attacks. The extent of danger is the test in this case, which would require suspending *habeas corpus* if there is a reasonable suspicion that a detainee is a terrorist. However, questions arise such as: Are there other ways the public can be made safe? How dangerous are these people? How long can someone be detained before a legal review takes place? What are the criteria of independence as well as the quality of evidence mandated by such a review?

Facts of the Case

On November 9, 2004, the Respondent Western Country was attacked by the Islamic Jihad terrorist network, which targeted a large commercial center in

New Providence and the headquarters of the nation's Ministry of Defense, while attempting, but failing to strike another target in the capital city of the Western County. The attacks perpetrated by agents of Islamic Jihad involved the hijacking of commercial aircraft which were then flown directly into buildings. All told, over 3,000 people were killed, including 400 emergency response personnel; thousands more were injured; billions of dollars of property was destroyed; and trillions in economic costs were incurred. These deadly attacks became known worldwide as the "11/9" attacks.

Shortly thereafter, the National Assembly of the Western Country enacted legislation granting the President the ability to use "all appropriate means" to kill, capture, detain and interrogate, and where desired, to hold legally accountable those responsible for the 11/9 attacks.[1] As a consequence, the Western Country invaded and then occupied two countries: Tajmenistan and Qari, where Islamic Jihad, was located. The attempts of the Western Country to capture the leader of Islamic Jihad, Amaso nib Nedal, an infamous international terrorist responsible for planning the 11/9 attacks, hiding in Tajmenistan under the protection of the Nabilat, has thus far been unsuccessful. At the time these briefs were filed, nib Nedal remained at large and continued to threaten the Western Country through videotaped statements.

The 2004 legislation enacted by the Western Country also granted the President the ability to suspend *habeas corpus* provisions for "alien enemy combatants" detained within the jurisdiction of the Western Country. The suspension of the writ of *habeas corpus* by the President of the Western Country was widely publicized throughout the world at the time.

Subsequent to the passage of this legislation, thousands of individuals were arrested and detained for their suspected connections to Islamic Jihad, the Nabilat, and any other terrorist organizations hostile to the security of the Western Country. Most detainees were transported to a territorial possession of the Western Country for interrogation and detention. Some of these detainees are citizens of Applicant Middle Eastern Country. The detention and interrogation of those suspected of involvement in the 11/9 attacks or of having connections to Islamic Jihad has enabled the Western Country to claim that it foiled a number of additional attacks, as the Respondent's brief indicates, though it did not provide any hard evidence for this claim.

Following the January 7, 2005 ruling by the High Court of the Respondent Western Country, which held that the indefinite detention of "unlawful enemy combatants" by the Western Country was unconstitutional, the National Assembly passed legislation in February 2005 which stripped federal courts in the Western Country of jurisdiction over detainee *habeas corpus* actions, creating in their stead a Detainee Review Commission (DRC).[2] The DRC, which consists of three military judges, is charged with reviewing the status of detainees held by the Western Country. If following a hearing before the DRC, it were determined a detainee poses no threat to the Western Country, he or she would be released. In hearings held before the DRC, due process rights are limited at best. As the Respondent's brief indicates the legality of the DRC was, at the time of the Respondent's brief, being addressed by the Supreme Judicial Court of the Western Country.

The Respondent Western Country and parts of the international community recognize the continued threat Islamic Jihad poses to the safety and security of developed and developing countries around the world though most countries have not accepted that the legal paradigm of armed conflict is the only relevant law and believe that human rights international law and criminal justice law domestically are relevant if not more relevant to regulating suspected terrorists. Allies of the Western Country have nevertheless also been attacked by Islamic Jihad. In late November 2004 a commuter train was bombed in the capital of the United Realm, the Western Country's closest European ally, injuring and killing over two hundred civilians. It was determined that the attack was orchestrated by individuals from several countries in the Middle East, including the Applicant Country, who were living in these European countries and affiliated with Islamic Jihad. Lastly, despite early military victories in Tajmenistan, it has been recently reported that Islamic Jihad has gained strength and influence in its sanctuary area along the Tajmenistan/Kapistan border. Terrorists, who are part of or sympathetic to the Islamic Jihad network, continue to take refuge in countries such as Gafhanistan, Tajmenistan, Qari, Nadroj, and the Middle Eastern Country, where they continue to plot terrorist attacks against the Western Country and its allies.

Lastly, the Western Country is a signatory to the ICCPR and the four Geneva Conventions, as well as the American Convention on Human Rights.

Legal and Other Issues for Discussion

Unlike the previous cases in this book, the crimes addressed in this set of briefs are not *jus cogens* violations, as such they do not automatically translate into crimes for which individuals will be held accountable.[3] The case in this section, held before the ICJ, concerns the legality of a state's derogation from the common law provision of *habeas corpus* ("you have the body"), generally defined as the right of the accused to be brought before a judge or court to be informed of the reason(s) for his/her detention. The origins of the principle—enshrined in domestic as well as international law—have been traced to Roman law; specifically the notion of *de homine libero exhibendo* ("produce the person").[4] Enshrined in the Magna Carta, the Habeas Corpus Act of 1679, and the U.S. Constitution among others, the principle of *habeas corpus* has been referred to as "one of the most precious and fought over principles of justice" and a "bulwark of personal liberty."[5]

Although considered a universal human right, it is possible to derogate (or detract) from the provision of *habeas corpus* under certain conditions. Given the fundamental importance of the right these conditions must be *extremely* serious. According to Article 4 of the ICCPR, for example, this must amount to a "public emergency which threatens the life of the nation."[6] This is not an expansive power however. States must ensure that their derogation is "not inconsistent with their other obligations under international law and [does] not involve discrimination solely on the ground of race, colour, sex, language, religion or social origin."[7] In any event the Respondent Western Country maintains that the circumstances of the day—the global war on terror—justify derogation as a matter of national security.

Moreover, once states choose to derogate from Article 9 of the ICCPR, they must "immediately inform the other States Parties to the present Covenant, through the intermediary of the Secretary-General of the United Nations, of the provisions from which it has derogated and of the reasons by which it was actuated."[8] One of the issues with which parties in the present case are addressing is whether or not the Respondent Western Country adequately followed these requirements for proper notification. Students and instructors can discuss whether or not, in times of public emergency (war, insurrection, etc.) states need adhere to this additional international requirement. Can they not just act as they see fit given the dire circumstances in which they find themselves? Is informal notice—through the actions taken by a country, their widespread acknowledgment by scholars and the media—enough? Or in the alternative is Applicant correct in suggesting that derogation without proper notification (informal and *post hoc* such as that of the Respondent) creates a slippery slope that permits countries to perpetrate a host of crimes against detainees in the name of national security? This topic also touches on a second larger subject for classroom discussion and which has been previously addressed in this book (see chapter 2): the relationship between international human rights law and the laws of war.

Under the Article 1, Section 9 of the U.S. Constitution the writ of *habeas corpus* can only be suspended "in Cases of Rebellion or Invasion, the public Safety may require it."[9] The federal writ of *habeas corpus* was suspended by President Abraham Lincoln in 1861 during the Civil War; narrow suspensions with respect to non-U.S. enemy combatants have also taken place in other wartime situations prior to the "war on terror" of the twenty-first century. Student lawyers would benefit from reading *Ex Parte Merryman* (1861), *Ex Parte Milligan* (1866), *Johnson v. Eistentrager* (1950), more recent U.S. Supreme Court decisions including *Hamdi v. Rumsfeld* (2004) and *Rasul v. Bush* (2004), as well as other relevant U.S. Supreme Court decisions in which questions associated with the principle of *habeas corpus* were debated.[10] Student lawyers should be mindful of not just the majority opinion in these and other cases, but concurring and dissenting opinions as well. These will serve as useful guides for the construction of legal arguments for and against the necessity of *habeas corpus* provisions during times of conflict. On a separate but related note, it will useful for instructors to inform students about the manner in which to obtain and cite U.S. cases. An excellent source to aid students is *The Bluebook* citation guide.[11]

As mentioned above, the present case raises interesting questions about the connection between international human rights law and international humanitarian law, IHL or the laws of conflict. Even if the human rights protection of *ha-*

beas corpus is derogable, certain procedures are required for legal derogation, and even then, IHL may not permit such derogations if Common Article Three of the Geneva Conventions is deemed to apply (not just to internal armed-conflicts, but also as the minimum standards for all international armed conflicts). If *habeas corpus* is a universal human right—in other words a right that applies to everyone by virtue of their status as a human being—should it not also apply during times of war, particularly given the propensity of states to engage in serious human rights violations during wartime? Unfortunately there are numerous examples instructors can point to demonstrate this latter phenomenon, including human rights abuses perpetrated by government forces in several sub-Saharan African and Latin American countries among others (past and present).

As obvious from the above statement of facts, the legal issues raised by the Western Country's restrictions on civil liberties resemble U.S. detention of supposed terrorist suspects in Guantánamo Bay and other secret locations.[12] Domestically, in the immediate days after the 9/11 attacks, over a thousand Arabs and Muslim immigrants were rounded up by the government and detained absent the provision of *habeas corpus*. As Welsh comments: "Under U.S. criminal law, these individuals would have been charged within twenty-four hours, while the more expansive Patriot Act allows for a seven-day detention based on reasonable grounds in the belief that an immigrant is engaged in terrorist activities. However, new regulations permitted many of these individuals to be held for months."[13]

Many prisoner of war detainees would subsequently be detained indefinitely in Guantánamo Bay as part of a program of "preventative detention."[14] Their status and treatment as "unlawful enemy combatants" was reinforced by Congressional legislation including the Military Commissions Act (MCA) of (2006). Section 948a of the MCA defines "unlawful enemy combatant" as either

> a person who has engaged in hostilities or who has purposefully and materially supported hostilities against the United States or its co-belligerents who is not a lawful enemy combatant (including a person who is part of the Taliban, al Qaeda or associated forces)"; or one who has already officially been found to be an "unlawful enemy combatant.[15]

Moreover, unlawful enemy combatants were to be tried by a military commission for "violations of the laws of war and other triable offenses under a military commission"[16] and they could *not* invoke the Geneva Conventions as a source of rights.[17] Much of this was attributed to the fact that, unlike conventional armed forces, these combatants did not wear uniforms or carry arms openly.[18]

The Bush Administration's use of this appellation was widely criticized as an attempt to circumvent the prisoner of war (POW) protections provided by the Third Geneva Convention.[19] The right of foreign or "alien" detainees at Guantánamo to challenge their detention was prohibited by the Detainee Treatment Act of 2005 (DTA).[20] Simply put: alien detainees had no standing to challenge their detention in U.S. courts. In a similar vein, the Respondent Western Country contends that derogation from *habeas corpus* protections provided by the ICCPR is permissible given the Applicant's lack of legal standing to request relief, that suspects are being detained in an area *outside* of the Western Country jurisdiction (hence the inapplicability of the ICCPR),[21] in addition to the fact that the Western Country's derogation from its obligations to provide *habeas corpus* is legal anyway under international law. As mentioned above, sources of law on state derogation include the ICCPR. Also included in these sources are the European Convention on Human Rights and the American Convention on Human Rights.[22]

Returning again to the example of the United States, although certain provisions of the DTA were ruled unconstitutional by the U.S. Supreme Court in 2006 in *Hamden v. Rumsfeld, Secretary of Defense et al.*,[23] Congress soon thereafter enacted the MCA which also proscribed *habeas* protections for alien enemy combatants, authorized the President to establish military commissions to try the "unlawful enemy combatants," and also authorized the Secretary of Defense to establish a Court of Military Commission Review to hear appeals.[24] The issue finally came to a head in *Boumediene v. Bush* (2008) wherein the Supreme Court held, among other things, that that federal *habeas* jurisdiction applied to Guantánamo detainees because they were being held in a U.S.-controlled area.[25] In any event despite the Obama Administration's efforts to comply with the Geneva Conventions and other relevant international law, not to mention the "flood" of lawsuits filed after *Boumediene*, the indefinite detention of terrorist suspects at Guantánamo and other places including the U.S. Air Force base in Bagram, Afghanistan, not to mention trials by military commissions, continue.[26]

In *Boumediene*, the U.S. Supreme Court challenged whether Congress' suspension of *habeas corpus* for detainees met the required level of "Rebellion or Invasion."[27] This would be a good place for a classroom discussion regarding the types of circumstances that warrant such a severe restriction of due process rights. Is rebellion or invasion required? Can some lesser event be just as critical to public safety, national security etc.? These are questions with which student-lawyers for the Respondent Western Country will no doubt have to contend.

Finally, another interesting topic for classroom discussion concerns the meaning of "indefinite detention." Does it mean detention abroad until hostilities have ended or perhaps longer?[28] Moreover, how does one measure the "end of hostilities," by unconditional surrender, collapse of a regime, the killing of every last known enemy combatant (lawful or unlawful)? It would appear from the circumstances of the present case, similar to the current war on terror, prolonged detention abroad is almost entirely arbitrary.

MEMORIAL FOR THE MIDDLE EASTERN COUNTRY

COMES NOW the Middle Eastern Country and for their Memorial to the Court, asks the following:

QUESTIONS PRESENTED

Is a derogation from the right under Article 9(4) of the ICCPR to judicial determination of the lawfulness of a detention effective if retroactive?

Is such derogation from the stipulated ICCPR right to due process legally effective if notice of a derogation is not directed formally to either the other ICCPR states parties, its treaty body, the Human Rights Committee, or the UN Secretary General?

Is there currently an "armed conflict not of an international character in the territory of one of the High Contracting Parties," in which case Common Article Three of the four Geneva Conventions would still apply? If there is an international armed conflict, would the rights accruing to those detained by a state party under the Third Geneva Convention also be guaranteed?

If so, was the denial of a "judicial determination of the lawfulness of a detention" carried out by the right under Common Article 3 of "a regularly constituted court, affording all the judicial guarantees which are recognized as indispensable by civilized peoples" invalid?

Does the Western Country's hearing procedure measure up to the standard of "a fair and public hearing by an independent and impartial tribunal, in the determination of his rights and obligations," the right to *habeas corpus* practiced since the Magna Carta?

Can domestic legislation prevail over binding treaty law just because the subject of the legislation has been called "terrorism"? Are the prohibitions of incommunicado or secret detentions effective in either an international or non-international armed conflict? If yes, should such secret detention invalidate the right of a state party to continue to detain someone?

STATEMENT OF LAW

From human rights law, the Respondent Western Country has ratified the ICCPR and is legally obligated by its terms.

Article 9(4) of the ICCPR states that "Anyone who is deprived of his liberty by arrest or detention shall be entitled to take proceedings before a court, in order that that court may decide without delay on the lawlessness of his detention and order his release if the detention is not lawful."[29]

Derogation from Article 9(4) of the ICCPR is permitted under Article 4(1) of the ICCPR *only* in cases "of public emergency which threatens the life of the nation"; provided that the measures taken by the derogating party are consistent with international law and are limited to those "required by the exigencies of the situation."[30] Per Article 4(3) of the ICCPR, derogating parties are required to notify other ICCPR states parties through the UN Secretary General of their intention to derogate. With its arbitrary detention of citizens of the Middle Eastern Country, without notifying the Secretary General of its intention to derogate from Article 9(4), the Respondent Western Country has violated all of these legal requirements.

The Respondent Western Country claims that it has the right under international humanitarian law to suspend *habeas corpus* provisions for "alien enemy combatants" detained within its borders as a matter of national security, since lawful combatants can be held as prisoners of war until the armed conflict ends, and unlawful combatants who are dangerous can be held even longer, until they are no longer a threat. The Western Country claims that the 1949 Geneva Conventions are *lex specialis*, which excludes the application of human rights law and its requirement of *habeas corpus*. The Western Country also claims that "unlawful combatants," under the provisions of the Third 1949 Geneva Convention are not eligible for *habeas corpus* and other rights. It claims that under this international humanitarian law, an unlawful combatant is only eligible to be treated humanely. All of these assertions fly in the face of international law, beginning with Article 27 of the Vienna Convention on the Law of Treaties, which is accepted as binding under customary international law, so that the Western Country is still bound by its rules. Article 27 mandates that domestic laws cannot override treaty obligations. Moreover, Article 31 holds that the interpretation of treaty law should be conducted in good faith and begun with the ordinary meaning of the text. With respect to treaties under international humanitarian law, the Western Country has ratified the 1907 Hague Conventions. Its Martens Clause states in case of any ambiguity in treaty law governing armed conflict, the interpretation should be made in favor of the humanitarian objectives of that treaty, namely reducing the severity of treatment. This would be particularly applicable in situations where an ex-combatant is a protected person *hors de combat* and subject to the control of the state party.

Rather than provide detainees from the Middle Eastern Country with access to its national courts, the Government of the Western Country created a Detainee Review Commission (DRC) to review the legality of detention. The review process is inconsistent with international law, including Common Article Three of the four 1949 Geneva Conventions, and Articles 10 and 71-73 of the Fourth Geneva Convention on the rights of Civilians under Occupations. The Respondent Western Country is a party to all four of the Geneva Conventions. Even if the Court were to accept the Western Country's argument that only international humanitarian law is binding, to the exclusion of human rights law or customary international law, the Third Geneva Convention only states that prisoners of war may be held to the end of the conflict, not unlawful combatants. Moreover, the rights under Common Article Three apply to all combatants and civilians, and do not distinguish between lawful and unlawful combatants.

The Respondent's actions were also in violation of international customary law, which now includes the 1948 Universal Declaration of Human Rights (UDHR), general principles recognized by the civilized world, and scholarly opinion, all of which are recognized as sources of law in this Court's statute.

Without a notice of derogation to other ICCPR states parties, the derogation in null and void.

Under Common Article 3, which legally regulates "armed conflict not of an international character in the territory of one of the High Contracting Parties," rights are listed which are non-derogable and inalienable, even for detainees who do not qualify for the protections of prisoners of war under the Third 1949 Geneva Convention. Most legal scholars argue that the rights under Common Article 3 of all four Geneva Conventions also apply to international armed conflicts.

The denial of a "judicial determination of the lawfulness of a detention" carried out by "a regularly constituted court, affording all the judicial guarantees which are recognized as indispensable by civilized peoples" is one of the inalienable rights listed under this Common Article 3.

The Western Country's DRC review hearing procedure does not measure up to the standard of "a fair and public hearing by an independent and impartial tribunal, in the determination of his rights and obligations," as mandated under the UDHR's binding customary international law.

Finally, the domestic legislation of the Western country does not prevail over its ratified treaty law, including its obligations to comply with the four Geneva Conventions and the ICCPR, just because the subject of the domestic legislation concerns "terrorism." Many UN treaty bodies, including the Human Rights Committee of the ICCPR, as well as the UN Human Rights Council's Special Rapporteurs on the Promotion and Protection of Human Rights while Countering Terrorism, have reaffirmed that the right of states to prosecute a war against terrorists does not relieve them of their fundamental obligations under both international human rights and humanitarian law.

STATEMENT OF JURISDICTION

As stated in the Order of the Court, jurisdiction is established pursuant to Article 36(2) of the Statute, according to which "states parties to the present Statute . . . declare that they recognize as compulsory *ipso facto* and without special agreement, in relation to any other state accepting the same obligation, the jurisdiction of the Court in all legal disputes concerning: a. the interpretation of a treaty."[31] In addition, the Western Country accepted the Court's jurisdiction voluntarily.

SUMMARY OF ARGUMENTS

The Respondent admits having deprived detainee of the hearing required by Article 9(4) of the ICCPR and Common Article 3 of the four 1949 Geneva Conventions. It claims to have derogated from that provision and having notified the ICCPR states parties, but did so only retroactively and therefore ineffectively.

Even if the Respondent had effectively derogated, its having deprived the detainees of a hearing required under the ICCPR violated other international laws, especially under Common Article 3 of the four 1949 Geneva Conventions, which this Court "shall apply" under Article 38 of its Statute, which lists its four sources of law, as follows:

> a. International conventions, whether general or particular, establishing rules expressly recognized by the contesting states; b. International custom, as evidence of a general practice accepted as law; c. The general principles of law recognized by civilized nations; d. Subject to the provisions of Article 59, judicial decisions and the teachings of the most highly qualified publicists of the various nations, as subsidiary means for the determination of rules of law.[32]

ARGUMENTS

I. International Conventions, Whether General or Particular, Establishing Rules Expressly Recognized by the Contesting States

The Respondent admits having deprived the detainees of the hearing on the legality of that detention, which is required by the ICCPR. Its attempted justification is a claim to have derogated from that requirement. This claim fails for several reasons.

First, there was no "public emergency which threatens the life of the nation and the existence of which is officially proclaimed."[33] Sabotage in one nation does not threaten the life of all other nations. The Respondent has not proclaimed any such emergency; its purported and invalid, retroactive derogation is too late to apply to these detainees and constitutes a separate act from any proclamation of emergency, had any proclamation been issued.

The Respondent has not justified its purported derogation by proving that it is limited "to the extent strictly required by the exigencies of the situation," as specified by the Human Rights Committee's general comment governing derogations under the ICCPR. Nor has the Respondent shown that "such measures are not inconsistent with their other obligations under international law and do not involve discrimination solely on the ground of race, colour, sex, language, religion or social origin." The Human Rights Committee's General Comment on ICCPR Article 4 on Derogation requires:

> measures taken under article 4 are of an exceptional and temporary nature and may only last as long as the life of the nation concerned is threatened and that, in times of emergency, the protection of human rights becomes all the more important, particularly those rights from which no derogations can be made. The Committee also considers that it is equally important for states parties, in times of public emergency, to inform the other states parties of the nature and extent of the derogations they have made and of the reasons therefore and, further, to fulfill their reporting obligations under article 40 of the Covenant by indicating the nature and extent of each right derogated from together with the relevant documentation.[34]

Moreover, the Respondent's purported derogation was long after the start of the victims' incarceration without the independent review hearing required by the ICCPR and the Third Geneva Convention. If retroactive derogation of ICCPR derogable rights were recognized, all manner of oppressive acts could take place without advance notice to citizens of the same or other countries. If armed conflict rights could be suspended, then indefinite, incommunicado detention would be mistakenly, or even malevolently, perpetrated against foot soldiers without any connection to terrorism because the party arbitrarily detains large groups, suspecting that a terrorist might be among their midst, but not knowing who within a group was a terrorist and who was not.

The Respondent has never notified other ICCPR states parties through the UN Secretary General in a timely manner of its purported derogation. Without such detailed notice in advance of the derogations, the claim of derogation lacks credibility, since there is no public record of the occurrence of the derogation outside of the Respondent's own (very likely secret) records. Without notice, any country could claim to have derogated at any convenient time in the past. Nor has the notice to states parties detailed the reasons for the emergency and the necessity justifying derogation from *habeas corpus* rights.

Additionally, notice must, by being sent world-wide, become public within the derogating country; lest the public there be unaware of the added risk to their liberty from unaccountable, arbitrary detentions without any opportunity to test in a regular court the grounds for their incarceration.

The Vienna Convention on the Law of Treaties, which is declarative of customary international law, establishes in Article 27 that, "A party may not invoke the provisions of its internal law as justification for its failure to perform a treaty."[35] Therefore, the Respondent's legislative apparatus for branding individuals as "terrorists" so as to deprive them of their fundamental rights has no effect on the Respondent's obligations under the ICCPR.

Apart from the ICCPR, further requirement for an ICCPR-type hearing is found in Common Article 3 of the Geneva Conventions, by which both parties are bound. Common Article 3 prohibits "the passing of sentences and the carrying out of executions without previous judgment pronounced by a regularly constituted court, affording all the judicial guarantees which are recognized as indispensable by civilized peoples."[36]

Derogation from these requirements is recognized only by agreement between governments, not by unilateral fiat. Article 11 of the Fourth Geneva Convention provides that:

> No derogation from the preceding provisions shall be made by special agreements between Powers one of which is restricted, even temporarily, in its freedom to negotiate with the other Power or its allies by reason of military events, more particularly where the whole, or a substantial part, of the territory of the said Power is occupied.[37]

Articles 71-73 provide detailed due process requirements; notably Article 72 states:

> Accused persons shall have the right to present evidence necessary to their defence and may, in particular, call witnesses. They shall have the right to be assisted by a qualified advocate or counsel of their own choice, who shall be able to visit them freely and shall enjoy the necessary facilities for preparing the defence.[38]

Due process, in other words, requires that persons detained be taken without delay before an impartial and independent judge in a regular court where the detaining authority has the burden of proving a valid basis for their detention. It goes without saying that the truncated procedure provided by the Western Country denies due process in a number of crucial ways.

II. International Custom as Evidence of a General Practice Accepted as Law

The UDHR in the years since its adoption and proclamation by the United Nations General Assembly in 1948 "as a common standard of achievement for all peoples and all nations," has been recognized as a firmly embedded part of customary international law.

Article 9 of the UDHR provides that: "No one shall be subjected to arbitrary arrest, detention or exile."[39] Article 10 provides that: "Everyone is entitled in full equality to a fair and public hearing by an independent and impartial tribunal, in the determination of his rights and obligations and of any criminal charge against him."[40]

III. General Principles of Law Recognized by Civilized Nations

By 1776, when decolonization of the British Empire began, the rights provided by the writ of *habeas corpus*, which closely resemble those provided by the ICCPR, were firmly embedded in the English common law. Almost a hundred years earlier, in 1679, Parliament had adopted the *Habeas Corpus Act*, which severely penalized any judge who refused without good cause to issue the writ as well as any person who failed to comply with it. This climaxed a century of struggle in Britain over arbitrary arrest and detention.

During the next two centuries following dozens of British colonies followed America's lead and emerged into independence, equipped with the mother country's common law system including the basic protection of individual liberty found in the writ of *habeas corpus*. Thus *habeas corpus* is, for those countries, a key part of the "general principles of law recognized by civilized nations" as the ICJ Statute puts it. For the other civilized nations that did not inherit the British common law, there is the similar remedy of *amparo*.

Accordingly, the type of hearing provided by the ICCPR is a fundamental requirement of most of the world's legal systems, entirely apart from the ICCPR itself, and applies with or without an ICCPR derogation.

IV. Judicial Decisions and the Teachings of the Most Highly Qualified Publicists of the Various Nations, as Subsidiary Means for the Determination of Rules of Law

In view of the overwhelming authority referred to above, there is little need to recall the intense litigation that swirled around President Abraham Lincoln as a result of his suspension of *habeas corpus* during the American Civil War. The drafters of the Constitution of 1789 had included Article 1, Section 9, the provision that, "The privilege of the writ of *habeas corpus* shall not be suspended, unless when in cases of rebellion or invasion the public safety may require it." The language "rebellion or invasion" may be contrasted with the ICCPR wording: "public emergency which threatens the life of the nation." The ICCPR formulation places the bar *higher* than the U.S. Constitution for governments wishing to suspend *habeas*-type hearings, since neither rebellion nor invasion necessarily threatens the life of a nation.

The sanctity of the right to a prompt hearing by a regular court with the aid of one's own counsel to contest the validity of one's incarceration was heroically proclaimed by Winston Churchill with these words in the dark days of 1943: "The power of the Executive to cast a man into prison without formulating any charge known to the law, and particularly to deny him the judgment of his peers, is in the highest degree odious and is the foundation of all totalitarian government whether Nazi or Communist."[41]

SUMMARY AND PRAYER FOR RELIEF

For all the compelling reasons set forth above, Applicant prays that this Court should declare and decree that the Respondent's denial to a citizen of Applicant country of the type of review described in the ICCPR for testing the validity of her incarceration is null and void, and that such citizen and any others similarly situated must be forthwith released with full and fair compensation for all violations of their fundamental rights.

RESPONDENT'S COUNTER-MEMORIAL

COMES NOW the Respondent Western Country for their Counter-Memorial to the Court and asks the following:

QUESTIONS PRESENTED

Whether the Middle Eastern Country is barred from seeking relief in this Court under the equitable doctrine of unclean hands where it has consistently discriminated against women, and ethnic and religious minorities in violation of the Universal Declaration of Human Rights or UDHR, and has tolerated, within its borders, the harboring and training of terrorists, such as those who attacked the Western Country, by failing to take adequate measures to prevent it.

Whether the ICCPR and Geneva Convention Common Article 3 apply in this case where the Respondent is in a state of public emergency which threatens the life of the nation, the existence of which was officially proclaimed and where the Respondent was attacked by foreign nationals having no fixed or recognizable signs, not carrying arms openly, and not conducting their operations in accordance with the laws and customs of war.

Whether the Respondent should be sanctioned by this Court for procedural defects in derogation, where the entire world was on notice that the Western Country had derogated from the procedures of Article 9(4) of the ICCPR within days after the Respondent was attacked, but the Respondent failed to give formal notice of such derogation in a timely fashion and then failed to perfect that notice by effecting service through the intermediary of the Secretary General of the United Nations and where no State Party to the ICCPR was prejudiced by these technical failures, for which the Respondent has apologized.

Whether the Petition is ripe for adjudication where issues concerning the validity of the Respondent's detention and hearing process are currently being adjudicated in the Respondent's domestic courts, and the Respondent has not taken a final position on those issues, and where detainees have not exhausted their remedies under the Respondent's domestic law.

Whether the hearing procedures the Respondent has implemented are consistent with ICCPR Article 9 and basic principles of international law under the facts and circumstances of this case.

PROCEDURAL HISTORY

On January 4, 2008, the Court served the Respondent by e-mail with an undated Order which stated that Applicant had filed a Petition claiming that the Respondent had failed to fulfill its duties under Common Article 3 of the 1949 Geneva Conventions and Article 9(4) and (5) of the ICCPR. The Order incorrectly stated that the Respondent had filed its Memorial, but correctly stated that the Respondent admitted that it has detained without charge, trial, or hearing under *habeas corpus*, certain persons identified as "terrorists" under its legislation claiming that such detention is not covered by said Convention but by the Respondent's domestic legislation. As stated below, the Respondent has implemented a hearing procedure, but with fewer rights for detainees than under traditional *habeas corpus* proceedings.

The Order said that the Court will hear arguments on March 27, 2008. The Order did *not* say that the Court would take *evidence* on March 27, 2008.[42]

On February 13, 2008, the Respondent gave notice to this Court and to Applicant that the Respondent had derogated pursuant to ICCPR Article 4. It has now been brought to the Respondent's attention that the Respondent failed to give notice through the intermediary of the Secretary General of the United Nations as required by ICCPR Article 4(3). The Respondent hereby apologizes for this oversight.

On February 18, 2008, the Respondent requested by e-mail that the parties stipulate to certain facts and on February 19, 2008, the Court requested that Applicant respond to the proposed stipulation. Applicant declined to do so.

On February 26, 2008 the Respondent sent a second proposal to the Court and to Applicant that the parties stipulate to certain facts prior to the filing of memorials and prior to the hearing in this matter and stated that the Respondent was willing to stipulate to these facts as long as the Court and the parties agreed to so stipulate by the morning of March 3, 2008.

On February 28, 2008, Applicant rejected the Respondent's proposed stipulation, but admitted a limited set of facts relating to derogation (set forth above) and relating to the hearing procedure the Respondent has established for detainees. Rather, than agreeing to a more fulsome stipulation or compromise, Applicant, relying on the Rules of Court Article 50(1) and 57 took the position that evidence could be submitted by means of documentary evidence and, contrary to the undated Order, which provides that the hearing would consist of argument, that evidence could be introduced by testimony at the hearing.

The Court has not ruled on the Respondent's proposed stipulation. Therefore, no compromise has been entered in this case, beyond an informal agreement to the facts relating to derogation and the Respondent's hearing process.

On February 27, 2008, the parties agreed to a schedule whereby Applicant would file its Memorial on March 7, 2008, the Respondent would file its Memorial on March 14, 2008, and Applicant would file its Reply Memorial on March 21. Applicant filed its Memorial on March 7, 2008.

STATEMENT OF LAW

The Respondent submits that the ICCPR does not apply in this case as the ICCPR is a treaty between states, The terrorists who attacked the Western Country are members of a rouge organization. They are neither a State nor representatives of a State. If this Court should find that the ICCPR does apply, derogation from Article 9 is permitted under the facts of this case. The Respondent has derogated and neither Petitioner nor anyone else has been prejudiced by the Respondent's delay and failure to follow the technical notice requirements in connection with its derogation.

The Applicant's argument relies heavily on Common Article 3 of the 1949 Geneva Convention. However, Common Article 3 does not apply to unlawful combatants—those who do not follow the rules of war—such as the detainees being held in this case.

The Petition is not ripe for adjudication. The Respondent's Supreme Judicial Court is currently addressing the issue of whether or not the procedures of the Detainee Review Commission (DRC) and the rights thereunder are subject to further judicial review and are sufficient under the domestic law of the Respondent. A decision has not yet been reached on this matter.

The Respondent has implemented alternative hearing procedures consistent with Articles 9 and 10 of the ICCPR and basic principles of international law.

STATEMENT OF FACTS[43]

I. Facts Concerning Western Country

On November 9, 2004, the Islamic Jihad terrorist network launched a vicious, co-coordinated attack on the Respondent Western Country, attacking a large commercial center in New Providence and the headquarters of the nation's Ministry of Defense. Islamic Jihad attempted but failed to strike another target in Capital City. These attacks became known as the 11/9 attacks and "11/9" has become synonymous with terrorism throughout the world. These attacks were carried out by Islamic Jihad agents hijacking commercial aircraft and flying them or attempting to fly them into buildings. Approximately 5,000 people were killed and thousands were injured. The destruction of billions of dollars of property and trillions in economic costs severely damaged the economy of the Western Country. It was the deadliest foreign attack on the Western Country's soil in one day in the nation's history.

In response, the President of the Western Country, acting as Commander in Chief, took action to defend the country and to prevent additional attacks. In a resolution passed on November 11, 2004, the National Assembly supported the President's use of "all necessary and appropriate force against those nations, organizations, or persons he determines planned or authorized, or aided in the terrorist [November 9] attacks . . . or harbored such organizations or persons." The National Assembly also emphasized that the forces responsible for the 11/9 attacks "continue to pose an unusual and extraordinary threat to the national security" and that "the President has authority under the laws of the Western

Country to take action to deter and prevent acts of international terrorism against the Western Country."

Subsequently, the Western Country attacked Tajmenistan and Qari, two countries that harbored, supported, or failed to adequately restrict Islamic Jihad and Nabilat forces, a supporter of Islamic Jihad's terrorist training, conspiracies, and acts. The Western Country was informed that the leader of Islamic Jihad, who planned the 11/9 attacks, was Amaso nib Nedal, an infamous international terrorist hiding in Tajmenistan under the protection of the Nabilat. The invading Western Country forces have been unable to kill nib Nedal, who is presently at large.

Subsequent to the 11/9 attacks, the Western Country thwarted a number of other attempted attacks. Three of these received wide publicity: an attempt by a terrorist to hijack an airplane using a bomb hidden in his baseball cap, an attempt by terrorists to hijack airplanes using explosives disguised as bottles of Snapple Iced Tea, and an attempt by terrorists to smuggle explosives across the border from the country of Adanac into the Western Country. Other terrorist attempts have been made which the Respondent has discovered through investigation and has prevented. The Respondent is unwilling to disclose information concerning these attempts because the disclosure of such information itself would jeopardize the security of the Western Country and jeopardize ongoing investigations.

Subsequent to the 11/9 attacks, a commuter train was bombed in the capital of the Western Country's closest European ally, injuring and killing a number of individuals. It was determined that this attack was orchestrated by individuals from several countries in the Middle East residing in European countries and affiliated with Islamic Jihad.

Despite some early success in the Western Country's military operations, it was reported just this week that Islamic Jihad has gained strength in the last two years in its sanctuary area on the Tajmenistan/Qari border.

Shortly after the 11/9 attacks, the Western Country, by public order of its President, arrested and detained certain individuals determined by the Western Country's investigation to be terrorists affiliated with Islamic Jihad, the Nabilat, or other terrorist organizations. The detainees were transported to a territory possession of the Western Country and detained pending further proceedings. Some of these individuals were apprehended in Tajmenistan and Sadamistan, some were apprehended in other countries supporting terrorist cells, and others were arrested as they attempted to travel to the Western Country from various ports of entry. A number of these individuals include citizens of Applicant Middle Eastern Country. The detention of these terrorist suspects was based on an investigation into their activities, and in no case was an individual's detention based solely on race, color, sex, language, religion, or national origin. Detention was strictly limited as required by the exigencies of the threats to the Respondent. Where a suspect was apprehended and investigation determined that he posed no threat of terrorism, he was released.

The President of the Western Country stated publicly that the Western Country's writ of *habeas corpus* had been suspended under its domestic law, and the Western Country's national assembly enacted legislation legalizing and supporting these actions.

The suspension of the writ of *habeas corpus*, which coincided with the detention of the earliest of the detainees, was widely publicized throughout the world at the time.

On February 1, 2005, in response to a ruling by the Respondent's Supreme Judicial Court, the Respondent's national assembly passed legislation creating a Detainee Review Commission and creating review procedures as a substitute for *habeas corpus*.

The DRC consists of three military judges, one of whom must be an attorney, that will provide review of the status of detainees, with hearsay evidence permitted and no right by detainees or their counsel to conduct cross examination or see the evidence against them. The DRC may release detainees or it may order continued detention. The detainees have limited access to court-appointed or voluntary attorneys. No hearings have been held yet under this procedure.

All of the above events and facts were widely publicized throughout the world. They are common knowledge.

Currently pending before the Respondent's Supreme Judicial Court are various issues relating to whether or not detainees are entitled to judicial review in the Respondent's federal courts of the decisions of the DRC and whether or not procedures followed by the DRC failed to give detainees the rights to which they are entitled under the Respondent's Constitution.

As noted above in the Procedural History on February 13, 2008, the Respondent, in the alternative to claiming that *habeas corpus* is governed by domestic legislation, and without waiving its right in that regard, stated that it had derogated from its alleged duty under the ICCPR to provide *habeas corpus*-type hearings and so notified Applicant. Of course Applicant had long been aware of the facts of this derogation, regardless of whether it had been technically termed "derogation" or whether precise technical requirements of derogation under the ICCPR had been followed.

II. Facts Concerning Middle Eastern Country

In the Middle Eastern Country, the government has prosecuted and imprisoned politicians and writers for expressing their nonviolent opinions. Women in the Middle Eastern Country are routinely denied the same educational benefits and other privileges as men. The Middle Eastern Country's government failed to take action to prevent the persecution of religious minorities by the religious majority, and such persecution is widespread. The Middle Eastern Country has also held so-called elections in which the incumbents encouraged rampant voter fraud. Women and religious minorities were intimidated and prevented from voting. Finally, and perhaps most importantly to the analysis here, the government of the Middle Eastern Country has failed to take steps to root out and prosecute terrorist cells within the Middle Eastern Country. These terrorists have stated goals of attacking the Western Country and its allies. Despite a stated policy of intolerance to such groups, the Middle Eastern Country's efforts against these groups have been woefully inadequate, amounting to little more than lip service.

SUMMARY OF ARGUMENT

The Respondent contends that the Petition should be dismissed or that Judgment should be entered in its favor for the following reasons. First, Applicant's claim is barred because Applicant comes into Court with unclean hands. It is a longstanding principle of law that he who seeks equity must do equity and a party with unclean hands may not seek relief in a court of equity. The Respondent has a long standing history of failing to take adequate action to prevent the harboring of terrorists and a history of denying women, religious minorities, and ethnic minorities fundamental human rights. Although these acts do not rise to the level of state sponsored terrorism, they nevertheless bar Applicant from seeking relief in this Court.

Second, the ICCPR does not apply in this case. The ICCPR is a treaty between States, and the terrorists who are members of a rouge organization are not a State or representatives of a State. Geneva Convention Common Article 3 does not apply to unlawful combatants, such as the detainees being held in this case. That is, the protections of Article 3 do not apply to those combatants who engage in acts of terror against citizens of a State who are not combatants and are not engaged in an armed conflict. Rather, the Geneva Conventions apply to States Parties who have agreed among themselves that the treaties require combatants to be legal to have their rights protected.

Third, in the alternative to the second argument, if this Court should find that the ICCPR does apply, derogation from Article 9 is allowed under the facts of this case. The Respondent has derogated and neither Petitioner nor anyone else has been prejudiced by the Respondent's delay and failure to follow the technical notice requirements in connection with its derogation.

Fourth, in the alternative to the second and third arguments, the Petition is not ripe for adjudication. The Respondent's Supreme Judicial Court currently has under consideration, with a decision pending, the issue of whether the procedures of the DRC and the rights thereunder are subject to further judicial review and are sufficient under the domestic law of the Respondent. Detainees have not exhausted the hearing rights they have been granted or may be granted. It is entirely possible that detainees will have additional rights after the Supreme Judicial Court rules, and indeed, they may be judged to have all the rights Applicant seeks to have declared on their behalf in this action. In any event, this action is not ripe, and there is no case in controversy, until there has been a final determination by the government of the Respondent as to what rights detainees have.

Fifth, in the alternative to the second and third arguments, the Respondent has implemented alternative hearing procedures consistent with Articles 9 and 10 of the ICCPR and basic principles of international law.

ARGUMENTS

I. Applicant is Barred from Seeking Relief under the Equitable Doctrine of Unclean Hands

It has been long established in the English Common Law and in the Law of the United States that a party is barred from seeking equitable relief if it comes into court with "unclean hands." Applicant here comes into this Court with unclean hands. Applicant has tolerated wide-spread discrimination against women and minorities, has suppressed freedom of expression, and has imprisoned its citizens for political reasons. In doing so, Applicant has acted contrary to Articles 1, 2, 7, 9, 10, 18, 19, 21, and 26 of the UDHR.

It is particularly disturbing that Applicant has imprisoned non-violent political dissenters, yet complains because the Respondent has detained those who pose a threat of violence to its citizens and to its national security.

Perhaps more to the point, Applicant has failed to take action to prevent terrorists such as those who attacked the Respondent from training, arming, and obtaining material support within its borders. The Respondent does not allege that Applicant has supported such terrorists, but the evidence shows that Applicant has passively tolerated them. In fact, citizens of Applicant are among those who have been detained by the Respondent and have been determined upon reliable information to be terrorists or terrorist supporters.

Under these circumstances, Applicant is barred by the unclean hands doctrine from seeking equitable relief, that is relief in the nature of a declaratory judgment or an injunction, in this Court.

Although the Respondent has not found a case in which this Court has invoked the unclean hands doctrine to bar a party from seeking relief, this Court has clearly recognized the existence and applicability of that doctrine. In so doing, it has only failed to apply the doctrine to bar relief because the facts of the case in which the doctrine was raised, unlike the facts of this case, do not justify it.

For example, in *La Grand*, Germany complained that the United States failed to allow its citizens consular assistance in connection with their case in which the death penalty was sought. The United States contended that Germany's submissions were inadmissible on the ground that Germany sought to have a standard applied to the United States that is different from its own practice. In other words, the United States contended that if Germany objects to the practice of the United States, Germany has unclean hands in this regard.

The Court recognized the validity of this principle but declined to decide the issue because the cases in which Germany failed to allow consular assistance were not death penalty cases but "entailed relatively light criminal penalties and are not evidence as to German practice where an arrested person, who has not been informed without delay of his or her rights, is facing a severe penalty as in the present case."[44]

In sharp contrast, in this case, the Middle Eastern Country has imprisoned without hearing individuals under circumstances that would have to be considered benign compared to the circumstances of the individuals that the Respondent has detained.

II. The ICCPR and the Geneva Convention do not Apply in This Case[45]

A. THE ICCPR AND THE GENEVA CONVENTION ARE INAPPLICABLE TO DETAINEES BECAUSE THEY ARE NOT STATES OR REPRESENTATIVES OF STATES.

Generally, treaties cover legal relationships between States. "[T]reaty means an international agreement concluded between States in written form and governed by international law."[46] The U.S. Supreme Court recognized this principle in *Banco Nacional de Cuba v. Sabbatino*, stating, "The traditional view of international law is that it establishes substantive principles for determining whether one country has wronged another."[47] Consistent with this principle, the ICCPR and the Geneva Conventions govern legal relationships between states, not between a state and a terrorist organization or its members.

Common Article 2 states that the Geneva Conventions are to be implemented in times of "war or any other armed conflict which may arise between two or more of the High Contracting Parties."[48] Thus, terrorist organizations such as Islamic Jihad and the Nabilat are not covered by Common Article 2 because they are not "High Contracting Parties," but non-governmental organizations.

B. ARTICLE 3 OF THE GENEVA CONVENTION IS INAPPLICABLE BECAUSE THE CONFLICT WITH THE TERRORISTS IS NOT AN "ARMED CONFLICT NOT OF AN INTERNATIONAL CHARACTER."

Common Article 3 is inapplicable because it is limited to times of civil war. As a complement to Common Article 2, Common Article 3 covers, "armed conflict not of an international character occurring in the territory of one of the High Contracting Parties."[49] A scholar writing contemporaneously with the preparation of the Conventions said, "a conflict not of an international character occurring in the territory of one of the High Contracting Parties . . . must normally mean a civil war."[50]

The Islamic Jihad attacks on the Respondent do not amount to a civil war. Although the attacks occurred on the Western Country soil, contrary to the requirement of Common Article 3, the conflict is actually of an international character because it was instigated by non-national terrorists. The Islamic Jihad leader, Amaso nib Nedal, is a foreign national. Further, nib Nedal and other Islamic Jihad leadership took refuge in countries including Tajmenistan, Nemey, Kapistan and the Middle Eastern Country, and were planning future terrorist attacks in the Western Country from those countries.

Applicant apparently contends, but does not argue in its Memorial, that Article 3 applies because the Western Country is not in an "armed conflict not of an international character."

Under the facts noted above and the applicable authority, it is clear that the conflict within the Western Country *is* of an international character rendering Article 3 inapplicable.[51]

At the 1949 Geneva Conference, the International Committee of the Red Cross (ICRC) presented the following text (known as the "Stockholm Draft") to the delegates for their consideration: "*In all cases of armed conflict which are not of an international character*, especially cases of civil war, colonial conflicts, or wars of religion, which may occur in the territory of one or more of the High Contracting Parties [emphasis added]."[52]

The proposed text proved to be very controversial:

> From the very outset, divergences of views became apparent. A considerable number of delegations were opposed, if not to any and every provision *in regard to civil war*, at any rate to the unqualified application of the Convention to such conflicts . . . It was said that [the proposal] would cover all forms of insurrections, rebellion, and the break-up of States, and even plain brigandage . . . To compel the Government of a State *in the throes of internal conflict* to apply to such a conflict the whole of the provisions of a Convention expressly concluded to cover the case of war would mean giving its enemies, who might be no more than a handful of rebels or common brigands, the status of belligerents, and possibly even a certain degree of legal recognition [emphasis added].[53]

At the Plenary Meeting on April 26, 1949, the articles common to all four conventions (which included Article 3) were referred to the committee known as the "Joint Committee."[54] At the first meeting of the Joint Committee to consider extending legal protections to victims of non-international conflicts, the Stockholm Draft's call for applying the Conventions' provisions to "*all* cases of armed conflict which are not of an international character" elicited a number of concerns.[55] Ultimately, because the language was so controversial, a separate, Special Committee was formed to deal specifically with Article 3.

Because of delegates' concerns about the breadth of the Stockholm proposal, the *Special Committee decided to abandon the Stockholm language*—to wit, that the Convention would apply "in *all cases* of armed conflict which are not of an international character [emphasis added],"[56]—and to define more clearly to which cases of armed conflict not of an international character the Conventions should apply.

Throughout their discussions, the concerns of the various delegations centered solely on civil wars and other significant *internal* conflicts, such as insurgencies and rebellions.[57] No delegation anticipated any type of conflict like the ongoing threat of international terrorism. As a result, all discussions are centered on civil wars and similar internal conflicts. It stretches credulity to the breaking point to conclude that delegates knowingly agreed that Article 3 was to apply to situations which they *neither anticipated nor discussed.* The language in the Joint Committee report to the Plenary Committee confirms this view.

Following many weeks of meetings and discussion, the Joint Committee delivered its report to the Plenary Committee for consideration by all delegations to the Conference. The portion of its report concerning Common Article 3 read, in pertinent part, as follows:

> In the Stockholm Draft, the fourth paragraph of Article 2 [what ultimately became Common Article 3] stipulated that, in *all* cases of armed conflict not of an international character, each of the Parties to the conflict should be bound to implement the provisions of the Conventions.
>
> At the present Conference, the question immediately arose of deciding what as to be understood by 'armed conflict not of an international character which may occur in the territory of one of the High Contracting Parties.' *It was clear that this referred to civil war,* and not to a mere riot or disturbances caused by bandits. States could not be obliged as soon as *rebellion arose within their frontiers,* to consider the rebels as regular belligerents to whose benefit the Conventions had to be applied. But *at what point should the suppression of the rising be regarded as a civil war?* [emphasis added].[58]

Nowhere in the Final Record is there any indication that any *other* types of conflict were considered other than serious *domestic* conflicts. Moreover, the delegates had consciously and intentionally removed the term "all" from the phrase proposed at Stockholm, "In *all* cases of armed conflict which are not of an international character."[59] They adopted the following phrasing instead: "In the case of an armed conflict not of an international character occurring in the territory of one of the High Contracting Parties, each Party to the conflict shall be bound to apply, as a minimum, the following provisions"[60]

Moreover, throughout the process, the majority of delegates to the 1949 Conference sought to narrow the reach of Article 3, not expand it.[61]

Civil wars, insurrections, rebellions, and the like are serious armed conflicts occurring within one country. This concept fully comports with Article 3's current language: "in the case of armed conflict not of an international character *occurring in the territory of one of the High Contracting Parties* [emphasis added]"[62] Hence, it is fully reasonable that the language adopted by the High Contracting Parties in Geneva was meant to limit Article 3's reach to civil wars and the like and to exclude any type of conflict similar to today's conflict with Islamic Jihad, the Nabilat, and other global terrorist groups. To conclude that Article 3 was meant to apply to such broader conflicts contradicts both the language and the negotiating history of Article 3 and is clearly erroneous.

C. THE GENEVA CONVENTION IS INAPPLICABLE BECAUSE THE TERRORISTS DO NOT MEET THE ELIGIBILITY REQUIREMENTS OF ARTICLE 4(A)(2)

To be eligible for treatment as a prisoner of war under the Third Geneva Convention, a captive must meet the eligibility requirements of Article 4(A)(2). Members of irregular forces entitled to this status must (i) be commanded by a person responsible for his subordinates, (ii) have a fixed distinctive sign recognizable at a distance, (iii) carry arms openly, and (iv) conduct their operations in accordance with the laws and customs of war.[63] Islamic Jihad and Nabilat members and other terrorists who aided in the attack of the Western Country or were planning such attacks are rogue individuals who fail to meet this standard, and are thus not eligible to receive the benefits of POW status.

These terrorists who attacked the Western Country did not carry arms openly. These attacks were done by stealth, with the obvious intent of preventing the Western Country from defending itself. Furthermore, those terrorist attacks were committed by use of commercial aircraft which should not be considered "arms." Finally, by committing terrorist attacks and killing civilians, the terrorists did not comply with the laws and customs of war.

D. APPLICANTS ARGUMENTS ARE WITHOUT MERIT

In the alternative to arguing that the ICCPR and the Geneva Conventions apply in this case, Applicant relies on the English Law on *habeas corpus* in an effort to argue that the Respondent has violated "general principles of law recognized by civilized nations." This argument is misplaced.

Of course the term *habeas corpus* is found nowhere in the ICCPR or the Geneva Conventions. Rather, it is a creation of English law. Under English law, the common-law writ of *habeas corpus* did not extend to aliens detained as prisoners of war or as international terrorists.[64]

Under English law, "one generally understands by a prisoner of war a person captured during the warlike operations by the naval or military forces of the Crown."[65] The detainees are not "prisoners of war" within the meaning of the Geneva Convention because, as noted above, Islamic Jihad is not a party to the Convention, and neither Islamic Jihad nor the Nabilat satisfies the requirements of Article 4(a)(2) of the Convention, such as having a fixed distinctive sign and "conducting their operations in accordance with the laws and customs of war."[66] Nevertheless, as confirmed enemy combatants they fall within the common-law understanding of "prisoners of war" as to whom *habeas* was traditionally unavailable. Indeed, given the greater protections available to prisoners of war, the historic unavailability of *habeas* to vindicate those protections would apply *a fortiori* to enemy spies and unlawful combatants who did not qualify as prisoners of war.

Under common law, prisoners of war did not have to be captured on the battlefield; "real danger to the realm may . . . exist . . . at distances far from where the actual clash of arms is taking place."[67] Nor did it matter where the prisoner was held; even those detained in England had no right to *habeas*. The "Rights of Prisoners taken in War" were determined by the "Judicial Power" of military officers, not by the civilian courts.[68]

Thus, in the *Case of Three Spanish Sailors*,[69] the court held that *habeas corpus* did not apply for sailors "taken as prisoners of war on board of a Spanish privateer" and subsequently transported to England.[70] The Court concluded, "[A]lien enemies and prisoners of war . . . [are] not entitled to any of the privileges of Englishmen; much less to be set at liberty on a *habeas corpus*."[71]

Similarly, in *Rex v. Schiever*,[72] the court denied the writ to the "subject of a neutral power, taken on board of an enemy's ship" and transported to Liverpool, even though the Swedish petitioner claimed to have been detained against his will on the French vessel and to have had no hostility to England. The mere fact that he had been on board the French ship was enough for the court to conclude that the petitioner was, "upon his own showing, clearly a prisoner of war, and lawfully detained as such."[73]

Prisoners of war lacked an entitlement to *habeas* because "the Crown in making a man a prisoner of war is acting under the royal prerogative (under which it wages war) and . . . its act, like certain other acts as a belligerent, is not examinable by the Courts."[74] Accordingly, when presented with a petition from a prisoner of war, "a complete answer to the writ will be that the applicant is both in fact and in law a prisoner of war detained by authority of the Crown."[75] Thus, in *Schiever*, the court looked no further than the fact that the petitioner had been found aboard an enemy ship. His status as a subject of a neutral power, and his protestations that he had been forced to serve against his will, did not alter his status as a prisoner of war.[76]

Applicant also relies on the Universal Declaration of Human Rights, which it has consistently violated itself, for support, ignoring the complete disregard and utter contempt for these human rights exhibited by the brutal killing of innocent civilians including women and children by those aided by the detainees. This argument merits no further response.

Finally, Applicant resorts to reliance on "teachings of the most highly qualified publicists." This argument establishes nothing, because for every "highly qualified publicist" Applicant cites, the Respondent can cite a "highly qualified publicist" who holds a contrary position.

In sum, Applicant has failed to advance a single credible argument to counter the unassailable fact that the ICCPR and the Geneva Conventions simply do not apply to international terrorists and those who aid them.

III. The Respondent has Derogated from any Duty it Might Have to Provide Habeas Corpus Procedures Under the ICCRP and to the Extent that Such Derogation May Not Have Been Timely or May Not Have Followed the Technical Notice Requirements Specified in ICCPR, Neither Applicant nor any Party State has Been Prejudiced Thereby

A. DEROGATION OF *HABEAS CORPUS* IS ALLOWED UNDER THE ICCPR UNDER THE CIRCUMSTANCES OF THIS CASE

Article 4 of the ICCPR provides as follows:

> In time of public emergency which threatens the life of the nation and the existence of which is officially proclaimed, the States Parties to the present Covenant may take measures derogating from their obligations under the present Covenant to the extent strictly required by the exigencies of the situation, provided that such measure are not inconsistent with their other obligations under international law and do not involve discrimination solely on the ground of race, color, sex, language, religion or social origin.[77]

Moreover, standards of international law have recognized that when the fight against terrorism takes place in a situation of war or public emergency which threatens the "life of a nation," a State may adopt measures temporarily derogating from certain obligations under international protection of human rights to the extent strictly required by the exigencies of the situation.[78]

Notably, in Article 4(2), the ICCPR states that no derogation from Articles 6, 7, 8 (paras. 1 and 2), 11, 15, 16, and 18 may be made under this provision. Therefore, by express exclusion from these exceptions, derogation may be made with regard to Article 9 of the ICCPR, the article which Applicant alleges the Respondent violated. Clearly, therefore, any obligation the Respondent had under Article 9 of the ICCPR is derogable. The standards for Article 4(1) are met in this case. The terrorists' attacks on the Respondent and the continuing threat of terrorist attacks clearly constitutes an emergency which threatens the life of the nation, as set forth in the Statement of Facts above. The President, and National Assembly of the Respondent have officially proclaimed the existence of this emergency.

It is in the realm of power for each Contracting State, with its responsibility for the life of its nation, to determine whether or not that life is threatened by such a "public emergency" and, if so, how far it is necessary to go in attempting to overcome the emergency.[79] Because of their direct and continuous contact with the pressing needs of the moment, national authorities such as the Western Country's President are better positioned than an international judge to decide both the presence of such an emergency and the nature and scope of derogations necessary to avert it.[80] Accordingly, in this matter a wide margin of deference should be granted to national authorities.[81]

This Court has recognized this principle in *Legal Consequences of the Construction of a Wall in the Occupied Palestinian Territory*,[82] In that case Israel proclaimed that it had taken "measures to the extent strictly required by the exigencies of the situation,"[83] and this Court made no further inquiry.

Applicant also argues that the Vienna Convention on the Law of Treaties establishes that a party may not invoke provisions of its internal laws as justification for its failure to perform a treaty. Applicant goes on to say that the Respondent's legislative apparatus for "branding" individual's terrorists so as to deprive them of their fundamental rights has no effect on the Respondent's obligations under the ICCPR.

Aside from the improper implication Applicant makes by using the pejorative term "branding" where the determination that these individuals posed a threat of violence to the Western Country was made upon a good faith investigation, this argument misses the point. The point for this Court is not whether Respondent has properly derogated under its legislative enactments. The point here is whether or not the Respondent has derogated under the terms of Article 4 of the ICCPR. The Respondent's Supreme Judicial Court is considering whether the Respondent's President properly suspended the right of *habeas corpus* under the Respondent's constitution, and that issue is not before this Court.

Applicant's final substantive argument is that derogation is not allowed under the Geneva Convention. The Respondent has derogated under the ICCPR, not the Geneva Convention. The Geneva Convention is clearly inapplicable to this case. Applicant's argument based on Article 10 of the Fourth Geneva Convention is misplaced. Terrorists, including Islamic Jihad and the Nabilat, are not State Parties or "Powers" signatory.

B. NEITHER APPLICANT NOR ANY OTHER PARTY STATE HAS BEEN PREJUDICED OR HARMED BY RESPONDENT'S FAILURE TO FOLLOW THE TIMING AND NOTICE PROVISIONS FOR DEROGATION UNDER ICCPR ARTICLE 4(3) AND FOR THE COURT TO DISALLOW DEROGATION FOR THOSE PROCEDURAL FAILURES WOULD BE TO ELEVATE FORM OVER SUBSTANCE

Despite the Respondent's failure to state that it had derogated under ICCPR Article 4, to the extent that the ICCPR may be applicable, at the time it began detaining terrorist suspects, and despite the fact that the Respondent failed to notify the party states through the Secretary General of the United Nations, it should not be sanctioned for these procedural failures. In fact, complying with the procedures would have served no purpose because the entire world knew of the action that the Respondent had taken. This derogation under the ICCPR is substantively identical to the Respondent's suspension of the writ of *habeas corpus* under its domestic law, which has been widely publicized from the time that it occurred.

Applicant does not, and cannot, claim any prejudice due to these procedural failures. Applicant does not claim that it would have filed its Application any earlier had the Respondent given notice of derogation. In fact, Applicant filed its application before the Respondent officially stated that it had derogated.

Applicant advances three arguments concerning the Respondent's belated derogation. First, the Respondent points out that derogation was long after the event of incarceration, and if retroactive derogation were tolerated, all manner of oppressive acts could take place without advance notice to citizens of the same or other countries. Citizens of the same or other countries had notice, they simply did not have notice through the technical mechanism that Applicant would prefer.

Second, Applicant claims that because the Respondent did not notify other countries of its purported derogation, the claim of derogation now lacks credibility. This argument is a *non sequitur*. Rather, Applicant's claim that other countries were "without . . . notice" itself lacks credibility.

Finally, Applicant argues that notice must be sent worldwide and become public within the derogating country lest the public be unaware of the added risk to their liberty. In fact, the public was not unaware of the added risk. More importantly, the public of the Western Country supported the actions undertaken on its behalf to reduce the risk to their life and safety from future terrorist attacks by the President and National Assembly to apprehend and detain suspected terrorists.

There is a well-established principle of law that where there is no harm, there need be no remedy. No harm has occurred to Applicant or any member state by the Respondent's failure to follow the technical timing and notice requirements of derogation. Therefore, no remedy or sanction should be imposed.

The Respondent has apologized for its failure to follow these technical requirements and that apology is more than sufficient to end this issue.

IV. The Petition is not Ripe for Adjudication Because the Issues in the Petition are Currently Being Adjudicated in the Respondent's Domestic Courts, and the Respondent has not Taken a Final Position on the Issues in this Case

Assuming arguendo contrary to the arguments above, that the ICCPR and Geneva Convention hearing provisions are applicable and that the Respondent has not derogated from them, the question arises as to whether the alternative hearing provisions under the DRC process are sufficient to comport the spirit of the ICCPR and the Geneva Convention under the facts and circumstances of this case. This Court, however, should dismiss the Application without addressing this issue. That issue is not ripe for adjudication for two interrelated reasons.

The statute creating the DRC process simply states:

> A Commission shall be established that will provide review for the status of detainees. Hearsay evidence shall be admitted. The detainees shall have access to attorneys but that access shall be limited. The detainees and the lawyers for the detainees shall have no rights to cross examine witnesses and no right to see the

> evidence against the detainee. Each case shall be judged by a three judge panel consisting of military officers, at least one of whom shall be a trained lawyer.[84]

Thus, the legislation creating the DRC process is bare bones. Much is left to be fleshed out by the judges as they make rulings during the DRC hearings for each individual. Furthermore, issues concerning the nature and extent of the DRC process are currently being litigated in the Western Country's domestic courts. In short, this Court cannot rule on whether the DRC process complies with the ICCPR and the Geneva Convention because this Court does not know what the DRC process is.

The DRC legislation leaves many questions open which will not be answered until the courts of the Western Country rule on the issues before them an until the judges interpreting the statue apply it in practice.

For example, we do not know what standards the judges will apply in admitting or excluding hearsay. We do not know what limitations the judges will place on the detainees access to counsel. We do not know the extent to which the judges, in their discretion, will allow detainees to see the evidence and cross examine witnesses, despite the fact that the detainees have no right to do either. Since the legislation is silent on the issue of judicial review, we do not know whether the decisions of the DRC are subject to judicial review and, if so, what the standard of review will be.

In its statement of questions presented, the Applicant asks: "Does the Western Country's hearing procedure measure up to the standard of 'a fair and public hearing by an independent and impartial tribunal, in the determination of its right and obligations?'" Applicant never addresses this question in its Memorial or by submitting evidence about the nature of the DRC hearing process. The likely reason for this is that Applicant does not know what the DRC process is.

Just as the Applicant does not know enough about the DRC process to address it in written argument, the Court does not have sufficient evidence before it to address it by a judicial decision.

No detainee has yet availed himself of the DRC process. Instead, detainees have chosen to attack that process in court. As a result the issue of whether the DRC complies with domestic law and the issue as to whether the DRC process is subject to judicial review is pending before the Respondent's Supreme Judicial Court.

Because detainees have not exhausted their remedies under the DRC, the exact nature of DRC review remains uncertain. This Court should not attempt to evaluate the adequacy of the DRC until the Western Country's domestic courts have had an opportunity to construe the statute establishing the DRC and this Court can examine its operation in a concrete setting. Indeed, important questions remain subject to consideration or elaboration as to the scope of the review available under the DRC and will be fleshed out on a case-by-case basis. Significantly, the Supreme Judicial Court of the Western Country will soon decide whether decisions of the DRC are subject to further judicial review and, indeed, whether the DRC process comports with the Western Country's Constitution.

Under these circumstances, there has been no final decision by the Respondent as to the nature and extent of the hearing that will be offered to detainee.

Therefore, the issue of whether detainees have been deprived hearings under any applicable international law standards is not ripe. It is a basic principle of law that a court should not decide an issue until the issue is ripe for adjudication. Because the detainees, whose rights the applicant seeks to protect, have not exhausted their remedies, and because this case is not ripe for adjudication, the application should be dismissed.

V. The Respondent has Implemented Appropriate and Lawful Procedures for Determining the Legality of Limitation, Consistent with Articles 9 and 10 of the ICCPR and the Geneva Convention[85]

If this Court reaches the issue of whether the hearings provided by the Respondent are legally sufficient, based on the limited information available at this time, it should rule that they are.

A. MILITARY COMMISSIONS SUCH AS THE DRC CONSTITUTE A WELL-ESTABLISHED METHOD AMONG CIVILIZED COUNTRIES TO ADJUDICATE ALLEGATIONS OF TERRORISM

Military commissions such as the DRC have been recognized as regular judicial proceedings.[86] When it comes to military-like actions, such as acts of terrorism, they are particularly the norm since the military is "a specialized society separate from civilian society" with "laws and traditions of its own."[87] Military commissions have been likened to "common-law war court[s] . . . recognized by statute law."[88] Indeed, their validity and use are so established as to remain recognized "even after peace has been declared."[89]

One commentator has noted that a number of Western countries have used military commissions similar to the DRC.

> Following World War II, the governments of the United States, the French Republic, the United Kingdom and the Union of Soviet Socialist Republics established an International Military Tribunal ("IMT") for the trial and punishment of war criminals of the European Axis. IMT was governed by a Constitution which was signed on August 8, 1945. IMT consisted of four members, each with an alternate, appointed by each of the four governments. Neither the IMT, its members nor their alternates could be challenged by the prosecution, or by the defendants or by their counsel. Before any trial could commence, the members of IMT were required to agree among themselves upon the selection from their number of President. The IMT Presidency rotated based upon the votes of its members. Decisions were made by majority vote, except that convictions and sentences require a 75% affirmative vote. Trials in absentia were authorized. Procedural rules were drafted by the prosecutors. In addition, the Constitution of IMT expressly provided that:
>
> The Tribunal shall not be bound by technical rules of evidence. It shall adopt and apply to the greatest possible extent expeditious and nontechnical proce-

> dures, and shall admit any evidence which it deems to be of probative value. [IMT Constitution, Article 19]
>
> The judgment of IMT as to the guilt or the innocence of any defendant was final and not subject to review. [IMT Constitution, Article 26][90]

With respect to the rights of a defendant, the international community has recognized that the reality of the fight against terrorism may justify derogations, particularly in regard to arrangements for access to counsel and the case-file, as well as the use of anonymous testimony.[91]

B. UNDER WELL-ESTABLISHED PRINCIPLES, MILITARY TRIBUNALS ARE NOT REQUIRED TO PROVIDE ALLEGED TERRORISTS THE RIGHT TO CONFRONT ALL THE EVIDENCE AGAINST THEM AND TO CROSS-EXAMINE WITNESSES

The use of anonymous witnesses is not necessarily incompatible with principles of international law.[92] For example, it may be legitimate "to preserve the anonymity of an agent . . . for his . . . protection and so as not to impair his usefulness" later.[93] Moreover, disclosure of evidence is "not an absolute right," particularly in the case where there "may be competing interests, such as national security or the need to protect witnesses . . . or keep secret police methods of investigation."[94] Furthermore, it is not the role of the international courts to rule on the rationale for non-disclosure since, "as a general rule, it is for the national courts to assess the evidence before them."[95] Instead, the international court's task is "to ascertain whether the decision-making procedure applied in each case complied . . . with the requirements of adversarial proceedings and equality of arms, and incorporated adequate safeguards."[96]

This is particularly true in the national security context.

> Classified information cannot be disclosed to those not authorized to receive it. To force the government to disclose its methods and techniques for information gathering against terrorists in open court would be foolhardy at best and would compromise its effectiveness permanently. Disclosing identities could result in the loss of intelligence agents at home and abroad. The myriad of evils which could flow from public disclosure of national security information cannot be overestimated.[97]

C. THE ADMISSIBILITY OF HEARSAY EVIDENCE IS APPROPRIATE IN THE CONTEXT OF TERRORISM AND DOES NOT VIOLATE ACCEPTED PRINCIPLES OF DUE PROCESS

As noted above, the IMT Constitution permitted the use of hearsay by allowing "any evidence which [the Tribunal] deems to be of probative value."[98]

The Dutch government's use of hearsay evidence in criminal trials has been approved in some contexts by the European Court of Human Rights.[99]

Allowing probative hearsay evidence in the informed judicial discretion of the tribunal is particularly important in international terrorism cases. An example by Crona and Richardson, writing in a journal no less prestigious than the *Oklahoma City University Law Review*, is persuasive.

> A relaxation of the hearsay rule might become critical in a prosecution for terrorism where it may be impossible to produce live witnesses to an event which occurred years earlier in a foreign country. For example, the indictment in the Pan Am Flight 103 case details the alleged purchase of clothing, by Libyan intelligence agent Abdel Bassett, for placement in the suitcase with the bomb. The clothing was used to disguise the contents of the suitcase containing the bomb, which was placed inside a radio-cassette player. Under the rules of evidence applicable in U.S. District Court, the prosecution would have to produce in person the Maltese shopkeeper to identify Abdel Bassett as the man who allegedly purchased the clothing back in 1988, as opposed to producing the investigator who tracked down the shopkeeper and showed him a photograph of Abdel Bassett. Even if we assume that the shopkeeper could be located six years or more after the fact, we recognize that it is nearly impossible to secure involuntary testimony from a witness who is a citizen of a foreign country, especially one that historically has been less than sympathetic to the United States. The reach of a federal court subpoena simply does not extend to Malta.[100]

The judicious admission of hearsay by a legally trained judge is not only consistent with fundamental fairness, it is necessary for the protection of those whom terrorists threaten.

D. THE HISTORICAL RECORD PROVES THAT MILITARY TRIBUNALS WITH PROCEDURES SIMILAR TO THE DCA DO NOT MAKE CONVICTION A FOREGONE CONCLUSION

Applicant cannot be heard to complain that the DRC will be biased against the detainees, if history is any guide. Again, Crona and Richardson make this point persuasively.

> In the Nuremberg war crimes trials, three of the twenty-two major defendants were acquitted, four were sentenced to twenty years in prison or less, and three received life sentences. Thus, the International Military Tribunal spared nearly half of the accused architects of Nazi policy that led to the Holocaust, World War II, and other forms of barbarism. These trained jurists sought to make determinations based on the evidence presented to them.
>
> The same was true of the United States military tribunals, composed solely of American judges, which tried 177 other Nazi officials and members of the SS, found 142 guilty of crimes against the law of nations, but executed only twelve. There is no reason to believe that a modern military commission would be less circumspect. In fact, such a commission would likely be less susceptible than civilian jurors to decisions based on "inflamed passions" rather than evidence.[101]

Applicant has offered no reason to believe that the detainees will not be treated fairly by the DRC process.

E. IN BALANCING THE THREAT OF TERRORISM AGAINST THE RIGHTS OF DETAINEES, A STATE IS ENTITLED TO A WIDE MARGIN OF DISCRETION

As noted above, it is the responsibility of a contracting State to determine how far it is necessary to go to prevent further harm to the state when it is threatened by a public emergency.[102] Because of their superior knowledge of the needs of the moment, national authorities with the day-to-day responsibility for the safety of their citizens are in a better position than an international court to decide the nature and the scope of the measures necessary to protect the country from terrorism.[103] Therefore, a wide margin of deference should be granted to national authorities in this regard.[104]

Military commissions are simply another valid tool of the Chief or State in an armed conflict as an instrument of national security. "An important incident to the conduct of war is the adoption of measures by the military commander, not only to repel and defeat the enemy, but to seize and subject [them] to disciplinary measures."[105] Therefore, the right to employ such a tool in times of emergency is therefore implied in a sovereign's right to exercise its national defense powers to preserve the foundation of all the Western Country's liberties.

CONCLUSION

For the foregoing reasons, the Respondent respectfully requests that this Court enter an Order dismissing the Application.

DECISION

The Applicant argues that because this was an international armed conflict that the Geneva Convention applies to those individuals detained. Since they were in fact removed from the physical location of the battlefield and moved to a secondary site, they were no longer combatants regardless of their status at the time of detainment. These individuals were entitled to a trial to determine their status which they were denied. Without a trial to determine their actual status they were denied the rights that are afforded to them under the Geneva Convention.

The Respondent argues that, due to their failure to adhere to the ICRC, that the Geneva Conventions do not apply to those arrested and therefore they are unlawful combatants and that only International Humanitarian Law (IHL) applies.[106] The Court finds in favor of the Applicant in regards to the nature of the armed conflict. While the terrorist organization failed to distinguish themselves from the civilian population, war tribunals should have been conducted to accurately determine the status of individuals prior to their detention. The fact that tribunals were not conducted leads the Court to believe that due diligence wasn't taken by the Western Country in regards to determining the war time status of the individuals. The Court also finds that the failure of Respondent to establish war time tribunals brought about unnecessary suffering to the civilian population. This Court finds that the Western country be required to provide reparations and compensation to the Middle Eastern Country.

Human rights law is relevant to this case. The view of some human rights NGOs is that even though you can derogate from due process, *habeas corpus* is not one of the areas of due process that is derogable. And one interpretation of the General Comments of the UN Human Rights Committee is that while due process is derogable, if you follow the rules for announcing a national emergency in the forum of the United Nations, you still have to give *habeas corpus* rights. This is because, for example, the Geneva Conventions require battlefield tribunals to determine prisoner status in cases where there is any doubt as to the status of a combatant.

"Show me the body" is *habeas corpus* in Latin. The original criteria and the normal criteria in criminal justice trials is probable cause of a crime. Already in Western Country, law holds that standards far less than acceptable for due process is acceptable because of the irrelevance of human rights law. The Western Country holds that IHL applies and that its protections for suspected terrorists are interpreted through subjective lens, that is, only that the Western Country suspects terrorism is the relevant legal criterion of intent, not what is reasonable objectively.

This Court maintains that human rights law applies to peacetime or armed conflict. Therefore, as a state party to the ICCPR, the Western Country had to comply with the rules established by the Human Rights Committee in General Comment 29 on States of Emergency.[107] Paragraph 2 states clearly:

> Measures derogating from the provisions of the Covenant must be of an exceptional and temporary nature. Before a State moves to invoke Article 4, two fundamental conditions must be met: the situation must amount to a public emergency which threatens the life of the nation, and the State party must have officially proclaimed a state of emergency. The latter requirement is essential for the maintenance of the principles of legality and rule of law at times when they are most needed.

Since the Western country maintains that an indefinite state of armed conflict is in effect and has not derogated from its due process requirements, it is in violation of Article 4 of the ICCPR. Moreover, the Human Rights Committee's jurisprudence holds that *habeas corpus* is a part of due process rights which are not derogable. While this view is not legally binding, and is contested by relevant state parties, including Western Country, this Court cannot hold that the entire body of human rights law be rejected in this context. Clearly, both war and human rights law consider arbitrary detention to be illegal and inexcusable under any circumstances, including in any putative war on terrorism.

If human rights law applies, and it certainly does in this case, then the detaining power must provide access to an independent court with due process guarantees.[108] The Western Country maintains that a minimum review of the legality of detention has been established by the Detainee Review Committee (DRC). However, what this means is that anyone dangerous to the Western Country can be still held indefinitely under war law until the war ends. The Court rejects this interpretation of both human rights and war law. Continuing the practice of indefinite detention without charge or trial is a violation of human rights law. War law also does not envision that wars last forever, and that no one who was initially not dangerous, as determined by a legitimate court, can be deemed dangerous subsequently due, presumably, to his unfair treatment. Therefore, this Court orders the release or trial of all detained as suspected terrorists. Indefinite detention without charge or trial of even suspected terrorists, without review by an independent court is a violation that the International Court of Justice cannot countenance, unless there are more clear limits imposed by regulations against arbitrariness, including independent review.

Legitimate national security considerations do not include governmental interests and activities that constitute grave crimes under international human rights law, let alone policies that are precisely calculated to evade the operation of human rights law.[109]

According to section 2 of the resolution regarding detention in Western Country, continued detention is warranted for a detainee if it is "necessary to protect against a significant threat to the security of the Western Country." While the DRC has been established to review the situation of each detainee, it is to be noted that such a review pertains to an assessment of the necessity of the continued detention pursuant to section 2, rather than a review of the lawfulness of the detention as required by international human rights law under Article 9, para. 4, of the ICCPR. While the principle of detention of combatants during an international armed conflict is well-established in international humanitarian law, the actions by Western Country extend the possibility of long-term or indefinite detention without charge or trial beyond the context of such conflict and extends applicability to those persons who are not combatants or terrorists.

In the case of the United States as an example, while courts have decided in favor of some Guantánamo detainees, the political branches of the Government of the United States retain the power of release of non-citizens.[110] Para. 83 of the Working Group on Arbitrary Detention's report stated that

> For such remedy [to cases of arbitrary detention] to be effective, as required by Article 2 (3) of the ICCPR, detaining States are under an obligation to release the arbitrarily detained (foreign) detainee into their own territory even if they wish to deport the (foreign) detainee, but where deportation of the detainee otherwise liable for removal to the country of origin or to a third country accepting the detainee is not promptly possible.[111]

The aforementioned judicial and administrative remedies are not sufficient to meet the due process standards, as embodied in Article 9, paras. 3 and 4 of the ICCPR, as they do not constitute an effective court review, which entails the possibility of release. In this context, I would like to refer to recommendations made to your Excellency's Government during the Universal Periodic Review calling on the authorities to ensure that all remaining detainees be tried without delay in accordance with to international law or be released (A/HRC/16/11, paras. 92.156 and 92.160).

Again referring to the example of the United States, at the Bagram air base in Afghanistan, no judicial review, including in the form of *habeas corpus*, has been undertaken nor is currently permitted.[112] In this connection, the Concluding Observations of the Committee on the Rights of the Child expressed its concern at the number of children detained in U.S. administered detention facilities in Iraq and Afghanistan over extended periods of time, in certain instances for one year or more, without adequate access to legal advisory services.[113] The Court finds this Advisory Opinion to reflect customary international law because it views no justification for denying legal assistance to minors, who number prominently among those detained, even during armed conflict by an occupying power, especially since most of them have no plausible connection to terrorism, even as children. The Committee on the Rights of the Child recommended that the State guarantee periodic and impartial review of their detention and conduct such reviews at greater frequency for children than adults.[114]

More generally, this Court is deciding whether or not adults should be guaranteed the right to *habeas corpus* or *amparo*. We are convinced that the requirements for *habeas corpus* found in the general comments, state party recommendations, and the case law of the Human Rights Committee of the ICCPR, though technically not binding, does represent customary international law. The Committee regards an independent review as non-derogable, even though other due process rights are derogable, because the *jus cogens* prohibition against torture is ineffective in practice if individuals can be detained arbitrarily and without any legal procedure to check the lawfulness of that detention on a case by case basis. Furthermore, IHL applied to armed conflict, mandates that full legal protections must be applied to those accused of a crime. Terrorism is a crime, and both the civil law and common law traditions, which provide the domestic principles of law on which international law is based, would require prosecution for such a serious crime. Therefore, terrorists should be prosecuted with full due process protections and must meet the criteria of probable cause to be detained further, as determined by an independent court. Thus, the distinction between IHL and human rights law is a distinction without a difference: such independent judicial assessments should have been conducted with battlefield tribunals for those detainees captured in combat for whom there is doubt as to whether or not they qualify for prisoner of war status. For others, it is more reasonable to use an independent judge to make a determination on the legality of detention, through the laws off criminal justice, consistent with human rights law.

Thus, no one should be deprived of liberty except on such grounds and in accordance with such procedures as are established by law. The substantive grounds for arrest or detention must be prescribed by law, and should be defined with sufficient precision to avoid overly broad or arbitrary application.[115] Deprivation of liberty without such legal authorization is unlawful, and violates Article 9 of the ICCPR.[116] Detention in violation of a judicial order of release is also unlawful.[117]

The existence of armed conflict is not relevant because both bodies of law coexist for all circumstances, including armed conflict. IHL is not exclusive, even if applicable as more specific specialized law in particular circumstances. In addition, the Western Country's argument that IHL applies as *lexis specialis* is not just or legal. The decisions of the International Criminal Tribunal for the Former Yugoslavia, along with the International Criminal Court, are among the tribunals that have applied rules from both sources of law, even if the first rule to be applied would come from IHL if it exists from treaties or customary international law. If a specific rule already exists in IHL, then human rights law would not apply. In the absence of an IHL rule, or in situations that do not involve armed conflict, then human rights law would apply. The Vienna Convention on the Law of Treaties holds that the most relevant and recent treaty rules apply and that specialized law applies because of its specificity, but does not mean that entire bodies of international law are to be excluded. Even in situations of clear armed conflict, IHL would not be the exclusive body of law. However, the most important argument is that IHL also requires *habeas corpus* as a non-derogable right for those who are or should be charged with crimes, such as those relating to terrorism.

Procedures for carrying out legally authorized deprivation of liberty should also be established by law, and States parties should ensure compliance with their legally prescribed procedures. Not every violation of a domestic procedural rule, however, amounts to a violation of Article 9 of the ICCPR. In armed conflict, states must follow the requirements for derogation, including any measures undertaken as proportionate and necessary.[118] It is difficult to foresee that a state party could justify many circumstances where independent review of legality would be required, but in the absence of making that case on the grounds of necessity and proportionality, the deprivation of liberty without independent review would be unacceptable.

In the particular circumstances, the Western Country not only did not justify the denial of *habeas corpus*, it also did not exhibit strict scrutiny to assure that substantial numbers of individuals were not deprived of their liberty. Each individual must be judged as a combatant or non-combatant civilian. It is quite apparent that many of those detained were non-combatant civilians, who must be afforded the protections of human rights law. If emergency measures are to apply to non-combatant civilians, that means that they deserve distinct treatment required by the rules of the Committees on Human Rights and Against Torture, to which the Western Country is bound as a state party to the ICCPR and the Convention against Torture. In addition, many were not involved in any armed conflict in any specific way and should have been governed entirely according to the dictates of human rights law.

Article 9 of the ICCPR, to which the Western Country is a party, requires compliance with domestic rules that define the procedure for arrest by identifying the officials authorized to arrest,[119] or by specifying when a warrant is required.[120] It also requires compliance with domestic rules that define when authorization to continue detention must be obtained from a judge or other officer,[121] where suspects may be detained,[122] when the detained person must be brought to court,[123] and legal limits on the duration of detention.[124] It also requires compliance with domestic rules providing important safeguards for detained persons, such as making a record of an arrest,[125] and permitting access to counsel.[126]

Finally, there is the issue of whether or not it might be reasonable to suspect a civil right during armed conflict, based on an objective test of what the reasonable country should have done. Unlike with individuals, whose intent can be surmised, countries do not have a mental element of reasonability. They are expected to follow reasonable standards of lawful conduct. Thinking that excessive force is necessary is not lawful for countries, which are required to institute legal procedures guaranteeing that unreasonable conduct is checked. That government officials thought that a restriction on rights was necessary is not lawful unless it meets the objective standard of credibility and reasonableness.

The International Court of Justice finds that the Detainee Review Committee established by the Western country is neither legal, nor sufficient under International Humanitarian Law The evidence of hearsay being permitted, under the presence of three military judges with only limited access to lawyers have deemed the DRC a failure under the criteria of the ICCPR Article 14. Section 1: Stating the right to a fair trial, Section 2: Stating the presumption of innocence, and Section 3: The minimum guarantees in criminal trials, including the right to appeal convictions in a higher court. Such rights have clearly been held from the detainees with the establishment of the DRC.

The ICJ requires that Western Country's compliance to derogating retroactively, entitles the detainees to minimum rights under Article 14 of the ICCPR. Necessary reforms must take place in terms of appointing non partisan and impartial judges. Secondly, the decision also acknowledges the fact in dispute of the doctrine of unclean hands brought forward by Western Country, and recognizing that perhaps, this ruling will complement some of the Human Rights issues that are faced by Middle Eastern Country and their neighboring states. Unclean hands are not the basis for the Middle Eastern country to demand remedies for its citizens, whose rights are not forfeited by the human rights violations of their government. The right to independent review of detention is among the most important rights against tyranny, which the existence declared of a state of war cannot be presumed to allow those who are not prisoners of war to be put at risk of torture or arbitrary deprivation of liberty. There is no justification for rounding up the innocent if there is no evidence that a reasonable third party would not conclude justifies continued imprisonment of those not likely to be found guilty. They still can be interrogated, if unlawful combatants, and from this questioning, sufficient evidence can be adduced and judged by those without a vested interest in detaining everyone who remote might be a terrorist but for which there is no evidence justifying their imprisonment.

APPENDIX A: Examples of Questions from Actual Moot Court Trials

Q: In this case you mention the Geneva Conventions, but the heart of this case is the ICCPR. One body of law is international humanitarian law, the law of armed conflict; the other is international human rights law. Why would the ICCPR be relevant to what is clearly some type of armed conflict?
A: Because the ICCPR mentions anyone "deprived of his liberty by arrest or detention" and "anyone" would mean someone involved in armed conflict or not.
Q: So, human rights law applies to armed conflict?
A. Yes in this instance.
Q: In all instances correct?
A: Yes.
(space indicates a new topic)

Q: In the Western Country's constitution you mention that there has to be a rebellion or invasion that threatens the public's safety. Clearly the attack on 11/9 was something that threatened the public's safety. Several people invaded the country and hijacked airplanes why is that not an invasion that threatens public safety?
A: I would not call that an invasion because an invasion means taking over the whole country not entering the country illegally.
Q: In other words you can do anything except try to take over the whole country and if you don't try to take over the whole country its not an invasion?
A: Not anything but rebellion or invasion that threatens the public safety.
Q: So if there was a massive rocket attack, let's say a thousand rockets, no ground troops, no attempt to capture the country that would not be an invasion?
A: I would not call that an invasion.

Q: You mention that you thought that the payments provided were not relevant. Wouldn't reparations or payments provided to victims always be relevant and always come after the fact? You complain that they were retroactive but aren't reparations always retroactive? They're paid after the event.
A: My point was that was the derogation proclamation was retroactive.
Q: I thought you were taking about reparations.
A: No I did mention Article 5 as what the Western Country proclaimed they were derogating from, which does mention reparations. My point was that

the Western Country did not derogate until 2007 which was after the violations had been committed.

Q: What was the evidence of torture in 2004 from the International Committee of the Red Cross? They normally do not publish their findings publicly. There was a report that was leaked publicly in 2009. You mention ICRC evidence of torture of these detainees.
A: Well, the ICRC did provide evidence of torture in 2007
Q: Well, they did but not in 2007, you picked a different date.
A: You said 2004
Q: Sorry 2004 they did after 2007.

Q: With respect to review of detainees status what type of review is required?
A: Review as to whether they are competent or innocent.
Q: By whom?
A: By the Western Country.
Q: The Western Country already provides the CSRT. So what are you asking for? What qualifies for *habeas corpus*?
A: We are saying that the CSRT is insufficient as detainees are not being treated fairly and we want to bring this to the ICJ.
Q: What remedy are you asking the Court to give you? You're not only asking the judge if habeas is required but what at a minimum above CSRT is required. Civilian courts?
A: Civilian courts, not military
Q: Distinct courts in a trial or some administrative procedure? So, an administrative judge?
A: Yes
Q: So a civilian administrative judge using what law? Is a lawyer for the defendant required? Is the defendant allowed to see the evidence against him? Can the defendant cross-examine? All of this?
A: Yes.
Q: So what you're saying is that even during wartime there's no excuse for even a military commission?
A: Yes because, well now we're talking about 2007 and it's not necessarily wartime.
Q: So it's a civilian court and a military commission would not suffice. I'm sorry why wouldn't criminal charges before a military commission suffice at least for military combatants?
A: Well, because these detainees are labeled unlawful combatants. Some of them have been proven innocent.
Q: You have to have a full trial to determine whether someone is guilty or not. You're basically complaining that the review is confidential.

Q: Aren't there already trials to determine the status of detainees?

A: Yes they are trials, but we want these trials to accord with internationally accepted human rights standards.
Q: Would these hearings be open hearings? Would that not pose a threat to the national security of the Western Country?
A: The courts can decide which evidence they want to limit to the media and issue a gag order and suppress information they think might put national security in jeopardy. Also this should not be a factor in the denial of *habeas corpus* rights to the detainees because there are ways to suppress classified information from the media and the Western Country by violating international human rights law it is destroying its own national security in the long-run.
Q: So you believe that because of the actions of the Western Country we are harming are own civil rights?
A: Yes.

Q: You said that the doctrine of unclean hands means that Applicant has no standing before the International Court of Justice. You mention that the doctrine of unclean hands is a common law doctrine. Why would a common law doctrine be adequate for the ICJ when the majority of the countries of the world use civil law?
A: I refer to the doctrine of unclean hands as a generally understood legal principal.
Q: It's a generally understood principal in common law countries. Why should this Court introduce this doctrine? It's an interesting doctrine but it would also mean that probably no country of the world could come forward because no country has a perfect record when it comes to providing human rights. All countries have violations and sometimes they are considered crimes; unlawful acts. Other times they are official policy and this would apply to even developed liberal democracies.
A: Yes it would. I hold that the doctrine should be introduced in this case because of the large scale crime deviation practiced by the Middle Eastern Country.
Q: What about your own Western Country? Does your country practice respect for all human rights? There are allegations that are quite credible that the Western Country has tortured these detainees.
A: As you said before no country is perfect. I call for it to be used against the Middle Eastern Country in this case because of the large scale to which it has deviated from human rights law.
Q: What about the large scale to which the Western Country has deviated in terms of its use of torture?
A: The Western Country's practices of tortured fall under its domestic law.
Q: The question here is international law, not domestic law isn't it?
A: Yes it is.

Q: You say that your detention practices are acceptable even though there is no writ of *habeas corpus* because the Combatant Status Review Tribunals

(CSRTs) that were established meet the standards, according to at least one justice of the Supreme Court, Justice O'Conner, of due process. Didn't the *Hamdi* case to which you cited actually strike down the review process as not adequate?

A: Yes it did.

Q: In particular what's curious about that statement is that even if they were adequate there were no battlefield tribunals at the time and as a consequence the large majority of persons sent to Guantánamo, in fact, according to several studies by professors at Seton Hall and UC-Berkeley law schools based on official government documents were not guilty of any crime and were detained mistakenly.

A: I would like to defer talking about battlefield tribunals until my rebuttal.

Q: Well, I'm asking you now. They brought it up and it's on the table. Why is it that we're talking about the fact that these people were denied *habeas corpus* until you set up the CSRTs. So separate from the issue of whether the CSRTs constitute *habeas corpus* and whether *habeas corpus* is required, the Geneva Conventions which you say apply, instead of the ICCPR, still require battlefield tribunals be used any time there is doubt as to the status of a person and clearly there is some doubt because all of these people in Guantánamo have been found to have been innocent. Obviously there are 200 or so hard core terrorists, but the other 600 were not.

A: Your question I would like to break up into two parts. One that being we should have battlefield tribunals and the other that it should at least be in a timely manner. Well, the timely manner I don't really have an answer to that question. Battlefield tribunals specifically one could argue that the precedent for battlefield tribunals comes from so long ago that modern warfare is almost inapplicable.

Q: They used them in World War II and the Vietnam War.

A: But those were still traditional-style battlefields.

Q: The Vietnam War was traditional? It was guerilla warfare.

A: The captures that we conduct today I would argue are taken in smaller villages and through the intelligence that we have now are more specific. Raiding a village to find one individual in a backroom, I would argue, that the battlefield in question, where the battle is actually taking place, is such a hostile environment. It is filled with an unknown number of unlawful combatants that may be dressed as civilians, where stopping right there and holding court seems illogical.

Q: Well, then why is establishing CSRTs years later and having detained these people for a matter of years, not hours or days, considered to be in a timely manner?

A: Well, this is 2007 correct?

Q: Right and these people were captured in 2001, 2002.

A: The CSRTs began in late 2004.

Q: So that means a good two years of detention without any review at all.

A: Well, that would refer to the second part of your question, the "timely manner" aspect and I do not have a good answer for that.

Q: You say that the Universal Code of Military Justice (UCMJ) will be used to try military combatants so are you saying that there are criminal charges? In which case you are observing *habeas corpus*, because you have to have military charges of crimes?
A: To declare someone an unlawful enemy combatant you almost have to a criminal trial, correct?
Q: Right and I saw nothing in the facts that shows the intent to try them. That doesn't seem to be the crime with which most of them were charged because most of them were not unlawful combatants. According to independent studies that were foot soldiers for the Taliban and the Taliban was the national army of Gafhanistan when the Western Country invaded it.
A: Is it in the facts that they were members of the Taliban?
Q: The large majority of people housed in Guantánamo were foot soldiers not terrorists and therefore they were legal combatants. How are you going to maintain that you're going to charge people by respecting legal rights to *habeas corpus*, or you're not going to charge them and they're innocent. Either way, the Western Country's actions seem to be short of what's required because you don't want to provide *habeas corpus* and you charge them with a crime which is a solution to providing *habeas corpus*. On the other hand you don't charge someone with a crime because they're not guilty of being an unlawful combatant yet you say they're all terrorists when in fact they're not unlawful combatants. They're fighting for the national government of Gafhanistan.
A: The Government of Gafhanistan stands behind the attacks of 9/11?
Q: No the Government of Gafhanistan did not. They denied that they had anything to do with it.
A: Well, then how can the people responsible for the attacks be part of the Gafhanistan government?
Q: They're not considered part of the Gafhanistan government. They are considered a terrorist group that was based in Gafhanistan. The perpetrators were residing in Germany and then came to the United States.
A: I thought the argument was that they were foot soldiers for Gafhanistan.
Q: The people who were detained, the majority were foot soldiers. There were people on 9/11 who were clearly enemy combatants and unlawful combatants. The question here is the individual who was not involved in 9/11 but was captured because someone was offered a bounty by the U.S. government to turn people over on the grounds that they were allegedly terrorists. It turned out that people were prepared to turn over innocent people.
A: I still stand by the fact that the CSRTs are sufficient for reviewing the status of enemy combatants.
Q: But the CSRTs only released people on the grounds that they were no longer considered dangerous. They did not deal with the issue of whether or not

they were in fact enemy combatants. So how can the CSRT be ruling on the legality of holding somebody because the legality did not depend on whether someone is dangerous. The legality depends on whether they committed a crime.

A: I was under the impression that the CSRT tribunals were all criminal because they would read them charges and they can defend themselves and they can call witnesses.

Q: They don't read the charges. They enter evidence that they were involved with al Qaeda which is not necessarily the same thing.

A: I read transcripts from some of the hearings and in the first 2-3 pages they read the charges.

Q: Well, then how can all these people be charged who ended up not being part of al Qaeda? Why were they all released?

A: They released detainees on the basis of whether the terrorist organization they are affiliated is still armed against the Western Country. So if we have constant reviews and the initial CSRT review. Each detainee's case determines how many reviews they will get, the time and manner of same, and to decide whether the group they are affiliated with is still openly at arms against the Western Country. So they are reviewed often and they if decide if the terrorist group they are affiliated with is no longer a threat to the Western Country they are released.

Q: Well, the Taliban is still active. I'm surprised that any detainees were released.

A: So you're saying we should keep them?

Q: Well, you let them go, not on the criteria of no longer being part of an ongoing criminal conspiracy, but on the criteria that they were never part of this or any terrorist organization or conspiracy.

A: So we're wrong for letting them go?

Q: You're wrong for having kept them in the first place without a review by an independent body of their status. Does the military have a possible bias of not wanting to be shown to have captured people for several years with no basis for their detention?

A: What I will argue is that releasing these individuals shows that the CSRTs review cases and they decide if the evidence against the individual is good enough.

Q: But what you are saying is that the CSRTs were established after people had been detained for a minimum of two years.

A: Yes. It was late but they let them go.

Q: So you're admitting that the CSRTs were late? You say the CSRTs meet the criteria of *habeas corpus* so you're implying that *habeas corpus* is a right? You even quoted Justice O'Conner in saying that the CSRTs meet the standards of due process.

A: I would argue that reviewing your combatant status and deciding that they're no longer a dangerous combatant and letting them go . . .

Q: But you just said that they are charged with crimes based on the criteria being used.

A: I said they constantly review the cases and then when they decide that the terrorist group they are affiliated with is not a threat to the Western Country they let them go.

Q: How can you say that the Taliban is no longer a legitimate threat?

A: Maybe the terrorist organization that they were affiliated with or the individuals themselves are no longer a credible threat. I would argue that the CSRT is sufficient for *habeas corpus* and for letting people go.

Q: So you're saying that some right to *habeas corpus* exists for some combatants?

A: No I'm saying that the CSRT is sufficient. They don't need out-right, full-on *habeas corpus* rights because they have the CSRT.

Q: You said that common Article 3 does not apply to this conflict? It's an international armed conflict. So you're saying that the four Geneva Conventions do not condemn torture in international armed conflicts?

A: No I'm saying that common Article 3 does not apply to conflicts of an international nature.

Q: So, if Gafhanistan is an international armed conflict then you're saying the rights of Common Article 3 do not apply to international armed conflicts, including the right not to be tortured?

A: Well, I don't consider torture and *habeas corpus* to be the same thing. I consider *habeas* to be a matter of detention not treatment.

Q: Well, with your argument about common law dirty hands doctrine you couldn't ask for the Court to consider you as adequately providing an independent review when you yourself are not respecting the rights of international law including the ban on torture which you are alleged to have perpetrated against these detainees.

A: Well, as I said the only reason the unclean hands doctrine was presented was to address the large-scale deviations perpetrated by the Middle Eastern Country as opposed to small-scale deviations.

Q: Like torture?

A: Yes absent organ failure or death.

Q: You said that a competent tribunal is needed to determine detainees' status and the CSRT is a competent tribunal. If the Court were to accept that legal argument, we do not have to provide reparations for the two year delay in which they were not provided access to the CSRT?

A: I thought we determined that we were not going to determine reparations in this hearing or whether reparations had already been paid.

Q: What I'm asking is that are you're conceding therefore that something at least like the CSRT at a minimum is required on the battlefield?

A: I won't concede that what this Court considers to be a battlefield tribunal should be used.

Q: At what point does the CSRT standard apply, after someone is in detention?

A: Yes.
Q: So what you're saying is that there was at least two years of unacceptable delay?
A: I don't mean two years. I would concede that two years is too long but I will not concede that we should have tribunals on the battlefield just because it puts the Western Country's servicemen in danger.

Q: Could you please explain to this Court why you think human rights law does not apply? Clearly you did not ask the Secretary General of the UN to derogate from its obligations to provide the rights of duly constituted courts until well after a delay. Your country has ratified the ICCPR, why doesn't it apply? It applies to wartime and peacetime.
A: I don't know.
Q: The US says it doesn't apply on the grounds of *lex specialis* or specialized law. Is that what you're saying?
A: I'm saying that human rights law doesn't apply, humanitarian should.

Q: You say that there is an abundance of military intelligence. If so why were the detainees held for so long?
A: Military intelligence can provide us with a reason to hold detainees for lengthy periods of time.

Appendix B: Alterable Facts that Students and Faculty Could Adopt to Change the Legal Arguments

1. The detention of terrorist suspects from the Middle Eastern Country was or was not based solely on race, color, sex, language, religion, or national origin.
2. The Western Country's suspension of the writ of *habeas corpus* was or was not widely publicized throughout the world at the time, as was the creation of the Detainee Review Commission.
3. The detention of terrorist suspects by the Western Country followed or did not follow specific provisions of the four Geneva Conventions, the Universal Declaration of Human Rights, general principles recognized by the civilized world, and scholarly opinion.
4. The arrest and detention of terrorist suspects by the Western Country was or was not wholly consistent with the domestic laws of the Western Country. The terrorists pose a national security threat to the Western Country and as such the laws of the Western Country should prevail.

5. The Western Country followed or did not follow all, some, or none of the appropriate procedures for notification of derogation outlined in Article 4 of the ICCPR.
6. The Western Country was correctly or incorrectly identifying the suspects as terrorists when they were captured and exaggerated or accepted the public emergency faced by the Western Country. This emergency, the threat to national security posed by Islamic Jihad and *Nabilat*, did or did not really threaten the life of the nation.
7. Public officials of the Western Country, and not international judges, are or are not in a better position to determine what is and is not a threat to the life and well-being of the Western Country. The detention and interrogation of those suspected of involvement in the 11/9 attacks or of having connections to Islamic Jihad has or has not enabled the Western Country to claim that it foiled a number of additional attacks. Hard evidence of actionable intelligence from interrogation was or not provided to the public.
8. Grave national threats, including those posed by international terrorist networks such as Islamic Jihad resulted in reasonable responses or excessive terms of detention of suspected terrorists.
9. The Western Country's derogation was or was not strictly limited by the "exigencies of the situation." Only those with suspected ties to Islamic Jihad, the *Nabilat*, and their associates or who actually participated in the 11/9 attacks were detained, or the Western country thought that they were terrorists, when a reasonable response would have concluded that they were an overreaction.
10. The Middle Eastern Country's own human rights record on detention was or was acceptable and may or may not have invoked the doctrine of unclean hands, prevents a valid claim from being asserted. The Middle Eastern country has or has not failed to investigate and prosecute terrorist suspects residing within its borders.
11. Those detained were or were not entitled to Geneva Convention III protections for prisoners of war because they did or did not have fixed or recognizable signs, did or did not carry arms openly, and did or did not conduct their operations in accordance with the laws and customs of war. Islamic Jihad, the *Nabilat*, and their associates were or were not unlawful combatants.
12. The Western country did or did not accept human rights law as binding on suspected terrorists. Islamic Jihad, the *Nabilat*, and its affiliate organizations did or did not fit these criteria. Islamic Jihad is or is not a global organization that transcends boundaries.
13. The attacks by only Islamic Jihad on the Western Country did or did not constitute only intra-state conflict, thereby excluding most of the Geneva Conventions, other than Common Article III, governing international armed conflict.

14. The hearing procedures before the Detainee Review Commission were or were not consistent with existing international law, including Articles 9 and 10 of the ICCPR. Military Commissions, such as the Detainee Review Commission did or did not limit provision of due process, part and parcel of military commissions, is appropriate given the circumstances faced by the Western Country.
15. Detainees did not did not in fact generally receive a fair hearing before the Detainee Military Commission. Their conviction by the Commission is or is not an absolute certainty.
16. The case before the ICJ was or was not ripe for consideration at the present time as the constitutional validity of the Western Country's hearing and detention processes have not yet been established by the Supreme Judicial Court of the Western Country. Detainees have or have not exhausted their claims before the courts of the Western Country.
17. Neither the Middle Eastern Country nor any other country has or has not been prejudiced by the Western Country's delay in notification of its derogation from the provision of *habeas corpus*.
18. *Habeas corpus* under British law does or does not have exceptions under the constitution of the Western Country. Under British law *habeas corpus* provisions were or were not granted to "alien combatants" detained as prisoners of war.
19. Hearsay evidence was or was not included in the conduct of the detainee review processes of the Western country and was or was not permitted to have probative value.

Notes

1. The legislation discussed above is similar to the Authorization for the Use of Military Force (AUMF) passed by the U.S. Congress after the September 11, 2001 attacks and continues to be the basis for the prolonged detention of terror suspects in Guantánamo, Cuba. Tyler L. Sparrow, "Indefinite Detention after *Boumediene*: Judicial Trailblazing in Unchartered and Unfamiliar Territory," 44 *Suffolk U. L. Rev.* 261, 263 (2011); also U.S. Congress, The Authorization for the Use of Military Force, Pub. Law No. 107-40, 107th Congress, (2001).

2. The DRC is analogous to the Combat Status Review Tribunals (CSRT) established by the Bush Administration in 2004. See Memorandum from Deputy Secretary of Defense Paul Wolfowitz re: Order Establishing Combatant Status Review Tribunals, July 4, 2004, http://www.defenselink.mil/news/Jul2004/d20040707.review.pdf (accessed July 16, 2011). For discussion about the US Supreme Court's criticism regarding CSRTs in *Boumediene v. Bush*, see Edward F. Sherman, "Terrorist Detainee Policies: Can the Constitutional and International Law Principles of the *Boumediene* Precedents Survive Political Pressures?," 19 *Tul. J. Int'l & Comp. L.* 207, 224-226 (2010-2011).

3. Chandra Lekha Sriram, Olga Martin-Ortega and Johanna Herman, "War, Conflict, and Human Rights," in *The International Studies Encyclopedia,* ed. Robert A. Denemark

(Blackwell Publishing; Blackwell Reference Online, 2010), http://www.isacompendium.com/subscriber/tocnode?id=g9781444336597_chunk_g978144433659721_ss1-1 (accessed November 15, 2010), 13.

4. For an excellent discussion about the historical evolution of the writ of *habeas corpus*, see Albert S. Glass, "Historical Aspects of Habeas Corpus," 9 *St. John's L. Rev.* 55 (1934-1935); also see James Robertson, "*Quo Vadis*, Habeas Corpus?" 55 *Buff. L. Rev.* 1063 (January 2008).

5. Glass, "Historical," 55.

6. International Covenant on Civil and Political Rights (1966), Art. 4(1), http://treaties.un.org/doc/Treaties/1976/03/19760323%2006-17%20AM/Ch_IV_4p.pdf (accessed July 6, 2011). The provision of *habeas corpus* is a right guaranteed by Article 9(4) of the ICCPR.

7. ICCPR, Art. 4(1).

8. ICCPR, Art. 4(3).

9. U.S. Constitution, Art. 1, §9, clause 2.

10. *Ex Parte Merryman* Fed. Cas. 9,487 (1861); *Ex Parte Milligan* 71 U.S. (4 Wall.) 2 (1866); *Johnson v. Eisentrager* 339 U.S. 763 (1950); *Hamdi v. Rumsfeld* 542 U.S. 507 (2004); *Rasul v. Bush* 542 U.S. 466 (2004). For a full discussion of the latter two cases, as well as *Johnson*, see Sherman, "Terrorist Detainee," 211-214; 222-224.

11. *The Bluebook: A Uniform System of Citation*, 18th ed. (Cambridge, MA: Harvard Law Review Association, 2005).

12. David Welsh, "Procedural Justice Post-9/11: The Effects of Procedurally Unfair Treatment of Detainees on Perceptions of Global Legitimacy," 9 *Univ. N. H. L. Rev.* 261, 267 (2010-2011).

13. Welsh, "Procedural Justice," 276-277.

14. Welsh, "Procedural Justice," 277.

15. U.S. Government, Military Commission Act of 2006 (MCA), Pub. Law No. 109-366, 109th Congress, October 17, 2006, §948a(A)(1)(i) and (ii). The use of military commissions did not begin with the MCA of 2006, but were originally initiated via Executive Order by President Bush in November 2001. See Sherman, "Terrorist Detainee," 210.

16. MCA, §948(b); see also §948(d)(c) with respect to the determination of unlawful enemy status by a CSRT.

17. MCA, §948b(g).

18. This is in violation of Article 4 of the Third Geneva Convention. Convention (III) relative to the Treatment of Prisoners of War (Geneva Convention III) (1949), Art. 4, http://www.icrc.org/ihl.nsf/FULL/375?OpenDocument (accessed July 1, 2011); see also Sherman, "Terrorist Detainee," 210.

19. See specifically Common article 3 of Geneva Convention III.

20. See specifically U.S. Government, The Detainee Treatment Act of 2005 (DTA), Pub. Law No. 109-148, 109th Congress, December 30, 2005, §1005(e). This action followed the Supreme Court's ruling in *Rasul v Bush* 542 U.S. 466 (2004) which held the DC federal court had jurisdiction over writs for *habeas corpus* filed by alien detainees in Guantánamo. See Sherman, "Terrorist Detainee," 214. For a full analysis of *Rasul*, *Hamdi*, and *Hamden* and their impact on Congressional legislation see also Captain Aaron L. Jackson, "Habeas Corpus in the Global War on Terror: An American Drama," 65 *A. F. L. Rev.* 263, 271-280 (2010).

21. On this particular matter the ICJ and the Human Rights Commission have interpreted the ICCPR to apply extraterritorially, although neither is especially clear on the

matter of jurisdiction. For further discussion see Hugh King, The Extraterritorial Human Rights Obligations of States, 9 *Hum. Rts. L. Rev.* 521 (2009).

22. See *Human Rights Constitutional Documents*, American Convention on Human Rights (1969), Art. 27, www.hrcr.og/docs/American_Convention/oashr.html (accessed July 18, 2011); HR-NET *Hellenic Resources Network*, European Convention on Human Rights, Art. 15, http://www.hri.org/docs/ECHR50.html#Convention (accessed July 18, 2011).

23. *Hamden v. Rumsfeld.* 548 U.S. 557 (2006). Hamden was challenging the jurisdictional limitations of *habeas* challenges per the DTA. Specifically the Court ruled that Hamden's case, being filed prior to the enactment of the DTA, could be heard by the federal courts; in other words the stripping of *habeas corpus* could not be applied retroactively. See also Sherman, "Terrorist Detainee," 215.

24. See MCA, §948(b) and §950(f); see also §950(g) with respect to the of the U.S. Court of Appeals for the District of Columbia and the U.S. Supreme Court; also Welch, "Procedural Justice," 270; Sherman, "Terrorist Detainee," 218-219. The second issue was likely intended to deal specifically with the fact that *Hamden* had also raised issues regarding the President's authority to establish these military commissions. *Hamden v Rumsfeld* 548 U.S. at 594-595.

25. *Boumediene v. Bush,* 128 S. Ct. 2229 (2008). See Sherman's full discussion of *Boumediene* in "Terrorist Detainee," 219-227. It is important to remember that the Supreme Court's decision did not apply to detainees held by the United States elsewhere around the globe. This question is still relatively unanswered. For a critical analysis of *Boumediene* in particular its negative implications for the global war on terror see Jackson, "Habeas Corpus," 284-288.

26. As Walsh discusses Obama has since dropped "unlawful enemy combatant" as the accepted justification for detention now relying entirely on his powers under the AUMF. Walsh, "Procedural Justice," 262-263. For his full discussion see 269-275; see also Sherman, "Terrorist Detainees," 237-239. Much of the problem remaining post-*Boumediene* concerns the fact that the Supreme Court in its decision declined from providing "the proper standards to use in determining whether to grant the writ to a petitioning detainee." 'Procedural Justice," 273. Moreover, the Justices in *Boumediene* also did not hold that a writ of *habeas corpus* "could be used to challenge . . . designation and detention as an enemy combatant, [and] other such treatment as shipment to other countries, interrogation techniques, and conditions of confinement. Sherman, "Terrorist Detainee," 228; on trials by military commissions, 243-245.

27. *Boumediene v. Bush* 128 S. Ct. at 2272-2275.

28. This is what the U.S. Supreme Court ruled in *Hamdi v Rumsfeld,* 542 U.S. at 520 which was consistent with international law on the issue. However, as Hamdi was a U.S. citizen he was entitled to all available due process guarantees, including the right to file a writ of *habeas corpus*. For further discussion, see Sherman, "Terrorist Detainee," 212-213.

29. *International Covenant on Civil and Political Rights* (1966), Art. 9(4).

30. ICCPR, Art. 4(1).

31. *Statute of the International Court of Justice* (ICJ), Art. 36(2).

32. *ICJ Statute*, Article 38(1).

33. ICCPR, Art. 4(1).

34. ICCPR, Art. 4(1); GENERAL COMMENT 5, "Derogation of rights (Article 4), (Thirteenth session, 1981).

35. *Vienna Convention on the Law of Treaties* (1969), Art. 27.

36. For example see *Geneva Convention (I) for the Amelioration of the Condition of the Wounded and Sick in Armed Forces in the Field* (1949), Art. 3(d).

37. *Geneva Convention (IV) relative to the Protection of Civilian Persons in Time of War* (1949), Art. 11.

38. *Geneva Convention IV*, Art. 72.

39. *Universal Declaration of Human Rights*, G.A. Res. 217k, UN Dec. A/810 (1948). Art. 9.

40. UDHR, Art. 10.

41. Alfred William Brian Simpson, *In the Highest Degree Odious: Detention Without Trial in Wartime Britain* (Oxford: Clarendon Press, 1992).

42. The Order appears to have been drafted and presented to the Court by counsel for Applicant *ex parte* without notice to counsel for the Respondent.

43. This section ref;ects inferred facts from the case.

44. *Germany v. United States of America.*

45. Portions of the argument in this and the next section incorporate arguments from the Respondent's Memorial in the Jessup Moot Court ICJ case of *Advoca v. Rotania* and the briefs of the Respondents and Amicus Curiae American Center for Law and Justice in *Boumediene v. Bush*, Supreme Court of the United States Nos. 6-1195 and 1196.

46. Vienna Convention on the Law of Treaties, May 23, 1969, Art. 2. § 1(a).

47. 376 U.S. 398, 422 (1964).

48. Geneva Convention (I) for the Amelioration of the Condition of the Wounded and Sick in Armed Forces in the Field (1949) Art. 2; Geneva Convention (II) for the Amelioration of the Condition of Wounded, Sick and Shipwrecked Members of Armed Forces at Sea (1949), Art. 2, supra note 62; Geneva Convention (IV) Relative to the Protection of Civilian Persons in Time of War (1949), Art. 2 (collectively hereinafter "Common Article 2").

49. Geneva Convention I Art. 3; Geneva Convention II Art. 3; Geneva Convention III Art. 3; Geneva Convention IV Art. 3 (collectively hereinafter "Common Article 3").

50. Joyce A.C. Gutteridge, *The Geneva Conventions of 1949*, 26 *Brit. Y. B. Int'l L.* 292, 298-99 (1949).

51. The argument in the remainder of this subsection is taken from the Amicus brief of the American Center for Law and Justice in *Boumediene*.

52. Geneva Convention III cmt. at 3.1

53. Geneva Convention III at 32.

54. 2B Final Record at 128.

55. 2B Final Record at 10 (noting that applying international protections "to *civil war* would strike at the root of national sovereignty and endanger national security [emphasis added])."

56. Geneva Convention III cmt. at 31

57. 2B Final Record at 10, 13.

58. 2B Final Record at 129.

59. 2B Final Record at 45.

60. Geneva Convention III Art. 3.

61. Geneva Convention III cmt. at 30 (noting even before the Geneva Conference began that "[t]here was reason to tear that there might be objections to the idea of imposing international obligations on States in connection with their *internal affairs* **** [emphasis added]).

62. Geneva Convention III Art. 3; Geneva Convention II cmt. at 33 (noting that Article 3 applies to conflicts "similar to international war, but [which] take place within the confines *of a single country* [emphasis added]."

63. Geneva Convention III, Art. 4(2).

64. The argument concerning the English writ of *habeas corpus* that follows is taken from the Respondent's brief in *Boumediene*.

65. *The King v. Superintendent of Vine St. Police Station* [1916] 1 K.B. 268, 274 (Eng.) (*Vine St.*).

66. Geneva Convention III, Art. 4(A)(2)(b) and (d).

67. *Vine St.* [1916] 1 K.B. at 278.

68. M. Hale, *The History of the Common Law of England* 39 (1713).

69. 96 Eng. Rep. 775, 775 (C.P. 1779).

70. 96 Eng. Rep. 775, 775 (C.P. 1779).

71. 96 Eng. Rep. 775, 776 (C.P. 1779).

72. 97 Eng. Rep. 551, 551 (K.B. 1759).

73. 97 Eng. Rep. 551, 552 (K.B. 1759). See *Furly v. Newnham*, 99 Eng. Rep. 269, 269 (K.B. 1780) ("there could be no *habeas corpus* [ad testificandum] to bring up a prisoner of war").

74. Lord McNair & A.D. Watts, *The Legal Effects of War* 95 (1966).

75. Sharp 116.

76. An alien enemy includes citizens of neutral countries who have engaged in or supported hostilities against this country or associated with those who have. See *Vaughan's Case*, 91 Eng. Rep. 535, 536 (K.B. 1696) ("If . . . certain Dutchmen . . . fight under command of the French King, they are *inimici* to us, and *Gallici subditi*; for the French subjection makes them French subjects in respect of all other nations but their own."); *Miller v. United States*, 78 U.S. (11 Wall.) 268, 311 (1871) ("[T]hose must be considered as public enemies, and amenable to the laws of war as such, who, though subjects of a state in amity with the United States, are in the service of a state at war with them, and this not because they are inhabitants of such a state, but because of their hostile acts in the war.").

77. ICCPR, Art. 4.

78. Committee of Ministers, Guidelines of the Committee of the Council of Europe on Human Rights and the Fight against Terrorism, Possible Derogations, XV. 1 (2002).

79. *See Ireland v. the United Kingdom*, Judgment of 18 January 1978, Series A no. 25, 78-79, para. 207.

80. *Ireland v. the United Kingdom*, Judgment, 78-79, para. 207.

81. *Brannigan and McBride v. United Kingdom*, 26 May 1993, para. 43.

82. Advisory opinion of July 9, 2004 at 2004 ICJ Lexis 20, para. 127.

83. Advisory opinion, para. 127.

84. E-mail of Henry F. Carey dated February 14, 2008. This e-mail contains the only information available about the DRC process.

85. Portions of the argument in this section are adapted from the Jessup Moot Court Memorial in *Adoua*.

86. For a history of the use of military commissions, see Crona and Richardson, "Justice for War Criminals of Invisible Armies: A New Legal and Military Approach to Terrorism," 21 *Okla. City U. L. Rev.* 349 (1996).

87. *Parker v. Levy*, 417 U.S. 733, 743 (1974).

88. *See Madsen v. Kinsella*, 343 U.S. 341, 348 n. 10 (1952).

89. *Madsen v. Kinsella*, 343 U.S. 341, 348 n. 10.

90. Lathrop, M.L., "A Realistic Look at Terrorism Trials by Military Commission," http://news.findlaw.com/cnn/docs/terrorism/lathrop.trials.112001.html (November 2001).

91. Committee of Ministers, *Guidelines of the Committee of Ministers of the Council of Europe on Human Rights and the Fight against Terrorism*, Possible Derogations, IX.3 (2002).

92. *Doorson v. The Netherlands* (March 26, 1996), para. 69-70; *Van Mechelen and others v. The Netherlands* (April 23, 1997), para. 52.

93. *Van Mechelen and others v. The Netherlands*, at 57.

94. *Rowe and Davies v. United Kingdom*, 16 February 2000, para. 61.

95. *Turek v. Slovakia*, 57986/00 [2006] ECHR 138 (14 February 2006); Joseph M. Jacobs, *Civil Justice In The Age Of Human Rights* (Ashgate Publishing, February 2007).

96. *Rowe and Davis*, supra at para. 62

97. Lathrop, "A Realistic Look."

98. IMT Constitution, Article 26.

99. See Beijer and van Hoorn, Report on Anonymous Witnesses in the Netherlands (1997), 524, 547.

100. Crona and Richardson, "Justice for War Criminals," 383.

101. Crona and Richardson, "Justice for War Criminals," citing, Peter Calvocaressi, *Nuremberg: The Facts, the Law, and the Consequences* (1948) and David Lippert, The "Eichmann Case and the Nuremberg Trials," 48 A.B.A.J. 738 (1962).

102. *See Ireland v. the United Kingdom.*

103. *Ireland v. the United Kingdom.*

104. *Brannigan and McBride v. United Kingdom*, 26 Max 1993, para. 43.

105. *In re Yamashita*, 327 U.S. 1, 11 (1946).

106. ICRC Rule 106; "Combatants must distinguish themselves from the civilian population while they are engaged in an attack or in a military operation preparatory to an attack. If they fail to do so, they do not have the right to prisoner-of-war status."

107. General Comment 29, States of Emergency (Article 4), U.N. Doc. CCPR/C/21/Rev.1/Add.11 (2001).

108. UN Document (A/HRC/6/17/Add.3, paras. 55 to 60, 63).

109. Observations on behalf of the High Commissioner for Human Rights to the ECtHR in *El-Masri, op. cit.*, footnote 26, Geneva, 11 March 2011, at para. 38. A particularly egregious illustration of this is the practice of the Military Commissions in Guantánamo Bay to treat evidence confirming the torture of "high-value detainees" by the CIA as "classified information" on the spurious ground that the accused, having been subjected to waterboarding and other forms of torture, are thereby privy to information about classified CIA interrogation techniques which they cannot be permitted to reveal, in any proceeding open to the public, even to the extent of preventing their attorneys from providing the accused with Government classified materials about the ill-treatment to which they were subjected. See *e.g. United States v. Mohammad*, Appellate Exhibit 013AA, Amended Protective Order #1 (To Prevent Against Disclosure of National Security Information), 2g(4)-(5), dtd Feb. 9, 2013, "observations and experiences of an accused with respect to" their treatment by the CIA remains classified, such as details of their capture, information that would tend to reveal the foreign countries involved, the names and identifies of the persons involved, the enhanced interrogation techniques applied, and any descriptions of the confinement conditions This absurdist and amoral legal analysis carries the implication that the use of torture by public officials is *ipso facto* privileged from public disclosure.

110. See www.whitehouse.gov/the-press-office/2011/12/31/statement-president-hr-1540.

111. UN Document A/HRC/13/30, para. 83.

112. See also Al Maqaleh v. Gates, 605 F. 3d 84 - Court of Appeals, Dist. of Co-

lumbia Circuit 2010, 21 May 2010.

113. UN Document CRC/C/OPAC/USA/CO/1, para. 28.

114. UN Document CRC/C/OPAC/USA/CO/1, para. 30f.

115. See, e.g., Concluding observations Sudan 1998, para. [124] ("national security" vague), Philippines 2004, para. 14 (vagrancy law vague), Mauritius 2005, para. 12 (terrorism law vague), Russian Federation 2010, para. 25 ("extremist activity" vague), United Republic of Tanzania 2009, para. 12 (terrorism law vague), Honduras 2007, para. 13 ("unlawful association" vague).

116. 702/1996, McLawrence v. Jamaica, para. 5.5 ("[T]he principle of legality is violated if an individual is arrested or detained on grounds which are not clearly established in domestic legislation.").

117. 856/1999, *Chambala v. Zambia*, para. 7.3.

118. 1425/2005, *Marz v. Russian Federation*, para. 5.3.

119. 461/2006, *Maksudov et al. v. Kyrgyzstan*, para. 12.2.

120. 1110/2002, *Rolando v. The Philippines*, para. 5.5.

121. 770/1997, *Gridin v. Russian Federation*, para. 8.1.

122. 1449/2006, *Umarov v. Uzbekistan*, para. 8.4.

123. 981/2001, *Gómez Casafranca v. Peru*, para. 7.2.

124. 2024/2011, *Israil v. Kazakhstan*, para. 9.2.

125. 1208/2003, *Kurbonov v. Tajikistan*, para. 6.5.

126. 1412/2005, *Butovenko v. Ukraine*, para. 7.6.

Index

About the Contributors

George Andreopoulos is professor of political science at the John Jay College of Criminal Justice and the Graduate Center, City University of New York (CUNY). He is also founding director of the Center for International Human Rights, John Jay College of Criminal Justice, CUNY. He has written extensively on international organizations, international human rights, and laws of war issues. His forthcoming publications include *Human Rights in the Era of Counter-Terrorism: Thinking and Acting in an Emergency* and *The Uses and Misuses of Human Rights* (co-author and co-editor). He has served as consultant for intergovernmental and non-governmental organizations and is a past president of the Human Rights Section of the American Political Science Association (APSA).

Robert J. Beck is associate professor of political science at the University of Wisconsin–Milwaukee. He holds a Ph.D. in government from Georgetown University and has previously taught at Tufts University and the University of Virginia. Beck has participated in law institutes at New York University's School of Law, the University of Virginia's School of Law, and Dartmouth College. He is author of *The Grenada Invasion* (1993), co-author of *International Law and the Use of Force* (1993), editor of *Law and Disciplinarity: Thinking beyond Borders* (2013), and co-editor of *International Rules* (1996), *International Law and the Rise of Nations* (2002), and the *International Law* volume of the International Studies Association's *Compendium* project (2010). Beck's work has also appeared in such journals as *International Security, Review of International Studies, International Journal of Refugee Law, International Studies Perspectives*, and *Commonwealth Journal of International Affairs*.

Dave Benjamin is associate professor of global development, and chair of the M.A. in Global Development and Peace at the University of Bridgeport. He has authored articles on the responsibility to protect and human security. His current research projects include those addressing political corruption, and reform of the United Nations. An active member of the International Studies Association, ISA Northeast, and the New England Political Science Association, he is a graduate of University of Cambridge (Ph.D. and M.Phil.) and Carleton University (B.A. Hons.).

Brittany M. Bromfield is a M.A. candidate in political science at Georgia State University. She has professional experience working with immigrants, refugees, and other underrepresented populations in Atlanta, Georgia with NGOs like Refugee Family Services, DeKalb County Board of Health, and the Global Village School in Decatur. Her research interests include international human rights activism, democratization, and social development.

Henry F. (Chip) Carey is associate professor of political science at Georgia State University. He is the author and editor of over ten books and numerous academic essays on human rights, international law, and European integration. His most recently authored books are *Reaping What You Sow: A Comparative Examination of Torture Reform in the United States, France, Argentina, and Israel* and *Privatizing the Democratic Peace: Policy Dilemmas of NGO Peacebuilding*. He is editor or co-editor of *Trials and Tribulations of International Prosecution*, as well as *Human Rights, Civil Society and European Institutions: Thematic Debates*, and *Promotion of Human Rights and Democracy in the Balkans and Beyond: Country Studies*. He is currently editor of *United Nations Law Reports* and a regular foreign policy blog at worldpolicy.org.

Aaron Fichtelberg is associate professor in the Faculty of Sociology and Criminal Justice, University of Delaware where he specializes in international criminal justice, comparative criminal justice, and legal theory. He has published widely on aspects of international criminal law, and international criminal justice. He is the author of *Law at the Vanishing Point* (2008) and *Crimes Without Borders: An Introduction to International Criminal Justice* (2007). He holds a Ph.D. from Emory University in Atlanta where he wrote his dissertation on the philosophical foundations of international law. He also holds an L.L.M. degree from Utrecht University in the Netherlands (*summa cum laude*) where he wrote his thesis on the role of liberal values in international criminal law. He has been published in journals like the *Journal of International Criminal Justice*, *Criminal Law Forum*, and *Criminal Justice Ethics*.

Rick Crawford is assistant professor of political science at Shorter University in Rome, Georgia, and a Ph.D. candidate in political science at Georgia State University. Prior to joining the faculty at Shorter, he worked as an attorney in private practice. He has also served as a municipal court judge, magistrate court judge, and as a member of the Georgia House of Representatives.

Rebecca (Becky) Littleton Sims has taught for thirteen years and is an associate professor of political science at Georgia Highlands College. She holds a J.D. degree from Baylor University School of Law and a M.P.A. from Valdosta State University. She is a former elected prosecutor and is currently pursuing a Ph.D. at Georgia State University.

Dr. Stacey M. Mitchell is a lecturer at the University of Georgia, Department of International Affairs. She specializes in human rights and international criminal law and has written and published on the topics of genocide, genocide in Rwanda, and the *Gacaca* courts in Rwanda. She is also co-editor with Henry (Chip) Carey of *Trials and Tribulations of International Prosecution* (2013).

Robert Weiner received his Ph.D. from New York University. He is a center associate at the Davis Center for Russian and Eurasian Studies at Harvard University and a fellow at the Center for Peace, Democracy, and Development at the University of Massachusetts in Boston. His research interests include genocide, diplomacy and war, theories and concepts of international relations, and the European Union and the emerging democracies. He is the author of "The Law of Genocide," in Robert A. Denemark (ed.), *The International Studies Encyclopedia* (2010). He is the academic editor of *World Politics 12/13* (2013), *World Politics 13/14* (2013/2014) and *World Politics 14/15*. He is the author of *Romanian Foreign Policy at the United Nations* (1984) and *Change in Eastern Europe* (1994). His articles have been published in such journals as the *International and Comparative Law Quarterly*, *Orbis*, *Problems of Postcommunism*, *Sudost Europa*, and *Demokratizatsiya*.

Stephanie Wolfe, Ph.D., is an assistant professor at Weber State University, Utah. She received her Ph.D. in international relations at the University of Kent in Brussels, Belgium. She specializes in international relations, genocide, crimes against humanity, and human rights.

Lightning Source UK Ltd.
Milton Keynes UK
UKOW04n1617190514

231929UK00001B/32/P

9 780739 170656